1995

The Contemporary Relevance of History

THE
CONTEMPORARY RELEVANCE
OF
HISTORY

A Study in Approaches and Methods

SALO W. BARON

New York   COLUMBIA UNIVERSITY PRESS   1986

Columbia University Press
New York   Guildford, Surrey
Copyright © 1986 Columbia University Press

Printed in the United States of America

Library of Congress Cataloging-in-Publication Data

Baron, Salo Wittmayer, 1895–
    The contemporary relevance of history.

    Bibliography: p.
    Includes index.
    1. History—Philosophy.   2. Historiography.
3. History—Methodology.   I. Title.
D16.8.B3145   1986   901   86-2644
ISBN 0-231-06336-9

CONTENTS

PREFACE

THE PRESENT STUDY is, in some respects, an appendix to my comprehensive work, A *Social and Religious History of the Jews*, the second and enlarged edition of which, even after the publication of eighteen volumes and an Index to Volumes I–VIII, still awaits completion. As indicated in the Preface to the first edition, that work originated from a series of ten Schermerhorn Lectures, delivered by me, under the title *Jewish Society and Religion* at Columbia University in the Spring of 1931. While the term "social history" has been used by many authors in different meanings, in my treatment it referred to the entire range of demographic, economic, political, legal, and sociological developments. It was the interrelation of all these vital historic forces with the religious evolutions under different civilizations which was the major guideline in my presentation. The last two chapters of the present study deal, indeed, with Society and Religion as two major factors in their interrelations in most periods of human history and still continue to play a significant role even in our recent, secularized generations. The so-called secular ideologies, like modern nationalism, the idea of progress, socialism and communism, have often turned into varying forms of faith, with all the emotional and some ritualistic aspects of religion. I have partially analyzed these deep affinities in my *Modern Nationalism and Religion*, published in 1947 and in following paperbacks.

Like my analysis of the national-religious interrelations, the present essay aims at a better understanding of history in its double meaning as a factual world phenomenon and as a discipline also concerned with an outlook on its relevance to life in the present. It is not limited to one particular civilization but looks for examples from antiquity to modern times in the broader area of the Mediterranean and general Western worlds. If relatively more illustrations are quoted here from events, descriptions, and theories, borrowed from the past of the Jewish people, this is not only owing to the author's personal lifetime preoccupation with Jewish history, but also to the objective fact that that history extends over three millennia under different environments in both East and West. Under these circumstances, the concrete examples cited usually have some broader, sometimes even universal, connotations.

In conclusion, I may add that as in my other works of the last half a century, the present volume owes much to my wife, Dr. Jeannette Meisel Baron, who for decades has been my only research assistant and helpmate in all walks of life.

Salo Wittmayer Baron

Yifat Shalom
Canaan, Connecticut
May 1985

The Contemporary Relevance of History

INTRODUCTION

T HE "NOW GENERATION," especially that of the late 1960s, often
asked the question whether history—and particularly the history of
the Jews or of any minority—was still relevant "today." In its headlong
quest to throw off all traditional shackles in its pursuit of happiness, it
readily forgot that "today" is but a moment between a long and, in perspective, ever changing past, and an unforeseeable future. Even in Swe-
den, where the youth had not been confronted with an "unwanted" war as
had its American counterpart, a survey conducted in November 1972 by a
leading newspaper, the *Svenska Dagbladet*, among sixteen-year-olds,
showed that a large majority denied that history had any practical use. In
1967 a Swiss historian, too, tried to find some satisfactory answers to his
query, "What's the Point of History?", in a German article in *Der Monat*,
which was speedily translated into English in *The Journal of Contemporary
History* (JCH). To me even then the question "Is History still relevant?"
had no more justification than one of whether Beethoven was still relevant today. Certainly, Beethoven cannot be truly relevant to a person who
has no musical ear. Similarly, a person who possesses no historical sense
will not be genuinely interested in what happened in the past and still less
in using such knowledge as a guide for some future behavior.[1]

However, the majority of people usually evince some interest in past
events and developments, if for no other reason than to satisfy their
natural curiosity about their families, friends, and their local environment. Just as many a normal child would sometimes break his or her toy in
order to find out what makes it work, often without any interest in repair-
ing it, many people show curiosity about their ancestry as well as about
their own earlier experiences. Some of them are also fascinated by the
careers of outstanding personalities, especially those whom they are told
to revere because of their achievements for their people, or whose anniversaries are celebrated as national holidays.

Beyond such healthy curiosity there has long been a quest for ascertaining historic experiences as lessons in behavioral patterns; they might advantageously be imitated under similar circumstances or be avoided because of their inherent dangers. The ancient Romans spoke in the Ciceronian terms of *historia magistra vitae*, of history being the teacher of life. The British statesman, William Pitt, Earl of Chatham, instructed his son, William Pitt, Jr., who at the age of twenty-four was likewise to serve as British Prime Minister, carefully to study Thucydides' *History of the Peloponnesian War* (431–404 B.C.E.) as the best practical handbook for statesmen.[2]

Learning from history is not so much the effect of its frequent repetitions. Even if one does not literally take the old biblical saying that there is "nothing new under the sun" and inverts it to contend that "everything is new under the sun"—since nothing repeats itself in exactly the same fashion within a totality of differing circumstances—it has long been accepted as a truism that one can learn much from the vicissitudes of one's group or nation, just as an individual constantly learns from his own past experiences. To be sure, a wit has contended that the only thing history has taught us is that no generation has ever learned from history. But this generalization, like many others, is not literally true. Nor does it prevent future generations, or at least some perspicacious individuals among them, from learning a great deal from history.[3]

Ironically, the last generation which so insistently queried history's relevance to contemporary affairs happened to include a great many more individuals who underwent psychoanalytic treatment than had any preceding generation. Needless to say, one of the psychoanalysts' major objectives is to find out whether their patients' behavioral patterns are derived from their experiences in early childhood or even in their prenatal stage, experiences remembered only in the recesses of their subconscious minds. The spokesmen of the irrelevance of history also readily overlooked the numerous references to history by Sigmund Freud, the founder of the psychoanalytical approach. In elaborating, for instance, his doctrine on the Ego (*Ich*) and Id (*Es*) he wrote:

> One must not too sharply draw a line between the Ego and the Id, nor forget that the Id is an especially differentiated part of the Ego. The experiences of the Ego at first appear to be lost through inheritance. But when they repeat themselves frequently and strongly enough in a number of individuals over several generations, they

transform themselves, so to say, into the Id, the impact of which is perpetuated through inheritance.

This is also the generation which has evinced a tremendous scientific curiosity about genetics, trying to trace back many characteristics of living persons as the result of genes inherited from their parents or grandparents. Clearly, such pursuits are closely akin to historical investigations of the impact of past events and movements on the destinies of individuals, groups, or nations.[4]

It seems, however, that after reaching its climax in the student uprisings of the 1960s, the "now generation" has lost much of its vigor and influence on the majority of the youth. Its negative outlook of history had been but part of a general attitude to life eloquently described by Henry Steele Commager in the following passage:

> What were the stigmata . . . of the new school [in the period after World War II]? First, the rejection—on pseudoscientific grounds—of reason, meaning, normality, morality, continuity, and coherence, the rejection of civilization itself as eccentric and decadent. Second, a passionate interest in the subconscious and the unconscious. . . . Third, an obsession with sex, especially in its abnormal manifestations. . . . Fourth, a weakness for the primitive . . . and closely connected with this a predilection for violence in all forms. Fifth, an unqualified repudiation of all orthodox moral standards, of comformities and conventions, and acquiescence in a pervasive amorality. . . . And, finally, the formulation of a new language and a new grammar to express more faithfully the fitful impulses emanating from the subconscious.

This attitude has given way to a more conservative reaction. Many young persons today are far more appreciative of traditional values. The quest for "roots," in particular, has in many ways reversed the depreciation of history, too. Nor must we overlook the creative effervescence of new approaches to historical research and interpretation among historians, philosophers, and social scientists of the postwar period. Some of these innovative movements have brought forth new schools of historiography which have not only dominated much of the new historiographic literature but have also penetrated many classrooms throughout the Western world.[5]

At the moment the *Sturm und Drang* period of these innovative move-ments seems to be over; it is apparently to be followed by some years of consolidation and a search for a new consensus. Probably a synthesis of the best of all the newer trends with the imperishable achievements of the earlier generations of historians would now be in order. The following brief review of the older and newer methods and approaches, with special reference to my lifelong preoccupation with Jewish history and social sciences—always against the background of the great civilizations under which Jews lived for the last three and a half millennia—may be of some help to specialists and readers in other fields as well.

I
CHANGING PATTERNS

DISSATISFACTION with modern historicism has had deeper roots, however. For many generations the wide acceptance of single explanations of the course of world and national histories crumbled under the onslaught of contrary views. The assumption of the distinguished biblical or Graeco-Roman historiography, which long dominated historical writings in the Western world, broke down after the incursion of perceptions opposing the Judeo-Christian interpretation of history.

The prevalent view of the classical historical literature from Herodotus down was based upon the parallel of the phenomena derived from the human cycle: birth, growth, maturity, old age, and death. It was readily assumed that nations, too, were born, grew until reaching a flowering of varying duration, which was followed by their decline and temporary or permanent disappearance. This view of an internal cyclical repetition was clearly formulated by Thucydides when he stated that what happened in the past, "will happen again in the same or in a similar way" in the future. The cyclical conception of history found disciples also in the modern world. It was most eloquently and persuasively developed by Giambattista Vico (1668–1744), particularly in his *Scienza Nuova*, refined in three successive editions of 1725, 1730, and 1744 (the latter published posthumously). This view also underlay Hegel's well-known doctrine of the succession of a thesis, antithesis, and synthesis, followed by the start of another cycle, which influenced Friedrich Nietzsche and many others.[6]

Confronted by the long-lasting life of the Jewish people, the first modern Hebrew philosopher of history, Nachman Krochmal, adopted the Hegelian theory that the historical evolution consisted as a rule in a certain set of phenomena which were followed by a reversal toward the opposite direction and ended with the synthesis of both sets. But he added the major variation that Jewish history had consisted of repetitions of that cycle and that after the end of each synthetic phase the Jewish people did not vanish but was always reborn and started a new cycle. Krochmal supported his view by quoting the statement of the second-century rabbi Simon ben Yohai, "Come and see how beloved the people of Israel is to the Holy One, blessed be He: To whatever locality they went the Divine Presence (*Shekhina*) went with them. When they were exiled to Egypt the Divine Presence was there with them; when they were exiled to Babylonia, the Divine Presence was with them. Similarly, when they will ultimately be redeemed (and restored to their home country) the Divine Presence will be with them." Krochmal also took as his motto for the chapter dealing with this theory Malachi the Prophet's declaration: "For I the Lord change not; and ye, the sons of Jacob, are not consumed."[7]

In contrast, the ancient Judeo-Christian outlook was based on the assumption of a divine guidance of all history and fundamentally perceived mankind's evolution in terms of the original divine creation and the final messianic age; in the Christian case by two messianic periods consisting in the provisional First and the final Second Coming of Christ. Within that scheme there was room for a great break in the early history of man caused by the Deluge and such subsequent major events as the Exodus from Egypt, the Revelation of the Torah on Sinai, and the First and Second Fall of Jerusalem. All these events were considered to have been foreseen by the omniscient Deity, yet were in many details affected by men acting in obedience or disobedience to the divine commandments. For Christians the greatest events in history after Creation were the birth, crucifixion, and resurrection of Jesus. The entire history up to that point being regarded as a mere *praeparatio evangelica*. These points of view dominated the thinking of the members of both faiths throughout the Middle Ages down to early modern times. Christian and Jewish thinkers were also deeply influenced by the vision of Daniel concerning the four beasts which, for the most part, were assumed to symbolize the successive reigns of the four world powers; Assyro-Babylonia, Persia, Greece (with its Hellenistic successors), and Rome. Down to the early modern period Jewish writers like Don Isaac Abravanel argued against the specific Christian interpretations of these dates and offered their own individual explanations. But all agreed that at the close of the fourth realm, the Messiah would come. (In the Christian view, Christ would come again.)[8]

An early breach in this world outlook came with the initial secularizing trends of the Renaissance Age. Jean Bodin, especially, effectively argued against that chronological scheme in his *Methodus ad facilem historiarum cognitionem*. Soon thereafter came the new chronological sequence advocated particularly by Christopher Cellarius, who introduced the division into ancient, medieval, and modern history, before long generally accepted in the Western world.[9]

In Jewish history the modern chronological divisions replacing the old view differed from one another according to the individual historian's opinion concerning the significance of particular events. Almost all of them regarded the Second Fall of Jerusalem and the ensuing loss of both the Temple and national independence as the outstanding turning point from the ancient to the medieval history of the Jewish people. But there were considerable divisions in assigning a chronological end to the Jewish Middle Ages. In the eyes of the nineteenth-century founders of the Science of Judaism the period from 70 C.E. to the late eighteenth century marked the era of Jewish exilic or medieval existence. A new period of modernity set in only with the French Revolution. This division was accepted by most historians, including Martin Philippson and Simon Dubnow, each of whom published a three-volume work on modern Jewish history, beginning with 1789 C.E. (Dubnow later incorporated these volumes in his *World History of the Jewish People*.) Significant exceptions were that, owing to his penchant for intellectual history, Heinrich Graetz began the last part of his eleven-volume *Geschichte* with the Mendelssohnian period (about the middle of the eighteenth century), while the American authors Max L. Margolis and Alexander Marx started "The Age of Emancipation" with the American Revolution of 1776 and the Constitution of 1787. Finally, in view of the more recent appreciation of the State of Israel, that event has replaced Emancipation as the end of Jewish medieval history. In a large segment of the Jewish public the Diaspora life from 70 to 1948 C.E. was but an era of constant sufferings of the Jews as a perpetual minority among predominantly hostile majorities. Some historians allowed for the new period to have begun with the Zionist movement resulting in the rise of that state; in one extreme case, Benzion Dinur postulated the dating of the incipient liberation movement with the first modern group migration to Palestine under Yehudah the Pious in the year 1700.[10]

My own preference has been to see the great break in modern Jewish history at the beginning of the emancipatory movement set in motion by cumulative sociopolitical, economic, cultural, and religious factors around 1650. These factors included the general rapid growth of the Western population, the vast international migrations, the Commercial and Industrial Revolutions, the aftereffects of Humanism and the Reformation, producing the ultimate deadlock of the Thirty Years' War, which resulted in the Westphalian Peace Treaties' recognition in 1648 of the liberty of religious conscience. Correspondingly, Jewish life, too, was affected by the reversal of Jewish migratory movements from Poland and Turkey to the West, the rise of new centers in Holland, England, France, and the Americas, the Marrano dispersion, the Shabbetian movement, the appearance of personalities like Baruch Spinoza and Uriel Da Costa, and the spread of the Italian and Dutch Haskalah into Germany, and later into Galicia and Russia—all these tended to facilitate the gradual integration of the Jewish segments into the Western nations. The successive proclamations of the equality of the Jews' rights with those of their neighbors often were but confirmations—and further accelerations—of the dominant "historical tendencies" (to use a Humboldtian term) which had operated in West-Central Europe and the New World for several generations.[11]

More important than these chronological divisions was the undermining of the heritage of the Judeo-Christian historical outlook by the French philosophers and the leaders of Enlightenment in other lands. The major historical force was now recognized to be the secular "Reign of Reason." So convinced were the radical exponents that their Religion of Reason would speedily supplant all traditional religions that they celebrated the French Revolution as the beginning of a new world era and started dating their documents from the year one of that era, which began on September 22, 1790. (Yet, despite the ensuing secularization of their historiography, they maintained the basic Judeo-Christian hope in an ultimate messianic future in a Heavenly City.) These new approaches found an echo also among Jewish intellectuals. Only a small Jewish minority in France began worshiping the cultic images of the new faith. In St. Esprit-Bayonne a group of young Jewish revolutionaries went to the extreme of offering their community's Hebrew scrolls of law to be burned on the bonfire staged by the new rulers. Yet many Jews who rejected the newly founded religious cult nevertheless enthusiastically adopted the new slogans of the cosmopolitan embrace of the Rights of Man and saw in them a way of reconciling all conflicts between nationalities and religious denominations.[12]

This new world view profoundly affected most Jewish scholars also in the following generations. Deeply involved in the struggle for Emancipation, they hailed the French egalitarian legislation as the dawn of a new era and were even prepared to advocate the cultural, though not the religious, assimilation of the Jewish people to its neighbors. To be sure, the flowering of Jewish historical literature in the nineteenth century came after the submergence of the cosmopolitan ideas of the eighteenth century under the growing nationalist clashes of modern Europe. In fact, a Jew no longer had the choice, as a famous slogan of the Haskalah read, "To be a Jew at home and a man on the street." He now definitely had to be a Frenchman, German, Englishman, or member of another major nationality, among which he lived. This illusion was further nurtured by the replacement of the Reign of Reason by one of "Progress" as the dominant idea in historical thinking. For most Jewish historians of the period the gradual spread of Emancipation from one country to another appeared as the embodiment of progress in Jewish life among its neighbors. It is small wonder, therefore, that they drew a sharp line of demarcation between the discriminatory treatment of the Jews in the Middle Ages and early modern times and the egalitarian expectations of the postrevolutionary era, reinforced by the fact—whether they fully realized it or not—that Jewish emancipation was an even greater historic necessity for the modern state than it was for the Jewish people. Jews, whose traditional optimism had long been buttressed by their confident reliance (*bittaḥon*) on God and the messianic hope, now seized on the expectation of progress, believed to be, despite setbacks, inevitably leading toward the amelioration of the life of all men. It was even more true of their leaders than of their Protestant compatriots about whom Ronald Arbuthnott Knox wrote:

> Those who had lost the sense of religious certainty enrolled themselves under the banner of optimism, the world's future occupied their thoughts instead of a future world, and, by a kind of inverted Confucianism, they fell to worshiping their grandchildren. With this optimistic agitation, the leaders of religion . . . have readily associated themselves.[13]

Combining the faith in progress with the reign of Reason, historians were also generally ready to discard the power of historical myths as contrasted with genuine historical facts. For this reason the vast literature of the talmudic Aggadah and other legendary and folkloristic sources were often dismissed by Jewish students of antiquity and the Middle Ages as sources of historical evidence, as was also the case of the parallel treatment of ancient and medieval mythological sources by their non-Jewish confreres. In vain did Johann Wolfgang von Goethe protest against this denigration of the most beautiful legendary traditions preserved by older generations, because they allegedly were creations of pure fancy. Writing in the era of growing historical criticism, the great poet protested against its "displacing, through some pedantic truths, great things which are of superior value to us." Only some legal historians still appreciated elements of legal practice preserved in the traditional legends and folklore. Lucien Henri Lévy-Bruhl even went so far as to assert "that while historians wanted to know what happened, rejected apocryphal sources, jurists know that many a legend is truer than history." This disregard of legendary sources has been doubly significant in the history of the Jewish people, in which the legal traditions of the Halakhah were often blended with the "fanciful" homilies and narratives of the Aggadah, and had jointly played such an enormous role in its entire intellectual evolution. Moreover, in their enthusiasm for criticism, many historians were prone to forget an obvious fact. As stated by William H. Dunning, the historian "must keep in mind that the reversal [of an occurrence or assumption mentioned by an earlier writer] cannot be made retroactive so as to affect the thoughts and deeds of the generations who knew not the reality. He must remember, in short, that for very, very much history there is more importance in the ancient error than the new-found truth."[14]

The idea of progress generated also another mighty trend in modern historiography, a trend which, going beyond the confines of historical thought and writing, has deeply affected the destinies of the modern world: the Marxist conception of history. Karl Marx himself was ready to admit that some of the fundamental ingredients of "historical materialism" had been furnished to him by earlier historians and economists. In his letter to Joseph Wedemayer, of March 5, 1852, when his theories were still unfolding toward their fuller formulation in *Das Kapital* (1867–95), he wrote:

> As far as I am concerned I cannot claim the honor of having discovered either classes or class conflict in modern society. Bourgeois historians have described the historical development of class struggle long before I came along, and bourgeois economists had laid bare the economic anatomy of the struggle. My contributions were to prove: (1) that the existence of classes is directly linked to specific historical stages in production methods; (2) that class struggle will inevitably lead to a dictatorship of the proletariat; and (3) that this dictatorship itself forms only a transition to the abolishment of classes and to a classless society.

Today, more than two generations after the successful Communist Revolution in the Soviet Union and other countries, the promise of a classless society is still relegated to a nebulous future. Interveningly the expected dictatorship of the proletariat has become a dictatorship of a relatively small group of leaders of the new class of bureaucrats and technocrats. Yet the doctrines of historical materialism, with many variations, have continued to influence the thinking of many historians outside the Soviet orbit as well.[15]

From many other angles the idea of progress also dominated the minds of the masses, including many historians, to the end of the nineteenth century; and in the United States into the early decades of the twentieth century. However, as time went on a growing chorus of pessimistic voices denied that expectation in the face of the increasing crudity, even barbarism, of contemporary public life. It is enough to contrast the confident assertion made in 1787 by Antoine Nicolas de Condorcet that "the more civilization will extend over the earth, the more will wars and conquests disappear as will slavery and misery," with the perplexities reflected in Fernand Braudel's description of "The Positions of History in 1950." In that inaugural lecture at the Collège de France, this leader of the historical school of the *Annales, Économies, Sociétés, Civilisations,* contended:

> Nowadays history faces the responsibilities both redoubtable and exalting. Without doubt this happens because it has never ceased, in its very essence and changeability, to depend on the existing concrete social conditions. History is a daughter of its time; its disquiet is therefore a reflection of the very disquiet which heavily rests upon our hearts and our spirit.

Martin Heidegger went even further and, in his "atheistic existentialism," as his philosophy was often designated, he claimed that "No age has known so much and so many different things about man as ours. . . . And no age has known less than ours of what man is."[16]

It is not surprising, therefore, that a generation filled with such uncertainties, and possibly facing an apocalyptic, atomic destruction, has often lost patience with all historical lucubrations. Especially those young people who had studied history in schools with the dullest of teachers marshaling an endless array of facts and dates, without explanations of their importance for their day and ours, rejected all historical studies out of hand. In recent years it has been particularly the Jewish students in many lands, including Israel and the United States, who rejected the study of Jewish history in the form usually presented to them as a sequence of persecutions and massacres; some of them dismissed the entire period before the achievement of true Emancipation or even until the rise of the State of Israel as a constant nightmare. At the same time numerous young activists, referring especially to the Holocaust, insistently asked about the millions of Jewish victims: "Why did they allow themselves to be led like sheep to slaughter?" Not only were they completely alienated from the concepts of Jewish religious martyrdom and submission to God's will, but they even lent an unwilling ear to proofs of strong Jewish resistance in many areas.[17]

In the last few years, however, there has been a gradual reaction to the impatience and unlimited expectations which characterized much of the American and Western European youth in the late 1960s. Facing a much more serious situation in the job market and finding that hard preparatory work makes a great difference in achieving academic and other professional positions, many young people began studying with greater dedication and foresight. Many of them came to realize the truth of Page Smith's assertion: "If the teenager must have adult pleasures at once, he can never become an adult. It is a sad fact that 'too soon' means 'never.'" In the field of history, moreover, there appeared new popular trends, which, far transcending the professional preoccupation with history, awakened among the masses a new interest about their past. The great popularity of Alex Haley's *Roots*, spread through the press, film, and television to wide circles of the population, aroused a new interest in genealogy and other aspects of history much beyond the various ethnic groups. Similarly, the Holocaust, whether through the presentation of Anne Frank's *Diary* or through the recurrent accusations of both the Papacy and the Jewish and non-Jewish leaders in the free world for their passivity in the face of the mass murders, or finally through the enormous popular interest in the new novels, dramas, and scholarly works related to the Nazi "final solution," opened up a new understanding of the importance of history.[18]

Among historians, on the other hand, there was a revival in the search for historical methodology. The same German thinkers who at the beginning of this century spoke with disdain of the excesses of "historicism" began taking a renewed interest in the various approaches to the philosophy of history, whether stemming from philosophers like Hegel and Nietzsche or from among leading historians like Johann Gustav Droysen, Jakob Burckhardt, Wilhelm Dilthey, and Friedrich Meinecke. The great, if temporary, influence exercised by Oswald Spengler's *Decline of the West* upon the professional and lay public throughout Germany (despite its obvious shortcomings and heavy style, the book is said to have sold more than 120,000 copies in the first year) revived the interest in history because it appealed to the deep pessimism generated, among both Germans and the victors, by Germany's defeat in the First World War. In the United States the distinguished philosopher Morris R. Cohen chose in 1944 to analyze for the important series of Carus Lectures *The Meaning of Human History*, which, according to his daughter-biographer, "he considered . . . his magnum opus." For many years the historical explanations offered by Arnold Joseph Toynbee, especially in his multivolumed *Study of History*, aroused the interest of both partisans and opponents. Most recently courses in historical methods, now named *Historik*, as an important discipline at German universities has begun to be emulated in many lands. In Israel the Six-Day War—with the deep concern evinced by, and emotional participation among, all Jewries of the Dispersion in the perils and successes of the young State—evoked a new recognition of the intimate links between the Diaspora and the Homeland as forged by the people's unique history over the ages. All that led to an awakening of historical concerns and particularly also in the quest to derive from historic experience some lessons for contemporary action and future planning.[19]

II

PROBLEMS OF
HISTORICAL OBJECTIVITY

MODERN APPROACHES to Jewish and general history, represented by various schools of thought, have often been plagued by the problem of the extent to which historians can be truly objective in their evaluation of past events. Like students of other social sciences and humanities, they are confronted by a chaotic mass of available materials concerning modern times, in contrast to the frequent paucity of source materials for ancient and medieval history. Anatole France correctly stressed the difficulties of modern historians in ascertaining the accuracy of numerous details because of the contradictory testimonies of the authors of numerous memoirs alone. More fundamentally, the experience of Sir Walter Raleigh (Ralegh), doubtless repeated by many others, offers a serious warning. While writing his major historical work, we are told, the Elizabethan historian suddenly heard a tumult in front of his house. Looking out the window, he noted what was happening. In the evening he was visited by a friend who had chanced to be on the scene of that disturbance and described it to Sir Walter in considerable detail. Noticing the great discrepancies between the observation of that generally trustworthy eyewitness and his own, the historian threw up his hands in despair concerning the veracity of all eyewitness accounts. The difficulties of judges attempting to sort out the truth in frequently contradictory—even if apparently unbiased—testimonies of eyewitnesses testifying under oath are well known, while "hearsay" is often completely disregarded in courts. How much reliance, therefore, can be placed on reports in a single ancient or medieval source, which is evidently based on rumors or on second- or third-hand tales stemming from some unknown original eyewitness?[20]

At the same time, unlike students of pure science, historians cannot experimentally repeat the same phenomena to check whether identical causes would produce identical results. As we recall, in history one may paraphrase the old assertion of Ecclesiastes (1:9) that "there is nothing new under the sun" by contending that practically everything is new under the sun. When one views any historical event or development against its background of an ever varying environment and chain of circumstances, one realizes that nothing repeats itself exactly. Confronted with the great diversity of nonrepetitive individual or mass happenings, the historian must choose which "facts" he considers important and which he must discard as "irrelevant," and how to integrate such obviously disparate phenomena into a single, logical whole. Naturally such enforced selectivity may often become arbitrary and depend on the momentarily prevailing climate of opinion, the investigators' personal inclinations, their prejudices generated by their social background, their political and religious convictions, or even on purely adventitious circumstances.

A noteworthy example of how difficult it is to adhere to the postulate of historical objectivity, especially in cases of deep emotional concern, is offered by the great social scientist Max Weber. In many of his works he insisted upon the duty of historians and social scientists to avoid value judgments and to treat all phenomena in the past and present with total objectivity. Yet, when it came to vital issues of contemporary German domestic policies, his deeply rooted German patriotism made him frequently abandon his own principle of complete detachment. As was shown by Wolfgang Mommsen and Arthur Mitzman, in decisive moments, Weber, generally a foremost exponent of German liberalism, fully embraced German imperialism and became a ruthless advocate of national Realpolitik.[21]

It is not enough to say, therefore, that the historian should stick to his "facts." Some scholars have actually denied the existence of "brute facts" completely independent of their historical interpretation. This difficulty is aggravated by the very ambiguity of some fundamental historical terminology. Long ago Heinrich Rickert argued that, for instance, the important term "evolution" had seven different meanings, and hence one could not fully compare one thinker with another, "because the idea of evolution occupies such a dominant position in their thinking." Similarly, there have been numerous debates about the meaning of "objectivity." A recent scholar has offered five different definitions of that term, the third and fifth of which he accepted as particularly applicable to historical work. Nor has the meaning of the "quest for truth" been devoid of ambiguity, since opinions have varied as to what "truth" actually is. Other complications arise from the frequently unavoidable translations from a text in a foreign language. It has been pointed out that, for example, the German term "Reich" has different shades of meaning than its usual English equivalent "empire." Every language possesses, moreover, wholly untranslatable words. Hence, the presence of so many loanwords from other languages which sooner or later are "officially" sanctioned by their inclusion in a new edition of an authoritative dictionary. Another form of "subjectivity" arises from the tendency of creative scholars to overemphasize the preeminent role played by a single factor among the causes of certain new historical developments, such as Karl Marx's stress on the changes in the process of production; Henri Pirenne's attribution of the rise of the medieval Western society from a reaction to the speedy expansion of Islam; Frederick Jackson Turner's highly influential thesis on *The Frontier in American History*; or Max Weber's theory of *The Protestant Ethic and the Spirit of Capitalism* (by coincidence, the last two essays happened to appear in the same year, 1920). This conglomeration of different conceptions—or, to use the New Testament description of the multiplicity of voices in Acts 2:9 ff.—has been further aggravated by the numerous new techniques of historical research employed in recent decades (about which more anon), a situation which induced C. Vann Woodward to exclaim that it has "gone so far that it is doubtful whether the notion of 'history' has any core meaning at all, so various are the meanings which can be imputed to it." Nevertheless, without a deliberate and strenuous effort to be at least as objective as possible, a historian turns into a moralist, a social or political propagandist, a religious determinist, or else an incoherent writer.[22]

To begin with, Jewish and Christian historical writings were long dominated by their authors' religious outlooks. From biblical times on, the historians interpreted most of the contemporary and past phenomena as the effect of an often inscrutable divine will. As late as the nineteenth century the distinguished American historian George Bancroft could write: "History was the unfolding of a vast providential plan." Two centuries earlier, Sir Walter Raleigh had tried to explain the downfall of the Lancaster and Tudor dynasties by the biblical reference to God's punishment for sins down to the fourth generation. Since the relationships between state and Church played an enormous role in the history of the medieval and early modern world, these and other religious presuppositions affected the writing of many outstanding secular historians as well. To theologians the problem of *Glaube und Geschichte*, faith and history, involved puzzling decisions which, however, often proved totally unsatisfactory; for example, in the study of the Bible at times they had to construe a two-tier theory of historical and transhistorical (*übergeschichtlich*) truths. After reviewing the conflicting schools of thought in the mid-1940s, Chester Charlton McCown observed that "the relationship of Christianity and its doctrines of revelation to history is one of the most serious problems that the present generation of theologians has to face." Paul Tillich, too, has characterized history as "the problem of our age." About the same time another American theologian, Clarence T. Craig, noted that "the present revolt" against the excesses committed by many leading biblical critics earlier in the century

> is in grave danger of becoming a retreat to dogma rather than an advance to a truer insight into the permanent significance of the events recorded in the Old and New Testaments. That peril can be met only as men of sound historical training accept the challenge to interpret the meaning of Christian faith.

Nevertheless, as late as 1967 a scholar suggested that in the conflict between faith and history it is for the historian to decide "which questions are relevant in practice"—a desperate expedient. Jewish students also found themselves restricted in their judgments by the authority of sanctified sources. Purely objective research and attempts to impose general historical considerations as determining criteria on the study of biblical and other highly revered religious writings ran counter to deeply felt convictions of staunch believers.[23]

Such relations between Church history and general history also in the case of sacred Jewish literature frequently generated conflicts in one's religious conscience, and in earlier times stamped the historian as a heretic and an outlaw in his own community. Survivals of such intimate interrelations between Church and state have been preserved in the institutional recognition of theological faculties as integral parts of universities. One must not forget that some of the most revered institutions of higher learning such as the universities of Bologna, Salamanca, Paris, Oxford, Vienna, Prague, Cracow, and Harvard had originally started as schools of religious studies and only subsequently broadened their teaching programs to include the various other branches of learning. In the Jewish and Muslim areas secular institutions, as distinguished from yeshivot and madrases, have been altogether the fruits of modern secularization in the nineteenth and twentieth centuries. When in the 1830s the reformers Abraham Geiger and Ludwig Philippson sounded their clarion calls for the establishment of a department of Jewish studies at a German university, they spoke in terms of a "Jewish theological faculty," parallel to those of the Christian faith connected with the celebrated German schools of higher learning. Nor must we forget that even in recent years the critical study of the Bible, and particularly the Pentateuch, was sharply delimited in many supposedly secular Jewish schools to avoid instruction in biblical criticism along modern lines.[24]

Other shackles on the freedom of objective historical research were imposed by dominant political or social movements. In totalitarian countries especially, whether fascist, nazi, or communist, history was put into the service of a particular Weltanschauung allowing for few deviations. In fact, however, Marxism carried within itself a basic contradiction between theory and practice. On the one hand, the doctrine of historical materialism insisted that all historical developments are primarily determined by basic changes in production and other economic factors. In practice, on the other hand, Karl Marx himself and his successors propagated individual and group action by their adherents in order to bring about the necessary social changes. But these and other contradictions were readily reconciled by "dialectical" reasoning. Totalitarian indoctrination thus became a basic instrument of governmental operations. This did not prevent, for instance, the ruling circles in the Kremlin from changing their minds under new political exigencies. As a result certain historical treatments, originally approved by the authorities, were later suppressed and replaced by often contradictory evaluations. Such directed historiography came to the fore, especially in the treatment of minorities and particularly of the Jews. One need but refer to the descriptions, under governmental supervision, of the Jewish past and present in the various editions of the *Bolshaya Entsiklopedia* (Large Russian Encyclopedia). While in the first edition in 1932 the article "Evrei" was given an extensive (130-column) and moderately balanced, if preordained, coverage; in the second edition in 1952 the space allotted to the general subject of "Jews" was reduced to the insignificant total of two columns. The third edition in 1972 handled it even more deprecatingly, reflecting the growth of anti-Jewish feelings in the ruling circles. In contrast, the Soviet attitudes to the Russian Orthodox Church have undergone a sharp reorientation in the opposite direction. From open hostility in the 1920s came a growing rapprochement in the face of the rising Nazi menace in the 1930s and in the crucible of the Second World War. This reorientation also greatly affected the Soviet historiography with respect to Russian history of the Middle Ages and early modern times.[25]

Less authoritarian, but no less dogmatic, has been the self-imposed attitude of many Marxist historians in other countries. Less obvious, but quite pervasive, often were also some fundamental ideological assumptions in democratic societies. Without imposing any formal censorship upon the individual writers, the prevailing nationalist and other political orientations seriously affected a great many historians. When a patriotic Prussian like Heinrich von Treitschke insisted that "all history is primarily political history" and sweepingly asserted that "one can imagine English history without William III and French history without Richelieu, but the Prussian state is the work of its princes," he wrote as a partisan of the Prussian monarchy rather than as an objective historian. Truly distinguished Jewish historians like Heinrich Graetz and Simon Dubnow, too, did not try to hide their intense Jewish loyalites in all their treatments of the Jewish past. They often wrote as moralists judging what was good or bad for their people; it may be said that their great popularity was the result not only of their historical skills, but also of their patriotic Jewish interpretations which appealed to the Jewish public at large. It is small wonder, then, that Treitschke and Graetz publicly clashed on the Jewish issue, creating quite a furor in Germany and other countries.[26]

At the same time some biases reflected in modern historical writings were the result of involuntary assimilation of ideas and assertions underlying the existing historical sources themselves. We are, for example, so much better informed about the history of the medieval clergy and nobility and particularly of the various royal dynasties than about that of the masses of peasants, who often amounted to 80 or more percent of the population of each country. The reason was that most of the chronicles and other more or less contemporary sources were written by clerics or courtiers. The same holds true for much of the rich Muslim historiography of the Middle Ages and early modern times. In Jewish life, too, most of the material available to modern investigators originated from writings by scholars and rabbis who automatically reflected the attitudes of, and recorded events relating to, the life in their circle, rather than those regarding the people at large. Moses Maimonides merely revealed his equally narrrow view of history when he rejected the entire contemporary Arabic historical literature. He wrote:

It is sheer waste of time; as in the case of books found among the Arabs describing historical events, the government of kings and Arab genealogy, or books of songs and similar works which neither posssess wisdom nor yield profit for the body, but are merely a waste of time.

He himself maintained a keen historic interest only in the sequence of generations of rabbis as a major part of the Jewish tradition. In general, intellectual history remained the preoccupation of all medieval and early modern Jewish students; at the most they supplemented these concerns with the history of Jewish sufferings as did, for instance, Joseph ben Joshua ha-Kohen. After the broadening of modern historical research, the historians, Christian, Muslim, and Jewish, found themselves hampered by the nearly total absence of records pertaining to the life of the masses during many historical periods and had to supplement the existing information by more or less ingenious hypotheses.[27]

III

PREDICTABILITY

CONNECTED WITH the questions concerning both history's relevance and objectivity is that of the use of historical data for predicting the future. The biblical writers used descriptions of historical events so
as to fit them into the general scheme of a divinely ordered historical
process and for praising or condemning the behavior of rulers, as well as
for deriving from them lessons for the future. All along the "judgment of
history" has often been invoked by religious moralists or political propagandists to justify whatever action they proposed. In this respect historians shared with other social scientists the necessity of making many
value judgments. Although less frequently than the economists helping
prepare state or corporate budgets or foretelling the likely upward or down-
ward trends in the prices of commodities, they have also been called upon
to extrapolate from their analyses of contemporary or past events some
predictions for future planning.

On the other hand, opponents questioned the right to pass, or even
the possibility of passing, such judgments, and to apply them to future
actions. They attributed all efforts of this kind to the personal dispositions
of the particular historians accounted for by their individual tempera-
ments, their upbringing, their particular class, or their yielding to the
prevailing climate of opinion of their time. Still others, like Friedrich
Nietzsche, went to the other extreme of evaluating historical judgments
on the basis of their supposed usefulness to society. In a characteristic
passage he contended that "the falsity of an opinion is by itself not yet a
valid argument against it . . . . The question is how much it helps to
promote life, to preserve life, to preserve a species, perhaps even to breed a
species." This statement appears less extreme if one considers the long
established practice in the legal profession and its literature not to disregard juridical teachings overruled by the majority. The prominent Muslim mystic-jurist Abu Bakr Muhammad ibn ʿAli ibn ʿArabi (1165–1240)

voiced the prevailing opinion among his coreligionists that "the acceptance of one opinion as prevailing over another, does not entail the total exclusion of the latter. On the contrary, one ought to preserve it." A widespread adage summed up the accepted rule that "there exists a blessing in the divergences among the *imams*." As is well known, the Talmud, too, is filled with debates among the leading exponents of opposing views which often required the adoption of rules as to which of them were to be regarded as more authoritative in practical application, without completely ruling out the validity of the rejected view in specific cases.[28]

Nevertheless, attempts at prediction were made even by historians who argued against the very principle of historical predictability. Jakob Burckhardt claimed that "a future known in advance is an absurdity. Foreknowledge of the future is not only undesirable, it is probably beyond our power as well." He pointed out that at best man is hampered by the ignorance of the latent forces of future conditions, the confusion of our wishes, and some calculable mental categories. On the other hand, though living in the period of great optimism and general belief in progress, he himself predicted some of the storms which were to threaten civilization in the twentieth century. It may be said, that theoretically most historians would agree with R. G. Collingwood's insistence that "whenever historians claim to be able to determine the future in advance of its happenings, we may know with certainty that something has gone wrong with their fundamental concepts of history."[29]

Yet, to many others the temptation to forecast the future on the basis of their historical analyses often proved irresistible. If one or another prediction happened to come true, it could readily be quoted to encourage continued experimentation along the same lines. We need but cite the fairly recent nightmare of the seizure of the American embassy in Teheran and the year-long detention of American hostages by the revolutionary Iranian authorities. All that despite the warning sounded by an Israeli analyst more than eight years before. Writing in 1971, Yehezkel Dror stated:

> American citizens and property in areas [in which] United States activities and strength are evident, may become useful bargaining counters in the hands of the "Crazy State" in order to achieve its ends. Thus blackmail based on the taking of American citizens as hostages for the purposes of ransom . . . is a clear example of such a possibility.

Some other predictions have also turned out to be correct, while a great many others have been off the mark. Their realization depended in part on accidental configurations, but at times were indeed foreseen by a historian's insights and moral forebodings. Lord Acton was not wrong in asserting that a historian's morality "consists of those things which affect the veracity" of his findings.[30]

Moreover, all predictions are based on the assumption of the continuity of history. One need not completely agree with Gottfried Wilhelm von Leibniz's assertion that "nature never makes somersaults; this is what I call the law of continuity" and his general doctrine of "preestablished harmony" as a universal divinely ordained system, and yet acknowledge the tremendous impact of continuity in the historical evolution. I, myself, have on occasion tried to show that revolutionary movements, if successful, have usually reversed the historic process with respect only to their main objectives, while they have left unaltered most other phases of the historic evolution. Thus the Protestant Reformation, wherever it prevailed, succeeded in rejecting the supremacy of the Papacy, reverted to the biblical texts freely interpreted by the individual conscience, and enforced obedience to some of its other basic teachings. But it left other institutions and doctrines, including those which affected, for example, the Jewish status, without far-reaching alterations. Only ultimately, because Protestantism had failed completely to overcome Catholicism, did the resulting prolonged Wars of Religion, ending in the stalemate of the Thirty Years War, lead to the recognition of the liberty of religious conscience by the Peace Treaties of Westphalia. This toleration of the respective large minorities also indirectly became a major factor in the progress of Jewish Emancipation. I made a similar observation in the case of the Russian Revolution: it attained its major aims (such as nationalization of the means of production and the destruction of the Tsarist system based, according to Sergei S. Uvarov's famous definition, upon "Orthodoxy, Autonomy, and [Russian] Nationality"), but otherwise retained—or in time reverted to—the fundamental institutions and attitudes of the Russian people including its strong anti-Semitic feelings. In fact, some historians have actually questioned the ability of any kind of precise historical periodicization, since almost all dominant trends of any new period can be shown to have had some antecedents in earlier times. This is, indeed, the underlying assumption of any cyclical interpretation of history. Such forebodings of things to come have been so frequent that one could paradoxically contend that many of the subsequently known historical "innovations" had been perceived as if "through a glass darkly" by primitive men living in caves.[31]

Cases of unpredictable historic consequences of events and actions of men are probably much more numerous than those which anybody had clearly foreseen. Suffice it to mention the "dominant tendencies" in American history since World War I. When the United States entered that war, the American public was generally convinced that this catastrophic confrontation—which was to end with the unprecedented total of 8,000,000 men killed in battle—was to be "a war to end all wars." The author of that watchword, Woodrow Wilson, was himself a social scientist of note, who should have known better than to predict such an outcome. In fact, what followed the Peace Treaties of 1919 was a series of wars in various parts of the world, climaxed by World War II, which justified the designation of the entire period of 1914–45, as that of a second Thirty Years' War.[32]

Similarly, the domestic policies based on long-range plans often proved highly disappointing. While they may have achieved a modicum of success in specific objectives originally anticipated, they also generated some unforeseen damaging side effects. For example, with its great emphasis on material well-being the American public had long cherished the belief that, by improving the material lot of the masses, all other difficulties would be greatly smoothed out. I still vividly recall that, soon after my arrival in the United States in 1926, I increasingly heard the slogan of "two chickens in every pot and two cars in every garage" as the panacea for all social ills. From politicians and economists one constantly heard the prediction that the wave of prosperity characteristic of the "roaring twenties" would never end. Although this expectation received a severe jolt during the Great Depression, the American public still continued to believe that by spending much money on worthwhile social projects one could not only achieve domestic happiness but also acquire friends in other countries. At one time President Franklin Delano Roosevelt and Henry Wallace, then the vice president, came out with a program of full employment and predicted that some day the American labor force would amount to 60,000,000 employed persons. (At this writing the number of employed exceeds 107,000,000 in addition to millions of workers from among the "undocumented" immigrants and others not counted in the census.) They spoke of this expectation in semimessianic terms. If many economists doubted the feasibility of such a program, they were later humbled when in the turbulent 1960s more than 80,000,000 people were employed. During that decade the ideal of two chickens and two cars, with the modern addition of two television sets, had become a reality among a large segment of the American people.

There is, indeed, no question that in the 1960s the country had achieved a height of prosperity unprecedented in its own history and, very likely, also in the history of the world. Yet, this was the decade of the greatest tragedies for the nation at large. For the first time in its history the United States had lost a war; for the first time it saw its cities burned by its own citizens. It also witnessed an unprecedented spread of a socially debilitating drug culture and soon also a crime wave of a totally unforeseen magnitude. Nor was it spared the spectacle of widespread student uprisings, aimed not as usual at seizing centers of political and military power, but at their own universities which in similar previous uprisings elsewhere had served as shelters for the student revolutionaries. Equally horrifying was the more permanent impact of that prosperity on the work ethic and the working habits of the American people. The resulting drop in productivity, combined with widespread absenteeism, made the United States, despite its advanced technology, less and less competitive in the world markets. At the same time, the generation's constantly rising expectations, which could not be met, created a mass of welfare clients many of whom ultimately lost all hope of ever emerging from that status. The example of Britain and other countries went totally unheeded, although more than a century ago Alexis de Toqueville had already pointed out the difference between England—then the most prosperous nation in the world—which had thousands upon thousands of "paupers" in its population, and Spain, then the poorest country in Europe, which had none. Now we have a large third generation on welfare which, through various quirks in the country's legislation and administration, occasionally includes paupers with a higher standard of life than that enjoyed by some hard-working wage earners. Yet, it may not be too late for the nation to learn some other sounder lessons from its own heritage.[33]

We must not overlook, however, the intrinsic connection between predictability and objectivity. Quite apart from the human tendency toward wishful thinking often leading to complete self-delusion, predictions from past events and developments necessarily depend on the interpretation of what has actually happened. Any inexplicable prejudgment of the past naturally leads to projections into the future based upon these distorted premises. Nevertheless by an occasional historical irony such distorted projection into the future may come true, if there are enough strong-willed persons or groups wishing to make them become a reality. In such cases the predictions may easily become self-fulfilling, offering but another illustration of the power of "illusions" in shaping historical events.

Understandably, therefore, historical predictability, as well as objectivity, has played a much smaller role in societies with strong religious or political convictions, unless they sought through oracles or prophecies to ascertain God's will, or through more secular means to learn about the plans and intentions of a powerful ruler. Even when they were conscious of their lack of historical objectivity, some spokesmen of an exclusively religious point of view usually buttressed their position by an appeal to the "higher truth" offered by supernatural revelation or its derivatives, contrasted with the admittedly fallible human reason.

Not surprisingly, therefore, in the 1960s many Americans living in the midst of that plenty were filled with anxiety about the future of their civilization. Some people were despondent enough to leave the United States, whether as draft dodgers or because they lost faith in the future of their country and tried to build up new careers elsewhere. All along historians were often asked whether the future was indeed as dismal as it appeared to many thoughtful onlookers.

A characteristic admission to this effect was made even by the totalitarian ruler Benito Mussolini who, in 1934, at the acme of his power, stated:

> From Diocletian to Bismarck [the whole history of Western civilization] teaches us that whenever there is a conflict between the state and religion it is always the state that loses the battle. A battle against religion is a battle against the imponderable. It is open warfare against the spirit, at the point where the spirit is deepest and most inward. It is proven to-day that in the course of such a battle even the sharpest weapons at the disposal of the state are ineffectual mortally to wound the Church. The Church, and more especially the Catholic Church, emerges from the bitterest battles unchanged and victorious.

Out of these considerations the Duce had concluded in 1929 a Concordat with the Vatican designed to bridge over the break between the Church and the state which had characterized the first half century of the nationally unified Italian regime (since 1870). In the same vein the formerly liberal philosopher, Giovanni Gentile, as a Fascist Minister of Education, demanded that the schools emphasize the "perennial philosophy" of Thomas Aquinas, rather than the short-lived systems of the modern thinkers. In a famous encyclical, *Studiorum ducem*, of June 29, 1923, Pope Pius XI wrote: "It is to be hoped that the doctrine of Aquinas concerning the ruling of peoples and the laws which establish their relations with one another may be better known, since they contain the true foundations of that which is termed the League of Nations." Similar attitudes occasionally came to the fore also among deeply religious persons in democratic countries. I remember that once, in addressing an interdenominational audience on the subject of "Liberty" I mentioned, among other matters, that, next to liberty of conscience and freedom from state interference in religious affairs, one ought to consider also liberty *within* the religious bodies. In the following discussion a Monsignor asked a question: "You spoke about Liberty in the treatment of divergent religious views, but what about Certainty?"[34]

Yet, in 1941 Mussolini himself, now under the strong influence of his Nazi allies, expressed surprise that Hitler had not abolished Christmas, a holiday "which reminds us only of the birth of a Jew who gave the world debilitating and devitalizing theories, and who had contrived to trick particularly Italy through the disintegrating power of the popes." In fact, through the exercise of a sharp censorship combined with a vigorous indoctrination of the people in the new racialist theories through the schools, press, radio, and public meetings, the National Socialists in Germany were able to persuade most of the German public to abandon its traditional historical views and to adopt the new racialist doctrines preached by their party. Long before Hitler's rise to power a determined Jew-baiter like Paul de Lagarde had used his considerable knowledge of Semitic languages to denigrate the basic doctrines of the Scripture, long cherished by all Christian denominations. "Catholicism, Protestantism, Judaism, naturalism," he wrote, "must give way to a new conception of life so that they be remembered no more than are the lamps used at night after the sun shines over the mountains." Other German Bible scholars like Friedrich Delitzsch and Gerhard Kittel were prone to pervert the meaning of the ancient and medieval sources in order to deny any originality to the Bible, insisting that all its admirable narratives and teachings were mere imitations of Babylonian or Egyptian prototypes. They concluded that throughout the ages the Jewish people represented an inferior and pernicious race. Finally, Alfred Rosenberg, the chief official ideologist of the

Nazi movement, could proclaim as one of the Nazis' basic interpretations of history that

> From the compulsory dogma of limitless love and the equality of everything human before God, on the one hand, and from the doctrine of democratic "rights of man," devoid of all racial feeling and all nationally rooted sense of honor, on the other hand, European society has "developed" into but a guardian of the inferior, the sick, and the crippled, of the criminal and putrid.

It is small wonder that Adolf Hitler himself expressed his great admiration for Sparta, because in that ancient Greek city-state the small elite of Spartans could dominate thousands of slaves. The chancellor's admiration may have been tempered had he known that the ancient Spartans and Second-Commonwealth Jews professed to have close family relationships.[35]

Equally arbitrary has been the rewriting of history under the Soviet regime. We recall their treatment of the Jews in the Large Russian Encyclopedia. Generally to enhance the prestige of the Soviet Union they claimed, as is well known, paternity for almost all scientific inventions and discoveries in the last generations. For this purpose they often manufactured evidence or offered completely untenable arguments. At some variance, however, from the National Socialists, the largely pragmatic Soviet leaders often paid attention to the demands of Realpolitik and were prepared radically to change their points of view and to adjust them to their new exigencies. Certain subjects nevertheless remained forbidden territory to scholarly investigation. The early defeats of the Soviet armies during the Nazi invasion of 1941 were either passed over in silence or reinterpreted to appear almost as victories of the Red Army. Even after Stalin's death and the so-called thaw in the strict supervision of all writings, many persons who had been condemned by the regime and executed, even if they were subsequently "rehabilitated," were never to be mentioned. Under these circumstances writing of modern history must have been extremely awkward for conscientious Russian scholars, not only because of the shackles from the outset imposed upon their productivity. They also had the wholly justified fear that any position taken at the time of writing which was fully consonant with the authoritarian outlook of the time might later be sharply disavowed by the upper echelons of the bureaucracy, and the author accused of undermining the Soviet regime.[36]

Such misreadings of history were not limited to dictatorial regimes. Even in democratic countries, political partisanship was often inspired by ardent nationalism. I noted personally how difficult it was for UNESCO, in its better days, to reconcile conflicting interpretations of historic events because of national biases. When this world organization adopted the project of preparing a supranational history of mankind, it found that, for example, the Napoleonic wars, especially in their latest phases, were treated in the respective French and German textbooks in a wholly irreconcilable manner. Such sharp divergences appeared during many wars already in the very original sources of information, such as the reportage about battles between the belligerent nations, whether in domestic or foreign combat. Finally, UNESCO decided to avoid political and economic history as far as possible and to concentrate on sponsoring the production of a History of Mankind: Cultural and Scientific Development which, on the face of it, appeared more amenable. In the execution, however, nationalist and other biases could not be completely suppressed. Despite the editors' efforts to maintain an impartial stance, they could only with great difficulty tone down the contributions of some collaborators by the use of their editorial pencils.[37]

An extreme tool for abetting religious and political interests or prejudices consisted of forging historical documents. One of the most enduringly successful forgeries consisted in the notorious Donatio Constantini, the alleged privilege granted the Papacy by Constantine the Great, which was fabricated four centuries after the supposed event. Although it is recorded as having been known as a forgery in certain papal circles as early as the tenth century, this falsification was not publicly exposed until the brilliant researches of Lorenzo Valla half a millennium later (1440). Even thereafter its authenticity still found some scholarly defenders for several centuries. Similarly, the recent spread of The Protocols of the Elders of Zion, though repeatedly proved to be an outright forgery by competent scholars independently reaching the same conclusion, was not completely silenced by their incontestable proofs. It still enjoys wide circulation in some Communist and Arab countries. At times such forgeries were produced merely ad majorem Dei gloriam. In Jewish circles the presentation of numerous Karaite manuscripts by Abraham Firkovich to the Imperial Library in St. Petersburg caused a great stir both in the historical profession and among the public. Yet, it took many years for experts (beginning with Albert [Abraham] Harkavy and Hermann Strack) to segregate the kernels of truth out of the superimposed levels of interpolations and other alterations in the texts. Even now the authenticity of many passages cannot be fully proved or disproved. According to G. R. Elton, "no one ever forges documents to deceive historians." However, we know of some exceptions at least in the case of a Belgian scholar Eliakim Carmoly. If we are to believe such adversaries as Moritz Steinschneider, Carmoly's quotations of many passages from medieval sources or even one or another small tract published by him were based upon much fabrication. This was done as a rule not for any monetary gain or for the promotion of some partisan cause, but merely in order to enhance that author's scholarly prestige.[38]

Such extremes are, of course, avoided in most Western historical literature. However, the connections with contemporary movements are often quite evident and partisanship in favor of one or another of them is publicly admitted or at least clearly implied. To cite examples from Jewish historical writings, it suffices to cite one of the founders of the modern science of Judaism, Leopold Zunz. This distinguished historian of Hebrew letters could not avoid insisting that the study of the Jewish people and of its political and moral history must precede all efforts to ascertain what in the old conception is usable and what is obsolete, as well as which of the new trends appears most desirable. The entire stress on what I called the "lachrymose conception of history," so dominant in nineteenth-century Jewish historiography was consciously or unconsciously placed at the service of the Emancipation movement, since it helped refute the opposition's major argument that giving Jews full equality of rights would only hurt society by the expansion of Jewish usury. With the reiterated emphasis on the Jewish sufferings through the ages it could be explained that the lopsidedness of the medieval Jewish economic endeavors and other alleged shortcomings were the results of governmental oppression and societal discrimination and that they would disappear with the growing integration of the Jews in the Western societies. Similar presuppositions could easily be detected in the orthodox, nationalist, and Zionist historiography later in the century. Yet, such uses of history for both analysis and prediction, done with a modicum of objectivity, and without concealment of one's own preferential views, have long been accepted as fairly legitimate ingredients in analyzing the past in a coherent and plausible way.[39]

IV

HISTORY FOR
HISTORY'S SAKE

A GREAT MANY SCHOLARS chose history as their field of study out
of sheer love for the past without any partisan intentions whatsoever.
William Stubbs was not the only historian who felt that "the study of
history is . . . as Coleridge said of Poetry, its own great reward, a thing to
be loved and cultivated for its own sake." Moreover, like artists or writers
who could select subjects for their paintings or novels without any religious or political bias, some historians, too, are known to have selected a
particular branch of historical research because it appealed to them as a
profession or hobby. In fact, the old discussion as to whether history is an
art or a science has never been completely resolved. It obviously has
elements of both. Some observers have actually seen in this combination
that one of the great tasks of history is to serve as a bridge between these
two domains. In any case, as Norman Hampson observed, "historians are
normally too busy teaching and writing history and being people, to worry
very much about the nature of what they are trying to do. If . . . history is
primarily an art, this is reasonable enough. One expects painters to paint,
and to leave it to others to argue about the nature of painting." Many
historians have, indeed, just written history following Leopold von
Ranke's advice to describe "as it essentially was" (*wie es eigentlich gewesen
ist*) not quite realizing that the mere selection of the factors considered
significant was in itself a reflection of certain theoretical presuppositions
of which they themselves may not have been aware. At times such lack of
concern for the theoretical underpinnings was considered a blemish by
outsiders to historical research. For example, Hermann Cohen's censure
of Zunz's great historic contribution and his stating than "Zunz could have
been a great historian but alas he turned out to be no more than an
antiquarian" was based upon Zunz's neglecting to formulate and apply

some theoretical approaches to his work. Somewhat related, though more technical, was Heinrich Graetz's contention that "Zunz's more confusing than illuminating notes and his dry nomenclature have been of little help to me."[40]

In some respects the profession, overt or tacit, of great objectivity and noninvolvement in the ideological struggles of the day produced dire results for Jewish historiography in the latter part of the nineteenth century. Because modern Jewish history, like most other modern developments, usually left behind a multitude of sources and required much more selectivity than the relatively few preserved documents of ancient and medieval time such personal selectivity could be dismissed as "journalism" by Moritz Steinschneider and other scholars, whose greatest effort consisted in gathering and organizing notes, rather than reconstructing sequences of historical events and movements at large. Another criticism often heard in Germany and even Britain was connected with the publication of a historical work written in good literary style. Some readers, including historians unable to write well, saw in such successful literary efforts an indication that these authors lacked profundity and thoroughgoing research. As a result of such suspicions, the field of modern Jewish history was frequently neglected altogether or else was relinquished to professional journalists or littérateurs. An outcome of this primary preoccupation with the earlier periods was, for example, the undue neglect of the informative tenth volume in three parts of the *Geschichte der Israeliten* by Isaak Markus Jost, covering the period 1815–45. It was not until the beginning of the twentieth century that the diverse treatments of the modern period by Martin Philippson and Simon Dubnow saw the light of day. They were followed by such works as Ismar Elbogen's *A Century of Jewish Life*, designed as a supplement to Graetz's *Geschichte*, the final volume of which had stopped with the year 1848. The very failure of the historians to analyze the impact of the great revolutionary movements of 1848–49 (sometimes called the "Spring of Nations") on European Jewry during the second half of the nineteenth century well illustrated the growing indifference of those generations toward the history of their more recent past.[41]

Another effect of this extreme quest for nonpartisanship was the concentration of scholars of that time on critical editions of older sources with the avoidance of narrative and reconstructive history. Many historians felt that they would be on safer ground when they learned to read paleographically difficult manuscripts, reconstruct inscriptions, and unravel papyri—in other words, what Nietzsche called the "monumental" and "antiquarian" aspects of historical studies—transcribe them accurately; try to ascertain certain facts recorded in them by comparison with other sources; closely identify names of persons and localities; and pursue other such minutiae, and thus publish well-annotated, critical editions of important texts.

The typical remark of Ludwig Mitteis to Guido Kisch that "edition of sources belongs to the most gratifying tasks in scholarship" well mirrored the feelings of many leading scholars of the generation. Such works were, of course, great contributions to learning, and they laid memorable foundations upon which historians could build their future reconstructions. But at times these efforts represented only a failure of nerve to reshape such materials into constructive images of the past by more creative and intensive efforts to imbue the newly recovered details with broadly relevant meanings.[42]

It goes without saying that even such detailed investigations could not be pursued without basic theoretical decisions. One had to proceed, for example, in the study of the Bible and other ancient sources, from the "lower criticism" concerned with the verification of existing texts—wherever necessary with the aid of proposed serious emendations derived from speculation rather than from direct evidence—to "higher criticism." As is well known, the late nineteenth and early twentieth centuries marked the high points of literary criticism—both high and low, of all ancient sources. Criticism was indeed pushed to such extremes as to lead to the wholesale denial of the historicity of major events or personalities. By the beginning of this century scholars like the Germans Hugo Winckler and Arthur Drews, the Englishman John M. Robertson, the Italian Milesbo (Emilio Rossi), and the American William Benjamin Smith made a career of denying the historicity of Moses and the Exodus as well as that of Jesus and all the events connected with their work according to the Old and New Testament sources. Radical criticism of this kind may have abated in recent decades, but its heritage is still with us, as is the generally atheistic stance of Karl Marx and Vladimir Lenin—including Lenin's appeal to his Bolshevik Party to spread the French Enlightenment's antireligious writings among the masses. These trends helped to spawn the numerous new innovative "approaches" to biblical and other ancient sources, each represented by a different school of biblical criticism. Nor were even such allegedly independent examinations devoid of partisanship. Some of them were actually generated by outright antisemitism, as was the Bible–Babel controversy over Friedrich Delitzsch's theories.[43]

One of the major stumbling blocks for critics of the Bible and other

ancient sources has been their ambivalence toward the ancient oral traditions, especially in the legal field. Even those who realized that much of
the ancient literature had been derived from legal precedents, words of
wisdom, songs, and other creations of the popular mind first recorded
through oral transmission over many generations of sayings, narratives,
genealogies, and the like, were frequently quite hesitant to accept them at
their face value. Prejudiced by the modern conception that documentary
evidence, submitted especially to courts of justice, was much superior to
that based on recollections of bystanders, most historians automatically
assumed that in ancient times, too, alterations could more readily occur
through the failure of memory, human error, or the particular bias of the
individual oral transmitters than the facts or opinions recorded in written
documents. They did not quite realize that in the Middle East down to
modern times memory was cultivated to an extent unparalleled in the
West. Professional or amateur "memorizers" were often able to repeat with
considerable accuracy long passages, songs, and particularly brief epi-
grams, after hearing them once.

Suffice it to mention here the example of the Mughal (Indian) emperor Akbar the Great whom the modern historian, Vincent A. Smith
characterized as "a born king of men, with a rightful claim to rank as one
of the greatest sovereigns known in history." He had no formal education,
and actually was an illiterate. And yet he possessed such a prodigious
memory that, after once hearing the recitation of lengthy Persian poems,
he could repeat them verbatim without an error. Similarly, engaging in his
beloved pastime of assembling learned representatives of the various religious groups in his empire and listening to their debates about the respective merits of their faiths, he quickly absorbed the knowledge not only
of the basic teachings but also the innumerable theological and ritualistic
minutiae of Hinduism, Jainism, Zoroastrianism, Christianity, Judaism,
and Islam—including their numerous subdivisions. It is also very likely
that most spokesmen in their religious disputations presented their arguments from their own deep-rooted and long-cultivated memories. Hence it
was possible for the talmudic sages to insist that, while the written law,
the Torah, being divinely ordained down to the smallest minutiae, ought
not to be recited from memory, the reverse was true in the case of oral
traditions. Characteristically, the Talmud justified this decision by stating
that written documents may be subject to alteration, willfully or unwittingly, by the scribes, whereas records handed down orally through autho-

rized memorizers were far more reliable. The faith that the "Oral Law" had basically been revealed to Moses on Sinai as a supplement to the written law and that it anticipated in substance all the future elaborations in the various schools of priestly and rabbinic jurisprudence was so deeply rooted that the majority of the Jewish people readily rejected the important Karaite sect as utterly heretical because it had repudiated the validity of the Oral Law.[44]

The failure to recognize the relatively great dependability of ancient oral traditions, held sacred by trained memorizers, was a major weakness, for example, on the part of the distinguished school of biblical criticism led by Julius Wellhausen. It assumed that the so-called Priestly Code must have originated *after* the work of the Deuteronomist. However brilliant the spokesmen of that school were, and however significant their contribution to biblical studies has remained until the present day, they readily overlooked the possibility—even the likelihood—that at least a great many of the laws included in the Book of Leviticus had their origin in rituals and legal decisions accumulated during several preceding centuries. These "laws" had first been formulated by some priestly or lay judges responding to specific needs of their time and were later transmitted by faithful recorders for many generations before some selected portions were written down by one or another scribe. Similarly, a persuasive argument has been made in favor of the theory that even the Babylonian Talmud (although, in contrast to its Palestinian counterpart, it had gone through a careful editorial process during most of the fifth century C.E.) had remained unwritten for two hundred years or longer. Its text was essentially preserved only through the memorizers of the two Babylonian academies of Sura and Pumbedita. This serious oversight, as we shall see, was aggravated in the case of the Bible by the additional shortcoming of the Bible critics' appreciation of the speed with which the original Israelite conquerors of Palestine had changed, after their settlement in the Holy Land, from their alleged seminomadic to a more civilized mode of life.[45]

Remarkably, in recent years some historians, dissatisfied with the amount and type of information supplied by the available documentary evidence, have turned the whole cycle back to Oral History. According to one of its younger devotees, "historians have long felt that written documents lack human direction and spontaneity. . . . [They] also are innocent of the lives of the vast numbers of poor and working people." I remember my own and several other colleagues' pleasant surprise when, in

1938, Allan Nevins first advanced the idea of his well-known Oral History project at Columbia University. Nevins, to quote his assistant, Saul Benison,

> looked upon it as an organization that in a systematic way could obtain from the lips of living Americans who had led significant lives a full review of their participation in the political, economic, and cultural affairs of the nation. His purpose was to prepare such materials for the use of future historians.

The project was an instantaneous success and spread like wildfire into many countries. By 1970 a pertinent Dictionary listed no less than 230 such efforts in the United States alone. Five years later one of its practitioners estimated that their number had reached 450. Many universities now offer courses in Oral History. In the Jewish field, the collections assembled by some organizations, including the Hebrew University, produced much of that novel material. To be sure, because of their general selectivity in interviewing only "important" persons, the organizers have injected a strong subjective element into their operations, and for the most part have failed to supply data concerning the lives of the "silent majorities." They have also failed, as a rule, to take sufficient precautions against the inability of listeners to reproduce fully the shades of meaning conveyed by the speakers, the frequent capriciousness of the questions asked by the interviewers, and the distortions of human memory especially characteristic of highly active persons concerning their earlier actions or opinions. From the outset I mentioned to Nevins my experiences with newspaper reports about meetings which I had attended; they were, for the most part, at some variance with what I had heard, unless they quoted from a prepared official release or, more recently, from an electronically recorded text. I had also found that many active political leaders sincerely believed that they had some years before held and expressed opinions dramatically opposed to what the contemporary minutes had reported them as saying. Neither they, nor their original listeners, were trained "memorizers" of the ancient or medieval type. Yet, when used with great caution and applied with some of the stringent safeguards developed over the years through the criticism of written documents, including autobiographical memoirs, these new materials have provided the student of twentieth-century history with some valuable additional data. At the same time they have also increased the burden of subjective selectivity on the part of the narrators and analysts of recent developments for which there usually exists an overabundance of written materials, printed or as yet unpublished. It also makes doubly difficult the art of "forgetting" which, as Friedrich Nietzsche has pointed out, is a necessary counterpart to that of "remembering" among the tools of a historian.[46]

V

INTERDISCIPLINARY RELATIONS

PERHAPS THE GREATEST difficulty for any kind of consensus in historical methodology among twentieth-century scholars stems from the vast incursions of methodological elements from related disciplines such as philosophy, sociology, anthropology, archaeology, economics, and psychiatry. If one sometimes speaks of these disciplines as "auxiliary sciences" to history, this does not indicate, of course, that they are in any way inferior. In fact, history is, in return, an "auxiliary science" for each of them in a larger or lesser degree. But with the enormously rich and speedy development of each of these auxiliary disciplines, with their numerous subdivisions and ramifications, their impact upon historical research has been doubly irresistible as the resulting changes greatly appealed to generations bent upon "innovative" approaches. There is no question, indeed, that the cross-fertilization of ideas and tools of these varying approaches has greatly enriched the field of historical methodology and given rise to some significant new schools of historical research.[47]

From the outset the closest relationship has thus existed between history and philosophy. In time the study of philosophy itself was to a large extent devoted to the history of philosophy, which mainly meant an analysis of the individual systems created by great thinkers, often without relationship to one another. There even have been studies concerning the philosophy of the history of philosophy. At the same time the reciprocal philosophy of history has either overtly or tacitly influenced much of the other areas of historical writings. Needless to say, the term "philosophy" in English has had different shades of meaning from that in other languages; it often referred merely to one or another underlying attitude to life in general or to special situations. However, the general outlook on history as a part of either the illustration of the divine guidance of human destinies or as a part of the national tradition affecting even daily morality appeared in full bloom already in ancient times. We need but remember the injunction of the Deuteronomist (32:7): "Remember the days of old, Consider the years of many generations; Ask thy father and he will declare unto thee, Thine elders, and they will tell thee." According to traditional rabbinic interpretation this injunction referred to an inquiry from prophets (often called fathers) and from sages (often called elders). The superiority of the historical narratives of the Hebrew Bible over anything produced by its predecessors has long been recognized. Eduard Meyer, a leading historian of antiquity, has rightly observed that "no other oriental nation was able to create such an historical literature. Even the Greeks succeeded in producing one only at a much later stage in their development, in the fifth century." This statement still holds true now notwithstanding the more recent archaeological discoveries of additional Middle Eastern sources. But there remained a fundamental difference between the underlying Israelitic and Greek philosophies of history. To cite Hermann Cohen (1842–1918), the distinguished Neo-Kantian thinker who exalted the basic historical outlook of the biblical prophets:

> The concept of history is a creation of the [ancient] prophetism. It succeeded in what Greek intellectualism was unable to achieve. . . . The Greeks had always been oriented toward the past. . . . In contrast, the prophetic seers have created the concept of history as an anticipation of the life of the future. . . . The past and the present are submerged there in the impact of that expected future era.[48]

This view of the future dominated also the Jewish writings during the Second Commonwealth and after. Even the generally ahistorical "apocalyptic" preachers of doom tried "to find in the whole evolution of mankind a hidden meaning," history being "a long drama in which mankind involves itself ever deeper in sin and cruelty until the crisis comes, when the whole world explodes from excessive iniquity [opening the way for] redemption" (Israel Efros). Even the strongly hellenized Alexandrian Jewish apologists down to the Palestinian Josephus, though constantly invoking the past, partly in the Greek fashion, continued to look into the messianic future as the inevitable outcome of the divine guidance of history. It was this Jewish heritage which deeply influenced the medieval Christian philosophy of history as well. This heritage has continued until the present day to color many historical interpretations among the Jewish, Christian, and Muslim fundamentalists. A telling expression of the Catholic view was officially presented, for example, by Pope Pius XII in his address to the Tenth International Congress of Historical Sciences on September 7, 1955, when he declared: "The Catholic Church is cognizant of the fact that events take place according to the will and the permission of the Divine Providence. God obtains His objectives through history . . . God is indeed the Lord of history." This point of view found an eloquent exponent and popularizer in the more detailed studies of the Neo-Thomist philosopher, Jacques Maritain. Even a secular thinker like Karl Löwith entitled his important contribution to the general philosophy of history *Meaning in History: The Theological Implications of the Philosophy of History.*[49]

At the highest flowering of the historical writings during the nineteenth century the thinking of many philosophers, and to a lesser extent of historians, was dominated by the Hegelian interpretation, in which the state had largely supplanted God as the major historical force. Among its numerous offshoots, Marxism's materialistic conception of history became a most important historical movement in both theory and practice. Exponents of other distinguished historical approaches with worldwide influence included Wilhelm Dilthey, Max Weber, Benedetto Croce, and Friedrich Meinecke. As time went on, however, the impact of some new trends in philosophy, as well as in science, proved less beneficial to historical research. In fact, in some respects, the considerable disarray in philosophic and scientific thinking caused by the epochal and speedily changing trends during the two World Wars and their aftermaths brought about a considerable disorientation among historians as well. As R. F. Nichols rightly observed:

> The historian found in some cases that he must modify his sense of certainty. He realized that his cherished objectivity and scientific accuracy were somewhat illusory and that he was bound to take into account the implications of relativism. . . . Such thinking in one sense was clarifying; it destroyed a specious optimism and sense of infallibility. On the other hand, it tended to create confusion in some minds, it lessened self-confidence and it caused some workers in the vineyard to espouse a doctrine of uncertainty.

This was part of a general dissolution of the long-accepted moral and intellectual standards, so aptly summarized, with reference to the American intelligentsia, by Henry Steele Commager: "The two generations after 1890 witnessed a transition from certainty to uncertainty, from faith to doubt, from security to insecurity, from seeming order to ostentatious disorder." As a result of this internal insecurity, as well as the growing perennial quest for innovation, there have emerged a number of new historical schools, only some of which enjoyed more than a temporary and more or less partisan acceptance among the actual writers of history.[50]

These divergent voices made themselves but little heard among Jewish historians. In general, neither Jewish philosophers nor Jewish students of history were particularly concerned with epistomological or methodological problems of historical research. Their main contribution to the debate was in their quest for the "meaning" of the events and trends in the different periods of Jewish history. Even Nachman Krochmal, who presented a philosophic reinterpretation of the entire Jewish historical evolution, employed the traditionally accepted patterns of analysis and argumentation. On the other hand, Heinrich Graetz prepared a general "construction" of his own historical thinking in advance of his eleven-volume work which became a classic in the field. (See his *The Structure of Jewish History and Other Essays*.) But neither his fellow historians nor the public at large, who evinced great interest in the work itself, paid much attention to its theoretical underpinnings. Similarly, Simon M. Dubnow's occasional observations in his general outlook on Jewish history and even his important series of philosophico-historical *Letters on Ancient and Medieval Jewish History*, which over a number of years appeared in the *Voskhod*, attracted far more general attention through their exposition of Dubnow's brand of Jewish Diaspora nationalism and its role in the political struggles of East European Jewry at that time than through their historiographical relevance.[51]

Other writers who sought to reformulate the meaning of Jewish history included Melkizedek (pseudonym for Katzenelson), Jacob B. Agus, Simon Rawidowicz, Nathan Rotenstreich, and to some extent Morris R. Cohen in an essay on "Philosophies of Jewish History," which preceded his general work on *The Meaning of Human History*. Remarkably, most Jewish historians did not bother to come to grips with the basic philosophical and methodological aspects of their craft, but merely devoted their energies to describing historical events and movements in some narrative or analytical fashion appealing to them. They also continued to issue critical editions from archival and library collections. This was the case with the majority of general historians, too. Some of them, when venturing into the realm of theory, had little success. A case in point was Eduard Meyer, whose analysis of the philosophical underpinnings of his own important work left much to be desired.[52]

Equally close have been the relationships between history and *sociology*. To be sure, while definitions of the term "history" have sometimes differed, those of sociology have been subject to almost constant debates ever since the introduction of both the discipline and its nomenclature by Auguste Comte (1798–1857). There also have been some differences between countries in the prevailing notions concerning methods and terminology. Suffice it to mention the work of the French sociologist Georges Gurvitch who, in his comprehensive study on sociology, quoted a number of definitions and approaches by outstanding thinkers in the field, especially Émile Durkheim, whose outlook he analyzed in some detail. He even offered a somewhat obscure definition of Durkheim's conceptions and also discussed the sociological contributions of John Stuart Mill, Georg Simmel, Alfred Vierkand, Robert Ezra Park, and Ernest Watson Burgess. The latter two published in 1921 their *Introduction to the Science of Sociology*, which speedily became the leading textbook in the United States, just as Franklin Henry Gidding's *The Principles of Sociology*, published in 1896, had served as the general sociological guide for the preceding generation. Gurvitch concluded his survey with his own two definitions of the discipline. To cite only the shorter one, he declared that sociology is a science

> which studies the totality of social phenomena within the wholeness of their aspects and their movements. [It achieves this aim] by subsuming [*captant*, otherwise used mostly in a rather derogatory sense] them under dialectizing types, microsocial, group sized, or global, in the process of making and unmaking them.

If this definition lacks clarity, the longer one leaves even more to be desired on this score. Nor is Charles Morazé's analysis, informative as it is regarding numerous details, sufficiently persuasive concerning its main topic: "The Application of the Social Sciences to History." G. R. Elton was, indeed, quite right in saying that "anthropology and sociology do not stand still; there are probably few disciplines in which the differences among the learned are more ineradicable and more ferocious." On the other hand, in his essay in Gurvitch's volume, Fernand Braudel made it clear that he did not agree with Gurvitch but referred rather to his own interpretation which followed those of his distinguished teachers Marc Bloch and Lucien Febvre. The term sociology had its vagaries in Germany, too. Understandably, it was the German usage that influenced most German Jewish scholars, such as Arthur Ruppin. His outstanding work,

Die Soziologie der Juden, hardly drew a line between social history and more contemporary sociology, a term he sparingly used in his other works, as also did his Yiddish-writing counterpart, Jacob Lestchinsky.[53]

If one may speak of any kind of consensus at all, the difference between these two disciplines has consisted in sociologists trying to set up some generalizations; they were basically "nomothetic" as opposed to the specific and individualistic or "ideographic" approach of historians. At times such generalizations, introduced by Wilhelm Windelband in 1894, are subject to numerous exceptions. As Robert K. Merton observed,

> The growing contributions of sociological theory to its sister disciplines lie more in the realm of general sociological orientations than in that of specific confirmed hypotheses. . . . Despite the many volumes dealing with the history of sociological theory and despite the plethora of specific investigations, sociologists (including the writer) may discuss the logical criteria of sociological laws without citing a single instance which fully satisfies these criteria.

Perhaps the differentiation between "historical laws" and "sociological laws" (the term in both cases used metaphorically) might best be defined by saying that historians assume that similar causes known to have existed at certain times would generate basically similar effects at other times, whereas sociologists look for a similarity of conditions found to exist simultaneously in diverse societies, or segments thereof, which presumably would result in the repetition of similar phenomena.[54]

In practical application the distinctions have often blurred, however. In sociological tracts based upon surveys, particularly if made with the aid of personal interviews or questionnaires, the material is often fundamentally individualistic and dependent on the experiences and training of the researchers, the precision of the questions in oral interviews or written inquiries, and the percentage as well as quality of the replies secured. This approach is very much akin to oral history projects, since it also leads to an ultimate analysis of the assembled material and to the drawing therefrom of some general conclusions. In both cases, moreover, the sample obtained may be much too small or haphazard to warrant definite conclusions. In any case, rechecking one's results by the use of inquiries with different methods may prove helpful, although the mere fact of publication of the results of the earlier investigation may be self-confirming. One must also beware of the frequently heard objections that, after assembling a lot of weighty materials, at considerable expense in time and money, the results of the projects merely confirm the obvious and thus contribute merely to the documentation of long-accepted views. In the Jewish field, in particular, many sociological studies have suffered from the meagerness or lopsided nature of the evidence on which the conclusions were based.

Nevertheless, the sociological methods and factual findings have greatly enriched the study of history, too. Even while denying its character as a "global science . . . which it is not yet but to which it will not cease to aspire," Fernand Braudel admits that history itself is not a one-track science. "There is no *one* history, *one* historical profession, but professions and histories, that is a sum total of interests, points of view, and possibilities." What this amounts to is an admission that there exists no consensus about the best historical methods but that historians must individually, or in cooperation wtih others, choose the topics; use their own inclinations for the best way of gathering materials and making personal decisions in the selection of the most relevant from an excessive plurality of sources; or extrapolate guesstimates or hypotheses from a paucity of sources; and finally present the findings in the best way they can according to the writers' talent and training. But whatever the theoretical discussions may lead to, there is no question that history and sociology have greatly influenced one another. Certainly, from the beginning of this century, partly under the influence of Marxism and the teachings of Max Weber, Émile Durkheim, and others, historians have often looked for the environmental influences on the historical trends of each period in sociological or near-sociological terms. In the Jewish field, too, much of the work of Simon Dubnow and his school, the study of Pharisees by Louis Finkelstein, and those of many others reflected their authors' recognition of the importance of social factors, even if most of them rejected the materialistic conception of history preached by Marxist scholars.[55]

The French school of the *Annales,* employed still another method, known as "Structuralism" in both its historical and sociological researches. The stimulus was given by the anthropologist Claude Lévi-Strauss whose *Structural Anthropology* greatly influenced the thinking of many sociologists and historians as well. The short definition of that technique given it by Georges Gurvitch is that it deals with "a systematic whole of self-regulating transformations." This basically means that the school emphasizes institutional studies above and beyond those of individual personalities or even of large groups of individuals. Its main advantages, described by Siegfried F. Nadel are: "first, that structural analysis lends to the social data a higher degree of comparability, and second, that it renders them more readily quantifiable." In this respect, structuralism is akin to the quantitative method, which will be analyzed below. During the early postwar years this school's program found followers not only in France but also in some other European countries and the United States. While generally this approach was closer to sociology than to history, it injected a fructifying element into pertinent inquiries—which usually included also half the answers—into the study of historical institutions as well. Jewish historians, however, seem on the whole to have avoided this approach because in recent decades they have been largely concentrating on uncovering—often under very trying conditions—or reconstructing from insufficient materials the history of many communities destroyed by the Nazis; these studies rarely lend themselves to drawing generalizations. Even in the younger communities of the Western Hemisphere they usually faced a dearth of material from which to present charts and statistical tables revealing the various "structures" within the organized Jewish communities. Not that the institutional approach was completely neglected. Long before the rise of the structuralist school I personally devoted much effort to the study of Jewish communities throughout their history and published in 1942 a three-volume work describing their evolution and variegated functions up to the American Revolution. The original plan to continue that study into the nineteenth and twentieth centuries has not yet been realized. However, even the several important histories of Jewish communities in the United States and England, such as those by Lloyd Gartner published in the postwar period, usually lacked the vast statistical apparatus characteristic of the structuralist treatment. So were in a different form some of the studies of Uriel Tal pertaining to Wilhelmian and Nazi Germany.[56]

Another closely related area of significance to history and particularly to Jewish history is the history of *languages* and *literatures*. Methodologically, these disciplines use only variants of the general historical tools long employed in other fields of historical research. However, by the nature of their subjects, most literary histories deal with poets and writers as individuals, describing largely their lives and works. Only in a subsidiary fashion do they also analyze the general background and the "regnant tendencies" in the literary movements contemporaneous with those authors, especially in such broad literary schools as those of the Classicists, Romantics, Realists, and the like. The same may be said about historians of art. They all resemble the basic aforementioned approaches of most historians of philosophy, except that the latter often expatiate more fully on the impact of a new system propounded by a great thinker on his successors and, as in the case of Plato, Kant, or Hegel, on students of their disciplines. In contrast, linguistic studies have mostly been concerned with groups rather than individuals, and share with the institutional historical approaches much emphasis on the speech characteristics of entire communities or of certain subcultures within them. In both cases the combination of the general historical and sociological methods has proved very helpful to linguists and philologists studying the various dialects or the linguistic aspects in literary work. Reciprocally, the philological criticism of sources and the folkloristic data gained by the study of local or regional linguistic peculiarities have frequently proved very helpful even to politically, legally, or philosophically minded historians.[57]

Intimately connected with the nexus between history and sociology is also that between these two disciplines and *anthropology*. Here again we have to deal with major divisions concerning the scope and approaches of that branch of learning, which, in some respects, have more intimate relationships with "pure" sciences than either history or sociology. Sometimes we actually speak of "physical anthropology" by which we mean the study of man with respect to his physical environment. If much of human history is affected by the climate, water supply, earthquakes, epidemics, and other phenomena primarily studied by natural scientists, such physical forces play an even greater role in scientific anthropology. Moreover, much of that science which deals with primitive peoples, even cave dwellers, has to take into account a diversity of living conditions which are not treated by social anthropology and are but occasionally mentioned in history or the social sciences.[58]

Scholars have often observed the tendency of anthropologists to draw rather hasty analyses between one primitive tribe and another, distant from it both in space and time. Because we have more opportunity to study Polynesian Islanders or Australian bushmen today than to investigate the behavior of the pre-Columbian Incas or ancient Israelites in the patriarchal period, there has been too much temptation to exaggerate the parallels in the behavioral patterns of these diverse groups. One of my major objections to the theories of Karl Budde and other biblical critics concerning the Israelitic prophets' alleged "nomadic ideals" going back to the assumed behavioral patterns among the Israelites of the patriarchal and Mosaic ages, refers to their being constantly compared with the primitive tribes of our times. I particularly pointed out that the Israelitic conquerors of Canaan had entered an area which had previously enjoyed a fair measure of civilization for some two thousand years—a length of time quite comparable with the duration of West European civilized life today. I also drew the parallel with contemporary Bedouins in Israel, whose lives only a short time ago had not differed greatly from that of their biblical ancestors. Nevertheless, any Bedouin taken out of his tribe into Jerusalem or Tel Aviv today may in a few years skip entire stretches in the general evolution of civilization by assimilating himself to his new Israeli environment. Nowadays even many Israeli Bedouins still dwelling in their ancient localities often live a life of luxury, with modern amenities and some modern ways of life. It is therefore doubly questionable to apply general anthropological observations among primitive peoples to the life of the ancient Jews, whether in biblical or talmudic periods. Yet, even in this area, by employing the requisite caution and critical observation, modern scholars may indeed learn something from anthropology for the history of ancient Jewry.[59]

Among the numerous disciplines related to anthropology, *archaeology,* and *ethnology* (including racial studies) are of special significance to Jewish history. The untiring work of numerous scholars in digging up ever new historically relevant materials from the Palestinian soil has not only greatly enriched our knowledge of ancient Israel, but has also shed much new light on later settlements, especially during the period of the Crusades. The prolonged Jewish life in the Diaspora as an ethnoreligious minority reaching back to remote antiquity has, of course, been an integral part of the historic experience of the Jewish people. The role of racial anti-Semitism in the Nazi seizure of power and pseudoscientific use of both anthropology and history to justify the National Socialist policies up to the Holocaust have been recent turning points in the destinies of the Jewish people. However, even today, when in many Western countries racial discrimination against "non-Aryans" has greatly lost its attraction among the masses, except for some "lunatic fringes," Jews, like members of other ethnic minorities, have frequently experienced the nagging feeling described by Michael Parenti,

> Even if full social acceptance is won without serious encounters with bigotry, it is unlikely that from childhood to adulthood one will have escaped a realization that some kind of stigma is attached to one's minority identity, that one is in some way "marginal." Ethnic identifications are, after all, rarely neutral.

Understandably, political scientists, as well as anthropologists and historians, have evinced keen interest in the great ethnic divisions in a country like the United States, aptly called by Louis Adamic "the nation of nations." They not only have begun intensively to study their contemporary effects on voting for elective offices, their impact on public education, and other political changes, but also have reached back to analyze similar manifestations in the eighteenth and nineteenth centuries for which source materials are still available.[60]

In fact, *political science,* and intimately related to it *historical* and *sociological jurisprudence,* have always been closely associated with history, especially since many historians from the days of Thucydides on have laid particular stress on political history, the dynastic changes, and the story of battles and peace treaties, together with some constitutional and legal elements of the states' historic evolution. One need but recall the enduring contributions made by constitutional historians like Bishop William Stubbs (1825–1901), Frederic William Maitland (1850–1906), Sir Paul Vinogradoff (1859–1925), and Sir Leon Bernstein Namier (1888–1960) to English historiography. Not surprisingly, we now also have a school of the "New Political History," the child of the twentieth-century concern for statistically attainable data such as had led to the development of the "New Economic Science" and the "Quantitative History" (see below). Principally represented by younger American scholars, this method lent special significance to such numerically ascertainable phenomena as size and voting patterns, or mutual relations of various ethnic groups. Clear differentiation between this new type of political science and traditional methods is still being developed. Perhaps most enlightening is the negative formulation by Darett B. Rutman: "The 'New Political History' is not to be identified by a simple count of charts and graphs or the number of numbers in the text. Nor should it be characterized by the degree of its departure from Art." Clearly, the requisite ample records for such investigations are available only in certain countries during recent centuries and depend to a large extent on their preservation in national or local archives. For most periods of history such data are simply nonexistent. Even methods more or less successfully employed in evaluating broad demographic or economic trends before the seventeenth century are for the most part extremely limited in the political arena. In general, moreover, at least the moderate exponents of that new political approach are reconciled to follow the traditional patterns of political science in their treatment of other statistically less dependable areas of their research. In many cases a compromise between the old and new political science has also proved helpful to historians, just as the various branches of history, including biographies and oral history data, have been of considerable aid to the political scientist in practically every phase of his work.[61]

In passing, we need but mention briefly the all-pervasive penetration of the political element into the ancient realm of *theology*. In the emotionally overheated atmosphere of the Nazi revolution, the Party's political ideology was early invested with a sacred character. The new "political theology" developed into a discipline using long-established scholarly techniques to justify the novel mythology and irrationality of the racist ideology. As Uriel Tal well expressed it, "Theology and religion were secularized while politics and the state became consecrated and served as a substitute religion. . . . Political myth was meant to establish a system of values that would penetrate into the realm of personal and family life, into culture, education, art, and economy." In the Nazi frenzy of the revaluation of all values, anti-Semitism played a preeminent role. Remarkably, even after the fall of the Nazi regime, the term "political theology" remained as a designation of a new approach to theological and historical thought.[62]

VI

PSYCHOHISTORY

AMONG THE VARIOUS auxiliary approaches to historical research two have made a special impression on recent authors and readers alike: the psychoanalytical and quantitative methods. As usual, they have found ardent admirers as well as sharp critics. Even William Langer, a distinguished historian of the older school, whose own works had achieved wide recognition through their use of conventional methods, nevertheless in his presidential address at the 1957 annual meeting of the American Historical Association urged his colleagues to give careful consideration to the psychoanalytical lessons in history. Alain Besançon of the Sorbonne who, on a previous occasion, had sharply criticized the work of a Dutch scholar, Jan Hendrik Van den Berg, on historical psychology, nonetheless himself pointed out the close affinities between the task of an historian and that of a psychoanalyst:

> Each of them is concerned with interpretation and with the search for meaning. They deal with *texts*, in the broader sense of the term: A countryside can be a text for the historian, as a silence can be for the psychoanalyst. . . . The most striking analogy is that both the historian and the psychoanalyst, are, each of them in himself, his own instrument for understanding.[63]

Clearly, human motivation, lasting or temporary, and hence their psychological drives in their significant public or private activities, were part of the historical literature from ancient times. To be sure, Robert George Collingwood, after calling Thucydides "the father of psychological history," immediately added that it

> is not history at all, but natural science of a special kind. It does not narrate facts for the sake of narrating facts. The chief purpose is to

affirm laws, psychological laws. . . . Thucydides is not the successor
of Herodotus in historical thought but the man in whom the historical thought of Herodotus was overlaid and smothered beneath anti-
historical motives.

This is a decided overstatement, however. Long before the Greek historian, the biblical narrators of the past of their people more concisely
depicted kings and other leading individuals according to a simple formula
as to whether their motives were in agreement with, or in defiance of, the
divine law. Some eminent historians, from Livy and Josephus to the Renaissance writers, including Joshua ben Joseph ha-Kohen (the sixteenth-
century author of both a world history and a history of medieval Jewish
sufferings), used a special technique to explain the factors which, in their
opinion, had motivated the leading personalities in doing (or occasionally
in failing to do) something specific. They inserted into their presentation
alleged statements, or even short speeches, by the persons concerned, not
in order to mislead their readers into believing that these speeches had
actually been delivered—most initiates were well aware of that artifice—
but rather to give some idea of what guided the particular "speakers" to act
the way they did.[64]

From another angle, Francis Bacon, in his *The Advancement of Learning*, Book VII, proposed certain divisions of historical science, which had
a considerable admixture of psychological motivations. He wrote: "All
history is either national history or civil history. Civil history has three
branches: history of learning, ecclesiastical history on church, prophecy
or providence, and civil history of action, also civil history of words." He
also emphasized that

> to speak the real truth, the poets and writers of history, are the best
> doctors of this knowledge [of emotions], where we may find painted
> forth with great life and dissected how affectations are kindled and
> excited, how pacified and restrained, how they disclose themselves
> though repressed and concealed; how they work, how they vary.

Some of the "heroes" in history, moreover, believed indeed that they owed
their successes to their own genius. For example, ever vainglorious
Napoleon Bonaparte had himself in mind when he obliquely asserted that
"an army of rabbits commanded by a lion is better than an army of lions
commanded by a rabbit." Medieval Islam, particularly, glorified some of

its imams supposedly chosen by the lord to lead their generation. Among
the Jews it was especially Saadiah Gaon (882–942) who applied this doctrine to himself and wrote:

> God does not leave His people in any generation without a scholar
> whom He inspires and enlightens so that he [the scholar] in turn
> may so instruct and teach the people as to make it prosper through
> him. And the occasion thereto has been what I have personally
> experienced in what God in His grace has done for me and for the
> people.

Such assertions were vastly overshadowed by the near apotheosis in which
most Italians, Germans, and Russians of a short time ago held their
exalted leaders, Benito Mussolini, Adolf Hitler, and Joseph Stalin. Even
some otherwise critical historians actually shared that belief in the extraordinary impact of "heroes" in critical moments of history. For instance, Thomas Carlyle unhesitatingly asserted that "Universal History,
the history of what man has accomplished in this world, is at bottom the
History of Great Men who have worked here."[65]
   Some more recent historians who have sought to emphasize above all
the dominant political, socioeconomic, and cultural factors in man's historical developments, often merely replace the old political and military
heroes by outstanding leaders in business, science, literature, or the arts.
Of course, in all such cases penetrating studies of the personality traits
and psychological impulses of such leaders have contributed much to the
understanding of major historical events.
   More complicated has been the use of psychoanalytical methods for
general historical research. There is no doubt that certain leaders—religious, political, economic, or intellectual—who have left behind much
biographical material, are fit objects for the quest to uncover certain less
obvious aspects of their emotional life; even their phantasies have often
deeply influenced their behavior in critical moments of both private and
public life. A good case in point is Martin Luther, whose numerous publications, table-talks, and letters offer a plethora of information on the
thoughts underlying his activities. Moreover, he seems to have "suffered
from an abnormally strong sense of sin and the immediacy of death and
damnation." In the Jewish field, Theodor Herzl, as the author of a large
collection of often unabashed and quite revealing *Diaries*, addresses,
feuilletons, plays, and letters, was likewise an inviting object for psycho-

analytical probings. On the other hand, in his early attempt to analyze the marriage of the prophet Hosea, known to us exclusively from a few biblical chapters, Adolph Allwohn had to be limited to a number of more or less persuasive hypotheses, which could neither be fully proved nor decisively repudiated.[66]

Freud himself faced many such difficulties whenever he ventured into the field of psychohistory, through the medium of psychoanalytical biography. If I may refer to a personal experience: some forty years ago I was confronted with the task of writing a review of Sigmund Freud's *Moses and Monotheism*. Despite my deep admiration for the master—many of whose lectures at the Vienna University Medical School I had been privileged to attend, but whose general theories I could not accept—I felt obliged to point out the basic weaknesses of the factual material upon which he had built his construction. Certainly, assertions like the following did not endear him to historians, among whose first prerequisites is a careful critical examination of the reliability of their sources:

> When I use Biblical traditions here in such an autocratic and arbitrary way, draw on it for confirmation whenever it is convenient and dismiss the evidence without scruple when it contradicts my conclusions, I know full well that I am exposing myself to severe criticism concerning my method and that I weaken the force of my proofs. But this is the only way to treat material whose trustworthiness, as we know for certain, was seriously damaged by the influence of distorted tendencies.

However ingenious his theories may have been, Freud relied in this book principally on biblical scholars writing before the First World War at the height of radical biblical criticism (the book on Moses was practically completed in 1912 and was revised for publication only in 1937–38). Their interpretations enjoyed little acceptance even in their own day and by the late 1930s had been repudiated by the majority of biblical scholars. Today their views are even more superannuated. Freud himself seems to have had some qualms about the validity of his theories concerning Moses. On the one hand, he considered Moses, though of Egyptian origin, the true creator of the Jewish people. On the other hand, he openly admitted that he did not find it easy, through his theory of the "Egyptian" Moses, to deny to a people its claim to a man it considered the greatest of its native sons, "especially if the writer himself belongs to that people." This reluctance must have been intensified during the final revision and printing of the book in 1937–38, when the world-wide Nazi antisemitic propaganda reached its greatest pre-War intensity. In fact, in its early formulation, the book had a subtitle: *An Historical Novel.* This designation might have reminded many readers of the widely quoted quip by the eminent nineteenth-century literary historian Georg Brandes, who compared historical novels generally with the then widely advertised *Feigenkaffee* (chicory or in its literal translation: fig-coffee) generally used in Europe as an admixture to coffee. According to Brandes, just as fig was not coffee, so an historical novel was fiction, not history. This inner uncertainty may have contributed to the master's postponement of the publication of this work from 1912 to 1938.[67]

Freud's admission of his occasional disavowal, "without scruple," of the historical evidence in favor of a broader theory reminds one of Nietzsche's aforementioned assertion of the legitimacy of "life-supporting" denials of historical truths. Such a procedure seems to be abetted by Sir Isaiah Berlin's sharp differentiation between the scientific and historical methods. "It is the scientist's business to fit the facts to the theory, the historian's responsibility is to place his confidence in facts over theories." Not surprisingly, the selective choice in the use of evidence has penetrated the field of history, especially in totalitarian states. Just as some Nazi writers occasionally invoked Nietzsche's authority in claiming the right to manipulate their evidence to fit their historical reconstructions, so did numerous Soviet historians build castles in the air with frequently spurious or at least incomplete verification. As Roland Mousnier and René Pillorget correctly observed:

> The greatest danger which threatens historical research at the present time does not consist of the too exclusive orientation toward the economic and social sphere. It exists much more in the establishment in the U.S.S.R. of a pseudo-science of history, which consists in illustrating a preestablished scheme by a selection of documents; and in the fact that this psuedo-science has been able, in a more or less diluted form, to infiltrate the West.

Understandably, because of their geographic proximity and unity of language, West German historians were at times subjected to the impact of similar attitudes among their East German colleagues.[68]

It was easier for Freud to reconstruct the personalities of Leonardo da Vinci or Woodrow Wilson, for whom much authentic material was available. In Leonardo's case, to be sure, much of the analysis was based merely on a youthful fragment from the great painter-scientist's hand. Yet, no less distinguished an art historian than Meyer Shapiro could claim that Freud was able,

> thanks to his theory and method and perhaps even more to his sympathy for the tragic and problematic Leonardo to pose altogether new and important questions which were unsuspected by earlier writers and to which no better answer than Freud's has as yet been given.

This assertion merely confirms the old adage that "a good question implies half the answer." In the case of Wilson's prolonged illness at the end of his presidency, there was a multitude of source material available; its sifting was far more of a problem than its availability. Moreover, the analyst enjoyed in this task the cooperation of William Christian Bullitt, an experienced journalist and diplomat who had many an opportunity to observe Wilson in action.[69]

Nor are the more conventional methods of assessing the characters and motivations of living persons sufficiently refined to establish reliable historical criteria. One need but refer to the divergent evaluations of political leaders by contemporaries, even close associates, of our time. A laudable effort of the Institute of Personality Assessment and Research of the University of California, Berkeley, to collect data by a number of trained and unbiased observers and then to seek out the elements of consensus among them is in some respects an improvement over the haphazard evaluations by individual reporters, friends, or enemies. Yet, even this method leaves a considerable amount of doubt behind. At times, the characterization of a single acute observer may prove to be historically more correct than the results of such a collective investigation.[70]

Of a different nature is the evaluation of the mass attitudes and movements in the past and present. The fairly refined method of sampling and polls of contemporary public opinion, despite its imperfections and accepted considerable margins of error, certainly is a great help. It rarely can be applied to the past, however, even where there still exists ample documentation. On the other hand, there is something peculiar in mass phenomena. One need but consider developments in family life. In each case, a boy may meet a particular girl as the result of a mere accident. They may or may not get together again, may fall in and out of love, become engaged and break an engagement, be and stay married or be divorced, have one child or many children—all apparently unpredictable chance happenings. And yet in the aggregate, the general statistics of marriages and divorces and of both birth and death rates in a particular society frequently show a steady curve during a particular period, which may even justify some cautious predictions about the future. Similarly, some mass movements in the past, especially those of an extraordinary kind, like the flagellants, the "children's crusade," the great mortality and mass reactions thereto during the Black Death and other great epidemics—in Jewish history the "Massada complex" or the mass suicides during the Crusades and the Cossack uprising of 1648–49, or the totality of the Shabbetian movement—can all be analyzed with almost a greater degree of accuracy than the psychological motivations of some individuals. However, these analyses likewise suffer from the shortcomings of all social sciences, in that they cannot experimentally be repeated at will and thus confirm, modify, or refute the original observations or conclusions. Had not Freud himself warned his overzealous followers of the great difficulty of analyzing the pathology of an entire culture since, in contrast to individuals, there is no standard of comparison of what constitutes a "normal" culture.[71]

Yet, all efforts, successful or unsuccessful, made in these directions have greatly fructified historical research, when treated as more or less probable hypotheses. If starting from different premises the hypotheses end in certain convergences, their ultimate conclusions may, indeed, lead to a broad concensus among specialists. Needless to say, such consensus may be controverted by new data or new interpretations and give way to a new consensus. But after all, in pure science, too, the Ptolemaic astronomy, generally accepted for a millennium and a half, ultimately was displaced by the Copernican system.[72]

In the Jewish field it was principally anti-Semitism which, from antiquity to the present, has generated diverse mass feelings, often a mass hysteria and major violence. Its manifestations have, of course, had many aspects of deviant mass psychology. To be sure, although he spent most of his life in the predominantly antisemitic atmosphere of Vienna—witnessing the rise to power of the avowedly anti-Jewish Christian-Socialist Party, which long dominated the municipal adminsitration of the city, and finally leaving it as a refugee to London at the end of his life—Freud himself did not feel the urge of submitting this movement, in all its political, socioeconomic, and cultural manifestations, to a searching psychoanalysis. But other scholars, prompted especially by Hitler's drive toward the "Final Solution" of the Jewish question and the Holocaust, did publish many books and articles on the subject. These and other mass phenomena have often been the subject of careful study by psychologists and psycho-analysts, as well as by historians. Of great psychological-historical interest have also been the various reactions to Jew-hatred over the ages on the part of its Jewish victims as well as of the philosemites, or of a more or less indifferent non-Jewish public. There have also existed various disguised forms of anti-Jewish agitation like the clearly absurd equation of Zionism with racism, even Nazism, as officially sponsored by Soviet propagandists and accepted by the mechanical majorities of the United Nations General Assembly. Despite the availability of a vast amount of documentation and secondary literature on these subjects, there still is much room left for further researches in depth.[73]

The antisemitic ambiance of Vienna in the early twentieth cen-tury was in some respects a permanent creative challenge and provocation to its intellectual circles, which included many outstanding Jewish schol-ars, writers and musicians. In some cases it led to self-hatred in such a degree that Otto Weininger, a very gifted young author of a much-dis-cussed volume about Geschlecht und Charakter (1903) actually committed suicide at the age of twenty-three in order to eliminate the Jew in him. In others as in Theodor Herzl it brought about a deep reaction (also stimu-lated by the Dreyfus Affair in France) to reassert the values of Judaism and the need for the revival of a Jewish homeland. Freud's attitude was some-what ambivalent. While he never denied his Jewishness, he steered clear of the controversies of his day. It might indeed be rewarding for someone to write a Freudian interpretation of the life and work of the founder of psychoanalysis—an attempt which, to my knowledge, has never been made despite the availability of considerable biographical material in his correspondence and other sources.[74]

The great variety of responses to the challenges of anti-Semitism and similar mass movements may perhaps reinforce the conclusion that psy-chohistory can only be of limited help in elucidating mass phenomena. Alain Besançon was right in contending that "the further historiography moves away from the old type of court history, which was essentially psychological, the less it matters whether Da Vinci was homosexual, or Napoleon jealous of his brother Joseph." He also pointed out that both psychoanalysis and history

are crafts rather than sciences, which call for apprenticeship equally long in both of them. This double apprenticeship cannot be divided;

nor should we neglect, however, what Ralph Linton said some time ago—that the most efficient collaboration between two disciplines takes place inside the same head.

At the present state of our knowledge between the two disciplines Bruce Mazlish's sanguine assertion that "it will be difficult for any really honest historian to evade a confrontation on this level with himself and consequently with his fellow men and their destinies," is definitely an exaggerated or, at least, a premature assumption. One may, however, more readily agree with Mazlish's other contention that "psychoanalysis adds to other explanations in history; it is no substitute for them."[75]

VII

QUANTITATIVE HISTORY

In their quest for some greater reliability and objectivity of the data found in their primary sources and for the reduction of subjective judgement by their investigators, including themselves, some recent historians have evinced a predilection for quantitative history. This method was largely borrowed from the speedily developing "econometric" school of economists and economic historians through the pioneering efforts of Simon Kuznets and others. The representatives of that trend among historians assumed that if they could marshal sufficient statistical data for demographic and economic developments, and if through counting the number of voters for certain parties they could ascertain their attitudes to budgetary expenditures, educational and welfare costs, and the like, they might also reach more valid, broader conclusions concerning the basic political and social trends prevailing at the time in the particular society under investigation. Such data could frequently be assembled quite independently of the judgment of their compilers.

Some enthusiastic exponents of the new, rapidly expanding movement, like Adeline Daumard and François Furet, could triumphantly assert that "there is no social history, except quantitative history." More moderately, Jean Marczewski, the leading early protagonist of quantitative history, contended that the new approach embraced three basic concepts: (1) it illustrated the historical narrative with statistical data; (2) it reviewed the results of econometric history or cliometrics since 1950; and (3) it analyzed the results of national accounts such as those relating to economic growth. In the case of such accounts, whenever available, the task of the economists consisted in deriving from them certain economic generalizations, whereas that of the historian was to point up certain specific phenomena including the exceptions to the general results and their causes. In all these matters the quantitative historian depended on the availability of a mass of detailed data such as are represented by the modern "national accounts" published annually and, in some countries, even quarterly. Marczewski agrees that "in the case of distant periods one has to be satisfied with five or ten yearly accounts, which considerably reduces the precision of the analysis." He fails to mention, however, that in most historical periods up to the very recent generations, such comprehensive national accounts are not available at all. Marczewski and other like-minded theorists have also freely admitted that quantitative history is more useful for an analysis of mass movements than for that of the actions by individual leaders (which is the opposite of psychohistory) and that it is applicable to economic history much more than to that pertaining to the history of ideas or specific historical incidents. Even more generally, Marczewski conceded that

> there can be no opposition nor even competition, between quantitative and qualitative history. They represent nothing more than two distinct but complementary approaches, both especially indispensable to historical research.[76]

Even more important than such technical difficulties is the fact that history, in its broad sense, tries to reconstruct the totality of human life in its almost endless variety of aspects. Many areas of history by their very nature do not lend themselves to the process of quantification. In his rejection of "quantitative magic," Arthur M. Schlesinger, Jr. cogently argued that "as a humanist, I am bound to reply that almost all important questions [in history] are important precisely because they are not susceptible to quantitative answers." It so happens that I have always (at times unwittingly) been in favor of some such quantitative approaches. Throughout my career as an historian I have constantly evinced great interest especially in population figures and quanititative economic data. I still vividly recall a discussion I had in the late 1920s with Stephen S. Wise and Judah Magnes in which I told them about my dream of someday writing a "Jewish History in the Light of Numbers." It was also at the time that I wrote, as a sort of first chapter, the long Hebrew article on "Jewish Population under the Kings of Israel" which, though written in 1928, did not appear until 1933. When I tried to revise that essay for an English translation published forty years later, I was amazed by the paucity of research in this field in the intervening years, as contrasted with the proliferation of publications on almost any other phase of biblical history. It must be admitted, to be sure, that except for the modern period, and even then only for certain countries, the complicated data needed for the reconstruction of the size and composition of the Jewish population are rarely available. In most other areas and periods we are confined to a few, more or less fragmentary, data and must supplement them with numerous hypotheses from various angles and degrees of plausibility. We are happy when these hypotheses converge at certain points and thus allow for conclusions approximating reality.[77]

In Jewish history and in the premodern period also in that of Christian and Muslim nations, where religion always played a preeminent role, the difficulties of quantitative and otherwise objective evaluation are compounded by the nature of religious life itself. It certainly does not do merely to ascertain the number of existing churches, mosques, and synagogues or of religious schools wherever that is possible; nor do we learn too much from figures concerning the number of worshipers on the respective Sabbaths and holidays, as compared with weekdays; or of children attending religious schools for a specified number of hours a week. All these data are in themselves quite valuable and should be pursued wherever possible. However, they do not give us even an inkling of the nature and intensity of religious feelings characteristic of certain periods or localities. More importantly, there are some basic difficulties in dealing with sources which at least for numerous students include "revealed" Scriptures. Even in later periods, the sources of which are less "sacred" and therefore supposedly more subject to doubt, the importance often attached by large and influential segments of the population to the uncritical acceptance of religiously hallowed traditions make efforts at coming to grips with objective reality doubly difficult. Similar complications have arisen—perhaps even to a greater extent—in the efforts toward quantitative evaluation of the Catholic education in parochial schools and theological seminaries and of comparable other religiously oriented school systems. This is no less true with what may paradoxically be called the "secular" faiths of Communism, Fascism, Nazism, and other modern isms.[78]

This difficulty is not completely removed by the presence in the same society of another more critical, or even diametrically opposed segment in the population, and by giving to all parties complete freedom of expression so as to allow the "truth"—or whatever anyone regards as such—to prevail. The optimistic assertions of the Enlightenment era as was voiced by Thomas Jefferson in his aforementioned 1821 letter to the Savannah Jewish leader, Jacob de la Motta, is not altogether convincing today. The former president wrote about his "gratifying reflection" of "the maxim of civil government being reversed in that of religion where the true form is 'divided we stand, united, we fail.' " Even those convinced of these "truths" may not only doubt the full reversal of the doctrine regarding the unity under civil government—which may lead to totalitarianism—but also may be hesitant in deciding how far they may go in interpreting events and sayings, recorded from earlier periods. This is particularly true in the case of many talmudic and rabbinic sources. It has long been recognized that the specific rabbinic dialectic is basically different from the Western, more or less Aristotelian, categories of thinking. Only a student of the halakhah deeply imbued with the talmudic way of thinking can really do justice to the intrinsic meaning of many ancient sayings and debates. That is why a methodological work like Zacharias Frankel's Darkei ha-Mishnah (An Introduction to the Mishnah), although written more than a century ago, is so much closer to the true meaning and intentions of the ancient sages than is the somewhat similar work by the otherwise well-informed, more modern scholar Hermann Strack. To some extent this is also true of many Western students of medieval Islam. Though in many areas their Western techniques have proved far superior to the tradition-bound lore of the older sages of the Al-Azhar University in Cairo, in some other areas the old-fashioned ulama of the Eastern mosques more accurately perceived the genuine intent of the Muslim shari'a (system of law). The reputed assertion of an old-type rabbinic critic of Leopold Zunz's significant biography of Rashi that "if you want to learn when Rashi sneezed, you read Zunz, but if you desire to understand what Rashi really said, you better come to me!" was not completely unreasonable.[79]

Another major difficulty in analyzing a history like that of the Jewish people is the unusual frequency with which most of the historical evidence was derived from hostile sources. Because of the instability of Jewish life in many lands few Jewish archival documents from the older periods have been preserved. We learn, therefore, about many events and developments in the Jewish communities only from governmental ecclesiastical, or literary sources, originally written with an obvious anti-Jewish bias. The occasional brief references to the same happenings in the Jewish chronicles, written many years, even generations, later offer only sporadic corrections. In another context I pointed out that, for example, the same Roman Emperor Titus, whose name is rarely mentioned in the talmudic sources without the epithet ha-rasha', the evildoer, is at the same time glorified by the ancient Roman historians as a man of extraordinary humanity. We are told that he asked himself every evening what good deed he had performed during the day; if he had not done so, he considered that a lost day. But here we at least have the testimony of the Jewish historian, Josephus Flavius, to balance the accounts of the great Roman-Jewish war by Tacitus and other Roman and Christian writers. We are worse off with the conflicting appraisals which were given by Hebrew and Latin sources with respect to Hadrian. Until the recent archaeological discovery of some contemporary documentary material relating to the highly important Bar Kocheba Revolt of 132–35 C.E., we were almost entirely dependent on the Roman reports by Dio Cassius and later Christians. The very basic issue underlying that conflict remained long obscured: Hadrian, though of provincial Spanish descent, was often described in the annals of Roman history as a great ruler who largely succeeded in unifying the multi-ethnic, multi-racial, and multi-religious Roman Empire. Evidently, for this very reason, the Jewish sources mention only his attempts to break down the ethnoreligious "separatism" of the Jewish people by prohibiting the practice of circumcision as a barbaric custom, and by outlawing Jewish public assemblies for the study of Torah. To the Jews of the talmudic age he appeared, therefore, as the most cruel oppressor who tried to undermine the Jewish religious observance in its most vital manifestations. Similarly great figures in medieval European history, such as St. Louis and Philip IV of France, Edward I of England, and particularly Ferdinand and Isabella of Spain, who in the history of their own nations appeared as the great architects of their national states, also were the monarchs most responsible for the many discriminatory anti-Jewish laws and ultimately for the expulsions of the Jews from their countries and the total destruction of centuries-old Jewish communities.[80]

In almost all of these crucial events of ancient and medieval Jewish history the new innovative historical methods are of little assistance. There is hardly enough material available to subject the anti-Jewish actions of most ancient Roman and medieval monarchs, statesmen, or clergymen to a careful psychoanalytical scrutiny. This discipline may shed new light on some bizarre manifestations of the Crusader movements, just as it may produce some hypotheses concerning such complex personalities as St. Louis. But it cannot be expected to elucidate greatly the rather simple and rational reactions of the Spanish royal pair in 1492 to the Jewish and Moorish minorities, despite their involvement in the Spanish Inquisition—in itself a rather fertile ground for psychohistorical research—and the availability of an unusual amount of contemporary or near-contemporary non-Jewish and Jewish sources. Nor can quantitative history be of much help, when even the bare outlines of the number of Jews who had lived in Spain in 1492, of those who after the decree of expulsion left the country or remained behind and either became genuine Christians or else swelled the ranks of the more or less permanent group of *conversos*, are still subject to much guesswork. Nor can structuralism furnish us more than certain general models for religious persecutions. Even the ever ready Marxist explanations of the shortcomings of the feudal order, their emphasis on the imbalance of the Spanish-Jewish economic structure, and the class struggles within Spanish society at large, have contributed little more than a few additional insights into the underlying causes for the manifestations of the general religious intolerance of Spanish society. But at least thus far the materialistic interpretation of history has shed little new light on the epochal transformation of Jewish life during that crucial period.[81]

The same limitations apply also to many other ethnoreligious minorities. More imporantly, large areas of the globe have a paucity of information available even for modern times. Certainly many "developing" nations have preserved much too few archival and other dependable sources to be used for psychoanalytic, quantitative, and some of the other novel approaches to historical research about their past. Even the Muslim world, with its vast historical literature written in the medieval and early modern periods, finds this material so concentrated on the narrow confines of dynastic, military, and legal histories, as well as biographies of outstanding individuals, that broad areas of economic, social, and even political history are but incidentally mentioned. These data rarely lend themselves to research with the new methods. In any case even in the advanced societies the older historical writings from Thucydides to Gibbon, Ranke, and Michelet have not lost their freshness, depth of insights, and elegant writing. Whatever one may learn through the novel approaches must be regarded as merely supplementary to the achievements of these outstanding predecessors. Just as in the aforementioned example of Zacharias Frankel's methodological work on the Mishnah, which remains much superior to the work of most of his successors, so it is true of many historical classics from antiquity to the nineteenth century that they will retain much of their validity long after the newer "fashionable" approaches will have been forgotten.

E. E. G. Vermeulen has rightly pointed out that "the theorist of history must also bring to the attention of those who always seek to bring something new into the exercise of their craft that they may still learn a good deal from the contemplation of the old and familiar achievements." Moreover, without minimizing the worthiness of the new innovative approaches and their rounding out of the amount of human knowledge also in the historical field, we must bear in mind the predominantly short-lived character of most of these temporarily fashionable trends. Alexander Gershenkron once observed, with respect to the "New Economic History" about which he spoke in laudatory terms, that

> after a decade or so of assiduous work, diminishing returns will set in, and the lure of new problems and new methods will lead economic historians to other yet indiscernible tasks. The innovators of today may well become the conservators of tomorrow. But this is their day, and its splendor should be neither beclouded nor begrudged.

Such diminishing returns have also been noticeable in the leading protagonists of innovative historical approaches, the school of the *Annales*. As early as 1967, some twenty years after the postwar resuscitation of this important journal, under its new name of *Annales: Économies-Sociétés-Civilisations*, it took up the struggle for a comprehensive reform in historiography from Fèbvre and Bloch (the latter had been murdered by the Nazis during the Second World War) especially under the guidance of their pupil Fernand Braudel. After flourishing for about two decades the school's influence began to stagnate, especially under the direction of Charles Morazé and his associates. Similar slowdowns may also be observed in the innovative methods of other areas of history. Yet, they all ought to be welcomed for whatever new insights they have offered without in any way denigrating the achievements of the millennial historiography of past ages. One may perhaps compare the progress in historical methodology to the geological layers in which every new layer—which usually contains many elements of the older layers—adds some new elements and together they form the crust of the earth.[82]

VIII

SOCIORELIGIOUS APPROACH

UNDER THESE CIRCUMSTANCES it is probably wisest to return to some basic elements which have dominated men's historical outlook for a very long time and to try to fit into them the newer approaches wherever they may prove to be most useful. Probably the most enduring institutions in human history have been society and religion. Each of them has consisted of a variety of elements which have differed from area to area and period to period. Some of these components have shown great historical endurance and have been an essential part of their respective histories. Society, too, has been composed of such basic, often concentric, units as (1) families (frequently expanded into clans), (2) communities, (including villages, towns, and their subdivisions by occupation, descent, wealth, or ethnic characteristics), (3) tribes, some of which by themselves or in combination with others were growing into (4) nationalities and/or states which at times developed into (5) empires or other regional entities such as races or even large-scale civilizations. Religion, too, took on a variety of forms, beginning with small family, clan, or tribal rituals and ultimately growing into large regional faiths and even world religions. The relations between the societal organisms and the religious confessions have always been very close and, at times, served as the main propelling factors in human history. A closer examination of these interrelations has long preoccupied some of the best minds in the historical literature and still offers vast new opportunities for research.

To be sure, in the last several centuries of growing secularization many thinkers were prone to overlook, or to minimize, the role of religion in human history. Begun with some Renaissance philosophers postulating the existence of a "double truth" (derived from Revelation and human reason, respectively) and others emphasizing the *raison d'état* as the supreme criterion for international action, secularism found its most eloquent spokesmen among the eighteenth-century French *philosophes*, particularly Voltaire. This widely admired writer could with impunity declare that "religion is the chief cause of all sorrows of humanity. Everywhere useless, it has served to drive men to evil. . . . It makes of history . . . an immense tableau of human folly." The modern communists and other anti-religious spokesmen have often praised the stance of the French En-lightenment and encouraged their followers to read its published works as offering the most effective refutation of the religious "prejudice," or "opiate." On the other hand, many thoughtful Frenchmen have shared the sentiments of Ernest Renan, who condemned Voltaire as the author "who has done more damage to historical studies than had the barbarian invasions." Moreover, even those who disagree with the outright condem-nation of free-thinking must admit that the very persistent and inflama-tory anti-religious harangues in themselves are a vivid testimony to the strength and unbroken continuity of the role of religion in the destinies of humanity.[83]

The dethronement of religion as the guiding principle in the historic evolution of man was subsequently adopted by many modern observers, even those who evinced great appreciation for the historic importance of religious beliefs and practices. For example, Hermann Cohen could insist that "however central religion appears to us modern men within the gen-eral compass of history, it is nonetheless merely a concentric specialty within the unity of ethical culture. It is the state which occupies for us the focal position in human civilization." At the same time Cohen himself published the distinguished work entitled *The Religion of Reason from Jewish Sources* in which, among other matters, he extolled the great his-toric role played by the ancient Israelitic prophets. He wrote:

> The conception of history is a creation of Israelitic prophecy. . . . It succeeded in what the Greek intellectuals were unable to achieve. . . . . The Greek outlook was exclusively aimed at the past . . . . The ancient [Israelitic] seers have, on the contrary, emphasized the concept of the future existence. . . . The past and the future were thus blended in the realm of the future.

Such a sweeping assertion is not entirely contradicted by Jakob Burck-hardt's aforementioned exclamation that "a future known in advance is an absurdity." Of course, the Israelitic prophets were not historians and their foremost concern was not only with certain details in contemporary events but even more with their meaning within great historic epochs of human and Jewish destiny. Unlike the Greeks who glorified the "golden age" of the past, they expatiated in particular on the golden age of the future.[84]

Messianism had, indeed, become one of the dominant forces in the history of the Judeo-Christian and Muslim worlds. It underlay the various reformatory, as well as utopian, trends, both religious and secular. The messianic idea deeply colored even such secular expectations as were proclaimed in the Renaissance Utopian literature, the French Revolution's short-lived Religion of Reason, and the various modern socialist and anarchist doctrines.[85]

In recent centuries, it appeared, the centrality of religion in public life of the Western peoples was completely supplanted by that of the state. The German idealistic philosophy, particularly the school of Hegel and such offshoots as the teachings of Ludwig Feuerbach and Karl Marx, have emphasized the supremacy of the state. Combined with the new stress laid upon the intensification of nationalism, which increasingly dominated the outlook of the world societies, the secular expectations connected with political actions seemed to relegate religion into a less and less significant corner of public and private life. This tendency obtained its constitutional expression in the separation of state and Church, proclaimed by the American Revolution and followed by France in 1906. It also led to a formal condemnation of religion in the Soviet Union which profusely used the Marxian term that religion was but "an opiate of the people." This antireligious policy was frequently emphasized by Lenin even before he became the supreme ruler of the Union. For instance, in his essay on "Socialism and Religion" written in 1905, he bluntly declared:

The impotence of the exploited classes in the struggle against the exploiters engenders faith in a better life beyond the grave just as inevitably as the impotence of the savage in his struggle against nature engenders faith in gods, devils, miracles, and so forth. To him who toils and suffers want all his life religion teaches humility and patience on earth, consoling him with the hope of reward in heaven. And to those who live on the labor of others religion teaches charity on earth, offering them a very cheap justification for their whole existence as exploiters and selling them a suitable price ticket for admission to heavenly bliss. Religion is the opium of the people . . . . Our programme is entirely based on the scientific, that is the materialistic world outlook . . . . Our propaganda necessarily includes the propaganda of atheism.[86]

Nevertheless, the Soviet ruler and his associates were restrained from totally outlawing religion in the Union by the failures of the French Religion of Reason and Bismarck's *Kulturkampf*. Their compromise was defined in the so-called Constitution of 1936 (Art. 124), which stated that "freedom for the conduct of religious worship and freedom for anti-religious propaganda is recognized for all citizens." This meant that even teaching religion, being classified as religious propaganda, was sharply curtailed. On the other hand, there was much official support given to the atheistic propaganda of the Godless Society which in 1932 reached a membership of some 5,500,000 adults. The persecution of the clergy of all denominations, from the outset placed among the "declassed" segments of the population, speedily reached frightening dimensions. According to one computation no less than 32 Orthodox bishops, 1,560 priests, and more than 7,000 monks and nuns lost their lives in the first fifteen years of the revolutionary era. For a time it appeared, indeed, that the Soviet Communist Party would achieve its professed goal of

the complete withering away of religious prejudice. The Party strives towards a complete destruction of the relation between the exploiting class and the organization of religious propaganda, thus effecting the actual liberation of the toiling mass from religious prejudice, and towards organizing a most extensive scientific, educational and antireligious propaganda.

While thus sharply combating the Russian-Orthodox faith of the majority (though granting somewhat greater freedoms to some sectarian trends within it, or to such Protestant denominations as the Baptists, as well as to the large Muslim minority), the Party indoctrinated the Soviet youth in communist teachings with the fervor of missionaries for a rival religion. Quite early Nicholas Berdaev rightly recognized that "Communism, both as a theory and as a practice, is not only a social phenomenon, but also a spiritual and religious phenomenon. And it is formidable precisely as a religion."[87]

However, just as the Religion of Reason of the French Revolution provoked an anti-governmental reaction among the masses of the population, part of which staged an active uprising in the Vandée, so did the unbridled propaganda of the Communist "faith" elicit widespread discontent among the Russian people. As in France of the 1790s, the international complications in the 1930s increasingly caused the Soviet regime to fall back on Russian nationalism, with its strong religious underpinnings. The public glorification of such national heroes as Dmitri Donskoi, Aleksander Nevskii, and even Ivan the Terrible—all prominent fighters for the Orthodox faith—illustrated the growing realization in the leading communist circles of the deep religious roots of Russian nationalism now so badly needed for Russia's defense against the Nazi menace. Ultimately, during World War II, the Red Army was forced to admit the presence of numerous Orthodox and Catholic clerics among the troops. Early in 1945 the government itself promoted the festive installation of the newly elected Patriarch Alexei as head of the Russian Orthodox Church. These impressive ceremonies were attended by representative Orthodox ecclesiastics invited by the government from other lands. Thereafter, the overt antireligious propaganda was greatly toned down. Of course, the official census does not record the number of true believers nor are there any satisfactory methods to ascertain how many Russians or members of minorities more or less regularly attend church or otherwise demonstrate their religious loyalties. But, according to Gerhard Simon, writing in 1974, "one particularly well-informed Soviet church writer who tends, if anything, to make conservative estimates, puts the number of religious believers (not only Christians) in the Soviet Union at 30 million, which is about 12 percent of the population." This estimate, or perhaps rather guesstimate, may be too low, since that percentage is probably exceeded among the 50,000,000 Muslims, mostly living beyond the Urals, who have felt less pressure to give up their ancestral faith than did the Greek Orthodox majority. Clearly, the "realists" among the Soviet leaders had good reasons not to antagonize public opinion in the Arab and other Muslim countries supporting their international policies. It was, again for international political reasons, that only the Jewish religious community has continually suffered from major persecutions, at times reaching dimensions of a sharp religio-cultural intolerance.[88]

In many ways different was the evolution in the neighboring totalitarian state, National Socialist Germany. Hitler and his companions had inherited from the Prussian tradition the deeply rooted acceptance of the state's centrality in history, preached especially from the days of Hegel and Marx. We recall the abovementioned emphasis on statehood even in Hermann Cohen's outlook on life. Needless to say, German Protestantism had entered an early "Erastian" alliance with the state which was later to pave the way for the intensification of German nationalism during the Wars of Liberation in the Napoleonic era. Johann Gottlieb Fichte, who had originally extolled the uniqueness of the German nation because it had grown up "without a state" (he referred to a nationally unified state) and "without history," in his last years came close to preaching the idea of the supreme centralized national state. In a little known essay, published more than thirty years after his death, he almost became a harbinger of the later totalitarian Nazi structure. Ernst Moritz Arndt's famous slogan in his call to arms against Napoleon in the name of "German freedom, a German God, German faith without a scoff," had all the earmarks of an appeal for a national German faith. This idea was later propagated by an influential sector of the National Socialist Party. Suffice it to cite here the proclamation of the National Socialist Student League of 1935, published, as everything else in Germany of that period, with overt or tacit official approval; it insisted that

> there are now in Germany three basic conceptions of life, the Christian, the Marxist, and the National Socialist. One uncompromisingly excludes the other . . . . The National-Socialist conception is intended only for the Teutonic race, not like Christianity for all races . . . . We repudiate not only the hundred different forms of Christianity but Christianity as such.

The fuller realization of a new German national religion was probably prevented only by the short duration of the Nazi "Thousand-Year Reich," which went down in defeat after but twelve years of existence.[89]

In contrast to these two leading totalitarian regimes, that of Mussolini was generally rather friendly to the Catholic Church and fairly tolerant toward both the Protestant and Jewish minorities. The Duce's anti-Jewish racist legislation emerged only a short time before the outbreak of World War II as a result of Italy's alliance with Nazi Germany, despite his own aforementioned earlier recognition of the futility of governmental persecution of religious beliefs. The explanation of this sympathetic treatment of the Church lay partly in the inherited Italian pride of having in its midst the Bishop of Rome, heir and successor to St. Peter, and head of a great international Church. The Fascist regime not only acknowledged the Pope's sovereignty over a small area in the city of Rome as a wholly independent Vatican state, but in 1929 Mussolini also concluded a formal Concordat with the Papacy. As a result, religious instruction has been given in all Italian public schools until the present day. Certainly even the twentieth-century history of the Italian kingdom and later the republic cannot be treated without due consideration of the impact of Catholicism on the country's public and private life.[90]

Nor have democratic countries of the last generations become completely secularized. England, with its "mother of Parliaments," is the oldest continuous democratic Commonwealth. Nevertheless, it still has an official Anglican (in America called Episcopalian) religion in which the king or queen serves as head of the Church and Parliament passes judgment on major ecclesiastical matters. At the same time, full legal equality has been granted to Dissenters, Catholics, Jews, and other denominations. Another highly democratic society, that of the State of Israel, established by and for ethnic Jews, is often considered for that reason as being a religious-minded Jewish state, although until recently the majority of the leaders, and perhaps also of the population, consisted of semi-agnostic Jews. If in matters of highest personal concern (marriage, divorce, inheritance, and the like) the fundamental law of the country still separates the population according to the respective religious communities to which they belong, Jewish, Christian, and Muslim, this was not an innovation introduced by the "Jewish State," but rather a heritage from the old Ottoman *millet* system; it had been continued by the British regime under the Palestine Mandate and it remained unchanged under the State of Israel. This has been, indeed, the regnant system in many Muslim lands until today. Such an important legal division of the citizenry is an emphatic testimony of the persistently great influence of religion on the legal systems and the daily life in the large Muslim world. It is actually increasing now through the more extreme manifestation of the "Islamic Revolution" spreading from Iran into the rest of the *dar al-Islam*.[91]

Most remarkably, even in countries of formal separation of state and Church, religion has continued to play an incalculable historic role. In the United States, where that constitutional separation has gone to such lengths as to exclude religion from the decennial population census (though it permits the government to institute separate censuses of religious bodies), forbid religious instruction as part of a regular public school curriculum, outlaw the recitation of even interdenominational prayers, and the like, religion has nevertheless been a mighty factor in the American civilization. As early as 1837 Harriet Martineau could comment "that the event has fully justified the confidence of those who have faith enough in Christianity to see that it needs no protection from the State, but will commend itself to human hearts better without." The independent flowering of religious bodies in the United States, which had also struck such other acute observers as Alexis de Tocqueville and James Bryce, has influenced the federal, state, and municipal governments to grant tax exemptions to religious bodies throughout the United States. These bodies also induced many states to enact a variety of "blue laws." The federal government has granted clerics and students of theology of all denominations automatic exemption from military service but deemed it expedient to employ some of them as chaplains in the armed forces. This general interplay of religious and secular factors permeating the entire fabric of society led many writers to call the United States a "Christian nation"—a legally rather debatable designation; it is even questionable in the case of England. In any case, non-Christian groups, including outright atheists, are guaranteed full equality of rights at the same time. Within the religious bodies there is formal freedom of preaching and practicing of a huge variety of observances and doctrines. Only in America could censuses of religious bodies, as did those taken in 1926 and 1936, reveal the increase in the number of religious denominations during a single decade from 212 to 256. In fact, 47 new sectarian movements were reflected in these data, since interveningly 3 religious groups had been dissolved. The great importance of religion, in practice even more than in theory, could not have escaped the attention of leading American historians in the twentieth century. For one example, John Franklin Jameson, in his day called the "dean of the historical guild in America," emphasized the ramified significance of the numerous local religious writings as sources of historical information about the American people; he considered them more instructive than the entire range of *belles lettres*. In his presidential address to the American Historical Association of 1907 he stated that

he who would understand the American of past and present times, and to that end would provide himself with data representing all classes, all periods, all religions, may find in the history of American religion the closest approach to the continuous record he desires. Not that all or even most Americans have been religious, but there have been religious men and women in every class, every period, every subdivision of America, and multitudes of them have left individual or collective records of their thoughts, and ways, and feelings.[92]

France, on the other hand, has had a heritage of widespread free thought since the eighteenth century. A large segment of the population could be counted among the agnostics in the nineteenth century. Yet at that time the government was actually paying the salaries of the Catholic priests as well as of Protestant pastors and Jewish rabbis. Religion was indeed so deeply imbedded in many circles of French society that, even in the political sphere, one could not overlook its power over the minds of the Catholic majority. During the heated debates over the Separation of state and Church, which ultimately was accomplished in 1906, its protagonists argued that because of the influence of the clergy and pious lay leaders, much of the population lived under the spiritual subservience to a foreign power, the Bishop of Rome. It was in this connection that, to placate the opposition, the influential statesman Aristide Briand, who was to serve ten times as Prime Minister of France, expounded on November 9, 1906, the theory that the Pope was not really a foreign sovereign, but rather the domestic sovereign (*souverain intérieur*) in each country with a large Catholic population. In a similar vein the German Chancellor Otto von Bismarck had announced in the Reichstag (on November 30, 1881) that "the Catholic Church in Germany, together with the papal superstructure belonging to it, had long been a native institution of the German Confederate States or of the German Reich." On its part, the Papacy tried to meet the onslaught of extreme nationalism by stressing its own universal character. After World War II, for example, Pius XII felt it necessary in his Christmas allocution of 1945 to reassure the Catholic world that, as a mother of all its adherents, the *Sancta Mater Ecclesia* "does not and cannot belong exclusively to this or that people, or even more to one than to others, but equally to all."[93]

Nor has modern nationalism, that overpowering force in international and domestic affairs of the last two centuries, been devoid of deep religious ingredients. Outwardly secular in nature, the national movements sometimes appeared as a rivaling force to religion. National consciousness, especially if nurtured by the unity of language—which, as was ingeniously observed, often "formed man more than man formed language"—was frequently able to overcome religious disparities and to forge, for example, a united German nation of Protestants and Catholics. But even in such cases the nationalities took over certain fundamental religious teachings. The very concepts of a "chosen nation," of its "manifest destiny," and the like have sprung from the belief in the superior truth of one's religious conceptions against the presumably "false" teachings of other faiths. The chief spokesman of Italian nationalism in the era of the *Risorgimento*, Giuseppe Mazzini, went so far as to denigrate the doctrine of Rights of Man as benefiting only the individuals. Using religious terminology he declared:

Right undermines sacrifice and eliminates martyrdom from the world. In any theory of individual rights interest alone predominates and martyrdom becomes an absurdity. No interests could survive one's death. Nevertheless, it is martyrdom which serves as the baptism of a new world and the initiation of progress.

Here Mazzini spoke partly under the influence of the great Polish poet Adam Mickiewicz who, together with the mystic Andrzej Towiański, saw in the partitions of their Polish fatherland a sign that, like their brotherly stateless nation of Israel, the Polish people was chosen for the role of a "suffering messiah" for the salvation of the world. Mazzini used the same phraseology for his "chosen" nation, Italy. Even among adherents of the same world religions like Christianity or Islam, nations have often retained their beliefs of being chosen by God for a special superior mission.[94]

A similar doctrine could, on the other hand, be voiced already by leading thinkers of the ancient Roman Empire bent upon conquest of the entire Mediterranean world. So convinced were they of the superiority of their own culture that they considered any resistance to their "civilizing" efforts a sinful defiance of their divinely ordained system. In 59 B.C.E., four years after the first Roman occupation of Palestine, Cicero sharply condemned the Jews' insistence upon the preservation of their national-religious independence. He argued:

> Even while Jerusalem was standing and the Jews were at peace with us, the practice of their sacred rites was at variance with the glory of our empire, the dignity of our name, the customs of our ancestors. But now it is even more so, when that nation by its armed resistance has shown what it thinks of our rule; how dear it was to the immortal gods is shown by the fact that it has been conquered, reduced to a subject province, made a slave.

Basically similar arguments, though couched in somewhat milder language, have also been voiced by some modern defenders of expansionary imperialism as when Christopher Columbus embarked upon what was to become the discovery of America in order to enhance the glory and might of Christendom. Later it was Rudyard Kipling who, for a similar justification, coined his renowned slogan of "the white man's burden." It ultimately led to the extreme aberrations of racial superiority as in the doctrine of the Nazi conquering "superman." At the same time in a more moderate and creative form religious differences have often helped to maintain ethnic minority cultures, especially in such multinational empires as the United States' "nation of nations" or in the multitude of internationally sanctioned "national minority" rights.[95]

Such frequently close interrelations between nationalism and religion manifested themselves even under the avowedly anti-religious Soviet regime. Once they formally recognized the national minority rights in order to reduce the theretofore sharp national animosities in the Tsarist Empire, the early Soviet leaders necessarily helped to maintain the identities of the various religious denominations, especially in Asia. In the United States, too, Catholicism and Protestantism, with its various subdivisions, were mutually reinforced by the internal bonds of the ethnic groups of Irish, Italians, Scandinavians, and so forth. Not to speak of the Jewish Americans who, for the most part, have been treated by their neighbors as adherents of the Jewish faith, even if individually many of them were agnostics or atheists. Only secondarily were they also considered members of a distinct ethnic group. This evolution has had a long history behind it. Even in antiquity monophysitism was highly instrumental in maintaining the ethnic identity of the Egyptian and Armenian peoples who otherwise might have been totally submerged under the Byzantine power structure. "The ancient Church of Alexandria," states Edward R. Hardy, Jr., "has an important place both in the general history of Christianity and in the national history of Egypt. Its rise and decline is on the whole a glorious story of resistance to either pagan or officially Christian imperialism, and a valuable exhibition of the strength and limitations of a predominantly national form of Christianity." Similarly, in the Late Middle Ages Hussitism helped nurture the national feelings of the Czech people. In Belgium it was Flemish Catholicism (even more than the Flemish language) that preserved the Flemish nationality from being absorbed by their ruling neighbors during the political, military, and economic hegemony of the flourishing Dutch culture. "Flemish villages," writes Thomas Harrison, "have confronted French-speaking villages, the Flemish side of the street, the French side, time out of mind, without one tongue gaining on the other, and without any tendency toward the formation of a common speech." The same held largely true also for the later Catholic-Protestant divisions in the era of the Protestant Reformation.[96]

Corresponding developments and similar effects could be observed also in the large Muslim world. For one example, Shi'ite Islam of the "Twelver" variety helped create the modern national state of Persia, especially during the Safavid period of the sixteenth and seventeenth centuries. Today it serves as the mainspring of the "Islamic Revolution" of

Ayatolah Khomeini and his Iranian followers. This attempt at reversing the long-lasting powerful trends toward secularization, steadily reinforced by the economically overwhelming needs of westernization of the Middle Eastern cradles of Islam, now offers a most serious challenge to world peace. In contrast, the Ottoman Empire's policy of toleration of religious diversity, its communal system which granted the ethnic religious minorities considerable self-government in religious and cultural affairs, contributed greatly to the maintenance of a measure of internal peace among the numerous nationalities. As soon as the Empire was destroyed under the blows of World War I and the new Turkish Republic emerged as a smaller national state, however, the repression of its national minorities (in defiance of its explicit pledges in the Peace Treaties) became so serious that the League of Nations had to arrange an exchange of the Turkish and Greek populations. As a result 400,000 Turks are said to have left Greece for Turkey while 1.5 million "Greeks" were taken from Turkey to Greece. This masterly performance of Fritjof Nansen and his associates earned the distinguished explorer a well-deserved Nobel Peace Prize (1922). It must be remembered, however, that the essential criterion in the designation of "Turks" and "Greeks" was not linguistic but religious. The large majority of Muslims were thus expatriated from Greece, while the majority of Greek-Orthodox had to leave Turkey, whether they came from Turkish or Greek speaking households.[97]

This exchange of populations has offered a clear illustration of the importance of the historic religious divisions even in our highly secularized twentieth century. Looking back on the entire course of human history the profound and enduring impact on humanity of such religious "heroes" as Moses, Jesus, and Mohammed (although called the three great "impostors" by a twelfth-century opponent), Buddha, and Confucius has no parallel in that of any secular leader. Back in the twelfth century Yehudah Halevi, in his defense of the political and military "powerlessness" of the Jewish people, pointed out that masses of both Christians and Muslims venerated their great prophets and saints rather than their conquerors, statesmen, or thinkers. Jenghiz Khan and his family may have built in the course of a few decades the greatest empire of all times under the watchword that there be "one God in Heaven, and one ruler on earth." It extended from the Pacific to Central Europe. But because they offered no new spiritual underpinnings for their expansive powers, the Mongols themselves were quickly submerged within the Chinese and Islamic civilizations. In contrast, Hitler's "Thousand-Year Reich," though proclaimed with pseudo-religious fervor, vanished after a dozen years. Will anti-religions, or perhaps also intrinsically pseudoreligions, such as the profession of the Marxist-Leninst creed, prove very much more enduring? Only the future will tell. In any case, through the millennia of human history religion in one form or another has served as a sort of "soul" animating the various societal "bodies" throughout human history.[98]

IX

SOCIORELIGIOUS HISTORICAL
METHODOLOGY

THE ACTUAL APPLICATION of the socioreligious method to historical research, particularly of the modern period, has peculiar characteristics and difficulties of its own. In the ancient and medieval periods kings, statesmen, army commanders, as well as thinkers and writers, basically spoke the same language as the priests and prophets. They all shared the assumption that they lived under a divine guidance of history. Even the superficially purely secular "Mongolian flood" of Jenghiz Khan and his successors, which was not combined with efforts to uproot the established religions of the conquered populations and to replace them with Mongolian Shamanist beliefs and practices, nonetheless bore with it some religious coloring. In his drive for world domination the Great Khan is said to have used the aforementioned slogan that there should be "one God in heaven, and one ruler on earth." According to K. C. Chandry, the situation in India in the beginning of the twentieth century was such that "in politics, too, religion is the strongest fibre in the stuff of which patriotism or nationalism is made." Throughout much of recorded history, moreover, many rulers enlisted priestly and prophetic help by seeking to ascertain the divine will before embarking on a major enterprise. Nor did they as a rule deny the right of "saintly" persons to warn them against violations of the established religious and social order, or even to censure them for such deviations after the event. Residua of such interrelations between basic religious thinking and sociopolitical aspirations and actions have persisted in many countries in the religious formulas of the oaths taken by officials, high and low, at their installation in office as well as in various other oaths of allegiance, the saluting of the national flags, and the singing of patriotic hymns. This is in sharp contrast with the performance of daily chores where purely secular attitudes and utterances prevail even among such personally religious persons as the American "born again" Baptist President Jimmy Carter.[99]

So long as modern historiography concentrated on the political and, in recent generations, on the economic developments of localities, regions, or states, historians could neglect the impact of religion in these areas of life with relative impunity. But when their attention has increasingly been focused on the social and daily life of all classes, including the masses of poor and underprivileged, the religious factor should have loomed much larger than it did. Before the twentieth century, the large majority of population in most countries consisted of peasants, whose daily life and even more, their celebrations of festive occasions such as their Sabbaths, holidays, and family anniversaries, were deeply affected by their prayers, religious ceremonies, and preachments. Religious concerns came particularly to the fore on such crucial occasions as baptisms or circumcisions, Bar Mitzvahs, confirmations, betrothals, weddings, funerals, and the like. Even in countries where the population was known to be lax in attending church, synagogue, or mosque services (for instance in Latin America), the influence of the clergy, even in political affairs, has been quite marked. Nowadays, too, the mere arrival of the pope to celebrate a public Mass suffices to attract millions, and often results in the rekindling of the flame of faith. In a country like Poland, living under a communist regime, it has been the Church alone which has offered some counterpoise to communist totalitarianism. Similarly in Germany, in 1932—one of the most "advanced" industrial, democratic, and enlightened nations—upon Hitler's accession to power, the political organs, the army, the press, and the universities were speedily integrated (*gleichgeschaltet*) into the ruthless Nazi bulldozer. Only the religious bodies succeeded in maintaining a measure of continuity and independence into the new postwar era of democratic revival.[100]

Until recently the religious establishments have also played a major role in the economic life of each country. Through their ownership of much land (on which at least in the early Middle Ages they had actually pioneered in methods of cultivating the soil) and urban property on the one hand, and through their preeminent share in the religiously inspired charitable institutions and in other forms of aid to the poor on the other, they were an important segment of each country's economy. Before the relatively recent welfare states most hospitals and clinics, soup kitchens, family counseling services, and the like were run as denominational institutions by voluntary religious societies. Before the spread of the governmentally maintained public school systems during the last two centuries, schools were largely controlled by religious authorities. Even today, we still have a variety of parochial schools, day schools, and other educational institutions from nursery schools to universities run by denominational bodies in the United States and elsewhere. Nor can we overlook the impact of the widespread discrimination against religious minorities (in practice frequently defying the theoretical equality of all citizens) and the defensive measures adopted by these minorities against social ostracism or discrimination in public and private employment which deeply affected both the minorities and the majorities of the population. One need but remember the role of antisemitism in its various manifestations throughout the ages to realize that even in the modern "secular" societies religious and ethnoreligious disparities have played a far from negligible role in the historic evolution of many lands. One need but consider the extraordinary historic experience of the Jewish people, which for thousands of years had lived in a "divided world" of one kind or another. In antiquity it was the alternating struggle for hegemony between Egypt and the powers of the "Fertile Crescent," and later between Rome and Achaemenid Persia– Parthia–Sassanian Persia which greatly influenced the Jews of Palestine and their growing dispersion. Later on, the Jewish people found itself drawn into the conflict between Christendom and Islam, between colonial empires and the native populations, and more recently between the communist East and the free enterprise West.

All such conflicting influences and changing loyalties not only led to frequent complications and challenges, but also developed a variety of creative remedies. Discussing, for instance, the ethnocultural role in the votes cast in the United States at elections to political offices, James E. Wright correctly points out that

> religion is a more crucial variable than the ethno-cultural model, that is national stock. It is religion that provides the key to descriptions of differential behavior in the interpretive framework to understand it.

There is, of course, the great difficulty in achieving accurate quantitative assessment of the votes cast by various denominations or even in estimating their percentage among voters in particular districts. The data on church membership offer only one practical criterion; its rise and decline, which is often misleading as to the intensity of religious feelings and their effects. These psychological factors may be far more significant than the mere formal profession of belonging to one or another denomination. The few available studies on the percentage of the population formally joining congregations, though showing an upward trend, revealed that even in the nineteenth century there were many religiously unaffiliated persons. For example, a study of three states showed that in 1890 the Wisconsin and Ohio church membership embraced only 85 percent of the population, having increased from 60 and 75 percent respectively in the preceding twenty years. On the other hand, in Michigan the growth was merely from 65 to 75 percent during the same period. Moreover, these estimates are not altogether dependable, since another investigator, using somewhat different criteria, estimated in 1890 the Wisconsin church membership at only 52 percent, while in Iowa simultaneously the total supposedly reached no more than 46 percent.[101]

There is general agreement that these figures do not indicate that those who had failed to join any congregation were either atheists or agnostics, nor that those who joined were necessarily devout believers. To begin with, congregations in the United States—being purely voluntary associations for the most part maintained by their membership dues and other voluntary donations—have had to charge their members high amounts, which many persons could not afford. At the same time the need to attract worshipers, occasionally on a competitive basis, induced many a congregation to offer better services to members. In fact, there has been a long-standing debate as to whether the voluntary American Episcopalian Church is religiously more or less effective than its English counterpart, the state-supported Anglican Church. In any case, despite its financial dependence on the state, the Church of England has retained much political power in the country. Even today one still hears the old adage warning all British governments not to tangle with the monarchy, the Church, and the coal miners. However, I have been told that among the Jews, some members, especially in the American Southwest, joined two or even three congregations—Orthodox, Conservative, and Reform— merely because they were solicited by some friends for a gift, which they considered tantamount to a donation to some charity. On the other hand, at High Holiday services, which attracted the greatest numbers, the synagogues often could not accommodate the overflow of all would-be worshipers. This situation left an opening for private entrepreneurs to rent large halls, engage rabbis and cantors to conduct services, and admit without much ado anyone willing to pay a modest entrance fee. These crosscurrents have often been confusing and have made any kind of numerical estimate extremely difficult.[102]

A much more serious ambiguity facing a historian in connection with the designation "Jew" is its combination of ethnicism and religion. This difficulty, also in connection with such other designations, as Hebrew or Israelite, dates back to antiquity and the Middle Ages. A name combined with Judeus, Juif, or Ebreo did not always connote that the person was Jewish. There were some aristocratic individuals in both Western and Byzantine Christendom who used it as their family name. Even more difficult was the identification of a professing Jew who outwardly was, or appeared to be, a convert from Judaism. To discover and convict such New Christians (*conversos*, or Marranos), kept the tribunals of the Catholic Inquisition busy for centuries throughout the Spanish Empire with its Afro-Asian and American colonies. Even some genuine converts everlastingly lived under a cloud of suspicion. An outstanding example, even before the establishment of the Spanish Inquisition, was offered by Pope Anacletus II. A scion of the distinguished Roman Pierleoni family, he was born a Christian and as such was able to make a career in the Church. In 1123, as the papal legate, he presided over the distinguished ecclesiastical synods in Chartres and Beauvais. But when seven years later he was elected pope, some cardinals voted for the antipope, Innocent II. The widespread opposition throughout Western Europe was led by St. Bernard of Clairvaux who in his letter to Emperor Lothar complained that "it is well known that a Jewish offspring now occupies the see of St. Peter to the injury of Christ." Innocent II has thereafter been treated in the ecclesiastical records as the legitimate Pope, while Anacletus appeared as a mere antipope. Even in modern times Benjamin Disraeli, the famed novelist-statesman and one of Britain's empire-builders, although officially baptized at the age of thirteen, was often denounced by his opposition as a "Hebrew conjuror" and the like. In his reply, he declared, on more than one occasion, that he was indeed a Jew, but one of both Sinai and Calvary. He also pointed out that according to the historical record God had directly spoken only to Moses, the Hebrew prophets, Jesus, and Mohammed—all men of the Semitic race. A similar position was also taken, though in a somewhat more subdued tone, by some leading churchmen of Jewish origin. One need but invoke the example of the present Archbishop of Paris, Aaron Jean Marie Cardinal Lustiger. Born in 1926 to two Polish Jews, later survivors of the Holocaust, he rose to the rank of Archbishop of Paris, an office which for centuries has been considered second only to the bishopric of Rome (the Papacy) in the canonical structure. Yet, one day after his nomination to the College of Cardinals (February 1, 1983) Lustiger declared to a reporter:

> I have always considered myself a Jew, even if that is not the opinion of some rabbis . . . I was born Jewish, and so I remain, even if that is unacceptable to many . . . . For me the vocation of Israel is bringing light to the goyim [Gentiles].[103]

A telling example of the possible variations even in the censuses of religious bodies is offered by those of the Jewish communities of the United States. During the period of the great immigration, especially of Jews from Eastern Europe (1870–1914), many new arrivals (not counting the minority of determined atheists) failed to join any organized Jewish congregation. As a rule they regularly prayed in small private chapels (known in Yiddish as *shtiblekh*). These were often formed by associations of persons of common origin from a particular European locality or region, or by followers of one or another hasidic rabbi. Regrettably, our statistics in this field are very deficient. Our main source of information on the general membership in churches and synagogues throughout the country stems from the none-too-regular official Census of Religious Bodies. Unfortunately these findings were greatly affected by frequent changes in the methods employed in collecting the necessary data and inconsistencies in the basic definition of terms from one census to another. A particularly crass alteration took place in the Jewish censuses of 1916 and 1926. Since they were instructed in 1926 that each organization should "report the number of its members according to the definition of member used in that particular church or organization," the census takers completely reversed their previous methods of counting Jews. They admitted that

> the Jews, in contrast with the definition employed in earlier census periods [when only actual congregational members were counted], now consider as members all persons of the Jewish faith living in communities in which local congregations are situated.

The result was an endless chain of guesstimates of how many Jews lived in particular localities. The census thus furnished more or less approximate data in the case of small Jewish communities where the local Jewish leaders knew most of their coreligionists. This criterion completely broke down, however, in larger cities and metropolitan areas, where the overwhelming majority of American Jews were living. The outcome was that the new figure presented in the 1926 census, giving a total Jewish population of 4,081,242 persons allegedly residing in the United States, was disproportionately larger than the number published in the 1916 census. As it happened, the intervening decade, which included the years of World War I and its aftermath, had witnessed a great decline in Jewish immigration. Hence such an enormous disparity appeared ludicrous to the census takers themselves so that they had to insert the following caveat:

> Obviously it would be fallacious to assume that this immense increase of 3,724,107 represents the growth of Jewish membership during the decade. Because of this fact, it was decided to entirely omit the Jewish figure when computing the membership growth during the last two decades.

The situation was quite different in most other countries, including neighboring Canada, where the general population censuses, unhampered by the strict interpretation of the separation of state and Church, included an inquiry concerning the religious affiliation of the individuals counted.[104]

Since 1926, the situation in the United States has greatly improved through a number of special studies. Using more refined tools covering many localities and larger regions some private individuals and organizations have furnished more adequate information about the Jewish population in the country. However, there are still numerous lacunae which must be filled. Without any government aid, some Jewish organizations, especially the American Jewish Committee, the Conference on Jewish Social Studies, and more recently the Council of Jewish Federations and Welfare Funds, have tried to come to grips with the difficult methodological problems of first how to identify persons as Jews and second how to locate them in particular areas. Using all sorts of approaches, such as the long-lasting experiment with the Yom Kippur census (the counting of the excess number of absentee pupils from the public schools on the Day of Atonement and then multiplying the resulting figures by the general ratio of school children to the total population), the number of Jewish burials, and occasional visits to areas known to be inhabited predominantly by Jews, the investigation of ten Jewish communities in the late 1930s reached certain tentative but valuable conclusions. Details of that investigation were described in typescript memoranda, which were then summarized in a volume provided with an enlightening introduction on the merits and demerits of the respective methods by Sophia M. Robison. Entitled *Jewish Population Studies*, it was edited by her with the assistance of Joshua Starr. Subsequently a number of other communities undertook such surveys of their own, often in consultation with the Conference on Jewish Social Studies. More recently, the Council of Jewish Federations and Welfare Funds has initiated studies toward a new comprehensive census using some further refined methods.[105]

In short, the impact of religion on society in the public, and even more in the private life of a great many citizens, has always been enormous. This was true in ordinary times, and doubly so in periods of crisis, especially during wars. Such a ramified influence, both positive and negative, exerted by religious denominations even in the "secular" era of modern history has not yet been adequately studied, especially in its different forms and potency observable from country to country and period to period. Suffice it to cite here the example of Austria, a generally progressive Western country. Vienna, one of the great centers of secular culture before World War I and the birthplace of psychoanalyis and psychohistory, during most of Freud's lifetime had been dominated by the Christian Socialist Party with its strong Catholic orientation combined with outspoken antisemitism. In the early twentieth century the law of the land still provided that Christians could not legally marry adherents of any non-Christian faith. Since mixed Judeo-Christian marriages had become quite common, it usually was the Jewish bridegroom who either converted to Christianity or else formally declared before state authorities to be "without religion" (*konfessionslos*). A Viennese journal published weekly lists of persons who in this fashion severed their membership in the Jewish community, lists which at times counted several hundred Jewish names a year out of a population of some 200,000 Jews. Remarkably, this system continued to operate in Austria which, in its preparation for the law of 1890 regulating the legal status of the Austrian Jewish community as a part of the governmental structure, had been forewarned by neighboring Prussia that some wealthy Jews had been leaving the Jewish community of Berlin and other Prussian cities merely in order to evade the obligatory Jewish communal taxes. It was in reply to an Austrian inquiry that in 1883 Otto von Bismarck, in his capacity as Prussia's prime minister, had instituted a formal inquiry about the practices generated by the Prussian law of 1876 concerning Jewish community life. This law, adopted by the Prussian Diet under the combined pressures of Orthodox and agnostic Jews, had allowed Jewish members to sever their ties with their religious communities under the excuse of some (undefined) "religious scruples."[106]

It is small wonder, then, that as late as in the nineteenth century so profound a thinker as Johann Wolfgang von Goethe could declare that "all wars are wars of religion." To some extent the same assertion could still be made throughout the modern period, if for the concept of the established God-worshiping religions one substitutes at times some such deeply emotional entities as the "religion of progress," the apotheosis of Nazi racism and its Führer, Adolf Hitler, or of communism and its leader, Joseph Stalin. Very enlightening also is the career of the distinguished American historian, Henry Charles Lea. Although a competent student of biology and chemistry, as a Quaker, he became interested in problems of religious toleration. Before long he began to concentrate on medieval history.

> In his medieval studies [asserts Lea's biographer, Edward Sculley Bradley] he was gradually impressed by the fact that in whatever direction he turned he was confronted by the Church. It was omnipresent and frequently omnipotent, not only in spiritual but in temporal affairs, and no one could comprehend the antagonizing forces which moulded the evoluton of our civilization without understanding the sources of ecclesiastical power and the use to which it was put.

Even later during "enlightened absolutism" it was the more specifically religious doctrine of the "divine right of kings" which served to legitimize excessive monarchical power. This doctrine of the sacral nature of kingship had deep roots in many civilizations from antiquity to the modern period. It played a great role in England during the seventeenth century and it was not fully abolished by the revolution of 1688. It was still the subject of a serious debate at the International Congress of the History of Religions held in 1959 entirely devoted to the various aspects of Sacral Kingships (*La Regalità Sacra*). Throughout the millennia of earlier history in the minds of a large majority of people God (or the gods of polytheistic nations) loomed far above any earthly rulers in determining the fate of their nation, tribe, or individual members. The state usually shared its role with other institutions such as the military establishment, the economic system, the class structure, and particularly the Church or Mosque. All of these, though generally conceived as man-made societal forms, subject to man-made changes, were nevertheless regarded by most people as having been created and guided throughout their existence by an outside supernatural power, omnipotent and omniscient, which in the ultimate sense decided whatever happened on earth or elsewhere in the universe.[107]

The primitive tribes who worshiped their respective gods and in the case of defeat in war, assumed that the gods of the victorious tribe had proved to be superior and therefore deserved to be adopted as the gods of the vanquished tribe as well, deeply believed in the supernatural forces dominant in nature and in the human world. A purely expansionist conqueror, like Jenghiz Khan, who strove to become the sole master on earth, recognized, as we recall, the presence of a superior master in heaven. Without trying to suppress, or even sharply to restrict, the various faiths professed by the conquered populations, he did not tolerate any direct offense against his own religion. Typical of the thinking of the Mongolian dynasty was the letter addressed in 1546 by Jenghiz' grandson, the Great Khan Göyük, to Pope Innocent IV. It included the characteristic exhortation:

> Jenghis Khan and the Great Khan [Ogotai] have both transmitted to me God's order [that all the world should surrender to the Mongols]. . . . You personally at the head of the [Christian] kings, shall come, one and all, to pay homage to me and to serve me; then we shall take your submission. If, however, you do not accept God's wish and act against Our order, we shall know that you are Our enemies.

Much more pronounced were, of course, the religious motivations behind the great expansion of Islam in the seventh century and the counter-offensive of the Christian crusades in the later Middle Ages, as well as behind the imperialist politico-economic expansion of the three greatest modern empires: Spain, Great Britain, and Russia.[108]

Certainly, from the standpoint of the millennia of human history, one might reverse Hermann Cohen's aforementioned statement and contend that the state has been but one of the concentric entities within the religious universe of the respective faiths. A more authoritative view of normative Judaism was once summarized by me as follows:

> In Maimonides' opinion, Jewish law, being divinely ordained is wholly independent of its territorial origin and of the state for which it was first enacted. Both the [Catholic] Church and Islam likewise gloried in the supernatural origin of their respective legal systems,

Canon jurists in particular stressing the *ius divinum* and the law of nature, which they often identified with the fundamentals of Old Testament Law. But for the medieval Jew, far more than for the medieval Christian, the state was the result of sin, although at the same time a remedy to sin.

Nor was the attitude of many Muslim theologians and the majority of laymen any friendlier to the idea of statehood. Although they must have realized that the rise of Islam had strong political as well as religious motivations, few of them were advocates of state power. "Religious people," observed Shelomo David Goitein, "shunned government service and regarded government in general as the very substance of the forces which opposed God's role on earth. A pious man would not accept an invitation to dine from a government official . . . since most of the government's revenue was thought to emanate from extortions, law-breaking and oppression of the weak." Of course, the religious establishment as such was but another such concentric entity within religion, but since it was believed to be closer to the Deity and in a better position to divine God's will, it was often assumed to be able to warn all earthly powers against defying that will. It also could threaten evildoers (including opponents) with punishment or promise righteous persons great rewards, both in this world and in the Hereafter. Religion thus was within nature and outside it, within society and a counterpart to it. For thousands of years it also served as the mainspring of culture and the leading force in individual and collective education. That is why a clear understanding of the interplay of religious and secular history in its numerous manifestations through the ages ought to receive much fuller consideration than it has had in the secular historiography of the eighteenth to the twentieth centuries, except perhaps in such works as those by Toynbee, who may have gone too far in the other direction.[109]

At the same time historians must beware of the pitfalls emerging from the combination of historical and metahistorical approaches in religious history. Because religion is so deeply intertwined with tradition as expressed in both "sacred scriptures" and inherited long-practiced rituals and mores, it often became enmeshed in the deep conflict between faith and reason or even—as queried by the aforementioned Monsignor—in the dichotomy between religious "certainty" and rational "liberty" in judging what is historically true. Certainly, a historian today cannot simply follow the criteria established by the biblical chroniclers—despite their great contributions to human historiography—and their explanations of all major events in national and world history through divine rewards or punishments for the peoples', or their rulers', good or sinful behavior. That approach, often leading to self-accusation, so frequently applied by the Israelitic prophets, has left its permanent mark on the Jews (and to a lesser extent on Christians and Muslims) of the following generations. Until today pious Jews recite the ancient prayer, "Because of our [or our forefathers'] sins we have been exiled from our country," attributing the destruction of the two Temples in Jerusalem and the loss of Jewish national independence to the misdeeds of their ancient forebears. Such attributions overlooked the fact that even before the First Exile ancient Israel had drifted away from the doctrine of the children's responsibility for the sinful behavior of their ancestors, at least beyond the fourth generation. As the prophets Jeremiah and Ezekiel graphically questioned why, if "the fathers had eaten sour grapes should the children's teeth be set on edge?"[110]

Nor have all pious Catholics, despite the pertinent resolution at the Second Ecumenical Vatican Council of 1962–65, relinquished the belief that Jews of all generations ought to suffer retribution as descendants of their alleged Christ-killing ancestors in Jerusalem almost two thousand years before. The venom of that myth, which had pervaded all Judeo-Christian relations through the ages has only to some extent been mitigated by the numerous historical studies written by outstanding Christian and Jewish scholars about the proceedings at the trial of Jesus.[111]

Not that mythology and legends as such are to be eliminated from the realm of historical research. Because they were in themselves a fact of life and sometimes also because of their intrinsic beauty and the light they shed on the peoples' psychology in various regions and periods (occasionally also because of some kernels of historic reality hidden in their legendary shells) they form a part—in some areas a major part—of the surviving resources for historical investigations.[112]

Another major difficulty confronting the historian using religious sources stems from terminological obstacles. To begin with, the very term "religion" is often used and abused through different applications. Morton Smith raised a serious question when he pointed out that

> the variety of ordinary usage [of that word] is so wide, that the number of terms which . . . were used has been used to translate in learned literature is *so enormous*, the special meanings which have been given it by individual thinkers are so many and so various, that the historical method is *unusable* because of the complexity of the problem.

Remarkably, moreover, there is the astonishing fact that the Hebrew Bible, a major source of religious inspiration, education, and endless controversies, does not have an exact Hebrew equivalent to the Latin term *religio*. In addition, much of the existing historical material, "sacred" to the religious persons, is written in languages which are foreign to the large majority of believers. We recall how difficult it is to reproduce all shades of meanings by translating from one language to another the simple German word "Reich" by using its English equivalent "Empire." It is also generally known that most languages contain words untranslatable into any other language. Similarly ambigious is the term History. Among its numerous meanings the most difficult has been the fact that it may refer to "the object of the description or the description of the object." Furthermore Western students using, for instance, Arabic sources are not only perplexed by the enormous variety of dialects spoken in the Arab world from Morocco to Iraq and Yemen, but also by the frequent double meanings of the same words. For instance, the word *mawla* may refer to a slave in one context and to his master in another. *Abbana* can at one time mean to blame a deceased person and on another occasion to indicate praise for his or her good deeds. Two scholars were actually able to compile a list of four hundred such heteronyms in the juridical field alone. This is the more astonishing, as in legal documents even minor deviations from an officially required formulation might nullify the pertinent testimony and thus inflict untold losses to innocent individuals. According to Jewish law, a small scribal error removes an entire Torah (scroll of law) from use in divine services, while any deviation from the language prescribed for a formal writ of divorce nullifies the whole act and renders particularly the wife incapable of remarriage.[113]

It is not surprising, therefore, that sometimes historians use evasive, even weasel words, to circumvent such perplexities or conflicts. Through a study of a selected group of modern Muslim historians Rotraut Wielandt has shown how, by using accepted historical terms, some of these scholars were able to turn them into ambiguous secular-sounding explanations. For example, Malek Bennabi, describing the "phenomenon called Qur'an" as "the religion of Abraham which embraces the deeds of the prophets . . . , one biography follows another from Abraham to Zechariah, John the Baptist, Mary and Jesus, the Qur'an has newly edited that chronology in a partially new form." By using the historical terminology of "biography," "chronology," and "edited," the author was able to camouflage the dogmatic character of the long-accepted Islamic tradition and the metahistorical claims of the Muslim Scripture.[114]

In practice, such difficulties can be avoided by the historian when he keeps the two domains clearly apart, a separation which has often been observed in political life. At the outbreak of World War II many Catholics in the United States and Canada may have shared the sentiments expressed by Cardinal Hinseley in his Pastoral Letter of 1940 about the need of a program for the postwar reconstruction of war-torn Europe. This high ranking churchman wrote:

> We have proof positive that in the present state of the world a system of secularist or materialist idealisms are built on sand, and great is the fall thereof when the storms and floods run down. Such collapse is inevitable unless, as Pius XI declared (in his Encyclical *Quadragesimo Anno*), all men's activities unite to imitate and, as far as is humanly possible, carry out the unity of the Divine Plan which places God as the first and supreme end of all created activities.

Yet, even a century earlier, Alexis de Tocqueville had asserted that "in the United States no religious doctrine displays the slightest hostility to democratic and republican institutions. The clergy of all the different sects hold the same language, their opinions are consonant to the laws, and the human intellect flows onward in one sole current."[115]

Of course, the historian must likewise carefully consider the reciprocal influence of society on religious life and thought. Because religion has been such a pervasive influence in many social domains, changes within society almost immediately had repercussions also in the religious sphere. Adjustment of some religious usages and even laws to such changing trends in social life in all its manifestations, political, economic, and cultural, has been an accepted method in almost all denominations. Even adamant traditionalists often had to make such concessions, as long as these did not encroach upon the fundamentals of their faith for which some of them were prepared to suffer religious martyrdom. A number of these adjustments in social life actually preceded the corresponding changes in formal religious laws and teachings. But such theoretical adaptations of the law to life merely resembled the similar revisions of the new secular laws enacted by the respective states or municipalities under the impact of changes already generated by practices in the ever fluid domestic and international situations. At times, however, religious visionaries or reformers, appealing to the masses from purely ethnoreligious motivations, have caused much friction within the religious bodies.

Apart from the numerous dogmatic, liturgical, and even textual controversies—we need but remember the streams of blood shed in the Christian world over the use of the word *filioque* in the liturgy and the differences in the worship of the Twelve Saints of the Iranian Shi'ites in variance from other Shi'ite and all Sunni sects in the world of Islam—there also were nationalistic, dynastic, and other political interests which sometimes resulted in the emergence of permanent new sects. Such sectarians usually functioned in opposition to the majority of their own denomination. The historian need not be a well-trained theologian to examine the endless minutiae in the frequently obscure and conflicting ecclesiastical records in order to perceive the fine points and the broad trends in some historically relevant changes in socioreligious interrelations. The burden is certainly not alleviated by the presence of enormously rich source materials, mostly written from different premises and with different objectives in mind from those often encountered in the documentation in the secular world. In each case, the historian must judge the intrinsic meaning of the source, not from some of his own scale of values, but from that of the original writer or speaker. One may only wish that, reciprocally, another scholar, approaching the same sources from his study of religion, will follow the direction indicated by Friedrich Daniel Ernst Schleiermacher (1768–1834), the famous Protestant theologian, when he asserted that

> every human institution, insofar as it essentially and genuinely mirrors the spirit of a people, is just as much law divine and revelation of divine power and majesty as were that law and those orders to which the people of the Old Covenant had given that name. For it is God alone and immediately who assigned to each people its peculiar calling on earth and imbues it with its peculiar spirit so that He may glorify himself by each in its peculiar way.

Historians may disregard such theological justifications and even take the reactions to contemporary sociopolitical changes for granted. But in the real world these explanations fill an important void in the minds of numerous pious listeners and even at times have some direct ideological or practical consequences.[116]

In general, modern historians, even some of the best, have often neglected the religious factor in the history of the modern world. They were so involved in the political, economic, and social developments, that they often delegated even the significant changes in intellectual and scientific fields to specialists in the history of ideas or of science. The transformations in religious life and thought, even in the earlier periods when religion played a preeminent role, were left in the hands of theologians and, to a lesser extent, in those of lay students of religion, almost all of whom have approached the subject from different ideological, liturgical, or institutional, rather than historical, angles.

X

METHODOLOGICAL PLURALISM

IN SUMMATION one may note that each of the approaches and methods analyzed here have their merits as well as their serious disadvantages. Remarkably, the fullest treatment had to be given here to the oldest, namely the socioreligious, or perhaps religiosocial, "historicism." One may call it an "old-old-fashioned method," because the epithet "old-fashioned" has in the pertinent scholarly literature of the last decades been frequently attached to the totally secularized methods which had played such a dominant role in the nineteenth and twentieth centuries. In fact, modern historiography of the last three centuries has, in part, owed its rise to a rebellion against the earlier millennial tradition of God or gods as the ultimate determining factors on the destinies of all humanity, indeed of the universe as a whole. Under the prevailing secularist tendencies of scholars and students, represented by the large majority of secular-oriented individuals, the religious element was relegated into an ever-shrinking corner of the historical horizon. The history of religion, even more than those of literature, art, philosophy, or science, has become a specialty outside the training of most professional or amateur historians. It was almost entirely entrusted to theologians of the respective faiths, many of whom had no historical training. On the other hand, most historians have often forgotten that, unlike the other branches of learning which are fields of intensive preoccupation mainly by a small intellectual elite, religion in one form or another has been affecting multitudes of individuals and groups both in their daily lives and at many turning points in their development under diverse civilizations.

If I may be allowed to insert an observation from personal perspectives I should like to emphasize that all that is said here is not out of deep religious feelings which cannot understand the attitude of purely secularist historians who had never been "insiders" in the realm of religious beliefs and practices, or had consciously repudiated them as a way of life. This is not the place for personal "confessions." Suffice it to say, that in the stretches of my life under three different civilizations I have had many opportunities to observe, and even to participate in, a variety of experiments in social, communal, and intellectual life. As a child and adolescent I lived in the midst of a Galician community which had retained many characteristics of a medieval ghetto. I spent my young manhood enjoying the turbulent and pulsating life of Vienna during its last years of serving as the capital and intellectual center of the powerful Austro-Hungarian empire of 54,000,000 people belonging to a dozen different nationalities and cultures. I also participated in the traumatic experience of that city when it suddenly shrank to the position of a capital of a small state of 6,000,000 persons, a third of whom lived within its own confines. Even then for a while, Vienna continued to play its traditional role of mediation between the West and the East of Europe. Subsequently, for more than half a century I participated in the every-changing, often creative and always exciting crosscurrents of New York City which had suddenly become the center of the financial, and in many areas also of the cultural world. These experiences were enriched by my spending several months each year either in a characteristic environment of rural New England or on journeys to various lands in Europe, the Middle East, or other parts of the world. Because during these months abroad I spent some hours daily doing research in archives and libraries, sometimes also teaching and always exchanging ideas with local friends, I felt as being not merely a tourist looking at the diverse cultures from the outside, but rather as somewhat of a participant. Perhaps because of these muiltifarious experiences I have been drawn into consideration of numerous political, cultural, religious, and ethnic differences with a much greater sense of understanding of, and participating in, that unity within the diversity of mankind.

Basically it appears that most of the methods analyzed in this essay have their advantages and disadvantages dependent on the periods of history, the different geographic areas, and most of all, on the availability of dependable source material and the quality of research already done in the field. The choice of methods to be used depends not only on each historian's personal predilections, abilities, temperament, linguistic facilities, and mastery of research tools, but also on the subject matter under investigation. It has long been recognized that historical writing is mainly divided into *narrative* and *interpretive* approaches. The narrative part may consist of the gathering and marshaling of factual data and presenting them either in the traditional form of a story told in some chronological or other logical sequence, or in certain measurable areas by the use of statistical tables and charts. Since history has long been recognized as a discipline combining artistic with scientific elements, the narrative may be more or less elegant and readable. Such a narrative may be combined with more or less documentation from the sources, references to previous researches in the field, maps, and so forth. These additions are frequently relegated to footnotes and appendices in order not to disrupt the flow of the main presentation. On the other hand, interpretation may be interwoven into the narrative, treated separately, or even preponderantly throughout the text and the footnotes.

Another highly variable branch of historiography consists of locating, reproducing, editing, and publishing previously inaccessible documents, archeological artifacts, artistic objects (preferably with illustrations), and the like—all supplied with the necessary textual or other variants from different sources, and commentaries. Quantitative history has proved particularly helpful, wherever sufficient documentation was available, in the fields of historical demography and economic history. Linguistic and chronological methods, archeology, and epigraphy are especially useful in the publication of new texts, while philosophy, psychology and psycho-history, social sciences, and jurisprudence are preeminent aids in the interpretive parts. Religious history, finally, is not only contributing a wealth of original materials, including biographies of saints and many leading statesmen and thinkers. It also promotes the understanding of cultural, sociopolitical, and economic developments often reviewed from some independent angles and from other sources of influence. No historian can claim expertise in all these domains of historical endeavor. He or she must concentrate on approaches determined by personal inclinations and earlier experiences, without completely neglecting some of the other approaches necessary for the fuller understanding of the subject under discussion. This is a sort of "eclecticism" which has long become a "dirty word" in the study of philosophic systems, but is unavoidable in the treatment of the enormously variegated phenomena of human life in the past ages down to the present. It is the collective effort of many specialists, starting from different assumptions and using different tools of research and presentation, that offers an aggregate historical panorama which—ever subject to change and modification—to some extent at least may satisfy the curiosity of successive generations. Thus, aided and abetted by experts in related fields of knowledge, the historians may contribute their share to making the discipline an effective *magistra vitae* for their generation. The historians who still cherish the belief in the ultimate divine guidance of history may view the unfolding history of mankind as a new divine book which has opened itself before the eyes of the faithful so that its constant interpretations and reinterpretations would serve as a sort of new historical *midrash* and help answer some of the most perplexing questions of the present and the future.[117]

Abbreviations

AHR	American Historical Review
Annales ESC	Annales Économies, Sociétés, Civilisations
HT	History and Theory
HTR	Harvard Theological Review
HUCA	Hebrew Union College Annual
HZ	Historische Zeitschrift
JBL	Journal of Biblical Literature
JC	Salo W. Baron, The Jewish Community: Its History and Structure to the American Revolution, 3 vols., Philadelphia, 1942; reprinted Westport, Conn. 1972.
JCH	Journal of Contemporary History
JSS	Jewish Social Studies
MGWJ	Monatsschrift für Geschichte und Wissenschaft des Judentums
PAAJR	Proceedings of the American Academy for Jewish Research
PAJHS	Publications of the American Jewish Historical Society now abridged to American Jewish History
REJ	Revue des Études Juives
SRH	Salo W. Baron, A Social and Religious History of the Jews, 1st ed., 3 vols., New York, 1937; 2d ed., Vols. I–XVIII, New York, 1952–83. Reference is to 2d ed. unless otherwise indicated.
VSW	Vierteljahrsschrift für Sozial- und Wirtschaftsgeschichte

Notes

INTRODUCTION

1. *Svenska Dagbladet* of November 1972 quoted by Józef Lewandowski in his "Specific Historical Functions in the Lands of the Soviet System" (Polish), *Zeszyty Historyczne*, (Paris), XXIII (1973), 3–17, esp. p. 4; Herbert Lüthy, "What's the Point of History?" *JCH*, III/2 (1968), 3–22. See also below, nn. 3 ff. There are, of course, musicians who, because of their preference for atonal music, feel obligated to denigrate the immortal achievements of their classical predecessors. Some others may reject Beethoven's music for political reasons. I understand that Communist China under Mao outlawed all public performances of Beethoven's symphonies, because they allegedly were the outgrowth of the "corrupt" Western culture. Certainly, Schiller's triumphant paean for *freedom* in the ecstatic finale of Beethoven's Ninth Symphony, must have deeply disturbed the devotees of any dictatorial regime. It was only in the last few years that this prohibition was revoked, as part of the "thaw" in Chinese-Western relations.

2. The great prestige of Thucydides' *History* (below n.6) also in Prussia's official circles is well illustrated by a recollection of Friedrich C. G. von Raumer, secretary of Chancellor Karl August von Hardenberg. In 1811 he persuaded a high-ranking Treasury official to drop his proposal for the issuance of much new paper money by referring to some alleged evils of excessive circulation of paper notes in ancient Athens as supposedly described by Thucydides. In fact, however, ancient Athens did not have any paper money. See Raumer, *Lebenserinnerungen und Briefwechsel*, 2 vols., Leipzig, 1861, I, 118.

3. See Friedrich Nietzsche, *Vom Nutzen und Nachteil der Historie für das Leben* (first published in 1874 as a second installment of his *Unzeitgemässe Betrachtungen*), reproduced, among other editions, in his *Werke, Klassiker Ausgabe*, Vol. II, Stuttgart, 1921, pp. 125–232, esp. pp. 167 ff. In their note thereon (*ibid.*, pp. 439 f.) the editors point out that Nietzsche himself later on (in his *Genealogie der Moral*, published in 1887) referred to this essay by calling it a "contribution to the history of diseases of the modern soul." (See below, n. 6).

4. Sigmund Freud's essay "Das Ich und das Es" reproduced in his *Gesammelte Werke*, ed. by Anna Freud and Marie Bonaparte, 5th ed., Frankfurt a.M., 1967, XIII, 267. See also Dieter Groh, *Kritische Geschichtswissenschaft in emanzipatorischer Absicht. Überlegungen zur Geschichtswissenschaft als Sozialwissenschaft*, Stuttgart, 1973. Urban-Taschenbücher, 80/846, pp. 27 f.; and below, n. 62.

5. Henry Steele Commager, *The American Mind: an Interpretation of American Thought and Character since the 1880s*, New Haven, 1950, p. 122; Alex Haley, *Roots*, Garden City, New York, 1976. As far as Jewish history is concerned the enormously awakened interest in the past of both Jews and non-Jews and the outpouring of a vast literature, especially on the Holocaust and developments in the State of Israel, are a partial testimony of their revived historical interest.

CHAPTER I: CHANGING PATTERNS

6. Thucydides, [*History of*] *The Peloponnesian War* (Greek), with an English trans. by C. Forster Smith. 4 vols., London, 1928–35. Loeb Classical Library; Giambattista Vico, *Scienza nuova* in his *Opere Complete*, ed. by Giuseppe Ferrari, 7 vols., Naples, 1858–65 (Vols. IV–V: *Principij di una Scienza nuova*); with the comments thereon by Aloysius Robert Camponigri in his *Time and Idea: The Theory of History in Giambattista Vico*, Notre Dame, Indiana, 1968 (paperback). On the enormous bibliography on Vico's seminal work see Fausto Nicolini's *Bibliografia Vicchiana*, 2 vols., Naples, 1947–48; Georg Wilhelm Friedrich Hegel, *Vorlesungen über die Philosophie der Geschichte*, ed. with an Intro. and Notes by F. Brunstad, Leipzig, n. d., esp. pp. 95 ff. and the editor's comments, n. 10, pp. 574 f.; Friedrich Nietzsche, *The Use and Abuse of History*, English trans. by Adrian Collins, with an Intro. by Julian Kraft, New York, 1944, pp. 24 ff. It may be noted in this connection that, in many respects, Josephus Flavius was the first historian who succeeded in combining a basic biblical outlook with the use of the Greek historiographic technique. See P. Colombe, "La Place de Josèphe dans la technique de l'historiographie hellénistique," *Études historiques* of the Faculté des Lettres of the University of Strasbourg, 1947, pp. 81–92; and the literature listed in my *SRH*, I, 186, 378 f. n. 24; II, 38, 344 f. n. 46.

7. Bab. Talmud Megillah, 29a, quoting I Sam. 2:27; Isa. 43:14, and Deut. 30:3; Malachi 3:6; Nachman Krochmal, *Moreh nebukhe ha-zeman* (Guide for the Perplexed of Our Time), first published, with an Intro. by Leopold Zunz, in Lwów, 1851; now available in Krochmal's *Kitbe* (Writings), ed. with additional introductions by Simon Rawidowicz, 2nd ed. enlarged, London, 1961, esp. Chap. vii, pp. 40 ff.; and the comments thereon by the editor, pp. 113 ff. Rawidowicz also discussed the impact on Krochmal of such philosophers as Vico, Lessing, and Hegel. See also Rawidowicz's essays, "War Nachman Krochmal Hegelianer?" *Hebrew Union College Annual*, V (1928), 535–82 (answering in the negative); and "Nachman Krochmal als Historiker," *Festschrift zu Simon Dubnow's Siebzigsten Geburtstag*, ed. by Ismar Elbogen et al., Berlin, 1930, pp. 57–75, esp. p. 58, emphasizing that, "through his historical method Krochmal confronted both the representatives of traditional Judaism, for whom Judaism exists beyond time and space, and the 'frivolous mockers' who consider Judaism superseded." His task was aggravated by the neglect of centuries of his ahistorical predecessors in accumulating historical data.

8. See, for instance, Isaac Abravanel's Commentaries on Deut. 28:49; and particularly his messianic trilogy *Ma'aynei ha-Yeshu'ah* (Springs of Salvation), Fer-

rara, 1551; *Yeshu'ot Meshiḥo* (Salvations of His Annointed), Salonica, 1526; *Mashmi'a yeshu'ah* (Announcer of Salvation), Königsberg, 1861; and the comments thereon by Benzion Netanyahu in his *Don Isaac Abravanel, Statesman and Philosopher*, 2nd ed., Philadelphia, 1968, esp. pp. 195 ff.

Of considerable interest in this connection are the varying interpretations of the medieval historical outlook offered by modern historians. See, for instance, the complementary analyses by Hans Rudolf Guggisberg in *Das europäische Mittelalter im amerikanischen Geschichtsdenken des 19. und frühen 20. Jahrhundert*, Basel, 1973. Basler Beiträge zur Geschichtswissenschaft, XII; C. W. David, "American Historiography of the Middle Ages, 1884–1934," *Speculum*, X (1925), 125–36; Norman Cantor, "Medieval Historiography in Modern Political and Social Thought," *JCH*, III/2 (1968), 55–78; M. I. Knowles, "Some Trends in Scholarship (1868–1968) in the Field of Medieval History," *Transactions* of the Royal Historical Society of England, 5th ser. XIX (1969), 139–57; continued by Herbert Butterfield for "Some Trends . . . of Modern History," *ibid.*, pp. 159–84 (both these papers were delivered as Centenary Addresses before the Society). See also below, n. 100.

9. Jean Bodin, *Methodus ad facilem historiarum cognitionem* (1566), Chap. vii, Strasbourg, 1607 ed., p. 310; or in the English trans. by Beatrice Reynolds, entitled *Method for the Easy Apprehension of History*, New York, 1945. Records of Civilization, XXXVIII; Christopher Cellarius, *Historia universalis in antiquam et medii aevi et novam divisa*, Jena, 1696. See also Cellarius' earlier treatment of *Historia antiqua*, Jena, 1685; and *Historia medii aevi*, Jena, 1688. Incidentally, Bodin's *Methodus* represented in many ways the new approach to Jewish history on the part of the Renaissance Christian scholars. See Jacob Guttmann, "Über Jean Bodin in seinen Beziehungen zum Judentum," *MGWJ*, XLIX, 315–48, 459–89; and Samuel Ettinger's observations on "The Beginnings of the Change in Attitude of the European Society towards the Jews," *Scripta Hierosolymitana*, VII (1961), 193–219, esp. p. 197.

10. Heinrich Graetz, *Geschichte der Juden von Beginn der Mendelssohnischen Zeit (1750) bis in die neueste Zeit*, 2nd, ed., Leipzig, n.d. Foreword; Martin Philippson, *Neueste Geschichte des jüdischen Volkes*, Vols. I–II, 2nd ed., Frankfurt, 1922–30; Vol. III, 1911; Simon Dubnow, *Neueste Geschichte des jüdischen Volkes*, 3 vols., Berlin, 1920–23, later included in his *Weltgeschichte des jüdischen Volkes*, 10 vols., Berlin, 1925–29 as Vols. VIII–X; Max L. Margolis and Alexander Marx, *A History of the Jewish People*, Philadelphia, 1927, pp. 60 ff.: "The Age of Emancipation"; Benzion Dinur, "Modern Times in Jewish History" (Hebrew) reprinted in his *Be-Mifneh ha-dorot* (At the Turn of Generations; a collection of essays), Vol. I, Jerusalem, 1955, pp. 19–66.

11. See my Preface to *SRH*, Vol. IX, New York, 1965; the sequence from the Italian to the Russian Haskalah, explained in the first (1937) ed. of that work, Vol. II, pp. 205 ff. and the notes thereon in Vol. III, pp. 139 ff. nn. 13–17. The impact of these forces on the organizational forms and functions of the Jewish communities in the Western world, is discussed in my *JC* in Vols. I, pp. 3 ff.: "Quest for New Forms"; II, pp. 351 ff.; and in the notes thereon in Vol. III, pp. 3 ff., 219 ff. While these differences in periodicization reflect fairly the changing approaches to history, it must also be realized that, as Morris Raphael Cohen observed, "those who insist on the continuity of history . . . are prone to attack any division of history

into periods as arbitrary, as each important characteristic of the era in question had its prototype and origin at an earlier age." See his *The Meaning of Human History*, 2nd ed., pp. 71 ff.; and below, n. 49.

12. See Ernest Ginsburger, *Le Comité de surveillance de Jean-Jacques Rousseau*, Paris, 1934; idem, "Le Comité de surveillance de J. J. Rousseau et les sans-culottes de Nancy," *REJ*, XCVIII (1934), 91–93; Robert Anchel, *Napoléon et les Juifs*, Paris, 1928, pp. 14 ff.; and, more generally, Carl L. Becker, *The Heavenly City of the Eighteenth Century Philosophers*, New Haven, 1946. On its antecedents, see Adalbert Klempt, *Die Säkularisierung der universalhistorischen Auffassung. Zum Wandel des Geschichtsdenkens im 16. und 17. Jahrhundert*, Göttingen, 1960. Göttinger Bausteine zur Geschichtswissenschaft, XXXI; and the data on the Jewish developments of that period in my bibliographical essay, "Some Recent Literature on the History of the Jews in the Preemancipation Era (1300–1800)," *Journal of World History* (*Cahiers d'histoire mondiale*), VII (1963), 137–71.

13. See my "New Approaches to Jewish Emancipation" in UNESCO's *Diogenes*, no. 29 (1960), 56–81; and "Medieval Heritage and Modern Realities in Protestant-Jewish Relations," *ibid.*, no. 61 (1968), 32–51 (both essays are also available in French and Spanish translations in the trilingual publications of that journal); Ronald A. Knox, *God and the Atom*, New York, 1945, p. 59. See also, more generally, Albert Salomon, "The Religion of Progress," *Social Research*, XIII (1946), 441–62, and J. B. Bury, *The Idea of Progress: an Inquiry into Its Origins and Growth*, New York, 1932. Its roots, like many other "modern" concepts may be traced back to ancient thinkers. See Ludwig Edelstein's analysis in *The Idea of Progress in Classical Antiquity*, Baltimore, 1967, with the review thereof by E. R. Dodds in the *Journal of the History of Ideas*, XXIX (1968), 453–57.

14. See William A. Dunning, *Truth in History and Other Essays*, ed. by J. G. de Roulhas Hamilton, New York, 1937, esp. p. 20; Lucien Lévy-Bruhl, *Aspects sociologiques du droit*, Paris, 1951, p. 31. On the example of "Consequences of New Trends in the History of Ancient Law," see Arnaldo Momigliano's *Studies in Historiography*, London, 1969, pp. 39 ff.

The attitude of historians and other social scientists to myths varied over the ages. While in the hypercritical period of the turn from the nineteenth to the twentieth century even Andrew Lang, an eminent pioneer on the application of anthropological methods to legends and folklore, held legends to be mere survivals of savage societies (see his *Myth, Literature and Religion* [1882], new ed., London, 1899), more recent scholarship has evinced a much greater appreciation of the value of myths and general folklore as a reflection of the life and thought of the masses. See, for instance, Cora L. Daniels and C. M. Stevens, eds., *Encyclopedia of Superstitions, Folklore, and the Occult Sciences of the World*, 3 vols., Detroit, 1971; and a variety of observations which may be cited at random from the huge pertinent literature, such as Sir Moses I. Finley's "Myths, Memory, and History," *HT*, IV (1963), 281–302; or Ben Halpern's "'Myth' and 'Ideology' in Modern Usage," *ibid.*, I (1961), 129–39.

An interesting example of such dichotomies even among convinced religious traditionalists is offered by the varying attitudes of leading medieval and modern rabbis to the Aggadah. Since much of these materials, largely arising from pious homilies of revered preachers, had been incorporated in the Talmud, the authoritative guide for Orthodox Judaism, they could not be rejected outright even by more rationalistically oriented teachers. Typical of the ensuing compromises is the following excerpt from a responsum, written by Hai Gaon, a leading eleventh-century Babylonian sage, in reply to a query:

> Everything written in the Talmud is more correct than what is not included in it. Although *aggadot* written in the Talmud, if they prove untrue or distorted, need not be considered authoritative, because of the general rule that one does not rely on *aggadah*, yet we are obliged to remove wherever possible the distortion of any statement included in the Talmud. For if the statement had not contained some [worthwhile] hermeneutic interpretation, it would never have been incorporated in the Talmud. But if unable to remove the distortion, we shall treat it like any of the rejected laws. Statements not included in the Talmud, however, require no such exertion on our part. If one is correct and beautiful, we preach on it and teach it to pupils; if not, we simply disregard it.

See the text reproduced in *Teshubot ha-Geonim* (Responsa of the Geonim), ed. and annotated by Jacob Musafia, Lyck, 1864, No. 99; and other excerpts quoted in E. E. Hildesheimer's "Mystik und Agada im Urteile der Gaonen R. Scherira und R. Hai," *Festschrift für Jacob Rosenheim*, Frankfurt, 1931, pp. 259–86; and other sources and observations in my *SRH*, VI, 175 ff., 412 f. nn. 29 ff. See also the highly instructive collection and interpretation of *The Legends of the Jews* by Louis Ginzberg, 7 vols., Philadelphia, 1909–38.

15. Karl Marx's letter to Josef Wedemayer of May 5, 1852, in his *Werke*, 39 vols., Berlin, 1958–68, esp. XXVIII, 507 ff. It is reproduced here in the English translation by Ernst Nolte in "The Relationship between 'Bourgeois' and 'Marxist' Historiography," *HT*, XIV (1975), 57–73, esp. p. 66. See also below, nn. 50 and 72.

16. Fernand Braudel, "Position de l'histoire en 1950," reprinted in his *Écrits sur l'histoire*, Paris, 1969, pp. 15–38; Martin Heidegger, *From Kant to the Problem of Metaphysics* (cited by Martin Buber in his *Between Man and Man*, English trans. by Ronald Gregor Smith, London, 1917, p. 181). In quoting Condorcet's enthusiastic prediction, Braudel pointed out that today we must refer to civilizations in the plural. He might also have emphasized how quickly Condorcet's prediction was controverted by a quarter century of the Napoleonic wars, the greatest theretofore fought on the European continent in modern times; also how Condorcet himself had died a mysterious death in the turmoil of the Revolution. See also the essays from the school of the *Annales* assembled by Jacques Le Goff and Pierre Nora and published under the characteristic title, *Faire de l'histoire*, 3 vols., Paris, 1974. These volumes deal respectively with "New Problems," "New Approaches," and "New Objects."

17. See, for instance, Reuben Ainsztein, *Jewish Resistance in Nazi-Occupied Eastern Europe, with a Historical Survey of the Jew as Fighter and Soldier in the Diaspora*, London, 1974; and the literature listed there.

18. Page Smith, *The Historian and History*, New York, 1964, p. 213; Alex Haley, *Roots*. The tremendous recent outpouring of Jewish Holocaust literature has overshadowed in quantity, if not in quality, the vast accumulation of earlier publications listed in Jacob Robinson and Philip Friedman's *Guide to Jewish History under Nazi Impact*, New York, 1960 (Joint Documentary Projects of the Yad Washem in

Jerusalem and the YIVO Institute for Jewish Research, Bibliographical Series, No. 1). This volume was followed by a number of major bibliographical compilations by Friedman and associates. Because of Friedman's memorable share in laying the foundations for all subsequent serious research into that great catastrophe, the publication of a collection of his Holocaust studies (many translated from various foreign languages) was quite noteworthy. It appeared under the title, *Roads to Extinction: Essays on the Holocaust*, ed. by Ada J. Friedman, with an Intro. by Salo Wittmayer Baron, New York and Philadelphia, 1980. These essays written over many years have further inspired some younger scholars to engage in researches in-depth of that momentous event in Jewish and world history. Among the more recent publications one need but mention here Raul Hilberg's *The Destruction of the European Jews*, Chicago, 1967; idem, *Documents of Destruction: Germany and Jewry, 1933–1945*, Chicago, 1971; Lucy S. Dawidowicz, *The War Against the Jews, 1933–1945*, New York, 1975; idem, *The Holocaust and the Historians*, Cambridge, Mass., 1981.

19. See Oswald Spengler, *Der Untergang des Abendlandes, Umrisse einer Morphologie der Weltgeschichte*, Munich, 1920–22 (also in the English trans. by Charles Francis Arkinson entitled *The Decline of the West*, 2 vols., London, 1972); Morris R. Cohen, *The Meaning of Human History*, with the Preface to the Second Edition by Leonora Cohen Rosenfeld, p. x; Jörn Rüsen, *Für eine erneute Historik. Studien zur Theorie der Geschichtswissenschaft*, Stuttgart, 1976. Kultur and Gesellschaft, I, marking the beginning of an historiographic series, sponsored by the Werner-Reisner Stiftung in Bad Homburg. The term *Historik*, borrowed from Johann Gustav Droysen's work long considered authoritative in this field, is defined by Rüsen in the English section of his Preface, as being "understood as a systematic examination of theories, methods and purposes efficient in historical research and history writing." See also Ulrich Mühlock's comments in his review article, "Probleme einer erneuten Historik," *HZ*, CCXXVIII (1979), 335–64; and, more broadly, I. Kon, *Die Geschichtsphilosophie des 20. Jahrhunderts, Kritischer Abriss*, 2 vols., Berlin, 1964 (written from the Marxist point of view); and such monographs as *Historische Theorie und Geschichtsforschung der Gegenwart*, Berlin, 1964, reproducing six lectures by scholars analyzing the approaches to history by Arnold Toynbee, Peter Sorokin, Karl Jaspers, Friedrich Meinecke, and M. N. Pokrovskii. The revival of historiographic interests in America, too, has led to the publication of two special periodicals, *HT*, from 1960 on; and *Historical Newsletter*, from 1945 on. Some of their articles having a direct bearing on aspects discussed in the present essay, will be quoted in the forthcoming notes.

In the Jewish field, too, the turbulent 1960s saw one of the rare efforts of a philosopher coming to grips with underlying forces in the totality of Jewish history in Jacob Bernard Agus's *The Meaning of Jewish History*, 2 vols., London, 1964.

CHAPTER II: PROBLEMS OF HISTORICAL OBJECTIVITY

20. Anatole France, *Penguin Island*, cited by Morris R. Cohen in *The Meaning of Human History*, p. 19; Sir Walter Raleigh (Ralegh), *History of the World*, in his *Works*, ed. by W. Oldy and T. Birch, 8 vols., London, 1829; and E. Edwards, *Life of*

Sir Walter Ralegh, 2 vols., London, 1868. My diffidence in regard to eyewitness accounts was increased by an unusual personal experience. Back in 1937 I spent my first Sabbatical leave on an eight-month's research journey in Europe and the Middle East. On this occasion I spent for the first time a couple of months each in Palestine and the Soviet Union, both countries of great significance in Jewish history. Before reaching these areas I promised myself a sort of test of how my impressions on the spot would compare with what I had learned about them in extensive studies in the historical and contemporary literature over the years. I was not surprised to find that my eyewitness observations of life in Palestine fully confirmed my earlier appraisals; they merely filled in many lacunae in details. In Moscow and other Soviet cities, on the other hand, I was astonished time and again by how greatly many of my direct observations differed from all I had learned about these particular aspects of life from books, newspapers, and friends. But I received the shock of my life when, upon repeated deep reflection and weighing all the pros and cons, I came to the conclusion that many assumptions I had made before my arrival in Russia on the basis of various documentary and oral testimonies were much closer to reality than what I was seeing and assessing in real life. Somewhat later I even dared to communicate this "shocking" conclusion to my colleagues in Columbia's History Department when addressing their annual meeting in the fall of 1937. I hesitantly illustrated my contention by a few telling examples, for I knew that I was running counter to the widespread belief of the American public that any long-time resident in a foreign country was automatically a more trustworthy witness than anybody who had merely studied the situation from a distance.

21. See Wolfgang Mommsen, *Max Weber und die deutsche Politik*, Tübingen, 1954, esp. p. 311; Arthur Mitzman, *The Iron Cage: an Historical Interpretation of Max Weber*, New York, 1969, with Bruce Mazlish's comments thereon in his review of that work in *HT*, X (1971), 90–107. See also, more generally, Fritz Stern's essay on "German Historians and the War," in his ed. of *The Failure of Liberalism: Essays in the Political Culture of Modern Germany*, 1st ed, New York, 1972; 2nd ed., 1976.

22. Heinrich Rickert, *Die Grenzen der naturwissenschaftlichen Begriffsbildung*, Tübingen, 1921, pp. 298 ff.; the *Festgabe* for Friedrich Engel-Janosi, *Die Wahrheit der Geschichte. Versuche zur Geschichtsschreibung in der Neuzeit*, Munich, 1973, pp. 13 ff.; E. E. G. Vermeulen, "Was ist Objektivität?" *Saeculum*, XIII (1962), 394–400, esp. pp. 395 ff.; Adam Schaff, "Der Streit um die Objektivität der historischen Erkenntnis," in Jörn Rüsen, ed., *Historische Objektivität, Aufsätze zur Geschichtstheorie*, Göttingen, 1975, pp. 33–47, esp. pp. 36 f.; C. Vann Woodward, "History and the Third Culture," *JCH*, III (1968), 23–35, esp. p. 24; Irving Louis Horowitz, "Social Science Objectivity and Value Neutrality: Historical Problems and Projections," *Diogenes*, XXXIX (1962), 12–44.

An interesting collection of modern loanwords is assembled in Morris Kasriel Katz's "Hebrew and Yiddish Words in American English and the Impact of Aramaic, Greek and Latin on Hebrew," *The Jacob Dolnitzky Memorial Volume*, Skokie, Ill., 1980, pp. 79–91; see also Eliezer Weinryb, "The Justification of Causal Theses: an Analysis of the Controversies over the Theses of Pirenne, Turner, and Weber," *HT*, XIV (1975), 32–56; Charles E. Beard's rather despondent outcry about "That Noble Dream," *AHR*, XLI (1935–36), 74–87 with reference to Theodore Clarke Smith's "The Writing of American History in America," *ibid.*, XL (1934–35),

439–49; and Otto Friedrich Bollner, "Die Objektivität der Geisteswissenschaften und die Frage nach dem Wesen der Wahrheit," *Zeitschrift für Philosophische Forschung,* XVI (1962), 3–25. See also below, n. 38.

These concerns about objectivity did not include authors of historical works avowedly written for the purpose of indoctrinating readers, particularly in schools. Such an "applied form of history" has been practiced through the ages. Even in the early twentieth century, before the rise of the totalitarian regimes, much of the pedagogic literature was clearly permeated with patriotic teachings. For one example, a very popular German handbook bore the unmistakable title, *Angewandte Geschichte. Eine Erziehung zum politischen Denken und Wollen,* 10th ed. rev., Leipzig, 1910, which had a strongly racist and anti-Semitic coloring. Perhaps for this reason the first nine editions of that work had quickly disappeared from the market. Nor was it at all surprising that some early modern English historians, who ventured to dispute the long accepted myth about the English kings' direct descent from Julius Caesar or Brutus were regarded as lacking in patriotism not only by the masses but also by some of their confreres. See George Grote, *A History of Greece,* 12 vols., London, 1846–56, esp. III, 216 f. On the other hand, until the end of the nineteenth century the majority of Americans evinced little interest in serious historical writings; the emphasis of their authors on continuity and tradition clearly ran counter to the majority's immersion in a life of flux and innovation. See John Higham, "The Schism in American Scholarship," *AHR,* LXXII (1972), 1–21.

23. George Bancroft, cited by David Levin, *History as a Romantic Art: Bancroft, Prescott, Motley and Parkman,* Stanford, Cal., 1959, pp. 25 f.; Arthur Weiser, *Glaube und Geschichte im Alten Testament,* Stuttgart, 1931, BWANT, LV; Chester Charlton McCown, "In History and Beyond History," *HTR,* XXXVIII (1945), 151–75; Clarence T. Craig, "Biblical Theology and the Rise of Historicism," *JBL,* LXII (1943), 284–94; Reinhold Niebuhr, *Faith and History: A Comparison of Christian and Modern Views of History,* New York, 1949; and the additional literature with my observations thereon in *SRH,* Vols. I, pp. 296 f. n. 6; II, pp. 64, 354 n. 10. On faith versus history in the whole range of Jewish history, see Jacob Bernard Agus, *The Meaning of Jewish History,* with a Foreword by Salo W. Baron, 2 vols., New York, 1964.

24. See Abraham Geiger, "Die Gründung einer jüdisch-theologischen Fakultät, ein dringendes Bedürfnis unserer Zeit," *Wissenschaftliche Zeitschrift für jüdische Theologie,* II (1836), 1–21; and other sources analyzed in my "Jewish Studies at Universities: an Early Project," *HUCA,* XLVI (1975), 357–76; and my Hebrew Inaugural Lecture at the opening of the Chaim Rosenberg School of Jewish Studies at the University of Tel-Aviv, published by the University in a pamphlet entitled *Halom she-nitgashem* (A Dream Come True), Tel-Aviv, 1972. Understandably, the functioning of theological faculties at state universities created some legal problems in the face of the prevailing modern trends of separation of Church and state. See, for instance, Ernst Lüde-Solte's juridical tract, *Theologie an der Universität, Staats- und Kirchenrecht. Probleme der theologischen Fakultäten,* Munich, 1971.

25. See esp. my *The Russian Jew under Tsars and Soviets,* 2nd ed. revised, New York, 1976, pp. 273 ff., 423 ff. and the sources listed there. Another example of governmental direction of Russian historiography is offered by Matthew P. Gal-

lagher in *The Russian History of World War II: Myths, Memories and Realities*, New York, 1963. On the change in the Soviet attitudes to religion and particularly to the Russian Orthodox Church, see Robert Stupperich's brief survey, "Die deutsche Forschung über Religion und Atheismus in der UdSSR seit 1945," *Kirche im Osten*, XV (1972), 74–88; and Gerhard Simon, *Die Kirchen in Russland. Berichte, Dokumente*, Munich, 1970. See also, more generally, Jack V. Haney, "The Revival of Interest in the Russian Past in the Soviet Union," *Slavic Review*, XXXII (1973), 1–16; and the discussions thereon, *ibid.*, pp. 17–44. The relationships between state and Church in other communist Eastern European countries are discussed, among others, in Vladimir Csovski, ed., *Church and State Behind the Iron Curtain: Czechoslovakia, Hungary, Poland, Rumania*, with an Intro. on the Soviet Union, New York, 1955. Praeger Publications in Russian History, XVII; and Henryk Świątkowski, *Państwo a kościół w świetle prawa* (State and Church in Light of the Law: Selected Problems), 2nd ed., Warsaw, 1960; and Giovanni Cedenvilla, *Stato e chiesa nell'Unione Sovietica*, Milan, 1972. Archivi per la Russia, IV.

26. Heinrich von Treitschke, *Vorlesungen gehalten an der Universität zu Berlin*, ed. by Max Coricelius, 5th ed., Leipzig, 1922, I, 63; idem, *Deutsche Geschichte im 19. Jahrhundert*, Leipzig, 1927, I, 27; idem, *Ein Wort über unser Judentum*, Berlin, 1879–80, reprinted from *Preussische Jahrbücher*, XLIV–XLV; Heinrich Graetz, "Erwiderung an Herrn von Treitschke," *Schlesische Presse* (Breslau), December 7, 1879; idem, "Mein letztes Wort an Professor von Treitschke," *ibid.*, December 28, 1879.

27. See, for example, Franz Rosenthal's *History of Muslim Historiography*, 2nd ed. rev., Leiden, 1968; and, from another angle, the critical observations on *Historians of the Middle East*, ed. by Bernard Lewis and Peter Malcolm Holt, London, 1962. Maimonides' repudiation of the contemporary Muslim historical writings is found in his *Commentary* on Mishnah Sanhedrin, X, 1; his reconstruction of the historic succession of rabbis in the Introduction to his *Mishneh Torah* (Code of Laws); my "The Historical Outlook of Maimonides," *PAAJR*, VI (1935), 5–113; reprinted in my *History and Jewish Historians: Essays and Addresses*, compiled with a Foreword by Arthur Hertzberg and Leon Feldman, Philadelphia, 1964, pp. 109 ff., esp. pp. 110 ff., 349 n. 4; Joseph ben Joshua ha-Kohen, *'Emeq ha-bakha* (Valley of Tears); also in the English trans. by Henry S. May entitled *The Vale of Tears* (Emeq ha-bakha), with a Critical Commentary, The Hague, 1971.

CHAPTER III: PREDICTABILITY

28. See Gunnar Myrdal, *Value in Social Theory: a Selection of Essays on Methodology*, ed. by Paul Streeten, London, 1968. International Library of Sociology, pp. 58 f. (arguing that it is extremely difficult to ascertain the true motivations behind human actions, since even the same persons may on different occasions reach conflicting valuations); Friedrich Nietzsche, *Beyond Good and Evil*, trans. by Helen Zimmerman, in the Modern Library ed. of *The Philosophy of Nietzsche*, New York, 1937, pp. 4, 62, 80, with the remarks thereon in my *Modern Nationalism and Religion*, New York, 1947, pp. 76, 290 n. 14; and Detlev Junker, "Über die Legi-

timität von Werturteilen in den Sozialwissenschaften und der Geschichtswissen-schaft," *HZ*, CCXI (1970), 1–33. Ibn Arabi's statement and the adage concerning the blessing of divergence are cited by Jacques Berque in "L'Ambiguité dans le fiqh," in *L'Ambivalence dans la culture arabe*, ed. by Jean-Paul Charney, Paris, 1967, pp. 232–52, esp. pp. 235 f.; and other sources discussed in *SRH*, 2nd ed., XVII, 167 and 375 n. 52. A recent example of divergences between two modern Jewish scholars is the pertinent correspondence between Professor Samuel Atlas and Rabbi Yehiel Jacob Weinberg entitled "Differences of Opinion on Legal Matters" (Hebrew) in Atlas's *Netivim ba-mishpat ha-ivri* (Pathways in Hebrew Law), New York, 1978, pp. 130–55. On the talmudic controversies and the ultimate legal decisions, without total neglect of opposing views, see Hermann Strack, *Introduction to the Talmud and Midrash*, authorized Translation of the Fifth German Edition, Philadelphia, 1931.

29. Jakob C. Burckhardt, *Force and Freedom: Reflections on History*, English trans. and ed. by James Hastings Nichols, New York, 1943, pp. 90 f.; Robin George Collingwood, *The Idea of History*, Oxford, 1946, esp. pp. 54, 129, 220. Incidentally, unlike most of his contemporaries, Burckhardt (as well as Ranke) was no believer in the inevitability of progress.

30. Yehezkel Dror, *Crazy States: a Counterconventional Strategic Problem*, Lexington, Mass., 1971, p. 98; Lord Acton's saying quoted by Geoffrey Barraclough in his "History, Morals and Politics," *International Affairs*, XXXIV (1958), esp. p. 15.

31. Gottfried Wilhelm von Leibniz, *Nouveaux essais sur l'entendement par l'auteur de système de l'harmonie préestablie*, ed. by Carl H. Gebhardt, Berlin, 1882, V, 40; my "Medieval Heritage and Modern Realities in Protestant-Jewish Relations," *Diogenes*, no. 61 (January–March, 1961; also in the French and Spanish versions), reprinted in my *Ancient and Medieval Jewish History: Essays*, pp. 323–37, 544–48.

32. World War II offered major examples of men learning from or misapplying historical experience. For instance, the restraint in using chemical, especially gas, warfare was based on Germany's previous experience that the direction of the winds would generally favor the Allies. On the other hand, France's great reliance on the Maginot Line for its defense, as a result of the experiences of World War I, contributed greatly to its speedy downfall. In World War II such examples could easily be multiplied.

33. See Alexis de Tocqueville's *Democracy in America*, English trans., 4 vols., 1835–40, 2nd ed. rev., New York, 1945; and H. S. Commager's description of the situation in the 1960s, partially quoted above, n. 4. The prevailing revaluations of moral values among a large number of Americans at that time is further graphically described by him: "Paris became a symbol and Greenwich Village a synonym for nameless orgies. Americans unable to admire André Gide from attics on the Left Bank imitated him from attics in Bank Street. Reticence became pandery, modesty hypocrisy, and virginity a reproach" (*The American Mind*, p. 123). The hope that the extremely pessimistic mood of the American public characteristic of the late 1960s and early 1970s would be transitory was supported by many previous shifts in public opinion as a result of the recognition of long-range historical trends. To quote merely two experiences from the recent past: during the student uprisings of the 1960s many of my friends—like the public at large—believed them to have

become a long-lasting accompaniment of higher education in the United States. I recall that, when the disturbances reached their climax in the shooting of four students at Kent State University, one of my friends asked me: "How long do you think this movement is going to last?" My answer was: "I cannot predict the future, but I have a strong feeling that this period in American history will last no longer than the McCarthy era which, in its time, had likewise generated a legion of prophets of gloom." Similarly, several years later, after Yasir Arafat's triumphant entry into the United Nations, some of my colleagues were describing this event as "the end of the Third Jewish Commonwealth [hurban bayit shelishi]." I pacified them by referring to other critical moments in the struggle for Palestine which had come and passed away. I also mentioned, with great sorrow, the parallel with the League of Nations which, by allowing itself to become an organ of special interests and an instrument of worldwide propaganda saw its influence on world affairs rapidly declining. Of course, I have also had my full share of false predictions based on historical precedents.

34. Nathaniel Micklem, *National Socialism and the Roman Catholic Church. Being an Account of the Conflict between the National Socialist Government of Germany and the Roman Catholic Church, 1935–1938*, London, 1939, p. 104; Pope Pius XI's encyclical *Studiarum ducem* of June 29, 1929 in Harry C. Koenig's ed., *Principles for Peace (Selections from Papal Documents, Leo XIII to Pius XII)*, Washington, D.C., 1943, pp. 343, 347, 352 f., 364; C. S. C. Burtchell, *Catholic Theories of Biblical Inspiration since 1810: a Review and Critique*, Cambridge, 1969. On the other hand, advocates of full religious freedom and separation of state and Church saw in the diversity of religious views and interpretations a blessing for both religion and society. For example, in thanking, on September 1, 1820, the Jewish physician Jacob de la Motta for the copy of his discourse at the consecration of the Savannah synagogue (July 21), Thomas Jefferson observed that "it excites in him the gratifying reflection that his country has been the first to prove to the world two truths, the most salutary to human society, that man can govern himself, and that religious freedom is the most effectual anodyne of religious dissension; the maxim of civil government being reversed in that of religion, where its true form is 'divided we stand, united we fall.'" See Max J. Kohler, "Unpublished Correspondence between Thomas Jefferson and Some American Jews," *PAJHS*, XX (1911), 11–30, esp. p. 21; Joseph L. Blau and my ed. of *The Jews of the United States, 1790–1840: a Documentary History*, 3 vols., New York, 1963, I, 13 f. Nos. 10–11, 242 f. nn. 31–34 (includes a similar acknowledgement by James Madison); II, 572 ff., 660 f. nn. 165–68 (text of de la Motta's discourse). See also, more generally, Robert M. Healey, "Jefferson on Judaism and the Jews: Divided We Stand, United We Fall," *American Jewish History*, LXXIII (1984), 359–74; and my "American Jewish Communal Pioneering," reprinted from the aforementioned *PAJHS*, XLIII (1953–54), 133–50 in my *Steeled by Adversity: Essays and Addresses on American Jewish Life*, ed. by Jeannette M. Baron, pp. 127–40, 603–604, esp. n. 26.

35. Mussolini's crude remarks on Christmas uttered to a private group and reported by his son-in-law, Galeazzo Ciano, in the *Diaries, 1939–1943*, ed. by Hugh Gibson, New York, 1946, p. 423; Paul de Lagarde, "Diagnose" in his *Deutsche Schriften*, 4th ed., Göttingen, 1903, pp. 97 ff.; Alfred Rosenberg, *Der Mythus des*

20. *Jahrhunderts* or its English trans., *The Myth of the Twentieth Century, passim*; Adolf Hitler's 1929 peroration on Sparta, cited by Karl Ferdinand Werner in his "On Some Examples of the National-Socialist View of History," *JCH*, III/2, (1968), 193–206, esp. p. 193 (more fully in his *Das Nationalsozialistische Geschichtsbild und die deutsche Geschichtswissenschaft*, Stuttgart, 1967). See also Max Weinreich, *Hitler's Professors: the Part of Scholarship in Germany's Crimes Against the Jewish People*, New York, 1946. YIVO Translation Series; and my *Modern Nationalism*, pp. 76 ff., 290 ff. In his "Églises chrétiennes et totalitarisme national-socialiste," *Revue d'histoire d'Église*, LXIII (1968), 437–503, 868–948. Victor Canzenius was so impressed by the vast literature pertaining to the Nazi persecution of the Christian Churches, that he saw in it an indication "that a new chapter in Church history is now open to researchers studying the very recent past" (pp. 943 ff.). He also observed that now (in 1968), "thirty years after the event, we are still only at the beginning of research on this subject"—a deficiency not yet completely remedied even today after the passing of nearly two more decades. The same trend may be observed also in the Jewish camp with its proliferation of writings on the Holocaust now, more than a generation after the tragedy. To mention only one noteworthy example, the aforementioned collection of pertinent essays, *Roads to Extinction*, by the late Philip Friedman, often styled "the father of the Holocaust literature," shows that some aspects of his 1946 "Outline of a Program for Holocaust Research" (see his Appendix, *ibid.*, pp. 569–76), still belong to the category of "unfinished business."

36. See, for instance, the debate between Jack V. Haney in his "The Revival of Interest in the Russian Past in the Soviet Union," *Slavic Review*, XXXII (1975), 1–16; Thomas E. Bird in "New Interest in Old Russian Things: Literary Ferment, Religious Perspectives and National Self-Assertion," *ibid.*, pp. 17–28; George A. Kline in "Religion, National Character, and the Rediscovery of the Russian Roots," *ibid.*, pp. 29–40; and Haney's "Reply," *ibid.*, pp. 41–44. See also the numerous examples, including Ilya Ehrenburg's unusually successful *salti mortali* in adjusting himself to the ever changing regnant approaches of the Soviet bureaucracy, mentioned in my *The Russian Jew*, esp. pp. 242 ff., 269 ff., 282 ff. and the notes thereon. Of special interest also is the exchange of views in the 1960s between the Soviet and Italian historians in the correspondence reproduced by Franco Venturi in his *Historiens du XXᵉ siècle. Jarès, Salvemini, Namier, Maturi, Tarle et Discussions entre historiens italiens et soviétiques*, translated from the Italian by Maurice Chevalier, Geneva, 1966. *Études et documents* of the Institut d'Histoire of the University of Geneva, III. As usual, the debate ended with the participants firmly adhering to their original positions.

37. Apart from the question of guilt, as to which side was responsible for the outbreak and dimensions of World War I, a question heatedly debated in the 1920s by German vis-à-vis Allied historians—little of that kind of controversy was heard after World War II—there also were differences about the respective parties' war crimes. See Joachim Rohlf's, "Französische und deutsche Historiker über die Kriegsziele," *Geschichte in Wissenschaft und Unterricht*, XVII (1960), 168–74.

38. Lorenzo Valla, *De falso credita et ementita Constantini donatione declamatio* (1440), newly ed. by W. Schwahn, Leipzig, 1928 (Teubner Series), with the analy-

sis thereof and an English trans. by Christopher Bush Coleman entitled *The Treatise of Lorenzo Valla on the Donation of Constantine*, New York, 1922; and by Walter Ullmann in his *History of Political Thought: the Middle Ages*, Harmondsworth, 1965; G. R. Elton, *The Practice of History*, New York, 1967, pp. 74 ff.; Abraham Firkovich, *Abne zikkaron* (Stones of Remembrance, partially autobiographical), Vilna, 1872; Abraham Eliyahu Harkavy, *Altjüdische Denkmäler aus der Krim*, St. Petersburg, 1876; Hermann Strack, *Abraham Firkowitsch und seine Entdeckungen*, Leipzig, 1876. See also Zvi Ankori, *Karaites in Byzantium*, New York, 1959; and my *SRH*, V, 407 f. n. 56. On the accusations regarding Eliakim Carmoly's purported fabrications, see, for example, my "Moritz Steinschneider's Contributions to Jewish Historiography," reprinted from the *Alexander Marx Jubilee Volume*, 2 vols., New York, 1950, I, 83–148 in my *History and Jewish Historians: Essays and Addresses*: pp. 276–321, 449–70, esp. pp. 299 f., 459 f. n. 44. See also the general wide-ranging essays in Friedrich Engel-Janosi *et al.*, eds., *Denken über Geschichte. Aufsätze zur heutigen Situation des geschichtlichen Bewusstseins und der Geschichtswissenschaft*, Vienna, 1974. Wiener Beiträge zur Geschichte der Neuzeit, I; and the *Festgabe* for Engel-Janosi: *Die Wahrheit der Geschichte. Versuche der Geschichtsschreibung in der Neuzeit*.

39. Leopold Zunz, "Etwas über die rabbinische Literatur" (1818), reprinted in his *Gesammelte Schriften*, 3 vols., Berlin, 1875, I, 1–31, esp. p. 5. One must not forget, however, that Zunz himself from time to time engaged in political activities. Among his preserved public addresses are three delivered in 1848–49 under the impact of the Revolution and of the ensuing elections to the Prussian Diet and two in 1861 when he himself ran as a candidate for office (*ibid.*, pp. 301–325). But although he genuinely believed in the political watchwords of "Forward, Progress, Freedom, and Truth," on which he expatiated in his first electoral speech of 1861 and was convinced all along that the modern science of Judaism was part of the struggle for Jewish Emancipation, he never allowed his political views to encroach on his scholarly research. See, however, such modern analyses as Fritz Bamberger's "Zunz's Conception of History: a Study of the Philosophic Element in Early Science of Judaism," *PAAJR*, XI (1941), 1–25; and Luitpold Wallach's "Über Leopold Zunz als Historiker. Eine Skizze," *Zeitschrift für die Geschichte der Juden in Deutschland*, n.s. V (1935), 247–52. See also Paul de Lagarde's sharp attack on Zunz in his *Erinnerungen an Friedrich Rückert, Lipmann Zunz und seine Verehrer. Über einige Theologen und was von ihnen zu lernen ist* (1886), 2nd impression, Göttingen, 1897, with David Kaufmann's refutation thereof in his general denigration of "Paul de Lagarde's jüdische Gelehrsamkeit" (1887), reprinted in his *Gesammelte Schriften*, 3 vols., Frankfurt, 1908–1915, I, 207–257.

CHAPTER IV: HISTORY FOR HISTORY'S SAKE

40. William Stubbs, *Seventeen Lectures in the Study of Medieval and Modern History and Kindred Subjects delivered at Oxford . . . in the Years 1867–1868*, Oxford, 1886, new impression, New York, 1967, p. 27; Norman Hampson, *History as an Art: an Inaugural Lecture*, Newcastle-upon-Tyne, 1968, pp. 3 f.; H. Stewart Hughes,

History as Art and Science, New York, 1964; Heinrich Graetz, *Geschichte,* 1st ed., V, Preface (omitted in later editions). Neither did Graetz escape some of the critical strictures of his former pupil, Hermann Cohen. See Cohen's "Zur Jahrhundertfeier unseres Graetz," and "Graetzens Philosophie der jüdischen Geschichte," both published in 1917 and later reprinted in his *Jüdische Schriften,* II, 446–53; III, 203–212; and Erwin I. J. Rosenthal's perceptive study, "Hermann Cohen and Heinrich Graetz," *Baron Jub. Vol.,* II, 725–43. See also below, n. 51.

41. See Martin Philippson, *Neueste Geschichte des jüdischen Volkes,* 3 vols., Frankfurt a. M., 1907–1911, *Schriften* of the Gesellschaft zur Förderung der Wissenschaft des Judentums (Vols. I–II appeared in a revised and enlarged ed. in 1922–30); Simon M. Dubnow's *Die Weltgeschichte des jüdischen Volkes,* Vols. VIII–X, Berlin, 1925–29 (also in English, Hebrew, and Yiddish translations); Ismar Elbogen, *A Century of Jewish Life,* with an introductory "Appreciation" of the author by Alexander Marx, Philadelphia, 1944; Isaak Markus Jost, *Geschichte der Israeliten seit der Maccabäer bis auf unsere Tage, nach den Quellen bearbeitet,* Vol. X, Parts 1–3: *Neuere Geschichte der Israeliten von 1815 bis 1845 mit Nachträgen und Berichtigungen zur ältesten Geschichte,* Berlin, 1846–47. See also the analysis in my *History and Jewish Historians,* pp. 240 ff., 263 ff. On the role of the "Spring of Nations" in the historical evolution of European Jewry, see my "The Impact of the Revolution of 1848 on Jewish Emancipation," *JSS,* XI (1949), 195–248; and other essays listed by Jeannette M. Baron in her "Bibliography" of my writings in the *Salo Wittmayer Baron Jubilee Volume,* ed. by Saul Lieberman, 3 vols., Jerusalem, 1975, esp. I, 17 ff. Nos. 216, 224, 239, and 247.

42. See Ludwig Mitteis's observation quoted by Guido Kisch in his Review of Fritz Baer, *Die Juden im christlichen Spanien,* 2 vols., Berlin, 1929–36 in *Zeitschrift der Savigny Stiftung für Rechtsgeschichte,* German Section, LVII (1937), 712–26, esp. p. 726.

In the field of Jewish studies we need but refer here to the imposing array of critical editions published before World War I by the Mekize Nirdamim Society, the Historische Kommission für Geschichte der Juden in Deutschland, and of the Israelitische Kultusgemeinde in Vienna, the *Transactions, Miscellanies,* and special volumes issued by the Jewish Historical Society of England, as well as the numerous texts published in the *Monatsschrift für Geschichte und Wissenschaft des Judentums,* the *Revue des Études juives,* the *Jewish Quarterly Review,* the *Publications of the American Jewish Historical Society, Proceedings of the American Academy for Jewish Research,* and others. Needless to say that these laudable volunteer efforts are greatly overshadowed by such gigantic governmentally sponsored collections as the *Monumenta Germaniae Historica,* the *Publications from the Public Record Office* in London, and similar other national undertakings.

43. From the vast literature on these subjects, see, for example, Hugo Winckler (who in his *Altorientalische Forschungen,* 3 vols., Leipzig, 1893–1906 was able to discuss the general adoption of Jahwism in the age of King David without as much as mentioning the name of Moses); Arthur Drews, *The Church Myth,* translated from the German by C. Delisle Burns, Chicago, n.d., esp. p. 286; John M. Robertson, *The Historical Jesus: a Survey of Positions,* London, 1916; Bussi Milesbo (Emilio Rossi), *Le Christ légendaire n'a jamais existé,* trans. from Italian by Victor

Charbouriel, Conflana-Honorina, 1923; William Benjamin Smith, *Ecce Homo: Studies in Primitive Christianty*, Chicago, 1912. See also the analysis of these extreme contentions by Frederick C. Conybeare in *The Historical Jesus, or, An Investigation of the Views of J. M. Robertson, Dr. A. Drews, and Prof. W. B. Smith*, Chicago, 1914; the brief remarks in my *SRH*, I, 34 f. n. 32; II, 354 n. 10; and my *Modern Nationalism*, pp. 197 f. On the various schools of biblical criticism, see esp. Herbert Ferdinand Hahn's Columbia University dissertation, *The Old Testament in Modern Research*, Philadelphia, 1954; 2nd ed., expanded, with a "Survey of New Publications," Philadelphia, 1966.

44. See Vincent A. Smith, *Akbar the Great Moghul, 1542–1605*, 2nd ed., Delhi, 1966, esp. p. 256; Solomon Gandz, "The Dawn of Literature. Prolegomena to a History of Unwritten Literature," *Osiris*, VII (1939), 261–522; Jan Vansina's more recent analysis of *Oral Tradition: a Study in Historical Methodology*, English trans. by H. M. Wright, London, 1965 (or its French original *De la tradition orale*, published four years earlier); and his specific illustration in "Once Upon a Time: Oral Traditions as History in Africa," *Daedalus*, Spring, 1971, pp. 442–68. With respect to the biblical literature, see esp. the conflicting opinions of Harris Birkeland in his *Zum hebräischen Traditionswesen. Die Komposition der prophetischen Bücher des Alten Testaments*, Oslo, 1938. Ovhandlingen of the Norske Videnskap Akademie, I, arguing that most preexilic "writings" owed their origin to oral transmission, compared with the more moderate view expressed by Jan van der Ploeg in "Le Rôle de la tradition orale dans la transmission du texte de l'Ancien Testament," *Revue biblique*, LIV, V (1947), 5–41. On the development of the talmudic oral traditions and their ultimate written records, see Nehemias Brüll's pioneering study, "Die Entstehungsgeschichte des babylonischen Talmuds als Schriftwerkes," *Jahrbücher für jüdische Geschichte und Literatur*, II (1876), 1–123. On these complicated problems and the literature thereon, see also the frequent remarks and bibliographical references in my *SRH*, as listed in the *Index to Vols. I–VIII*, s.v. Oral Law, Transmission, oral; and so forth, as well as my views concerning the historical value of some traditions, even "legends," preserved by such "exotic" segments of the Jewish people as the Falashas in Ethiopia, the Bene Israel and the Cochin Jews of India, and the Jewish community of Kaifeng, China in *SRH*, Vol. XVIII, esp. Chap. LXXX. Nor must we overlook the significant role played by oral tradition in the preservation of ethnic minorities in the Western countries as well. See Jean Bouvier *et al.*, eds., *Tradition orale et identité culturelle*, Paris, 1980. Edition du Centre de la Recherche Scientifique.

45. See my observations in *SRH*, I, 142, 359 n. 12; and on the problem of the allegedly slow evolution of the ancient Israelitic tribes from a seminomadic to a civilized society, below, n. 59.

46. See Saul Benison, "Reflections on Oral History," *American Archivist*, XXVIII (1968), 71; Gary Shumway, *Oral History in the United States: a Directory*, New York, 1970; Alice Kessler Harris's Introduction to Ronald J. Grele, ed., *Envelopes of Sound: Six Practitioners Discuss the Method, Theory and Practice of Oral Tradition*, Chicago, 1975; Friedrich Nietzsche, *The Use and Abuse of History*, English trans. by Adrian Collins, esp. pp. 24 ff. Nietzsche's emphasis on the art of forgetfulness is contrasted with Jakob Burckhardt's stress on that of "remembrance"

by Friedrich Engel-Janosi in *Die Wahrheit in der Geschichte*, p. 15. Both these arts are, indeed, important for different aspects of historical research. They are particularly necessary in the face of a plethora or paucity of available evidence. See also the brief analysis of this crucial problem of the "Accuracy of Oral Interviewing" in William W. Cutler's pertinent essay in the *Historical Methods Newsletter*, III (1970), 1–7. See also *Oral History Evaluation Guidelines*, Report of the Winspread Conference July 27–28, Racine, Wisconsin, October 27, 1979, East Lansing, Michigan, 1980; *Oral History: New Directions, Oral Seminars*, Oral History Association, 1982–83, Columbia University. The frequently discussed role of autobiographical records and their relevance to contemporary history are analyzed by Wilhelm Berges in his "Biographie und Autobiographie heute. Aus Theorie und Praxis der Geschichtswissenschaft" in the *Festschrift für Hans Herzfeld*, Berlin, 1972, pp. 27–48. Veröffentlichungen of the Historische Kommission in Berlin, XXXVII.

CHAPTER V: INTERDISCIPLINARY RELATIONS

47. See my earlier studies in this field, "Emphases in Jewish History," *JSS*, I (1939), 15–22; "Newer Emphases in Jewish History," *ibid.*, XXV (1963), 235–48; "World Dimensions of Jewish History" in *Simon Dubnow—The Man and His Work*, ed. by Aaron Steinberg, Paris, 1963, pp. 26–40, all three reprints ed. with some revisions in my *History and Jewish Historians*, ed. by Arthur Hertzberg and Leon A. Feldman, Philadelphia, 1964 and the literature listed there. See also my "New Horizons in Jewish History" in *Freedom and Reason: Studies in Philosophy and Jewish Culture in Memory of Morris Raphael Cohen*, ed. by Salo W. Baron, Ernest Nagel, and Koppel S. Pinson, Glencoe, Ill., 1951, pp. 337–53. Among other matters I pointed out (*History and Jewish Historians*, pp. 70 ff., 346 nn. 2–3) the enormous difficulties in ascertaining the impact of natural forces like climate, earthquakes, plagues, and so forth, and their scientific studies in the history of the Jewish communities, particularly in the Diaspora. However, the constant broadening of both the historical and the scientific horizons offer some opportunities for penetration of the arcana of these interrelations.

48. Walter Ehrlich, *Philosophie der Geschichte der Philosophie*, Tübingen, 1965; Deut. 32:7 and Rashi's comment thereon taken from *Sifrei on Deuteronomy*, ed. by Louis Finkelstein, Berlin, 1939, p. 351; Eduard Meyer, *Die Kulturelle, literarische und religiöse Entwicklung des israelitischen Volkes in der älteren Königszeit*, Berlin, 1930 (reprinted from the *Sitzungsberichte* of the Berlin Academy of Science, 1930, Part ii), p. 4; Hermann Cohen, *Die Religion der Vernunft aus den Quellen des Judentums*, Leipzig, 1919, pp. 307 ff. (not sufficiently reproduced in Mordecai Kaplan's modern reformulation of Cohen's views in *The Purpose and Meaning of Jewish Existence: a People in the Image of God*, Philadelphia, 1964, pp. 170 ff. See also my remarks in *SRH*, I, 99 f., 195 ff., 340 n. 51, 383 f. nn. 37 ff. and the literature cited there.

49. Israel Efros, *Ancient Jewish Philosophy*, Tel Aviv, 1964, p. 34; Pius XII, "Discours au X. Congrès International des Sciences historiques [7. Septembre 1955]" in *Documents pontificaux de Sa Sainteté Pie XII*, ed. by S. Delacroix, St. Maurice, 1957, p. 287; Jacques Maritain, *On the Use of Philosophy: Three Essays*,

Princeton, 1961; idem, *On the Philosophy of History*, ed. by Joseph W. Evans, New York, 1957; Karl Löwith, *Meaning in History: The Theological Implications of the Philosophy of History*, Chicago, 1949. Some of the Catholic thinkers, like Maritain, Charles Maurras, or Giovanni Gentile, combined their Thomistic outlook with one or another form of integral nationalism, or outright fascism. See Emilio Rossi, *Il Pensiero politico di Jacques Maritain*, Milan, 1956; Charles Maurras, *Oeuvres capitales*, 4 vols., Paris, 1954; Henri Massis, *Charles Maurras et notre temps*, 2 vols., Paris, 1951; Giovanni Gentile, *La mia religione, conferenze*, Florence, 1943. Biblioteca del Leonardo, XXVI. See also Feruccio Perlo, *La Filosofia di Giovanni Gentile, genesi, sviluppo, unità sistematica, critica*, Florence, 1972.

50. Roy F. Nichols, "Postwar Reorientation of Historical Thinking," *AHR*, LIV (1948–49), 78–89, esp. p. 79; Henry Steele Commager, *The American Mind*, p. 407. See also I. S. Kon's comprehensive review of *Die Geschichtsphilosophie des 20. Jahrhunderts. Kritischer Abriss*. Despite its Marxist bias, Vol. I, describing the "crisis of historicism" and the theories of some leading, mainly German, historians, is quite valuable. On the other hand, a number of Marxist historians, especially in the Soviet Union and the German Democratic Republic, have evinced considerable interest in refining and updating the methodology of their school. For one example, Ernst Engelberg, inspired by a colloquium held in Berlin in 1970 with some international participation, assembled thirteen pertinent essays in a volume entitled *Probleme der marxistischen Geschichtswissenschaft. Beiträge zu einer Theorie und Methode*. First published by the communist Berlin Academy, it was reissued in 1972 in West Berlin for the benefit of the West German historians. These debates have often revealed far-reaching efforts to reconcile the Marxist with the prevailing "bourgeois" philosophies of history. They have lacked the often vituperative tone in which Marx and Engels themselves had often referred to, and even misquoted, their opponents; one example was Marx's calling the then leading and much-admired German historian, Leopold von Ranke, that "dancing dwarf Ranke." See his and Friedrich Engel's *Werke*, 1956 ed., Vol. XXX, p. 286; Ernst Nolte, "The Relationship between 'Bourgeois' and 'Marxist' Historiography," *HT*, XIV (1975), 57–73; Milorad M. Drachkovitch, ed., *Marxist Ideology in the Contemporary World— Its Appeals and Paradoxes*, New York, 1966; above, n. 15; and below, n. 72.

The few bibliographical references mentioned in our previous and forthcoming notes give barely an inkling of the vast recent output in many countries of books and articles in the field of the philosophy of history. This plethora testifies to the great interest of both philosophers and historians in the variety of approaches and methods relating to this brand of their disciplines. See, for instance, the *Bibliography of Works in the Philosophy of History—1962–1965*, compiled by Lewis D. Wurgaft and published in 1967 as Beiheft 7 of the journal *History and Theory*. See also the numerous other studies, reviews, and bibliographical aids in the field of the philosophies of history offered by that journal in the last two decades. The variety of views expressed by specialists at pertinent conferences is well illustrated by Sidney Hook, ed., *Philosophy and History: a Symposium*, New York, 1963 which includes Hook's own essay on "Objectivity in Reconstruction of History" (pp. 250–74). Of interest also are some studies of the work of contemporary individual thinkers, such as Gaston Fessard's *La Philosophie historique du Raymond Aron*, Paris, 1980. On the other hand, Le Goff and Nora's aforementioned (n. 16) fine collection of essays on history's interrelations with other disciplines includes no study on its ties with philosophy. Perhaps they felt that, in one form or another, elements of philosophy underlay all interdisciplinary relations.

51. Simon Rawidowicz, "Nachman Krochmal als Historiker," in *Festschrift . . . Simon Dubnow,* ed. by Ismar Elbogen *et al.*, Berlin, 1930, pp. 57–75; Heinrich Graetz, "Die Konstruktion der jüdischen Geschichte," *Zeitschrift für die religiösen Interessen des Judenthums,* III (1846), 270–73, 307–312, 349–52, now available also in an English trans. by Ismar Schorsch entitled *The Structure of Jewish History and Other Essays,* New York, 1975. See also Hermann Cohen's critical analysis of "Graetzens Philosophie der jüdischen Geschichte," *MGWJ,* LXI (1917), 356–66; and my "Graetzens Geschichtsschreibung. Eine methodologische Untersuchung," *ibid.,* LXII (1918), 5–15, reproduced in a revised English trans. entitled "Graetz and Ranke: a Methodological Study" in my *History and Jewish Historians,* pp. 269–75. On Simon Dubnow's outlook, see his *Die jüdische Geschichte. Ein geschichtsphilosophischer Versuch,* trans. from the Russian by Israel Friedlaender, Frankfurt, 1921; idem, *Pisma o starom i novom evreistvie* (Letters on Old and New Judaism), St. Petersburg, 1907 (reprinted from the *Voskhod*), revised English trans. by Koppel S. Pinson, and entitled *Nationalism and History,* Philadelphia, 1958; and my brief remarks on "Simon Dubnow's Historical Approach" (Hebrew), *Bitzaron,* II (1940), 212–15. See also, more generally, Ismar Elbogen's survey "Von Graetz bis Dubnow. Fünfzig-Jahre jüdischer Geschichtsforschung," *Festschrift . . . Dubnow,* pp. 7–23, and several other essays in that volume.

52. Yehezkiel Kaufmann, *Golah ve-Nekhar* (Exile and Alienation), 2 vols., Jerusalem, 1929–30; Melkizedek (pseud. for Katzenelson), *Probleme der jüdischen Geschichte und Geschichtsphilosophie,* trans. from the Russian by Elias Hurwicz, Berlin, 1928; Jacob B. Agus, *The Meaning of Jewish History* (above, n. 23); Simon Rawidowicz, *Studies in Jewish Thought,* with a Foreword by Abram L. Sachar, and a Biographical Intro. by Benjamin C. Ravid, ed. by Nahum N. Glatzer, Philadelphia, 1974; Nathan Rotenstreich, *Between Past and Present: an Essay on History,* New Haven, 1958; Morris R. Cohen, "Philosophies of Jewish History," *JSS,* I (1939), 39–72. Of great interest to the then burgeoning "science of Judaism" also was such a programmatic outline as Leopold Zunz's "Grundlagen zu einer künftigen Statistik der Juden," in his *Zeitschrift für die Wissenschaft des Judenthums,* I (1823), 523–32, reprinted in his *Gesammelte Schriften,* I, 134–41.

53. Georges Gurvitch, *Traité de Sociologie,* 3d ed., Paris, 1967. Bibliothèque de sociologie contemporaine, pp. 3–27, esp. pp. 11, 27; Fernand Braudel, "Histoire et sociologie," *ibid.,* pp. 83–98; Franklin Henry Giddings, *The Principles of Sociology,* New York, 1896; Robert Ezra Park and Ernst Watson Burgess, *Introduction to the Science of Sociology,* New York, 1921; Charles Morazé, "The Application of the Social Sciences to History," *JCH,* III/2 (1968), 207–213; Arthur Ruppin, *Soziologie der Juden,* 2 vols., Berlin, 1930–31 (also in Hebrew); Jacob Lestschinsky, "The Evolution of the Jewish People during the Last Hundred Years" (Yiddish), *YIVO Shriftn far Ekonomik un Statistik,* I (1928), 1–54; G. R. Elton, *The Practice of History,* p. 25. See also Pitrim I. Sorokin, *Contemporary Sociological Theories,* New York, 1928; and the historical survey of Heinz Mann, "Geschichte der Soziologie,"

Handbuch der Soziologie, Stuttgart, 1956, pp. 1–120 (from Graeco-Roman times to the twentieth century). It may be noted that the abridged English trans. of Ruppin's *Soziologie* bore the title *The Jews in the Modern World*, London, 1934. It was provided with an Introduction by the well-known English historian Lewis B. Namier, whose historical methods found both ardent admirers and sharp critics in both England and America. See John Brooke, "Namier and Namierism," *HT*, III (1964), 330–47. Ruppin's work differed little, in content and method, from similar works written some years later by the historian Israel Cohen, *Contemporary Jewry: a Survey of Social, Cultural, Economic and Political Conditions*, London, 1950.

54. See Louis O. Mink, "The Autonomy of Historical Understanding," *HT*, V (1966), 24–47; Wilhelm Windelband, *Geschichte und Naturwissenschaft*, 4th ed., Frankfurt, 1904; Robert K. Merton, *Social Theory and Social Structure: Toward the Codification of Theory and Research*, Glencoe, Ill., 1949, pp. 82, 92; supplemented, in part, by his *On Theoretical Sociology: Three Essays*, New York, 1967; Alfred Cobban, *The Social Interpretation of the French Revolution*, Cambridge, 1904, p. 13. See also Hugh R. Trevor-Roper's observations on "The Past and the Present: History and Sociology," *Past and Present*, No. 42 (1969), 3–17; and Émile Durkheim's widely accepted *The Rules of Sociological Method*, English trans. from the French by Sarah A. Solovey and John H. Mueller, Chicago, 1946.

55. See Fernand Braudel's "Histoire et sociologie," in Georges Gurvitch's *Traité de Sociologie*, p. 83; Georges Granais, "Techniques de l'enquête sociologique," *ibid.*, 135–51. Of considerable interest also are the diverse approaches, discussed at national or international conferences, such as those held at Birkbeck College in July 1963, as summarized in the "Conference Report: History, Sociology and Anthropology," *Past and Present*, XXVII (1964), 102–108; the two round table discussions held at the Casa de Velázquez in Paris, on December 28, 1968 and January 10, 1969, and reviewed by Pierre Conard and Bernard Vincent in the *Mélanges* of that Casa, V (1969), 479–502; as well as the special committees of the Social Science Research Council, New York, reported in the *Bulletins* of that Council, Nos. 54 (1946) on the "Theory and Practice in Historical Study," and 64 (1954) on the "Social Sciences in Historical Study." The respective methods of the two disciplines are analyzed, among others, in the papers ed. by Seymour Martin Lipset and Richard Hofstadter under the title, *Sociology and History: Methods*, New York, 1968. The Sociology of American History.

The blurring of the boundaries between Jewish and general history and sociology was noted in particular by the writers on Jewish history in the Soviet Union. Regrettably, these voices have been muted ever since Stalin's regime of terror in the late 1930s. It is also apparent in the works of the few avowed adherents to the materialistic conception of history in other countries, such as Raphael Mahler and Morris A. Shappes. See Mahler's Yiddish essay, "Historical Materialism and Jewish History: a Lecture," *Di Zukunft*, XLIII (1938), 60–67; and my review of Shappes's *A Documentary History of the Jews in the United States 1654–1875*, reprinted from *JSS*, XIII (1951), 77–80, in my *Steeled by Adversity*, pp. 74–79.

56. See Claude Lévi-Strauss, *Structural Anthropology*, English trans. by Claire Jambon and Brooks Grundfest, Frankfurt, 1967; Jean Plaget, *Structuralism*, English trans. from the French by Channah Mashler, New York, 1970, esp. p. 44; the

earlier essays by Georges Gurvitch, "Le Concept de structure sociale," *Cahiers Internationaux de Sociologie*, XXI (1955), 3 ff.; Siegfried Nadel, *The Theory of Social Structure*, with a Memoir by Meyer Fortes, Glencoe, Ill., 1957, pp. 125 ff.; several essays ed. by Roger Bastide, *Sens et usage du terme structure dans les sciences humaines et sociales*, The Hague, 1962; Theodor Schieder, "Strukturen und Persönlichkeiten in der Geschichte," *HZ*, CXCV (1962), 265–96; and in fullest detail Raymond Boudon, *À quoi sert la notion de structure? Essai sur la signification de la notion de structure dans les sciences humaines*, Paris, 1968. Les Essais, 136. See also Edith Kurzweil's overall review of *The Age of Structuralism: Lévi-Strauss to Foucault*, New York, 1980, which includes data on the opponents of this movement, such as Alain Touraine in his "Structure without Structuralism," pp. 113–34.

On its part, the *Annales ESC* devoted a special issue to the discussions of "Histoire et structure," XXVI (1971), 533–88; Günther Schiwy, *Neue Aspekte des Strukturalismus*, Munich, 1971; and Manfred Wüstemeyer, "Die 'Annales.' Grundsätze und Methoden der neuen Geschichtswissenschaft," *VSW*, LIV (1967), 7–45. See also Traian Stoianovich, *French Historical Method: the Annales Paradigms*, with a Foreword by Fernand Braudel, Ithaca, N.Y., 1976; and, more generally, Robert K. Merton's related analysis of *Social Theory and Social Structure*; Richard Bernstein, *The Restructuring of Social and Political Theory*, New York, 1976; and Edith Kurzweil's survey of *The Age of Structuralism*.

Of course, the study of institutions in both past and present, without bearing the label of structuralism, is very old and may, in some respects, be traced back to the ancient Roman jurists. As to my own modest contribution to the institutional history of the Jewish people see my *The Jewish Community: Its History and Structure to the American Revolution*, 3 vols., Philadelphia, 1942 (3d and 4th impressions, 1948). Its second volume, dealing with the *structure* and functioning of the Jewish communities in some ways anticipated the later "structural" approach to history. Several other communal studies are listed in my "Bibliography" compiled by Jeannette M. Baron and published in the *Salo Wittmayer Baron Jubilee Volume*, Jerusalem, 1974 [1975], esp. Nos. 66–67, 79, 84, 136 (462/9), 152 (450), 159, 171 (462 f.), 184, 193, 195, 205–206 (408), 213, 239, 243, 247, 266–67, (438, 450/7), 278, 313, 405, 466–68.

57. See, for example, Gustave Lanson, *Essais de méthodes de critique et d'histoire littéraire*, assembled and ed. by Henri Peyre, Paris, 1965; William James, "Great Men and Their Environment," reproduced in his *Selected Papers on Philosophy*, with an Intro. by C. M. Bakewell, London, 1958. Everyman's Library, 739, pp. 165–97; Winfred Philip Lehmann and Yakov Malkiel, eds., *Symposium for Historical Linguistics*, Austin, Texas, 1968 (papers submitted to the Symposium held at the University of Texas in the Spring of 1966, including those presented by Uriel Weinreich, William Lebow, and Marvin I. Herzog; pp. 95–108); and the related chapters by Jean Starobinski, "La Littérature, le texte et l'interprète," Henri Zerner, "L'Art," and Jean Claude Chevalier, "La Langue, linguistique et l'histoire" in J. Le Goff and P. Nora's *Faire de l'histoire*, II, 168–82, 183–202; III; 95–114. See also Edward Sapir's *Language: an Introduction to the Study of Speech*, New York, 1921; and his *Culture, Language and Personality: Selected Essays*, ed. by David S. Mandelbaum, Berkeley, 1949; Herbert Landar, *Language and Culture*, New York, 1964. The enor-

mous literature appearing every year about the history of letters and the methodology of literary history and criticism includes much material relevant also for the other branches of historical research and writing. It must be remembered, however, that much of Jewish history, in general, was written with a preponderant emphasis on leading individuals often considered the heroes of their people who molded its destiny more than any other force. We need but refer to Thomas Carlyle in general and to Heinrich Graetz in Jewish history. See below, n. 65, and from another angle, Jacob Schmidely, "La Statistique lexicale: un example du rapports entre mathématique, linguistique et littérature," *Les Langues Néo-Latines,* LXIII (1969), No. 190, pp. 3–10.

58. See, for instance, the collection of essays in *Anthropology,* ed. by Samuel Rapport and Helen Wright, in consultation with Joseph Brann, including Bronislaw Malnowski's "The Study of Man's Culture: Subject, Method and Scope" (pp. 97–114); Claude Lévi-Strauss, "Today's Crisis in Anthropology" (pp. 129–38); Ruth Benedict, "Religion" (pp. 221–38). Of particular interest to historians also are the beginnings of the modern studies of man as analyzed by Michele Duchet in *Anthropologie et histoire au siècle des lumières. Buffon, Voltaire, Rousseau, Helvetius, Diderot,* Paris, 1971. See also, more generally, Wilhelm E. Mühlmann, *Geschichte der Anthropologie,* 2nd ed. rev., Bonn, 1968; and the sources reproduced by Wolf Lepenies in his *Soziologische Anthropologie: Materialien,* Munich, 1971. Reihe Hauser, LXXX.

Closely related to the scientific aspects of anthropology and their impact on history are such studies as E. Le Roi Ladurie, ed., *Le Territoire de l'historien,* Paris, 1970; Jacques Duparquet, "Essai de cartographie historique: Le Peuplement de Bassin Parisien en 1711," *Annales ESC,* XXIV (1969), 976–98 (the tenor of this article is described by its motto: a statement by Louis Febvre: "historians become geographers"); Elsworth Huntington, *Civilization and Climate,* New York, 1915; Gustaf Utterström, "Climate Fluctuations and Population Problems in Early Modern History," *Scandinavian Economic History Review,* II (1955), 3–47; Emmanuel Le Roy Ladurie, *Histoire du climat depuis l'an mil,* Paris, 1967; John B. S. Haldane, "The Argumentation from Animals to Men: an Examination of the Validity for Anthropology," *Journal of the Royal Anthropological Institute,* LXXVI (1956), 1–14; or such attempts at seeing in class struggle a preeminent force in the historical evolution, as René Baehrel's "La Haine de classe au temps d'épidemie," *Annales ESC,* VII (1952), 351–60. Nor must we overlook the related schools of history emphasizing the impact of the natural environment on historical evolution as espoused especially by Henry Thomas Buckle in his *History of Civilization in England,* 2 vols., London, 1857–61 [with my comments thereon in "Emphases in Jewish History," *JSS,* I (1939), 15–38, esp. pp. 19 f., reprinted in my *History and Jewish Historians,* pp. 65–89, 345–46, esp. pp. 65 f.]; and many works cited in *Historical Demography.*

Of most direct relevance to the present study are, of course, all aspects of "historical anthropology" and its ramifications. See, for instance, Thomas Nipperding, "Bemerkungen zum Problem einer historischen Anthropologie" in *Die Philosophie und die Wissenschaften* (Simon Moses Jubilee Volume), ed. by Ernst Oldenmeyer, Meisenheim am Glan, 1967, pp. 350–70; and his broader analysis of

"Kulturgeschichte, Sozialgeschichte, historische Anthropologie," *VSW,* LXV
(1968), 145–64; Oskar Köhler *et al.*, "Versuch einer historischen Anthropologie,"
Seaculum, XXV (1974), 129–65; and the remarks thereon by Rolf Spranger in his
"Kritische Bemerkungen zu einer historischen Anthropologie," *ibid.*, pp. 247–50.
Because of the variety of its subdivisions, it is difficult to trace back the full
history of anthropology. See, for example, Heinrich Karpp's *Anthropologie der Bibel
und des Altchristentums;* and his *Probleme altchristlicher Anthropologie und philosoph-
ischer Psychologie bei den Kirchenvätern des dritten Jahrhunderts,* Gütersloh, 1956.
Beiträge zur Förderung christlicher Theologie, XLIV/3; or John Howland Rowe,
"The Renaissance Foundations of Anthropology," *American Anthropologist,* LXVII
(1961), 1–20. Yet, the last three centuries witnessed gargantuan steps made in the
broadening of the scope and ramifications as well as a great refinement of its tools
of what is sometimes called "modern anthropology."

59. See Karl Budde, "The Nomadic Ideal in the Old Testament," *New World,*
IV (Boston, 1895), 725–45, English trans. from the German essay published in the
Preussische Jahrbücher, LXXXV (1895), 57–79; Theophile James Meek, *Hebrew
Origins,* New York, 1936. Haskell Lectures for 1933–34; idem, "Primitive Mono-
theism and the Religion of Moses," *Review of Religion,* IV (1940), 286–303; idem,
"Monotheism and the Religion of Israel," *JBL,* LXI (1942), 21–43, commenting on
William F. Albright's *From the Stone Age to Christianity: Monotheism and the Histor-
ical Process,* Baltimore, 1940; and the literature discussed by Herbert F. Hahn in his
aforementioned work, *The Old Testament in Modern Research* (n. 43); and my
remarks in *SRH,* I, 32 ff., 301 f. nn. 3 ff.

60. Michael Parenti, "Ethnic Politics: Persistance of Ethnic Identification,"
American Political Science Review, LXI (1967), 717–26, esp. p. 723; Andrée Com-
brie, *La Philosophie des races du Comte de Gobineau et sa portée actuelle,* Paris, 1937.
Bibliotheque de philosophie contemporaine; Wilhelm Coermann, *Die
Rassengesetzgebung des nationalsozialistischen Staates,* Eisenach, 1939; Robert Deisz,
Das Recht der Rasse. Kommentar zur Rassengesetzgebung, Munich, 1938; Pierre
Charles *et al.*, *Racisme et catholicisme,* Paris, 1939; David Farbstein, *Die Stellung der
Juden zur Rassen- und Fremdenfrage,* Zurich, 1939; and, on the genetic aspects,
Franz Boas's succinct observations on "Heredity and Environment," *JSS,* I (1939),
5–14. See also above, n. 35; and below, n. 90.

61. See William Stubbs, *The Constitutional History of England,* 3 vols., London, 1874–78; Frederic William Maitland, *The History of English Law before the
Time of Edward I,* 2 vols., London, 1895 (written in cooperation with Frederick
Pollock); Paul Vinogradoff, *Outlines of Historical Jurisprudence,* 2 vols., London,
1920–23; Lewis B. Namier, *The Structure of Politics at the Accession of George III,*
London, 1929, and the numerous other works by these authors. See also the
stimulating essays on ancient and medieval aspects of legal history in *Società Ital-
iana di Storia del Diritto nel quadro delle scienze storiche,* Florence, 1966; and Lucien
Lévy-Brühl, *Aspects sociologiques du droit,* Paris, 1951.

Among the spokesmen of the "New Political History," we need but mention
Allan G. Bogue, "United States: the 'New Political History,'" *JCH,* III/2 (1968),
5–26; Darett B. Rutman, "Political History: the New and the Pseudo-New," *Journal
of Interdisciplinary History,* II (1972), 305–310, esp. p. 309; Paul Kleppner, "Beyond
the New Political History: a Review Essay," *Historical Methods Newsletter,* VI

(1972), 17–26. Examples of recent detailed studies in the spirit of this new approach are Malvyn Hammersberg's *The Indiana Voter: the Historical Dynamism of Party Allegiance During the 1870s*, Chicago, 1977; Joel Silbey *et al.*, eds., *The History of American Electoral Behavior*, Princeton, 1978; and Paul Kleppner, *The Third Electoral System, 1853–1893: Voters and Political Cultures*, Chapel Hill, 1979, with Stephen L. Hansen's comments on these three works in his "The Illusion of Objectivism: a Review of Recent Trends of the New Political History," *Historical Methods Newsletter*, 1979. See also Samuel T. Sameny, "Ethnic Groups, Ethnic Conflicts, and Recent Quantitative Research in American Political History," *The International Migration Review*, VII (Spring, 1973), 14–33; James E. Wright, "The Ethnocultural Model of Voting: a Behavioral and Historical Critique," *American Behavioral Scientist*, XVI (1973), 653–74, esp. pp. 659 ff. See also the literature cited below, n. 101.

Related to ethnic studies are those concerning the historical role of the family. See, for instance, the 1932 issue of *Annales ESC* entirely devoted to essays dealing with *Famille et Société*; and Theodore K. Rabb and Robert I. Rotberg, eds., *The Family in History: Interdisciplinary Essays*, New York, 1976 (Reprinted from their *Journal of Interdisciplinary History*), with the comments thereon by Robert Muchembled in his "Famille et histoire des mentalité (XVIe-XVIIIe siècles). État présent des recherches," *Revue des Études Sudest-Européens*, XII (1979), 349–69.

62. See Uriel Tal's lecture *Structures of German "Political Theology" in the Nazi Era*, Tel Aviv, 1979, with the literature listed there; and, on earlier antecedents of the new ideology, idem, *Christians and Jews in Germany: Religion, Politics and Ideology in the Second Reich 1870–1914*, trans. into English by N. J. Jacobs, Ithaca, 1975. A great many other pertinent studies, generated by the Holocaust (see above, nn. 4 and 18; and below, nn. 73 and 90), have gone far in elucidating the historical roots of German anti-Semitism. See esp. Paul W. Massing, *Rehearsal for Destruction: a Study of Political Anti-Semitism in Imperial Germany*, New York, 1949; Theodor W. Adorno *et al.*, *The Authoritarian Personality*, New York, 1949; and the other three vols. in that *Studies in Prejudice Series*; and Hannah Arendt, *The Origins of Totalitarianism*, New York, 1951. See also the various views expressed in *Deutsche und Juden. Beiträge von Nahum Goldmann, Gershom Scholem, Golo Mann, Salo W. Baron, Eugen Gerstenmaier und Karl Jaspers*, Frankfurt, 1967. These addresses, delivered in Brussels on August 4, 1966, were designated "ein ungelöstes Problem." Even now this problem still is largely unresolved.

Needless to say, long before the rise of the Nazi movement the political element played a considerable role particularly in the state and Church debates in Christendom and was, from the outset, an even more vital ingredient of the Islamic civilization. Nor could Judaism or any other major religion completely avoid the interpenetration of sacred and secular (including political) factors, which in various ways also colored the outlook of students of both history and theology.

CHAPTER VI: PSYCHOHISTORY

63. William Langer, "The Next Assignment," AHR, LXIII (1958), 283–304; Kurt Robert Eissler, "Freud and the Psychoanalysis of History," *Journal of the Ameri-*

can *Psychiatric Association*, XI (1963), 675–705; Alan Besançon, "Histoire et psychoanalyse à propos de Metabletica," *Annales ESC*, XIX (1964), 237–49 (a review of Jan Hendrik Van den Berg's *Metabletica ou la psychologie historique*, French trans. from the Dutch by M. Van Scherpenzeel, Paris, 1962); idem, "Vers une histoire psychoanalytique," *ibid.*, pp. 584–616; idem, "Psychoanalysis: Auxiliary Science or Historical Method," *JCH*, III (1968), 149–62, esp. p. 149. See also Saul Friedlander, *Histoire et Psychoanalyse*, Paris, 1975. Not surprisingly the number of publications in this field in various languages increased rapidly, and ultimately, the special periodicals *Journal of Psychohistory* and *The Psychohistory Review* opened their columns to pertinent essays and reviews. This proliferation is well illustrated by William J. Gilmore's "Critical Bibliography," *The Psychohistory Review*, V/2 (1976), 4–33; VI/1 (1977), 88–96; VI/2–3 (1977–78), 106–111; VI/4 (1978), 66–69; VII/2 (1978), 40–47; VII/3 (1979), 43–49; VII/4 (1979), 26–42; VIII/3 (1979), 55–60.

64. See Robin George Collingwood, *The Idea of History*, London, 1946; and Louis O. Mink's analysis of *Mind, History, and Dialectic: The Philosophy of Robin George Collingwood*, Bloomington, Indiana, 1969. On the function of alleged brief speeches used for explaining a certain behavior, see, for instance, Joshua ben Joseph ha-Kohen's *Emeq ha-bakha* (Valley of Tears: a Chronicle), ed. by Meir Letteris, Vienna, 1852; or in its English trans. by Henry S. May, *Vale of Tears*, The Hague, 1971.

65. Francis Bacon, *The Advancement of Learning*, Book VII, in his *Works*, collected and edited by James Spedding *et al.*, 15 vols., Boston, 1861, esp. IX, 220; George W. Nadel, "History as Psychology in Francis Bacon's Theory of History," *HT*, V (1960), 275–87; Napoleon Bonaparte cited in Sidney Hook's *The Hero in History: a Study in Limitation and Possibility*, New York, 1943, esp. pp. 14, 28 n. 4 and *passim*; Thomas Carlyle, *On Heroes, Hero-Worship, and the Heroic in History: Six Lectures*, reproduced with Emendations and Additions in his *Sartor Resartus* (1840) and in his *Works*, Centenary Edition, London, 1901, Vol. V. See Saadia ben Joseph Gaon, *Sefer ha-Galui* (Book of the Exiled), ed. by Abraham E. Harkavy in his *Zikkaron la-Rishonim ve-gam la-Ahronim* (Biographical Studies on Older and Later Scholars), 5 vols., St. Petersburg, 1879–82, V, 155; my "Saadia's Communal Activities" (1943), reproduced in my *Ancient and Medieval Jewish History: Essays*, pp. 119 f., 425 n. 110. See also William James, "Great Men and Their Environment" in his *Selected Papers on Philosophy*, with an Introduction by C. M. Bakewell, London, 1958. Everyman's Library, 739, pp. 165–97; and, from another perspective, Louis Gottschalk *et al.*, *The Use of Personal Documents in History, Anthropology and Sociology*, New York, 1945. Bulletin of the Social Science Research Council, XLV.

In his "Psychohistory and Intellectual History," *HT*, XIV (1975), 139–55, esp. p. 154, Gerald Izemberg has correctly pointed out that "the lesson to be derived from the pitfalls of overdetermination is that in intellectual history it is necessary to begin with a man's work rather than his life. It is the work, as [Jean Paul] Sartre has pointed out in his *Search for Method* that poses questions to the life, not the other way around." This method reminds one of the widespread long-time practice of East-European Jews to identify the distinguished ancestry of a person by referring to his or her descent from a famous man of learning through his work rather than his person. One was a descendent of the *SHLAH* (*Shnei Luhot ha-Berit*, or the Two Tablets of the Covenant) or of the *Tosefot Yom-Tob* (Yom Tob's Supplements), one a renowned work in Jewish mysticism and the other an extensively studied commentary on the Mishnah, rather than to their authors, Isaiah Horowitz or Yom Tob Lipman Heller, respectively.

66. See William Langer, "The Next Assignment," *AHR*, LXIII, 301 quoting Karl Holl's "Luthers Urteile über sich selbst," *Gesammelte Aufsätze zur Kirchengeschichte*, 3 vols., Tübingen, 1923–28, I, 381–419; Erik H. Erikson, *Young Man Luther: a Study in Psychoanalysis and History*, New York, 1962. See also in a revised form Erikson's *Psychology and Religion: the Case of Young Man Luther*, ed. by Roger A. Johnson, with contributions by Roland H. Bainton *et al.*, Philadelphia, 1977. A different interpretation of Luther was offered by Preserved Smith in his "Luther's Early Development in the Light of Psychoanalysis," *American Journal of Psychology*, XLIV (1913), 360–77. Erikson also published another searching psychoanalytical interpretation of the career of Mohandas Karamchand Gandhi, an equally controversial and amply documented character. See his *Gandhi's Truth*, New York, 1969. Of considerable interest also are such attempts as Otto Pflanzer's "Toward a Psychoanalytic Interpretation of Bismarck," *AHR*, LXXVII (1972), 419–44; and Peter Loewenberg, "The Unsuccessful Adolescence of Heinrich Himmler," *ibid.*, LXXVI (1971), 612–41, based, in part, on Himmler's correspondence, edited by Helmut Herber in his *Reichsführer! Briefe an und von Himmler*, Stuttgart, 1956, which raised in Loewenberg's mind the question whether "one could have predicted from his [Himmler's] adolescence that this youth would end up to be the greatest mass murderer of all time?" Quite different, of course, is Loewenberg's sketch, "Theodor Herzl: a Psychoanalytic Study in Charismatic Political Leadership," in Benjamin B. Wolman, ed., *The Psychoanalytic Interpretation of History*, with a Foreword by William L. Langer, New York, 1971, pp. 150–91; Adolf Allwohn, *Die Ehe des Propheten Hosea in psychoanalytischer Beleuchtung*, Giessen, 1926.

67. See Sigmund Freud, *Moses and Monotheism*, New York, 1939, esp. pp. 37 n. 5, 164 f. with my comments thereon in a review in *The American Journal of Sociology*, XLV (1939), 471–77. I also learned a great deal about the man and the thinker from some of my friends in Freud's entourage, especially his personal physician, Dr. Max Schur who was also my doctor (and close friend) in Vienna and later in the United States. Originally a specialist in internal medicine, Schur was later to become a psychoanalyst and the author of a highly informative biography, *Freud Living and Dying*, New York, 1972. For some reason my modest review of Freud's *Moses* attracted unusual attention in later years. It was not only (adversely) referred to in Ernest Jones's standard biography, *The Life and Works of Sigmund Freud*, 3 vols., New York, 1953–57, Vol. III, p. 370; but it was also reprinted in 1969 in *Monotheism and Moses: the Genesis of Judaism*, ed. by Robert J. Christen and Harold E. Hazelton, Lexington, Mass., 1969, pp. 39–43; in 1971 in *Psychoanalysis and History*, ed. with an Intro. by Bruce Mazlish, New York, 1971, pp. 50–55; and in 1972 in my *Ancient and Medieval Jewish History: Essays*, pp. 3–9. On the great difficulties in reconstructing from the existing biblical materials a realistic picture of Moses and his work even for post-World War I students by means of the long-

established conventional critical methodology, suffice it to mention, for one example, Rudolf Kittel's *Geschichte des Volkes Israel*, 5th ed. rev., 3 vols., Gotha, 1923–29, I, 306 ff.

By pure coincidence in 1939 I also reviewed the psychoanalytically interpreted biography of *Jacob Emden: a Man of Controversy* by Mortimer Cohen in *JSS*, I (1939), 483–87, with additional comments by Cohen and myself, *ibid.*, II (1940), 117–23. Incidentally, an equally critical review of that volume by Gershom Scholem appeared in Hebrew, in *Kirjath Sepher*, XVI (1939–40), 320–38. But I certainly did not intend then, or later, in any way to repudiate on principle the use of psychoanalytical methods in historical research.

68. See Sir Isaiah Berlin, "History and Theory: The Concept of Scientific History," *HT*, I (1960), 1–31; Roland Mousnier and René Pillorget, "Contemporary History and Historians of the Sixteenth and Seventeenth Centuries," *JCH*, III/2 (1968), 93–109, esp. p. 107. Not surprisingly, Russian historians disregarded, or rejected outright, the new historiographic approaches in the West. In a typical analysis of "The Contemporary French Historiography" (Russian), *Myśl i Nauka*, 1979, M. N. Sokolova condemned Marc Bloch and Lucien Febvre, the founders of *Annales ESC*, for trying "at any price with all the weight of their experience and interpretation of history to minimize the grave contradictions in the society of the time in order to find in the past a confirmation of the eternal and indestructible character of the regime founded on the system of private enterprise and on the rights of the bourgeoisie." Cited by Claude Sergio Ingerlom in his "Moscou, le procès des Annales," *Annales ESC*, XXXVII (1982), 64–71. See also Eliam Amado Lévy-Valensi, "Histoire et psychologie?" *ibid.*, XX (1965), 923–38, esp. p. 936.

69. Sigmund Freud, *Leonardo da Vinci: a Study in Psychosexuality*, Authorized English trans. by A. A. Brill, New York, 1947; idem, *Leonardo da Vinci: a Memory from His Childhood*, English trans. by Alana Tyson, with an Intro. by Brian Farrel, Harmondsworth, 1966 (A Pelican Book, No. 519); Meyer Shapiro, "Leonardo and Freud: an Art-Historical Study," *Journal of the History of Ideas*, XVII (1956), 47–76; Freud and William C. Bullitt, *Thomas Woodrow Wilson: Twenty-Eighth President of the United States: a Psychological Study*, Boston, 1966. See also Bernard Brodie's "A Psychoanalytic Interpretation of Woodrow Wilson," in Bruno Mazlish's ed. of *Psychoanalysis and History*," pp. 115–23, which, however, is essentially but a review of Alexander L. George and Juliette L. George's more conventional study of *Woodrow Wilson and Colonel House*, New York, 1956.

70. See N. H. Caskey *et al.*, "Assessing Historical Figures: the Use of Observer-Based Personality Descriptions. The Historical Assessment Collaborative of the University of California at Berkeley," *Historical Method Newsletter*, X/2 (1979), 66–76. There have also been attempts of intensive collaboration between a student of history and one of psychoanalysis, as in the study of Friedrich Nietzsche by George Morastis and Carl Pletsch. See their "A Psychoanalytic Contribution to Method in Biography," *Psychohistory Review*, VIII/2 (1979), 72–74; and Pletsch's "A Note on the Adaptation of the Psychoanalytic Method to the Study of Historical Personalities. Psychoanalysts on Schreber," *ibid.*, VIII/3, 46–50, referring to the much debated record on D. P. Schreber's *Denkwürdigkeiten eines Nervenkranken*, published in Leipzig, 1903. Of course, continuous efforts in these directions may

lead to the refinement of methods and even pave the way for retrospective observational techniques in the evaluation of the documentary evidence pertaining to personalities and events of the past.

71. Freud treated some of these problems in his *Group Psychology and the Analysis of the Ego*, English trans. by James Strachey, New York, 1925 (the German original, *Massenpsychologie und Ich Analyse*, published in Leipzig, 1921, bore the unmistakable imprint of World War I and the early postwar reactions); his *Civilizations and Its Discontents*, trans. from the German *Das Unbehagen in der Kultur* by Joan Riviere, London, 1949. International Psychoanalytical Library, XVIII; and other writings. See also above n. 3; and Erich Fromm, "Über Methode und Aufgabe einer analytischen Sozialpsychologie," *Zeitschrift für Sozialforschung*, I (1932), 28–34; Bruno Bettelheim, *Dynamism of Prejudice*, New York, 1950; Hannah Arendt, *The Origins of Totalitarianism*; and other sources cited by William L. Langer in his aforementioned "The Next Assignment," *AHR*, LXXIII, 28 ff. (reprinted in Mazlish's *Psychoanalysis and History*, pp. 94 ff.). On the other hand, the opposition has become increasingly vocal and persuasive. See, for example, Jacques Barzun, "History, the Muse and the Doctors," *AHR*, LXXVII (1972), 36–64; idem, *Clio and the Doctors: Psycho-History, Quanto-History and History*, Chicago, 1974; David I. Stannard, *Shrinking History: on Freud and the Failure of Psychohistory*, New York, 1980 (includes a condemnation of even the medical aspect of psychoanalysis); also his discussion with Michael Franz Busch, Fred Weinstein and Travis I. Crosby at a "Symposium" in *The Psychohistory Review*, IX (1980–81), 136–61; and Donald J. Dietrich, "Clio on the Couch or Off?" *Historical Methods*, XIV (1982), 83–90. See also Frank E. Manuel's general warning in "The Use and Abuse of Psychology," *Daedalus*, C (1971), 187–213.

72. Understandably Marxist historians had serious difficulties in accepting Freud and his psychoanalytical approach, which so fundamentally deviated from the materialistic interpretation of history. For a time the Soviet regime is said to have banned all psychological literature. But see Francis A. Bartlett's *Sigmund Freud: a Marxist Essay*, London, 1938; Erich Fromm, ed., "The Application of Humanist Psychoanalysis to Marx's Theory," *Socialist Humanism: an International Symposium*, New York, 1966, pp. 228–45; and Helmut Delmer, "Psychoanalyse und historischer Materialismus" in A. Lorenzen *et al.*, eds., *Psychoanalyse und Sozialwissenschaft*, Frankfurt, 1971, pp. 60–92.

73. On the extensive literature dealing with anti-Semitism through the ages, see, for example, my "Changing Patterns of AntiSemitism: a Survey," *JSS*, XXXVIII (1976), 5–38; my brief summary in the article "Anti-Semitism" in the *Encyclopaedia Britannica*, in various editions till 1971 (II, 81–90); the important studies included in the *Essays on Antisemitism*, ed. by Koppel S. Pinson, 2nd ed. revised; *Violence and Defense in the Jewish Experience*, ed. by Salo W. Baron and George S. Wise, Philadelphia, 1977; and more fully in my *SRH*, Vols. I–XVIII and the extensive literature listed in all these works. See also the more recent comprehensive listing in Robert Singer's *Antisemitic Propaganda: an Annotated Bibliography and Research Guide*, with a Foreword by Colin Holmes, London, 1982.

Among recent publications one needs to refer also to the enormous and still growing literature on the Holocaust. As mentioned before (n. 18) the initial articles by the pioneering scholar in this field, Philip Friedman, have recently been assembled and published under the title, *Roads to Extinction: Essays on the Holocaust.* Much of the additional pertinent literature has been noted in Jacob Robinson and Friedman's *Guide to Jewish History under Nazi Impact;* and the following series of bibliographies of the works published in various languages compiled by Friedman *et al.*

74. The Viennese background of Freud's work, with its pulsating cultural life in which Jews played an important role, and its intense anti-Semitic manifestations at the turn of the century, have often been described. See Carl E. Schorske's *Fin-de-siècle Vienna: Politics and Culture,* New York, 1980; Hans Kohn, *Karl Kraus, Arthur Schnitzler, Otto Weininger: Aus dem jüdischen Wien der Jahrhundertswende,* Vienna, 1962; Peter Gay, *Freud, Jews and Other Germans, Masters and Victims in Modernist Culture,* New York, 1978, esp. pp. 29 ff.; Frederic V. Grunfeld, *Prophets Without Honour,* New York, 1979; Philadelphia, 1983. On Freud's own attitude to his ancestral religion and contemporary Jewish life, see Ernst Simon, "Sigmund Freud, and the Jews," *Yearbook* of the Leo Baeck Institute, II (1957), 270–305 (one of the best of the various studies under a similar title). Simon shows that, despite numerous experiences with anti-Semitism from the age of twelve, Freud stayed away from the heated controversies on this score during his lifetime. He had particularly no appreciation at all for the Jewish religion, since "religion was for him nothing but an illusion which could be used as a narcotic" (p. 305), a term reminiscent of Marx's well-known dictum.

Sometimes the fact that not only many of Freud's disciples but also numerous psychoanalysts in other countries were Jews led some observers to explain the special interest of students of the impact of psychoanalytical teachings on those aspects of world literature which dealt with Jews. For instance, in his study of *Psychoanalysis in Shakespeare,* New York, 1966, Norwood Norman Holland suggested that "perhaps because many psychoanalysts are Jews, the *Merchant of Venice* has received a great deal of attention, more proportionately than some of Shakespeare's more important plays" (p. 231). But we must bear in mind that the complex personality of Shylock and other unusual features of that play's plot would have aroused the curiosity of non-Jewish writers as well, even if they were not interested in solving the riddle of whether the great poet, like many other English writers of that period before the admission of the Jews to England, betrayed some anti-Jewish feelings. See the large pertinent bibliography listed in *SRH,* XV, 435 ff. n. 70.

75. See Alan Besançon, "Psychoanalysis, Auxiliary Science or Historical Method," *JCH,* III/2 (1968), 149–62; Bruno Mazlish, "Group Psychology and Problems of Contemporary History," *ibid.,* pp. 163–77, esp. p. 174. Needless to say, similar assertions can be made in connection with other social sciences as well. See, for instance, Fred Weinstein and Gerald M. Pratt, *Psychoanalytic Sociology, an Essay on the Interpretation of Historical Data and the Phenomena of Collective Behavior,* Baltimore, 1973; and their earlier study, *Wish to Be Free, Psyche and Value Change,* Berkeley, 1969, which the reviewer Jacob I. Talmon somewhat facetiously called attempts "to marry Sigmund Freud to Talcott Parsons." See *HT,* XIV (1975), 121–37. See also Harold D. Laswell's judicious appraisal of the "Impact of Psychoanalytic Teaching on the Social Sciences" in *The State of the Social Sciences,* ed. by Leonard D. White, Chicago, 1956, pp. 84–115.

CHAPTER VII: QUANTITATIVE HISTORY

76. Simon Kuznets, "Quantitative Aspects of Economic Growth," *Economic Development and Cultural Change*, V/1, Pt. 4 (October 1956–July 1957); XI/2, Pt. 2 (January 1963); Adeline Daumard and François Furet, "Méthodes de l'histoire sociale. Les Archives notariales et la Mechanographie," *Annales ESC*, XIV (1959), 676–93, esp. p. 676; Jean Marczewski, "Histoire quantitative: But et méthode," *Institut de Science Économique Appliquée*, Série AF No. 1 (July 1961); idem, *Introduction à l'histoire quantitative*, Geneva, 1965; idem, "Quantitative History," *JCH*, III/2 (1968), 179–92, esp. pp. 181 n. 6, 190 f.; Maurice Lévy-Leboyer, "La 'New Economic History' (Frontières nouvelles économiques)," *Annales ESC*, XXIV (1969), 1035–69; and other publications of that period, surveyed in Charlotte Erickson's "Quantitative History: Review Article," *AHR*, LXXX (1975), 352–60. See also, from the technical point of view, Marshall Smelser and William I. Davisson, "The Historian and the Computer: a Simple Introduction to a Complex Computation," *Essex Institute of Historical Collections*, CIV (1968), 109–126. See also such related economic studies as Moses Abramovitz's "Resource and Output Trends in the United States since 1870," *American Economic Review, Papers and Proceedings*, XLVI/2 (May 1956), 5–23; idem, *New Views on American Economic Development*, Cambridge, Mass., 1965; and Paul Lebrun, "Structure et quantification," in Chaim Perelman, ed., *Raisonnement et démarches de l'historien*, Brussels, 1963, pp. 29–52. See also above, n. 52.

Devotees of this new approach have also aired their different views on its merits and deficiencies in the papers published by the Purdue Conference on the Application of Economic Theory and Quantitative Technique to Problems of Economic History; and other assemblies in the United States and Europe; for instance, an International Colloquium was held on November 13–16, 1973 at the Polish Academy of Science with the participation of 14 foreign and 100 Polish interdisciplinary scholars; its debates were reviewed by Halina Channowska and Stefania Kowalska in their "Quantitative Methods in Historical Sciences" (Polish), *Kwartalnik Historyczny*, LXXXI (1974), 459–63. See also some other expositions of these theories as reproduced by Don K. Rowney and James Q. Graham, eds., *Quantitative History: Selective Readings in the Quantitative Analysis of Historical Data*, Homewood, 1969.

On the other hand, some serious reservations of the new theories presented by Robert William Fogel, himself an able practitioner of the quantitative method, in his "The Limits of Quantitative Methods in History," *AHR*, LXXX (1975), 329–50; and such outright opponents of that movement as Carl Bridenbaugh, who in his presidential address at the American Historical Association, delivered on December 29, 1962 and published under the title, "The Great Mutation," *ibid.*, LXXVIII (1962–63), 315–31, esp. p. 326, rejected what he called the "worship at the shrine of that Bitch goddess: QUANTIFICATION." Similarly the respected economic historian Edward C. Kirkland, reacting to the vigorous onslaught of the new reforms of historiography, characteristic of that general period of rebellion against traditional ways, derided the typical "cliometrician" with his new manifesto: "retool, rethink, reform, or be plowed under." See his review of R. W. Fogel's

Railroad and American Economic Growth, Baltimore, 1964, in *AHR*, LXXII (1967), 1493–95.

77. Arthur M. Schlesinger, "The Humanist Looks at Empirical Social Research," *AHR*, LXVII (1962), esp. p. 770. In fact, long before the emergence of the "quantitative" movement, there appeared many demographic studies, with or without the plethora of graphs and statistical tables, but with ultimate findings and reasonings quite similar to those of the quantitative researchers. See, for instance, my "The Authenticity of Numbers in the Historical Books of the Old Testament," *JBL*, XLIX (1930), 287–91; "The Israelitic Population under the Kings" (Hebrew), *Abhandlungen zur Erinnerung an Hirsch Perez Chajes*, Vienna, 1933, pp. 76–136, reproduced in a revised English trans. in my *Ancient and Medieval History: Essays*, pp. 23–73, 380–99; "Reflections on Ancient and Medieval Jewish Demography" (Hebrew), *Aryeh Tartakower Jubilee Volume*, ed. by Yosef Shapiro, Tel-Aviv, 1970, pp. 31–45, also reproduced in an English translation in the *Ancient and Medieval Jewish History*, pp. 10–22, 373–80; "Population [Jewish]," *Encyclopaedia Judaica*, 16 vols., Jerusalem, 1972, XIII, 866–903; and the various chapters in *SRH* and my *Jewish Community*, as referred to below, n. 81.

78. See, for example, the *Tentative List of Jewish Educational Institutions in Axis Occupied Countries* by the Research Staff of the Commission on European Jewish Cultural Reconstruction affiliated with the Conference on Jewish Relations (subsequently renamed Conference on Jewish Social Studies), New York, 1946. Supplement to *JSS*, VIII, No. 3; Zosa Szajkowski, *Jewish Education in France, 1789–1939*, ed. by Tobey B. Gitelle, New York, 1980. *JSS*, Monograph Series, No. 2; the numerous articles and reviews related to Jewish education published in that journal as listed in the Cumulative Index 1939–1964, compiled by Max M. Rothschild, New York, 1967; and the "Preliminary List and Subject Index of Jewish Social Studies 1964 through 1978" by Tobey B. Gitelle, *JSS*, XLI (1979), 9–22, s.v. Education; the special periodicals *Jewish Education* and *Shebile ha-Hinukh* (Educational Paths) in the United States and corresponding publications in Israel.

Ironically, one may face similar difficulties with the application of quantitative methods to the study of the spread and effectiveness of the instruction in quantitative history at various colleges in the United States and elsewhere. Such courses as those offered by the Department of History of Johns Hopkins University in its annual Summer Seminar on Quantitative Techniques in Historical Research held in the 1970s can be much better evaluated with the conventional methods of educational research. This is, of course, not to deny the contribution of such instruction to the more effective employment of the quantitative techniques by students. On improvements of this kind see also, for instance, James I. Smith's suggestions in his "New and Simple Methods for the Creation of Computerized Historical Data," *Papers* submitted to the 1980 Meeting of the Social Science Historical Association, Rochester, N.Y.

79. Zacharias Frankel, *Darkei ha-Mishnah* (Introduction to the Mishnah), Leipzig, 1859, with *Tosafot u-mafteah* (Supplements and Index to the *Darkei ha-Mishnah*), Leipzig, 1867; Hermann L. Strack, *Introduction to the Talmud and Midrash*, English trans. from the German, Philadelphia, 1931; Leopold Zunz, "Salomon b. Isaac, genannt Raschi," *Zeitschrift für die Wissenschaft des Judenthums*, I

(1823), 277–384. Harry A. Wolfson called this particular type of talmudic logic the "hypothetico-deductive method of text interpretation" and contended that it also influenced most late medieval Jewish philosophers; for instance, Hisdai Crescas. See his *Crescas' Critique of Aristotle. Problems of Aristotle's Physics in Jewish and Arabic Philosophy*, Cambridge, Mass., 1929, pp. 24 ff. In recent centuries some rabbis went further and constructed regular dialectical castles in the so-called *pilpul* which, though in principle as legitimate as most of the medieval and early modern Christian casuistry, remained fairly incomprehensible to modern Western-trained scholars, Jewish and non-Jewish. On this type of advanced casuistry and the difference between *pilpul* and the related term *hilluq*, see Chaim Zalmon Dimitrovsky's searching analysis in his "On the Pilpulistic Method" (Hebrew), *Salo Wittmayer Baron Jubilee Volume*, ed. by Saul Lieberman with the assistance of Arthur Hyman, III, 111–81.

80. See my *World Dimensions of Jewish History*, New York, 1962. Leo Baeck Memorial Lectures, V; reproduced with additions in *Simon Dubnow, l'homme et son oeuvre*, ed. by Aaron Steinberg, pp. 26–40; and again in *History and Jewish Historians*, pp. 23–42 (also in a Portuguese trans. in my *História e Historiografia de Povo Judeu*, São Paulo, 1974, pp. 1–19); and, more broadly, on the impact of nationalism, my *SRH*, XI, Chap. L, pp. 192 ff., 379 ff.

81. See, for example, the computations of the victims during the great Roman-Jewish War of 66–70 (73), those massacred during the First Crusade, and those affected by the expulsion from Spain in 1492 and the forced conversion in Portugal, as well as of the general Jewish population in various periods in my *SRH*, Vols. I, pp. 167 ff., 369 ff.; II, pp. 90 ff., 368 f.; IV, pp. 94 ff., 289 ff.; X, pp. 199 ff., 388 f.; XII, pp. 4 ff., 243 ff.; XVI, pp. 190 ff., 405 ff.; XVII, pp. 160 ff., 361 ff.; XVIII, pp. 184 ff., 510 ff., etc. The varying attitudes toward the expulsion of Jews and Moors from Spain are discussed *ibid.* and in other references, scattered throughout these volumes.

82. E. E. G. Vermeulen, "Was ist Objektivität?" *Saeculum*, XIII (1962), 394–400; Alexander Gershenkron, *Continuity in History and Other Essays*, Cambridge, Mass., 1968, esp. p. 40; and for the interesting description of the story of the school of *Annales*, from the publication of the *Annales d'histoire économique* (the original name of its journal) in 1929, see Manfred Wüstemeyer, above n. 56. Perhaps it is yet too early to agree with Reginald Baker that "for whatever its merits and drawbacks the revolution in historical research is now over." See his "Teaching Quantitative History: a Review Essay," *Historical Methods Newsletter*, X (1970), 90–97 (a review of 8 recent books, 11 films, and 5 audiotape cassettes). On the one hand, at any moment there may arise a new group of brilliant young men and women who will discover new angles and approaches to answer old and new questions. After all, history is a discipline so comprehensive as to embrace almost the totality of life, public and private, in the past—and today's happenings quickly become parts of the past—so that there will always be followers of new trends even beyond their merits. At the same time there will also be less gifted historians who may find acceptance of any new method as an easy substitution for hard work, extensive linguistic training, patience in absorbing the fruits of earlier labors, and coming up with solid evidence for any new sets of assumptions. Out of the ensuing

welter of controversy some kernels of new truths and accesses to them may ultimately emerge which will doubly justify the old adage that every generation rewrites history in a new vein. This has also been the assumption of the ancient rabbis—who insisted on constant study and inventiveness for its own sake in order "to increase and exalt the Torah." They also claimed that "there is no study without innovation" (*ein bet-midrash beli hiddush*), although they did not attach to each such innovation some new name nor added for it some new nomenclature in the modern manner.

CHAPTER VIII: SOCIORELIGIOUS APPROACH

83. François Marie Arouet de Voltaire, *Essai sur les moeurs et l'esprit de nations*, Paris, 1962, elaborated, among others, by Max Nordau in *The Interpretation of History*, trans. from the German by M. A. Hamilton, New York, 1910, pp. 238 f.; Ernest Renan, *Nouvelles études d'histoire religieuse*, new ed., Paris, 1899, p. 462. In fact, Voltaire's extreme criticism of religion, particularly of the Catholic faith and, connected with it, his outspoken anti-Judaism, which in part stemmed also from his admiration for Graeco-Roman anti-Semitism, did not completely nullify the value of his contributions to general historiography. See Arthur Hertzberg, *French Enlightenment and the Jews*, New York, 1968 and the literature listed there. In his perceptive study *Die Entstehung des Historismus*, 2nd ed., Munich, 1946, pp. 74 ff., Friedrich Meinecke rightly pointed out that Voltaire's concept of a broader world history, in contrast with the far narrower outlook of his European predecessors, opened up new horizons for historical understanding. Nor must one overlook the secularizing trends which made themselves felt in earlier historical writings, such as are analyzed in Adalbert Klemp's *Die Säkularisierung der universalhistorischen Auffassung. Zum Wandel des Geschichtsdenkens im 16. und 17. Jahrhundert*, Göttingen, 1960. Göttinger Beiträge zur Geschichtswissenschaft, XXXI; and in Yves-Marie Bercé's "Historiographie des temps modernes. Travaux parus depuis 1950 sur l'histoire et les historiens français du XIVᵉ aux XVIIIᵉ siècle," *Bibliothèque de l'École des Chartes*, CXXIV (1966), 281–95. Yet, these indubitably regnant secularizing trends, expanding from eastern Europe to the rest of the world as a part of its progressive "Westernization," did not deter an author like John T. Marcus from writing his *Heaven, Hell and History: a Survey of Man's Faith in History from Antiquity to the Present*, New York, 1967.

84. The apparent contradiction in Hermann Cohen's emphasis on the primacy of the state over religion in historical development expressed in his *Die Jüdischen Schriften*, esp. II, 323, 331; and his glorification of ancient Israelitic prophets as the creators of "historicism" in his *Die Religion der Vernunft aus den Quellen des Judentums*, Leipzig, 1919, pp. 293 ff., and 307 ff. is easily resolved when one regards his first remark as a mere acceptance of the generally high appreciation of statehood by his German contemporaries. See also Clarence T. Craig, "Biblical Theology and the Rise of Historicism," *JBL*, LXII (1943), 284–94. Of course, Jakob Burckhardt's observation quoted in the text from his *Force and Freedom: Reflections on History* (with Karl Löwith's comments thereon in his *Jacob Burckhardt: der*

Mensch in mitten der Geschichte, Stuttgart, 1966) refers to historical prediction of events expected to occur in a none-too-distant future, whereas the most relevant prophetic predictions are aimed at the messianic end of days. See above, nn. 28 ff.

85. Norman Cohn, *The Pursuit of the Millennium, Revolutionary Messianism in Medieval and Renaissance Europe and Its Bearing on Modern Totalitarian Movements,* 2nd ed., New York, 1961. On the general aspects of historical predictability, see above, nn. 28 ff. We must bear in mind, however, that in the pulsating and innovative intellectual upsurge during the Renaissance and Enlightenment periods so many new seeds were sown, both complementary and contradictory, that later thinkers found a great variety of ideas to choose from to support certain thoughts of their own. Hence came also the diverse interpretations of the "regnant tendencies" in those periods, as are reflected, for instance, in Wallace Klippert Ferguson's survey of *The Renaissance in Historical Thought: Three Centuries of Interpretation,* Cambridge, Mass., 1948.

86. Vladimir Ilyich Lenin, "Socialism and Religion," in his *Selected Works,* 12 vols., ed. by J. Fineberg, New York, 1935–38, XI, 658, 681. On other revolutionary activists among Lenin's equally anti-religious contemporaries, see Adolf Ziegler, *Die russische Gottlosenbewegung,* Munich, 1932; and the literature discussed in my *Modern Nationalism and Religion,* New York, 1947, pp. 197 ff., 331 n. 62. Needless to say, agnosticism and atheism have had a long tradition going back to ancient times. See the extensive data assembled by John Bagnell Bury in *A History of Freedom of Thought* (1913), 2nd ed. with an Epilogue by H. J. Blackham, London, 1959; Fritz Mauthner, *Der Atheismus und seine Geschichte im Abendlande,* 4 vols., Stuttgart, 1920–22; and Hermann Ley in *Geschichte der Aufklärung und des Atheismus,* 2 vols. in 3, Berlin, 1966–71. But the successful Communist Revolution of 1917 enabled Lenin to set in motion the powerful machinery of his increasingly totalitarian regime to impose his doctrines on the predominantly Orthodox Russian population. He probably did not quite realize that his vision of a World Revolution, under the leadership of the Russian Communist Party, bore some striking resemblance to the medieval concept of Moscow as the "Third Rome." See below, n. 88. It may be noted, however, that more recently a Soviet historian, M. A. Alpatov, was able to publish a study entitled *Ruskoya istoricheskaya mysl a Zapadnaya Europa* (Russian Historical Thought and Western Europe [in the Twelfth to the Seventeenth Century]), Moscow, 1976, in which he expatiates on Russia's medieval conception of world history including the doctrine of Moscow serving as the Third Rome.

87. Nicholas A. Berdyaev or Berdiaev, *The Russian Idea,* trans. from the Russian by R. M. Freud, Boston, 1962, Beacon Pamphlets, 139, esp. pp. 29 f.; and, more generally, David Bonner Richardson, *Berdyaev's Philosophy of History: an Existentialist Theory of Social Creativity and Eschatology,* The Hague, 1968.

88. See Gerhard Simon, *Church, State and Opposition in the USSR,* trans. from the German by Kathleen Matchett in Collaboration with the Centre for the Study of Religion and Communism, London, 1974, esp. p. 101; Michel Bourdeaux, *Religious Ferment in Russia: Protestant Opposition to Soviet Religious Policy,* London, 1968; idem, *Patriarch and Prophet: Persecution of the Russian-Orthodox Church Today,* London, 1969; and his report (prepared with the assistance of Kathleen Matchett

and Cornelia Gersten) for the University Rights Group about the *Religious Minorities in the Soviet Union*, London, 1973; Alfred Abraham Greenbaum, "Soviet Nationality Policy and the Problem of the 'Fluid' Nationality," in *Jews and Non-Jews in Eastern Europe, 1918–1945*, ed. by Bela Vago and George L. Mosse, New York, 1974, pp. 257–70; and with special reference to the revival of the interest in the Russian past, see the succinct surveys by George A. Kline, "Religion, National Character and the Rediscovery of Russian Roots," *Slavic Review*, XXXIII (1975), 29–40; Jack V. Bird, "New Interest in Old Russian Things: Literary Ferment, Religious Perspectives and National Self-Assertion," *ibid.*, XXXII (1975), 17–28. See also above, nn. 22 and 33.

The situation in Russia was not completely duplicated in the satellite states. Since many of them joined the Soviet Union after World War II, the peak of antireligious propaganda had long passed and even the communists did not vigorously persist in their struggle against the Churches with the same intensity as they did in pre-war Russia. Each country, moreover, had a national-religious tradition of its own and the vigor and public influence of the local Churches differed from one area to another. The largest among them, Poland, actually witnessed the continuation of a very influential Church structure which has, in many ways, served as a counterpoise to the Communist Party. See Henryk Świątkowski, *Państwo a kościół w świetle prawa. Wybrane zagadnienia* (State and Church in Light of the Law: Selected Problems), 2nd ed., Warsaw, 1960; and, more generally, Vladimir Csovski, *Church and State Behind the Iron Curtain: Czechoslovakia, Hungary, Poland, Rumania*, with an Intro. on the Soviet Union, New York, 1955. Praeger Publications in Russian History, XVII. The recent enthusiastic reception of the Polish Pope John Paul II by millions of his former countrymen during his visit to Poland has confirmed the long-observed attachment of the Polish majority to the Catholic faith despite the decades of communist rule.

89. See Johann Gottlieb Fichte, *The Republic of Germans at the Beginning of the Twentieth Century under the Fifth Imperial Bailiff*, written in 1807 under the impact of Prussia's defeat and partition by Napoleon, though not published until four decades later by Fichte's son and reproduced in the author's *Sämmtliche Werke*, VII, 530–45; Ernst Moritz Arndt, *Eleusinen des 19. Jahrhunderts*, II, 22 f.; the students' proclamation cited by Waldemar Gurian in *Der Kampf um die Kirche im dritten Reich*, Lucerne, 1936, pp. 48 ff.; and for recent developments Hans Gerhard Koch, *Staat und Kirche in der DDR. Zur Entwicklung ihrer Beziehungen von 1945–1974. Darstellung, Quellen, Übersichten*, Stuttgart, 1975; Victor Conzemius, "Églises chrétiennes et totalitarisme national-socialiste," *Revue d'histoire écclesiastique*," LXIII (1968), 437–503, 868–948. Of considerable interest also are the studies by Uriel Tal, *Religious and Anti-Religious Roots of Modern Anti-Semitism*, New York, 1971; his *Christians and Jews in Germany—Religion, Politics, and Ideology in the Second Reich, 1878–1914*; his *Structures of German Political Theology in the Second Reich*, Tel Aviv, 1979; and his more recent lecture, *Law and Theology. On the Status of German Jewry at the Outset of the Third Reich (1933/4)*, Tel Aviv, 1982; Karl Ferdinand Werner, *Das National-Sozialistische Geschichtsbild und die deutsche Geschichtswissenschaft*, Stuttgart, 1967. Lebendiges Wissen; idem, "On Some Examples of the National-Socialist View of History." *JCH*, III/2 (1968), 193–206; above, n. 35.

90. See Giuseppe Calabrò, *La Dottrina religioso-sociale di Giuseppe Mazzini. La religione dell'avvenire*, Palermo, 1912; Armando Carlini, *Filosofia a religione nel pensiero di Mussolini*, Rome, 1934; and the ideological formulations of the religious policies of the Fascist regime by Giovanni Gentile in his *La mia religione, Conferenze*, Florence, 1943. and other studies collected in his *Scritti minori di scienza, filosofia e letteratura*, Florence, 1943. Biblioteca di Leonardo, XXVI. See also Feruccio Pardo, *La Filosofia di Giovanni Gentile. Genesi, sviluppo, unità sistematica, critica*, Florence, 1972; and below, nn. 93–94.

91. Rotraut Wielandt, *Offenbarung und Geschichte im Denken moderner Muslime*, Wiesbaden, 1971. The apparent inconsistencies of the British system have been the outgrowth of a long democratic evolution unbound by a written constitution. Legislation *ad hoc*, as well as judicial sentences based upon often contradictory facts of life, could often be utilized to "muddle through." One certainly does not need to quote a more striking example than the 1744 court decision in the case of Elias de Paz' will. That gentleman had left a testamentary bequest for the London yeshivah. However, the probate judge, Lord Chancellor Philip Yorke Hardwicke argued that, Jews not having been allowed legally to return to England after their expulsion of 1290, the testator could not possibly have intended to leave a sum of money to a school of a legally nonexistant community. He therefore decided to turn over that money to the supposedly nearest object of the testator's will, a Christian theological school. Apparently he acted as a pedantic jurist rather than out of any anti-Jewish animus. (Hardwicke in 1753 joined the sponsors of the pioneering Jew Bill, a major step toward Jewish emancipation.) Here he pointed out the incongruity of the existing legislation which "renders those religions [of the Christian Dissenters] legal, [but] which is not the case of the Jewish Religion, that is not taken notice of by any law, but is barely connived at by the Legislature."

All this happened while the famous Sephardic congregation had already been in full swing for nearly a century (its synagogue being filled at least during Sabbath services with devout worshipers) and even though in 1697 the London Stock Exchange had formally reserved twelve seats, or almost ten percent of its total membership, for London Jews. See H. S. Q. Henriques, *The Jews and the English Law*, Oxford, 1908, pp. 19 ff., 53 ff., 147 ff.; Lucien Wolf, "The First Stage in Anglo-Jewish Emancipation," in his *Essays in Jewish History*, ed. by Cecil Roth, London, 1934, pp. 115–43, esp. p. 134.

92. Harriet Martineau, *Society in America*, 3 vols., 2nd ed., London, 1839, III, 273; John Franklin Jameson, "The American Acta Sanctorum," *AHR*, XIII (1908), 286–302. Among the most overlooked *acta* of this type is the large body of funerary orations and other necrologies, many of them readily found in newspapers, magazines, and easily available pamphlets, which shed much light on both the deceased persons and the speakers or writers who produced them. See, for example, Rudolf Lenz, ed., *Leichenpredigten als Quelle historischer Wissenschaft*, 2 vols., Cologne, 1975–79. To be sure, this type of literature is subject to the shortcomings of most biographical writings and as a rule is even more laudatory of the individual mourned than is characteristic of the description of someone's "life and work," in consonance with the old adage, *de mortuis nil nisi bonum*. Nevertheless the necrologies often furnish many new insights into the character and activities of some

persons who had played a significant role in their days. At the same time they tell us also something about many average men and women, as well as about their family backgrounds, and the social circles within which they had moved.

It is not surprising, therefore, that notwithstanding the official separation of state and Church and, in some respects, because of it, American states have often been greatly preoccupied with religious problems. See, for example, Chester James Antieau *et al.*, *Religion in the State Constitution*, Brooklyn, 1963; the publication by the Commission on Law and Social Action of the American Jewish Congress, *Digest and Analysis of the State Attorney General's Opinions Relating to the Freedom of Religion and Separation of Church and State*, New York, 1959. Of a different kind are the concerns of the Latin-American states with religious problems as illustrated, for one example, by Antonio de Tomaso's *El Estado y la iglesia: escritos y discursos*, Buenos Aires, 1925. Reciprocally, the religious establishments of the various faiths often had to adjust their own structures and policies to the exigencies of the states in which their members lived. See, for instance, the German analysis of *Die Kirche und das Staatsproblem der Gegenwart*, 2nd ed., Berlin, 1935; the interesting essays in *Kirche und Staat*, Festschrift for Bishop Hermann Kunst, Berlin, 1967; and the selected documentation in Sidney Ehler and B. M. Morrall, editors and translators, *Church and State Through the Centuries: a Collection of Historic Documents with Commentaries*, London, 1954.

93. Louis Le Fur, *Le Saint Siège et le Droit de Gens*, Paris, 1930, pp. 202 f.; Hubert Bastgen, *Die Römische Frage. Dokumente und Stimmen*, 3 vols., Freiburg i. B., 1919, III, 19. On their part, Popes Pius XI and XII made similar declarations. See Pius XI's encyclical *Studiorum ducem*, reproduced in English trans. in Harry C. Koenig's *Principle for Peace (Selections from Papal Documents, Leo XIII to Pius XII)*, Washington, D.C., 1943, pp. 343, 347, 364; and Pius XII's discourse at the opening of the Xth International Congress of Historical Studies in Rome on September 7, 1955, reprinted in Simon Delacroix *et al.*, eds., *Documents pontificaux de Sa Sainteté Pie XII*, (1939–58), 20 vols., St. Maurice, 1950 ff. The enormous difficulties in which the Papacy found itself during the Nazi racialist regime led Pius XI, as part of his effort to save Jews in Germany, to exclaim in 1937 that "religiously we are all Jews." On the other hand, his successor, Pius XII, remained silent during the Nazi genocidal activities against the Jews of Rome. These contrasting attitudes have created a prolonged heated discussion in the press and the recent Holocaust literature. See, for instance, Pierre Charles *et al.*, *Racisme et catholicisme*, published in Paris in 1939 in the midst of the Nazi persecutions; and the stormy debates which followed the performances of Rolf Hochhuth's play, *The Deputy*, trans. by Richard and Clara Winston, with a Preface by Albert Schweitzer, New York, 1964 (in England entitled *The Representative*, London, 1963); and Pinchas E. Lapide, *The Last Three Popes and the Jews*, London, 1967.

94. Giuseppe Mazzini, *Scritti editi ed inediti*, Edizione nazionale, 89 vols., and Appendix of 4 vols., Imola, 1906–1940, VI, 263 f.; and Giuseppe Calabrò, *La Dottrina religioso-sociale di Giuseppe Mazzini*; Pius XII's allocution, *New York Times*, December 25, 1945, p. 14; and other data cited in my *Modern Nationalism and Religion*, pp. 48 ff., 91 ff.

95. Marcus Tullius Cicero, *Pro Flacco*, xxviii. 69, in the English trans. of his

Speeches by Louis F. Lord, Cambridge, Mass., 1946, Loeb Classical Library, p. 441. (See also the slight variants and note in Menahem Stern's *Greek and Latin Authors on Jews and Judaism*, ed. with introductions, translations, and commentary, Vols. I–II, Jerusalem, 1974–80, I, 196 ff. No. 68).

96. Sir Ernest Llewellyn Woodward, *Christianity and Nationalism in the Later Roman Empire*, London, 1916, pp. 43 f., 46; Edward R. Hardy, Jr., "The Patriarchate of Alexandria: a Study in National Christianity," *Church History*, XV (1946), 81–100, esp. p. 100; František Graus, "Die Bildung eines Nationalbewusstseins im mittelalterlichen Böhmen (Die vorhussitische Zeit)," *Historica*, XIII (1966), 5–49; other literature listed by E. Seibt in his "Hus und die Husiten in der Czechischen wissenschaftlichen Literatur seit 1945," *Zeitschrift für Ostforschung*, VII, 560–90.

97. Walther Hinz, *Irans Aufstieg zum Nationalstaat im fünfzehnten Jahrhundert*, Berlin, 1936; Jean Aubin, "Le Chiisme et la nationalité persane," *Revue du monde musulman*, IV (1908), 457–90. This interlocking of religious intolerance with imperialist ambitions also led to two waves of sharp persecution of Jews in seventeenth-century Persia. See my *SRH*, Vol. XVIII (1983), pp. 320 ff., 568 ff. nn. 29–37; and the forthcoming publication by Vera B. Moreen, *Iranian Jewry's Hour of Peril and Heroism: A Study of Babai ibn Lutf's Chronicle (1617–1662)*. On the Turko-Greek exchange of population, see Liv Nansen-Høyer, *Mein Vater Fridtjof Nansen: Forscher und Menschenfreund*, Wiesbaden, 1957, pp. 251 ff., esp. p. 253.

98. See Yehudah Halevi, *Kitab al-Khuzari*, Arabic text ed. together with its Hebrew trans. by Yehudah Ibn Tibbon, by Hartwig Hirschfeld, Leipzig, 1887; English trans. with an Intro. by Hirschfeld, and a Preface to a new ed. by Mordecai M. Kaplan, New York, 1927; and my "Yehudah Halevi: an Answer to a Historical Challenge," *JSS*, III (1941), 243–72, reprinted in my *Ancient and Medieval Jewish History: Essays*, pp. 128–48, 433–43, esp. pp. 143 f.

The extreme reverence for the prophets and saints extended also to the sacred Scriptures. Two sixteenth-century episodes are particularly enlightening. When in May 1556 the Roman Inquisition staged, in the harbor-city of Ancona, a public auto-da-fé with the burning of twenty-four New Christians for their secret observance of Judaism, some leaders of Turkish Jewry, led by Doña Gracia Mendes, proclaimed a commercial boycott on Ancona and tried to transfer their trade to the neighboring harbor of Pesaro. The opposition, led by the Istanbul rabbi, Joshua Soncino, pointed above all to a prank played by the brother of the Duke of Urbino who, to quote Soncino, "Because of our [the Jews'] numerous sins, dragged out the scroll of the law and tore it; took a pig, clad it in the scroll's mantle, and placed it in the ark." The ignominy of this act for the Jewish people, the rabbi implied, was even greater than the loss of the lives of twenty-four martyrs for the faith. In 1590 Rome's Jewish community, after being exempted from an earlier papal decree of expulsion, deplored the recurring confiscation and burning of the Talmud and other Hebrew books. In their appeal for assistance addressed to other Italian Jewish communities, the Roman leaders characteristically argued: "If you have done so much to prevent a threatened expulsion, how much more ought you to do for the preservation of the sacred writings which are 'Thy life, and the length of thy days' [a reference to Deut. 30:20]." In other words, the preservation of sacred books and the safeguarding of their honor is supreme in the scale of values. See Joshua

Soncino's *Nahlah li-Yehoshu'a* (Joshua's Heritage; Responsa), Constantinople, 1731 ed., fols. 44b f.; Abraham Berliner, *Geschichte der Juden in Rom*, 2 vols., Berlin, 1893, esp. II, 92 f., 100 ff.; and other sources cited in *JC*, I, 224; and *SRH*, Vols. XIV, pp. 37 ff.; XVIII, pp. 79 ff.

CHAPTER IX: SOCIORELIGIOUS HISTORICAL METHOD

99. See Berthold Spuler, *Die Mongolen in Iran. Politik, Verwaltung und Kultur der Ilchanenzeit, 1220–1350*, 3rd ed., Berlin, 1968, pp. 26, 167 f.; or in the English trans., *History of the Mongols. Based on Eastern and Western Accounts of the Thirteenth and Fourteenth Centuries*, trans. from the German by Helga and Stuart Drummond, Berkeley, 1972. The Islamic World Series; K. C. Chandry, *Role of Religion in Indian Politics (1900–1925)*, Delhi, 1928, p. 1. As Spuler points out, the Mongol rulers themselves often violated their belief in one God by worshiping from time to time some lesser deities and abandoned their insistence on a single ruler. The descendants of Jenghiz Khan in Persia and lands further West ceased to recognize the supremacy of the Great Khan in China and most clearly demonstrated their independence by adopting another religion, as did the Il-Khan Dynasty by embracing Islam in Persia.

100. Henryk Świątkowski, *Państwo a kościół* and the more up-to-date studies of *Poland's Church-State Relations*, ed. by Lawrence Biondi, Chicago, 1981, based on papers presented at an International Symposium on Poland's Church-State Relations, held in October 1979 at Loyola University in Chicago. The vitality of the Catholic faith in Poland has been demonstrated again during the turbulent years of the Polish "Solidarity" Movement and its suppression. Even in the Soviet Union, the archenemy of all established religions, the role of the respective faiths and their religious organizations has been growing since the 1930s. In addition to the literature mentioned above, nn. 22 and 83, see esp. Gerhard Simon's substantial documentation in his *Church, State and Opposition in the U.S.S.R.*, trans. by Kathleen Machett, London, 1974.

The universality of the religious impact on public and private life before the Age of Enlightenment in the seventeenth and eighteenth centuries is widely recognized in almost every important scholarly work by both contemporaries and modern investigators. For instance, the descriptions of the religious life of the Spanish masses in the early modern period by Julio Caro Baroja in *Las Formas Complejas de la vida religiosa; religión, sociedad y carácter de la España de los siglos XVI y XVII*, Madrid, 1978; and William A. Christian, Jr., *Social Religion in Sixteenth Century Spain*, Princeton, 1981, may with modification also be applied to most Christian and Muslim countries of that time. The impact of religious leaders was indeed enormous. Hence for one example, in choosing his highest types of heroes through the ages Thomas Carlyle divided them into six categories of (1) "the hero as divinity," (2) "the hero as prophet," (3) "as poet," (4) "as priest," (5) "as man of letters," (6) "as king." See his *On Heroes, Hero-Worship, and the Heroic in History*, reprinted with emendations and additions in his *Sartor Resartus*, in *The Works*,

Centenary ed. in 30 vols., Vol. V. Needless to say, the behavior even of the secular "heroes" was often deeply motivated by their religious beliefs.

Among recent historians who have laid particular stress on the influence of religion were Jacques Maritain and Arnold Joseph Toynbee. See esp. Emilio Rossi, *Il pensiero politico di Jacques Maritain*, Milan, 1956; Toynbee's *Study of History*, 12 vols., London, 1934–61. Toynbee's emphasis on the universal religious factor in its ramified manifestations, as well as his frequently provocative interpretations, attracted widespread attention also in the historical profession of many lands. By 1963 John C. Rule and Barbara Stevens Crosby were actually prompted to compile a lengthy "Bibliography of Works on Arnold Toynbee, 1946–1960," published in *HT*, IV (1963), 212–33. Among other challenging declarations one pertaining to Jews almost assumed the character of a *cause célèbre* because of its relevance for contemporary anti-Semitism, namely his designation of medieval and modern Judaism as a "fossil." In his irate condemnation of that "fossil," and its offshoot, the State of Israel, and his mainly theological arguments, Toynbee lost all composure in predicting that "On the Day of Judgment the gravest crime standing to the German National Socialist account might be not that they had exterminated a majority of Western Jews, but that they had caused the surviving remnant of Jewry to stumble" by the alleged "deliberate expulsion of the Arab population from districts conquered by the Jewish armed forces between the 15th May, 1948, and the end of that year." See his *A Study*, VIII, 290 f. Quoting this almost unbelievable comparison in his *Address* delivered at the Israel Institute of Yeshiva University in New York on January 18, 1955 and distributed by the Israeli Embassy to the United States (p. 20), Abba Eban derisively replied: "Professor Toynbee is not merely the historian of the twentieth century; he is the Attorney-General of the Almighty upon The Day of Judgment." From among the numerous other replies to Toynbee we need but mention Maurice Samuel's *The Professor and the Fossil*, New York, 1956; and more broadly Peter Kaupp, "Das Judentum in der universalhistorischen Lehre A. J. Toynbees," *Saeculum*, XVII (1966), 223–76; and James Hastings Nichols, "Religion in Toynbee's History," *Journal of Religion*, XXVIII (1944), 99–119. See also, more generally, Toynbee's *Civilization on Trial*, New York, 1948, with my review thereof in the *Political Science Quarterly*, LXIV (1949), 110–13; Herbert Butterfield, *Christianity in European History*, London, 1953. Riddell Memorial Lectures, 23; J. E. Faulkner, *Religious Influence in Contemporary Society*, Columbus, Ohio, 1972; Francisco Gabrieli, *L'Islam nella storia: Saggi di storia e di storiografia musulmana*, Bari, 1966; Gabriel Baer, ed., *Ha-'Ulama u-ba'ayat dat ba-'olam ha-islami* (The Religious Scholars and the Problem of Religion in the Muslim World). Papers Presented in the 1969 Jerusalem Colloquium in Memory of Uriel Heyd, Jerusalem, 1971; Raphaela Lewis, *Everyday Life in Ottoman Turkey*, New York, 1971, with some detailed corrections in F. Davis's review of that work in *Archivum Ottomanicum*, V (1973), 324–26; John T. Marcus, *Heaven, Hell and History: a Survey of Man's Faith in History from Antiquity to the Present*.

It may be noted that the much-discussed secularization and westernization of the countries of Islam was often quite superficial. Reviewing the attitude of the modern Muslim historians, Rotraut Wielandt observed that most of them could not quite share the critical attitude toward their Scripture, the Qu'ran, when compared with that of their Christian colleagues toward the Bible. See Wielandt's *Offenbarung in Geschichte und Denken moderner Muslime* and below, n. 114. Nor must we forget that even in the Age of Reason the very leaders of, and propagandists for, secularization of historiography still frequently spoke in religious terms when depicting what Carl L. Becker called *The Heavenly City of the Eighteenth Century Philosophers*, New Haven, 1946; and Fritz Wagner, "Kirchengeschichte und Profanhistorie im Spiegel Newtons und seiner Zeit," *Saeculum*, XVII (1966), 97–111; also in an English trans. in *HT*, VIII (1969), 97–111. See also Émile Callot's *Les Trois moments de la philosophie théologique de l'histoire: Augustin, Vico, Herder. Situation actuelle* Paris, 1974; and its characteristic juxtaposition of the three great moments in the "theological philosophy of history through the works of St. Augustine, Vico and Herder." The tenor of this study is well characterized by Callot's motto, borrowed from an 1838 work on Vico by Donoso Cortès: "Philosophy of history is impossible without God, for history is a chaos, if God does not establish its framework, directs its course, and shines through its structure."

101. See Paul Kleppner, *The Cross of Culture: a Social Analysis of Mideastern Politics, 1850–1900*, New York, 1970; James E. Wright, "The Ethnocultural Model of Voting: a Behavioral and Historical Critique," *American Behavioral Scientist*, XVI (1972–73), 653–74, esp. pp. 654 f.; Paul Goodman, "A Guide to American Church Membership Data before the Civil War," *Historical Methods*, X/2 (1977), 85–89; and above, n. 57.

For the last several decades American scholarship evinced an increasing interest in the voting patterns of various ethnoreligious groups. It clearly showed that despite the separation of state and Church religious interests and antecedents still influenced voters in purely political elections. See, for instance, Robert T. Bower, *Voting Behavior of American Ethnic Groups*, New York, 1941. The religious issue came to the fore in particular at the presidential elections. Alfred E. Smith's Catholicism played a great role in his defeat in 1928. By 1960, however, the atmosphere of religious toleration had advanced sufficiently for John F. Kennedy to win the election. See the analysis by Saul Brenner in his "Patterns of Jewish-Catholic Democratic Voting and the 1960 Presidential Vote," *JSS*, XXVI (1964), 169–78; Lucy S. Dawidowicz with Leon J. Goldstein, *Politics in a Pluralist Democracy. Studies in Voting in the 1960 Election*, with a Foreword by Richard M. Scammon, New York, 1963. Writing in 1969 after the presidential election of Richard Nixon, Kevin P. Phillips described the collapse of the Democratic coalition after the Kennedy-Johnson administration and observed: "In practically every state and region ethnic and cultural animosities and divisions exceeded all other factors in explaining party choice and identification." See his *The Emerging Republican Majority*, New Rochelle, 1969; Nathan Glazer and Daniel P. Moynihan, *Beyond the Melting Pot*, 2nd ed., Cambridge, Mass., 1970, p. xcv, n. 31; Guy Michelet and Michel Simon, *Classe, religion et comportement politique*, Paris, 1977, especially referring to the French elections of 1966. Of interest also is the very query raised by Alan M. Fisher, "Realignment of the Jewish Vote?" *Political Science Quarterly*, XCIV (1979), 97–110; and Timothy I. Smith's concise analysis of the broader problems of "Religion and Ethnicity in America," *AHR*, LXXXIII (1975), 1155–85. See also such diverse approaches as Michael Hechter's brief analysis of "The Political Economy of Ethnic Change," *American Journal of Sociology*, LXXIX (1974), 1152–56; and Nathan Glazer's *Ethnic Dilemmas, 1964–82*, Cambridge, Mass., 1983.

We must not overlook, however, one major weakness of ethnoreligious minorities which manifested itself many times throughout history; it stemmed from their lack of unity. Rather than uniting their forces even against a very oppressive majority, they indulged in reciprocal accusations and constant tensions. See, for example, the data presented in Donald E. Gelfand and Russell D. Lee, comps., *Ethnic Conflicts and Power, a Cross-National Perspective*, New York, 1973; and the numerous examples of such disunity under various civilizations in my *SRH*. Before long quantitative historians found a promising field for their endeavors to present the voting preferences of the electorate in the readily available quantitative terms. See especially Joel H. Silbey and Samuel T. McSeveney, comps., *Voters, Parties and Elections. Quantitative Essays in the History of American Popular Voting Behavior*, Lexington, Mass., 1972; and Silbey *et al.*, eds., *The History of American Electoral Behavior*, Princeton, 1978. Quantitative Studies in History. See also above, n. 61.

The Jewish vote showed many peculiarities of its own. On the one hand, for many years American Jewish communal leaders, always on the defensive against antisemitic attacks, tried to deny the very existence of a special Jewish group vote. They insisted that Jews, like most other voters, acted from political conviction or out of consideration for their economic or other secular concerns. However, with the deep emotional involvement of American Jews in the survival of the State of Israel, certain leanings of Jewish voters in favor of, or against, particular candidates could well depend on their assessment of the candidates' attitudes to the Middle East conflicts. See Lawrence H. Fuchs, *The Political Behavior of American Jews*, Glencoe, Ill., 1956; and such analyses of local elections as Maurice G. Guysenir, "Jewish Vote in Chicago," *JSS*, XX (1958), 195–214; and Edgar Litt, "Status, Ethnicity, and Patterns of Jewish Voting Behavior of Baltimore," *ibid.*, XXII (1960), 159–64.

102. The institutional and financial disparity between the Anglican and Episcopalian Churches did not prevent their frequent exchanges of views and occasional close cooperation. Such cooperation came to the fore particularly in the decennial Lambeth Conferences. Beginning in 1867, these meetings helped forge a certain unity in both the doctrinal and institutional aspects of the faith. The significant role played by the American clergy not only during these meetings but also in the intervening years was well illustrated by its part in the steering committee of eighteen bishops who passed judgment on various important problems on an interim basis. The share of the American Episcopal Church of four bishops equaled numerically the total representation of the Anglican Church of England and Wales. See Sidney Dark, *The Lambeth Conferences. Their History and Their Significance*, London, 1930. On the period until World War II and its aftermath, see the literature listed in my *Modern Nationalism and Religion*, p. 314 n. 68.

103. On "Judeus" and its equivalent as a family name or a technical term see, for instance, my *JC*, III, 185 n. 8; *SRH*, IV, 271 n. 84; V, 126. The story of Anacletus II has often been told, see the literature listed *ibid.*, IV, 237 n. 8; Joachim Prinz, *Popes from the Ghetto*, New York, 1966. See also W. F. Monypenny and G. F. Buckle, *The Life of Benjamin Disraeli, Earl of Beaconsfield*, 6 vols., Lon-

don, 1910–20; my Introduction to Georg Brandes' *Lord Beaconsfield: a Study of Benjamin Disraeli*, New York, 1966 (also in paperback); John Vinecur, "A Most Special Cardinal," *The New York Times Magazine* of March 20, 1983, pp. 29–31, 76–77, 88–90. On the complicated "Problems of Jewish Identity from the Historical Perspective," see my survey under this title in the *American Academy for Jewish Research, Jubilee Volume (1928–29/1978–79)*, ed. by Salo W. Baron and Isaac E. Barzilay, 2 vols., Jerusalem, 1980, I, 33–67.

104. See Harry S. Linfield, "Jewish Population in the United States," *American Jewish Year Book*, XXX (1927), 101–198; idem, "Statistics of Jews and Jewish Organizations in the United States: an Historic Review of Ten Censuses, 1850–1937," *ibid.*, XL (1937), 61–84; idem, "Jewish Communities in the United States: Number and Distribution of Jews of the United States in Urban Places and Rural Territory," *ibid.*, XLII (1940–41), 215–56.

105. Sophia Robison with the assistance of Joshua Starr, eds., *Jewish Population Studies*, New York, 1944. Publications of Jewish Social Studies, III (still a basic book in the field); followed by Ben B. Seligman and Harvey Swados, "Jewish Population Studies in the United States," *American Jewish Year Book*, L (1948–49), 651–90; and Uri Zvi Engelman, "Jewish Statistics in the United States Census of Religious Bodies, 1850–1936," *JSS*, IX (1947), 127–74, esp. pp. 158 ff. See also my *Steeled by Adversity*, esp. pp. 127 ff., 269 ff., 603 f., 625 ff. On the contemporary situation see, esp. the brochures published under the direction of Fred Massarik, Alvin Chenkin *et al.*, by the Council of Jewish Federations and Welfare Boards in New York, since 1974, *Jewish Identity, Facts and Planning; Demographic Highlights, Facts and Planning; National and Regional Population Counts, Facts and Planning;* and others concerning Jewish Education, Jewish Aging and Intermarriages. Another effort in this direction is being made at present by Marshall Sklare and associates at Brandeis University.

106. See my "Impact of Wars on Religion," *Political Science Quarterly*, LXVII (1952), 534–72; reprinted in my *Steeled by Adversity*, pp. 417–53, 679–85; and my "Freedom and Constraint in the Jewish Community: a Historic Episode." *Essays and Studies in Memory of Linda R. Miller*, New York, 1938, pp. 9–23. Mixed marriages between Jews and Christians were an extremely delicate subject in the long struggle for Jewish Emancipation. Typical of the attitude of the majority of the Austrian population in the nineteenth century was the analysis presented by the Austrian State Councillor, Josef von Knorr, in his extensive memorandum of 1834 about the problems of ameliorating the status of Austrian Jewry. Knorr admitted that in some provinces of the Empire, especially in Lombardy-Venetia and Dalmatia, Jews already enjoyed practically full equality of rights except for "admission to government posts and marriages to Christians." He invoked the old antagonism of the Christian majority toward Jews whom it considered "adversaries and declared enemies of its religion." He pointed out in this connection that for centuries a wall of separation had kept Jews away from Christians, "especially in that closest bond in societal relationships, namely marriage." See the text of that memorandum reproduced by A. F. Pribram in his *Urkunden und Akten zur Geschichte der Juden in Wien*, Part I, Vol. II, Vienna, 1918, pp. 348–62, esp. p. 350.

107. See Edward Sculley Bradley, *Henry Charles Lea: a Biography*, Philadelphia,

1931, esp. p. 118; and the older but still valuable analysis by John Neville Figgi in *The Theory of the Divine Right of Kings* (1896), new impression, New York, 1965. For this reason the assassination even of an oppressive monarch was considered not only a crime, but also a serious religious sin. Even the "regicides" of Charles I of England in 1649, though acting on the basis of a formal trial, after the Restoration in 1660 paid dearly for their role in the king's execution. See Cicely V. Wedgwood, *A Coffin for King Charles: the Trial and Execution of Charles I*, New York, 1964; and, more generally, Harold G. Nicolson, *Monarchy*, London, 1963. On the religious impulses within England's Commercial Revolution, see, for example, Louis B. Wright's *Religion and Empire: the Alliance between Piety and Commerce in English Expansion, 1558–1625*, Chapel Hill, N.C., 1943.

108. See the Great Khan Göyük's letter to Pope Innocent IV reproduced in Paul Pelliot *et al.*, "Les Mongols et la Papauté. Documents nouveaux, édités, traduits et commentés," *Revue de l'Orient chrétien*, XXIII (1922–23), 3–30; XXIV (1924), 225–335; XXVIII (1931–32), 3–84, esp. XXIII, 13 ff., here given in a variant from the English translation in Bertold Spuler's *History of the Mongols*, pp. 69 f. (also reproducing a contemporary Latin translation of Göyük's letter to Innocent IV). See also some other literature listed in my *SRH*, Vol. XVII, p. 366 n. 27.

109. See my addresses, "Maimonides, the Leader and Lawgiver," *Essays on Maimonides: an Octocentennial Volume*, ed. by Salo W. Baron, New York, 1941, p. 17; and "Some Medieval Jewish Attitudes to the Muslim State," in my *Ancient and Medieval Jewish History: Essays*, pp. 77–94, 399–403, esp. pp. 82 f.; Shelomo David Goitein, *Jews and Arabs: Their Contacts Through the Ages*, New York, 1955, p. 104. Some contemporary tensions between Church and state are analyzed in the aforementioned (n. 78), *Die Kirche und das Staatsproblem in der Gegenwart*, Berlin, 1975. See also above, n. 92.

110. See Jer. 31:29; Ez. 18:2; Emil L. Fackenheim, *God's Presence in History: Jewish Affirmations and Philosophical Reflections*, Containing the Charles F. Deems Lectures delivered at New York University in 1968, New York, 1970.

111. The trial of Jesus and the general responsibility of Jerusalem Jewry for the death of the founder of Christianity have been the subject of endless debates not only between Jews and Christians but also within Christianity itself. Modern scholars, using the usual techniques of historical research, have often doubted the reports in the Gospels by pointing out especially the recorded loss of capital jurisdiction by the ancient Sanhedrin *before* the purported trial. This controversy seemed to have largely been settled after the publication of Hans Lietzmann's "Der Prozess Jesu," *Sitzungsberichte* of the Preussische Akademie der Wissenschaften in Berlin, Philos.-hist. Klasse, 1931, pp. 313–22; and the subsequent discussion thereon by Martin Dibelius in "Das historische Problem der Leidensgeschichte," Maurice Goguel, "À propos le procès de Jésus," and F. Büchsel in "Noch einmal: Zur Blutsgerichtsbarkeit des Synhedrions," all in *Die Zeitschrift für Neutestamentliche Wissenschaft*, XXX (1931), 193–201; XXXI (1932), 289–301; XXXIII (1934), 84–87. The arguments of these Christian theologians were supplemented by such observations of Jewish scholars as those of the historian Elias Bickermann in his "Utilitas crucis: Observations sur les récits du procès de Jésus dans les Evangiles canoniques," *Revue d'histoire des Religions*, CXII (1933), 169–241; the rabbinic

scholar Solomon Zeitlin in his *Who Crucified Jesus?*, 2nd ed., New York, 1947; and the jurist Max Radin in his *The Trial of Jesus of Nazareth*, Chicago, 1931. Even from the Catholic side the tradition, at least insofar as it affected the Church's attitude to the alleged responsibility of modern Jewry for their ancestors' role in the crucifixion of Jesus, seemed to have been peremptorily disposed of through the pertinent canon of the ecumenical Second Vatican Council of 1961–65.

The new attitude of the Catholic Church has also come to the fore in a small but significant liturgical alteration. From ancient times the Catholic worshipers all over the Mediterranean world inserted into their services on Good Friday a prayer reading: "We pray also for the unbelieving [*perfidis*] Jews that their God and Lord should remove their veil from their hearts and they themselves should recognize our Lord Jesus Christ." This prayer, attributed to Pope Gelasius (92–96 C.E.), was greatly moderated in recent years by the omission of the adjective *perfidis*. See the text of *The Gelasion Sacramentary*, reproduced in J. P. Migne's *Patrologia Latina*, LXXIV, 1105, and the analysis thereof in Louis Canet's "La Prière 'pro Judaeis' de la liturgie catholique romaine," *REJ*, LXI (1911), 213–21; and in John M. Österreicher's "Pro Perfidis Judaeis," *Theological Studies*, VIII (1947), 80–96. See also the observations and further literature cited in my *SRH*, Vols. II, pp. 67 ff., 168 f., 358 ff., 395 n. 52; V, pp. 351 f. n. 68. The ensuing meager results are described by Pinchas E. Lapide in his *The Last Three Popes and the Jews*, pp. 301 ff.

112. Modern historical science has generally rejected this testimony of censured legends and myths. However, Johann Wolfgang von Goethe long ago opposed such indiscriminate repudiation as brought about by August Christian Niebuhr's researches in ancient Roman history through exclaiming, "if the Romans were great enough to invent such beautiful stories [as those related to Mucius Scaevola and Lucretia], we should at least be sufficiently great to believe them." See also Karl Löwith's *The Meaning of History*; and Adolf Allwohn, *Der Mythus bei Schelling*, Charlottenburg, 1927. Ergänzungshefte to the Kant-Studien, LXI. See also *SRH*, Vol. VI, p. 440 n. 99; and above, nn. 14 and 44.

113. Morton Smith, "Historical Method in the Study of Religion," in James S. Heller, ed., *On Method in the History of Religions*, Middletown, n.d. [1968]; *HT* Studies in the Philosophy of History, Beiheft VIII, pp. 8–16; Georg Faber, *Theorie der Geschichtswissenschaft*, 4th ed., Munich, 1978. Becksche Schwarze Reihe, LXXVIII, pp. 23 ff., Chapter: "Was ist Geschichte?"; Hans Grotz, "Der wissenschaftliche Standort der Kirchengeschichte heute," *Zeitschrift für Katholische Theologie*, XLII (1970), 140–66; S. Bonstany and D. Cohen, "Essai de traduction des *Ad'dad*," in Jean Paul Charney, ed., *L'Ambivalence dans la culture arabe*, Paris, 1967, pp. 452–61, and other essays in this volume; Robert Brunschvig, "Variations sur le thème du doute dans le *fiqh*," *Studi orientalistici*, in Honor of Giorgio Levi della Vida, 2 vols., Rome, 1952, Vol. I, pp. 61–82. See also my remarks and additional literature in *SRH*, Vol. XVII, pp. 167 f., 375 nn. 52–53; and above, n. 57.

114. See Malik Bennabi, *Le Phénomène coranique, essai d'une théorie sur le Coran*, Paris, 1948, p. 105; Rotraut Wielandt, *Offenbarung und Geschichte im Denken moderner Muslime*, pp. 119 ff., 129.

115. See Pius XI's encyclical, *Quadragesimo Anno*, reproduced in the English translation by Harry C. Koenig, *Principle for Peace (Selections from Papal Documents,*

Leo XIII to Pius XII); J. N. Moody *et al.*, eds., *Church and Society: Catholic Social and Political Thought and Movements*, New York, 1953, pp. 840 ff., 886 f.; Alexis de Tocqueville, *Democracy in America*, trans. by Henry Reeves, and ed. by Henry S. Commager, New York, 1947, pp. 195 ff. See also, from another angle, Raymond Collyer Knox, *Religion and the American Dream*, with an Intro. by Nicholas Murray Butler, New York, 1934.

116. Friedrich Daniel Schleiermacher, *Predigten*, 4 vols., Berlin, 1843 (*Sämmtliche Werke*, 33 vols., Berlin, 1835–64, Vols., XIV–XVII), I, 353 ff., 364 (1808); IV, 34 (1809), and other passages quoted in my *Modern Nationalism and Religion*, pp. 136 ff., 309 ff. nn. 42 ff. That the distinguished preacher could not completely live up to the noble sentiments expressed in the passage here quoted was not surprising. We must not forget that, from week to week, he had to voice feelings engendered by the rapidly changing political and military situations during the Napoleonic wars.

CHAPTER X: METHODOLOGICAL PLURALISM

117. See the first edition of my *SRH*, Vol. II, p. 451.

Index

I N HIS LATEST BOOK the author of the classic multivolume *Social and Religious History of the Jews* steps back from his usual close, archival work to survey the entire field of historical scholarship from a perspective possible only from someone with his long and vast experience. Salo Baron covers history from antiquity to today, from the Mediterranean region to the Western world, critically assessing the various approaches to the study of history that have come into (and fallen from) fashion during his own years of writing history. Included are psycho-history, quantitative history, the socio-religious approach, and social-cultural analysis. While many of Baron's examples are taken from his field of expertise, Jewish history, they often have universal connotations since the Jewish past spans three milennia and tremendous geographical distance.

Baron also looks beyond the methods of history to examine the meaning of historical study in a much broader sense, discussing "historical objectivity" and questioning whether it is even possible to achieve such a perspective. In his fascinating discourse he addresses the questions of why we study history to begin with, and what intellectual and psychological needs are fulfilled by continually

RUSH
OH!

RUSH
OH!

A Novel

Shirley Barrett

Little, Brown and Company
New York Boston London

Copyright © 2015, 2016 by Shirley Barrett

All rights reserved. In accordance with the U.S. Copyright Act of 1976, the scanning, uploading, and electronic sharing of any part of this book without the permission of the publisher constitute unlawful piracy and theft of the author's intellectual property. If you would like to use material from the book (other than for review purposes), prior written permission must be obtained by contacting the publisher at permissions@hbgusa.com. Thank you for your support of the author's rights.

Little, Brown and Company
Hachette Book Group
1290 Avenue of the Americas, New York, NY 10104
littlebrown.com

First North American Edition: March 2016
Originally published in Australia by Picador, a division of Pan Macmillan Australia Pty. Ltd., September 2015

Little, Brown and Company is a division of Hachette Book Group, Inc. The Little, Brown name and logo are trademarks of Hachette Book Group, Inc.

The publisher is not responsible for websites (or their content) that are not owned by the publisher.

The Hachette Speakers Bureau provides a wide range of authors for speaking events. To find out more, go to hachettespeakersbureau.com or call (866) 376-6591.

Illustrations (except for those on pages vii and ix) by Matt Canning / The Illustration Room

ISBN 978-0-316-26154-8
LCCN 2015952954

10 9 8 7 6 5 4 3 2 1

RRD-C

Printed in the United States of America

For
Sabrina and Emmeline

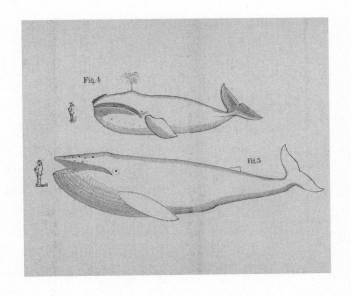

If you ever ever ever ever ever
If you ever ever ever see a whale
You must never never never never never
You must never never never touch its tail
For if you ever ever ever ever ever
If you ever ever ever touch its tail
You will never never never never never
You will never never see another whale.

ANON.

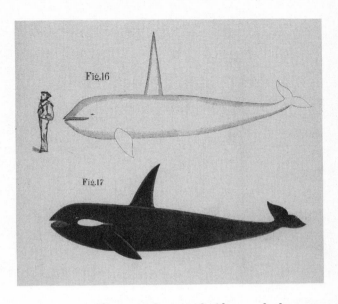

Fig.16

Fig.17

There are few people, if any, who have not
heard of the Killer Whales of Twofold Bay—
of the great help they render to the whaling
crews at Eden and the names they bear, such
as Tom, Hooky, Humpy and Cooper…
And yet those who have known these strange
creatures for a lifetime look upon them as
friends; yes, just as much friends to the
whaling crews as the cattle dog to the drover;
just about as much, if not a little more so.

EDEN OBSERVER AND SOUTH COAST ADVOCATE
27 NOVEMBER 1903

RUSH
OH!

A Visitor

OUR HOUSE WAS SITUATED UP THE HILL FROM THE TRY-works, which meant not only were we enveloped in the stench of boiling blubber for five months of the year, but also that our garden must needs incorporate various vestiges of dead marine life. The jaws of a large white pointer shark, in which the children liked to pretend they were being eaten, formed an ornamental feature near the front gate, while the path leading up to the house was laid with the pulverized remains of whale vertebrae, creating an effect not unlike pebbles, although considerably sharper underfoot. The towering rib cage of a ninety-foot blue whale sat amidst a winter display of jonquils; my father had had the men haul it closer to the house that he might contemplate its grandeur while enjoying his evening pipe. In a bid to soften its stark appearance (and incidentally create a kind of pergola), I had attempted to train a wisteria over it; however the wisteria had never taken to the task and its gnarled tendrils did nothing to dispel, in fact

3

seemed generally to enhance, the somewhat gloomy aspect of the mammal's parched remains. Certainly they cast an impression upon the visitor now standing before them, for he issued a low whistling sound through his teeth and shook his head slowly.

Before proceeding further, I should pause to mention that at the time my sisters and I were slave to a great many "kitchen superstitions," some of which we had learned from others, and many of which we had simply invented ourselves. For example, if when washing dishes a cup or a plate is overlooked, then that is a sign that you will soon hear tidings of a wedding. This particular superstition had failed us many times, but was later to come true in circumstances so close to home that we have persisted in believing in it, even in spite of the frequency with which we forget to wash things and the relative infrequency of hearing about weddings. Perhaps owing to our distance from the township of Eden, we had developed a whole series of superstitions regarding the impending arrival of visitors. If the kettle was accidentally placed on the fire with the spout facing backwards, then a stranger was coming to see us. If, after sweeping a room, the broom was left in a corner, then the sweeper would shortly meet her true love. Of course, as can be imagined, this led to a greater interest in sweeping and a good deal of leaving brooms about in corners, until we decided that the leaving of brooms had to be accidental or the effect was otherwise null and void. I convey this information simply for the purpose of setting the scene, for late that particular afternoon in June 1908, I had almost finished sweeping out the bedrooms when I glimpsed from the window the visitor gazing solemnly at the rib bones as I have just described. Throwing off my apron, I hurried out to the veranda, and in doing so, *I left the broom in the corner of that bedroom.*

"Good afternoon," the visitor called out to me. "I'm looking for George Davidson."

"He's in town," I responded. "He should be back before sundown."

"I hear he's putting together crews for his whaleboats," said the stranger, stooping to pluck a jonquil, which he proceeded to place in his buttonhole. (The jonquil display had been another of my attempts at "softening" the rib cage, yet in truth the effect was not entirely harmonious.) "Does he need another, do you know?"

"He does," responded my younger brother Dan, who had joined me on the veranda. "Tell me, can you row hard?"

"I can."

"Have you chased a whale before?"

"I've not," confessed the stranger, strolling up the path towards us, whale bones crunching underfoot. "But I can fish."

"They're bigger than fish."

"Much bigger?"

"Oh yes, quite considerably. Have you never seen a whale up close before?"

"I've not."

"Well then, you're in for quite a surprise." Dan took an old clay pipe from his pocket now, and tapped at it thoughtfully. "Mary, perhaps if you showed our visitor your artwork, it might convey more clearly some sense of their dimensions?"

At this, the stranger turned to me, and his face broke into a broad grin. I'm not sure what prompted this; perhaps Dan's lofty manner amused him (Dan was a small boy and looked younger than his twelve years).

"You sketch?" inquired the stranger.

"Yes, somewhat; mainly whaling scenes," I replied. My cheeks reddened. How dreary and bluestocking it seemed suddenly, to enjoy such a pastime. Nor was this impression helped by the fact that I was indeed wearing my blue stockings.

"One of Mary's depictions received a Highly Commended at the Eden Show just past," said Dan stoutly. "Go and fetch it, Mary," he encouraged, giving me a shove.

Although I am not usually one to put myself forward, I did as I was bid, for I felt an urge to cast an interesting impression of myself upon this gentleman. When I returned, I saw that Dan had perhaps been affected by a similar impulse, for he was now engaged in the act of demonstrating to the stranger the action of my father's whale gun. Dan had been expressly forbidden to so much as touch the whale gun since he and one of the Aboriginal children had used it for shooting minnows in the creek and only with the greatest good fortune avoided blowing away their own legs. Calmly I wrenched it from his grasp and placed it aside.

"My father rarely uses it," I explained to the stranger. "It scares the Killers away. Besides, it has a powerful kick that can knock you clear out of the boat and into the water. Dan here tried it once and had a bruise the size of a dinner plate on his chest."

"Show him your picture for God's sake, Mary," muttered

Dan, having no wish for me to go into further details on the subject.

"Very well," I replied.

"Stern All, Boys!" (which, as formerly mentioned, had received a Highly Commended in the Eden Show just past) depicts the moment when the whale receives the fatal lance and lashes the water in its death flurry. My father, the headsman, is standing at the bow of the boat applying the lance, and it is he who is calling out for the men to row hard astern in a bid to escape the fury of the tormented monster. You can see from the position of the whale's enormous flukes that its tail will crash down upon the boat at any moment. It is spouting blood; also, there is a fountain of blood issuing from the point where the lance enters the whale's vitals, spraying over the men and giving them a most ghoulish appearance. One of the striking features of the painting is the look of abject terror on the faces of the crew, with the exception of my father, who is known locally by the sobriquet of "Fearless." My brother Harry is the most terrified of them all. He is gazing up beseechingly at the giant flukes and wringing his hands like a girl (in fact, he was quite annoyed with me about this representation, and the subject was to remain a sore point between us). Amidst the commotion, one of the men has fallen into the sea and is in the throes of drowning, while another is depicted struggling valiantly for life in the grip of the whale's mighty jaws. Meanwhile, in the water circling the thrashing leviathan, are the Killer whales Tom, Hooky, Humpy, Typee, Jackson, Charlie Adgery and Kinscher—each of them identifiable by the distinguishing characteristics of their dorsal fins. Hooky is pushing at the whale from below to ensure it does not sound. Tom is jumping across the creature's

blowhole. Jackson is endeavoring to force open the jaws of the whale in a bid to tear out a portion of its tongue, while Humpy looks on approvingly.

All in all, it is quite a dramatic representation, and a great favorite with the children. Some considered it ought to have been awarded first prize; however, for reasons of their own which remain mysterious, the judges deemed otherwise. Admittedly, there were some small inaccuracies (the whale I have depicted started off as a humpback but, after some difficulty rendering the head, it ended up as a sperm whale; truth be told, however, sperm whales have never been sighted in Twofold Bay). It was rumored that the judges may have found the painting too gruesome—if this was the case, then I consider it curious, as I know that one of these judges was to be seen on the cliff tops cheering heartily whenever such a scene unfolded in real life. In truth, I suspect that the real reason *"Stern All, Boys!"* was deemed unworthy of a prize is that the subject matter was considered unsuitable for a young lady. Far better that I had employed my talents depicting three cows in a paddock at sunset, as did Miss Eunice Martin of Towamba, for which effort she received the coveted blue ribbon.

"Whales eat folk?" asked the stranger finally. He had been gazing steadily at the painting for some moments.

"Not commonly," I replied. "I have embellished a few small details."

"There's nothing to say a sperm whale wouldn't eat a man," said Dan. "Didn't Moby Dick eat Ahab?"

"I don't know. I can't remember," I said. "He may have done."

"Well, in any case, there's nothing to stop a fellow from falling into a whale's mouth," said Dan. "The whale may be just about to spit him out as so much gristle."

The stranger continued to study the painting in silence. I could see his brows knit and the muscles of his jaw tighten, and for a long time he gazed at it and said nothing. Evidently it was the first time he had seen whaling depicted in detail, and given that he had just volunteered for the job, perhaps he was experiencing misgivings.

Stern All, Boys!

"There's a lot of blood," he said finally. "Perhaps you could have shown less of it."

I stiffened. A surge of indignation rose up within me.

"Forgive me, but I felt it my responsibility to deliver an accurate pictorial representation. There *is* a lot of blood. Isn't there, Dan?"

"Oh yes," agreed Dan. "Whaling's not for the queasy."

"I never said I was queasy," said the visitor, seemingly slightly annoyed at the implication. "I just said how there's a deal of blood."

"Then perhaps you would prefer I confine my pictorial efforts to pastoral settings," I responded. "A cow or two in a paddock—would that be a more suitable subject for a young lady?"

"Leave it, Mary," said Dan.

"Never mind that one of Miss Martin's cows seemed for all the world to have five legs! I've never heard of a five-legged cow, have you?"

"There was a calf born in Bega with five legs," said Dan.

"That story was completely *apocryphal!*"

Just at that moment, our youngest sisters Annie and Violet cried out from the bottom of the garden—my father's motor launch, *Excelsior*, had rounded the headland and could be seen approaching. They galloped down to the jetty to meet him, followed by our dogs hot on their heels, anxious to convey the impression that they had remained vigilant and not spent the entire afternoon dozing in the sun. Forgetting his worldly manner, Dan stashed his pipe in his pocket and took off down to the jetty also. My father had been into Eden to pick up stores, and there was always the chance that he had thought to include some small confectionery or trifle.

"Well, sir," I ventured at last, turning to the stranger. "Are you still up for adventure, or has my painting put you off?"

"No," he said. "I mean, yes. In truth, it has scared the bejesus out of me."

A wave of alarm overtook me. I may not have yet mentioned that our visitor was remarkably handsome, and whalers as a rule were not celebrated for their good looks.

"Oh no, you mustn't let my picture deter you," I entreated. "Whaling is generally considered no more dangerous than fishing, albeit whales are larger than fish."

"Yes," he replied. "I think I am clear on that point now."

"Also, to be perfectly honest, we don't catch that many whales," I continued. "Oh, enough to get by certainly, and make a decent—well, a living of sorts, but…" Here I trailed off, for he glanced at me curiously. "The truth is, sir, my father could certainly use an extra hand at the oars."

I gazed at him imploringly and hoped that my spectacles were sitting straight. So often they sat askew, which gave me the appearance of a character in a musical comedy.

"This comment I made regarding the amount of blood," he said. "That was unwarranted. Forgive me."

"There's no need," I replied, surprised and, in truth, greatly pleased. "Your comment was perfectly understandable. However, I think you'll soon find that there *is* a lot of blood, perhaps more than one would reasonably expect."

"Yes," murmured the stranger, gazing off. "That is so often the case."

He fell silent now, apparently absorbed in his own thoughts. I strained to think of some additional remark that would assist my cause but could think of nothing, so instead stood sucking my lower lip between my teeth, a habit of mine when nervous. The dogs were barking furiously as my father maneuvered the *Excelsior* alongside the jetty; my brother Harry, at the bow of the vessel, tossed the rope to Dan, who jumped at it eagerly and missed. It ended up in the water. Harry pulled it out again, cursing Dan freely.

"Well, then," said the stranger at last. "Here goes for a cool, collected dive at death and destruction, and the devil fetch the hindmost."

And with that, he smiled at me, tipped his cap and strolled off down the hill to meet my father.

I stood for a moment and watched him go, then turned and hurried back inside. An odd feeling of distraction overcame me: I proceeded to sweep again with great thoroughness several rooms I had previously swept.

A Minister of the Methodist Church

GIVEN THE SHORTAGE OF WHALE MEN AFTER THE MIS-fortunes of last season, my father was pleased to make the acquaintance of John Beck (for that was the name of our visitor).

"And what kind of experience have you had?" he asked, after the initial introductions.

"Well, sir, up until recent times I was a minister of the Methodist church," John Beck replied. At this, the children stared and Harry embarked upon a series of snorting sounds (my brother had a problem with his adenoids). My father silenced him at once with a look.

"That is well and good," said my father, turning back to John Beck. "But what kind of experience as regards whaling?"

"Ah," said John Beck. "None, to be exact."

At this, both men gazed down sadly at the wooden boards of our jetty.

"It's a bad thing we lost Burrows," said Uncle Aleck that evening, as we sat around the kitchen table. "He was a good man when sober, and a fine oarsman. What makes you think this clergyman can row?"

"If he can't, then he'll learn soon enough," said my father.

"Perhaps he will row for Jesus," offered Dan, who was at the time a Junior Soldier with the Salvation Army. They would sometimes visit in a bid to minister to our Aboriginal whale men, but had so far only succeeded in recruiting Dan to their ranks. The Aborigines enjoyed the hymn singing, but that was about it.

"Also, Dad," said Harry, "I bumped into Robert Heffernan in town today and he mentioned to me that he would be very keen for you to consider him, if you are still short of oarsmen."

At this, my father turned and gazed suspiciously at my sister Louisa, but she continued to eat, paying no attention to the conversation around her. (I have not mentioned Louisa in detail yet, but I will get to her soon enough.)

"Well," he said. "I may have to at that, if we're to run two boats."

"God help us, George, two new chums and one an ex-clergyman!" cried Uncle Aleck. "You'll sink like a stone out there."

VOICES WHISPER

That the usual preparations for whaling in Eden will be ready by the 15th.

That the Killers, true to their custom, are about; and whales may be expected soon to show—or cry "hello," and bellow.

That Hopkins, our local butcher, who will never be beat in the dispensing of meat, in charge of bullocks whose fat would fill full street.

That our Eden horse, since last referred to, has masticated a fishing net and pair of boots.

That if he is not watched he will swallow a whale after the Killers are done with it.

EDEN OBSERVER AND SOUTH COAST ADVOCATE

A Good Fish Is Tom

WHILST IN TOWN, MY FATHER TOLD US, HE HAD HAD occasion to stop in at the Great Southern Hotel, where a gentleman recounted to him an amusing incident. It seems that very morning the gentleman had been fishing for snapper in the bay when all of a sudden he experienced a different "bite" to that which he had been anticipating. A group of Killer whales had materialized alongside his dinghy and, amidst the general spouting and breaching, one of their number had grasped the boat's kellick between his teeth and proceeded to tow the vessel at speed in the direction of the open sea. The man clung to the gunwales and began to weep, for he feared he might never again see his loved ones; yet just as they passed South Head, the kellick was dropped as summarily as it was taken and the Killer and his entourage departed. Finding himself thus abandoned, the unhappy fellow was then forced to row a distance of some several miles back to his starting point. "Whereupon I discovered that the snapper had long ago dispersed," he concluded, amidst general laughter in the front bar of the Great Southern.

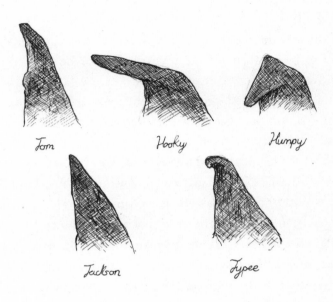

When the good-natured joshing had subsided, my father asked the gentleman if he could describe to him the appearance of the particular Killer whale who had taken the kellick.

"Why yes," the fisherman responded. "He was of about twenty-five feet in length, in rude good health, shiny black in color with gleaming white marks around his middle."

My father nodded thoughtfully. "And tell me, did you observe any peculiarity of the dorsal fin?"

"Well, sir, it was probably six feet in height and boasted a small knob or protuberance about midway up its trailing edge," replied the fisherman.

At this, many of the surrounding drinkers at once erupted into knowing chuckles.

"Then you should count yourself privileged," my father said, smiling. "For that was Master Tom himself who took your kellick."

Tom was the leader of the Killers, and his age was calculated to be upwards of sixty years old, for he had been my grandfather's lieutenant, just as he was my father's. In spite of his distinguished years, his demeanor was ever that of a cheeky schoolboy, the sort that might steal your apples or throw rocks at you from across the street, but nonetheless a good boy in his heart and loved by all who knew him. As well as his duties as Chief Scallywag and Rouseabout, it was Tom who would generally take it upon himself to alert my father and his men whenever he and his companions had herded a whale into the bay. Leaving his team to keep the hapless beast in check with their usual antics, he would make haste across the bay to our whaling station at Kiah Inlet, whereupon he would flop-tail vigorously in a bid to attract the attention of the whalers. There was no more welcome sound than the resounding *smack!* as Tom's mighty tail crashed down upon the water. The men would cry, "Rush oh!" and run to the whaleboats. Once the boats were put out, Tom (an impatient fish by nature) would lead them directly to the spot where his chums had corralled the whale. Occasionally, if engaged in a particularly exciting scrap that demanded his full attention, Tom would send an offsider to rouse us, but mostly he preferred to take this task upon himself. Rather like my father in this way, Tom was the sort of fish who liked to see a job done properly, even if it meant doing it himself.

Any account of Tom and the wonderful assistance he and his team provided our whalers, however, should not exclude the fact that this mischievous Killer whale could at times be as much hindrance as help. Several times over the years, we had experienced a number of incidents involving Tom and the whale line, resulting in the loss or near-loss of the whale. I shall endeavor to explain.

When stuck with a harpoon, a whale's natural response is to set off at great speed in a bid to escape the sting of the iron. The men chock their oars and are thus towed along behind it, great walls of water rising up on either side of their boat. Much skill is required to ensure that the whale has rope enough to run (and thus exhaust itself) without pulling the whale line out of the boat entirely. There is no more disheartening sight to a whale man than that of a whale swimming out of the heads with an iron in its side and fifty fathoms of rope trailing after it.

In all the danger and uproar of this hair-raising "sleigh ride," the last thing that is needed is for a Killer whale to suddenly attach himself to the whale line and hang on for grim life, and yet this is exactly what occurred on several occasions. As if losing his head in the excitement, Tom would throw himself upon the taut rope and hang there by his teeth, thus causing himself to be towed rapidly through the water along with the whaleboat. (I have never had the good fortune to witness this, but have had it described to me in detail; I had even attempted to re-create the scene in oils for the Eden Show the year previous, once again with little success.) Why Tom engaged in this behavior, no one could say; whether it was a bid to slow the whale's progress by adding his own body weight;

or simply for the enjoyable sensation of being pulled forcibly through the water. Whatever the reason, his antics were not well appreciated by the whale crew, as the sudden application of his weight could result in the line being pulled entirely from the boat and the whale subsequently lost. On several occasions, a stoush ensued between whale man and Killer whale; once a boathook was brought into play in a bid to dislodge the errant cetacean, but this annoyed Tom considerably and he hung on all the more tenaciously.

Another story involving Tom, and somewhat of an infamous one, concerns the time the Hon. Mr. Austin Chapman (the federal member for the region at the time) was hosting a pleasure cruise on the bay. Various visiting parliamentarians were on board, including the Hon. Mr. G.H. Reid and the Hon. Mr. Joseph Carruthers, the purpose of the excursion being to persuade the assembled dignitaries that, with its beautiful bay and natural harbor, the township of Eden was the obvious location in which to establish the national capital. With good fortune, they had chanced to witness the closing moments of a particularly exciting whale chase. Now that my father and his men were securing the carcass, Mr. Chapman took the opportunity to bring the pleasure craft over so that his guests might inspect the dead whale more closely. The visitors had a great many questions to ask of my father, and my father, a shy man but anxious to promote the attractions of Eden, responded to the very best of his ability. Yet all the while he was aware of the Killer whales' increasing agitation, and the growing urgency of securing the whale with anchors and marker buoys before they dragged the carcass to the depths below. As it was, they were already circling impatiently and tugging at its side fins.

"You certainly put on a fine show for us," said Mr. Chapman, after the initial introductions were made across the vast expanse of whale flesh.

"Yes, she led us on a bit of a dance, the old girl," said my father, with characteristic understatement. The chase had in fact been a desperate one and taken almost five hours, the men rowing from South Head to North Head and back again, with multiple diversions along the way.

"They call Mr. Davidson 'Fearless' in these parts, and I think you can now see why," Mr. Chapman remarked to his party. "I hope he won't mind me telling you that he has a wrought-iron constitution and a heart like a blacksmith's anvil!"

My father was always embarrassed by this sort of talk, but his men raised a hearty "Hear, hear!"

"Tell me, Mr. Davidson, what kind of whale is this?" asked the Hon. Mr. Reid, later to become the Prime Minister of Australia, if only for a period of eleven months.

"This is a southern right whale, sir, the most valuable of all on account of the whalebone."

"Is that so? And what would you estimate to be its worth?"

"Well, sir, the whale oil on a whale this size would be in the order of two hundred pounds, and the whalebone itself—well, we're talking in the league of a thousand pounds, sir."

The whalers raised an even louder cheer at this news, but my father could tell by the threshing of the water that the Killers were none too happy about the hold-up in proceedings.

"And tell me, Mr. Davidson—may I call you Fearless?—tell

me, Fearless, what are you up to here with the anchors and buoys and suchlike?" inquired the Hon. Mr. Carruthers.

"Well, sir, we let the Killers here have first dibs at the whale."

"It truly is quite remarkable," explained Mr. Chapman, eagerly. "The Killer whales will now take the carcass underwater and feast upon its tongue and lips—am I right, Mr. Davidson?"

"That's right, sir."

"How extraordinary," exclaimed Mrs. Reid. "I was not aware that whales had lips."

"Oh yes, ma'am," said my father. "A whale has lips all right."

"Then, some twenty-four hours later," continued Mr. Chapman, "after the Killers have enjoyed their repast, the remains of the carcass will fill with gas and rise to the surface, whereupon our stout-hearted friends here will tow the brute home and begin the process of rendering its blubber into whale oil."

"So you share the bounty, as it were," said Mr. Reid.

"That's right, sir. Well, the Killers help us catch the whales, and have done for sixty years. Also, to be honest, sir, I doubt we could get the whale off them now if we wanted to."

And just at that moment, as if to demonstrate this last point, Tom surged up out of the water and grabbed hold of the rope my father had in his hands, hanging on to it with his teeth for twenty seconds or thereabouts and crushing several of my father's fingers in the process. The assembled dignitaries cried out in horror; the whalers—terrified that the Killer would pull my father into the water—threatened Tom with whatever implements they had at hand until finally he relinquished his grasp and slid silently back into the water. Throughout the ordeal, my father's expression remained impassive, nor did he utter a sound; a slight wincing as he tucked his mutilated hand out of sight was the only hint of any discomfort he was experiencing.

"That's Tom," he said by way of explanation to the visitors, who were staring at him aghast. "He wants us to hurry up, by the looks of things. I daresay we'd best get back to work, if you'll excuse us."

"Yes, for heaven's sake, don't let us keep you," cried Mr. Reid, who was still recovering from the shock of this sudden attack. (Mrs. Reid had to sit down with her head between her knees.)

"Before we take our leave, one final question concerning Tom," said Mr. Chapman, anxious that the exchange end on a more cheerful note. "Would you agree with me in saying that there would not be a more loved and revered cetacean alive in the world today?"

My father paused to consider this. (It was always his custom to weigh matters carefully before giving an opinion.)

"He's a good fish is Tom," he said at last. "Though he has his funny ways."

Seeing that Mr. Chapman was smiling at him encouragingly and feeling that somehow something more was expected of him, especially in light of the incident they had just witnessed, he added: "He would be a tremendous asset to the nation's capital."

"Hear, hear!" cried the whalers.

Whenever I think of this story, I can almost see my father standing there atop the dead whale, a lean and wiry figure, yet somehow heroic with his bloody hand and his marker buoys and boathook, the sun setting behind him and the Killer whales circling and calling to one another with their high-pitched twittering. And even in spite of a subsequent infection and the amputation of the top two-thirds of his index finger, my father never went along with the thinking, popular amongst some in the township, that this particular episode contributed in no small way to the fact that Canberra was ultimately selected as the site of the nation's capital, and that therefore the blame could be sheeted home to Tom.

Non-appearance of Whales

THE SIGHTING OF TOM AND THE KILLER WHALES IN Twofold Bay (punctual as ever, for it was the first week of June) signified that the humpbacks and the right whales would soon be making their way up the coast. Whaling season was about to begin.

"He sounds to be in fine trim and looking for action!" chuckled Uncle Aleck, when he learned of Tom's escapade with the fisherman. "It's a good sign; it's a very good sign!"

The truth is, we had lately been feeling, in a more marked fashion than usual, an increasing anxiety as the season approached us. I experienced it as a gnawing sensation in the pit of my belly; in my brother Harry, it was evidenced by an outbreak of scaly eczema on his elbows. With my father, the anxiety manifested itself in his restless agitation, his endless inventory of ropes, lances and harpoons; also, unusually for him, in a shortness of temper. The fact of the matter was that the previous season had been the worst on record in sixty years of whaling at Twofold Bay. Not a single whale had been captured, and for this, I regret to say, the Killers had to bear some responsibility.

For reasons best known to themselves, the whales had elected to keep well clear of the coast that year, and from July through to October, barely a whale had ventured close enough to warrant the putting out of boats. Every morning at dawn my father and his crew would row over to South Head to keep lookout from the vantage point of Boyd Tower; every day their long vigils passed unrewarded. Week after week the *Eden Observer and South Coast Advocate* ran the same small item under *Voices Whisper*: *"That the whalers are wailing on account of the non-appearance of whales."* This did nothing to improve the morale of our whale crews. The men were grumbling and fighting amongst themselves; one of our best men absconded and it was all my father could do to keep the rest of them from following suit. The Killers, too, seemed restless and dissatisfied. Tired of toying with seals and grampus for their amusement, they took to cruising long distances out to sea, often staying away for days at a time. This was most unlike the Killers; their customary practice was to keep vigilant sentry at the heads, ready to escort the first unsuspecting whale into the welcoming waters of Twofold Bay. Even if a whale chanced to enter the bay without their initial encouragement, they could always be relied upon to join in the chase once they saw our whaleboats in the water. For the Killers to be absent without leave in the height of the whaling season was a most unusual occurrence.

Very late in the season, almost at the end of October, two

very large black whales unexpectedly hove to in the bay. My father and his crew put out at once and rowed hard in pursuit, expecting that at any moment the Killers would enter into the chase. The Killers, however, failed to present themselves. The crews toiled ceaselessly all day, rowing back and forth across the bay in futile pursuit, but were unable at any stage to gain sufficient proximity to engage the harpoon. Many times in their desperation my father and his men employed their usual means of summoning their assistants, by bringing the flat side of their oars down hard upon the water in unison. The Killers did not respond. Finally, as darkness descended, the whales escaped out to sea and the exhausted men made their way home. We later learned from the lighthouse keepers that the Killers had spent the day off Green Cape, idly tormenting seals for their amusement.

Rarely have I seen my father so despondent as when he returned that night. He sat at the kitchen table with his head in his hands and would take no supper. By all accounts, these two whales had been the largest seen in this vicinity for many years. Furthermore, they were right whales, the most greatly sought after owing to the immensity and value of their whalebone. These two whales, for their whalebone alone, were together worth possibly as much as three thousand pounds. This is without even taking into consideration the quantity of oil, which could be reasonably estimated at about sixteen tons. Hence it is not difficult to appreciate my father's disappointment.

The next day, the Killers were back, having a grand old time chasing a couple of worthless finbacks, right under the noses of the men on lookout, who cursed them bitterly.

Shortly thereafter, my father was forced to disperse his disgruntled crews. He and Harry kept lookout a while longer; however no more whales of any commercial value were sighted, and the fruitless season was closed by the middle of November.

Fastidious Diet of Whale Men

MY OWN FEELING OF ANXIETY REGARDING THE ONSET of whaling season was exacerbated by the fact that it seemed I was expected to be Cook again. It is true, my mother had cooked for the whalers along with all her other duties, but as I was only thirteen when she died, my father had gone on to employ a series of cooks. None of them lasted long at the post; it seemed they were either addicted to drink or inclined to run off with the first person who glanced at them sideways (usually one of the whalers). Three seasons ago, our cook (a bad-tempered redhead by the name of Ginnie) complained of tiny insects burrowing out of her skin and promptly took herself into town on a drinking spree with the money my father had given her to buy provisions. After two days she fell down dead in the back room of the Great Southern—a fitting end. However, I had little cause to celebrate, as I was thrown in at once to replace her.

I have read that cooking for shearers is a thankless job, yet

I would volunteer for it happily if offered a choice between that and cooking for whalers. Naturally, whalers are ill-mannered as a rule and boast enormous appetites—that is to be expected. What is less to be expected, however, is their extreme finickiness as regarding their "slops." It seemed that each one of them suffered from some manner of digestive imbalance which required the most fastidious tending. Bastable could not tolerate any form of marsupial, so kangaroo and wallaby were out of the question. Albert Thomas Junior complained that oysters gave him a terrific bellyache, which was unfortunate because oysters were abundant, and useful for stretching out many of their stews. Although rabbit was reasonably plentiful and cost nothing, the whalers became disgruntled when I served it too frequently; canned rabbit was out of the question. Mutton was tolerated if roasted in goose fat or fashioned into rissoles with finely chopped bacon and parsley. Stewed ibis, attempted once, was deemed unpalatable. Further, the whale men were extremely particular about seasoning and would pull me up sharply if they considered a dish under-salted. All meals were doused in vast quantities of Worcestershire sauce or golden syrup, with little thought as to the expense of such condiments.

Although I had no wish to add to his worries, I gathered my courage and asked my father if he would not hire a cook this season.

"They are too much trouble," he responded. "Besides, you are old enough now to take on the responsibility, and Louisa will help you."

"Louisa!" I scoffed. "She will be a lot of help, I must say. You might as well ask the cat."

"Then get the younger ones to help you."

"But they are completely useless!"

It was generally considered at the time amongst the immediate family that Annie and Violet, our youngest two, were not quite right in the head. For many years now, they had communicated mostly through a language they called "Whinny," which consisted of grunting and snickering and pawing the ground. This had been mildly amusing when they were small children, but now that they were nine and ten years of age it had frankly become rather tiresome. Oddly, they had little interest in our actual horse, Two Socks, but then he was always a very difficult horse to get along with.

"Well, Mary, it is up to you," said my father, rising to his feet. "You are the little mother of the household now. You will have to organize the younger ones accordingly. I have enough to deal with regarding the whales."

What a burden it is to be the firstborn daughter when your mother has died! It was not as if I was unused to work—I did almost all the cooking and all the washing (with some assistance from Louisa, admittedly) and cleaned the house and darned their clothes; I even taught the little ones their lessons as best I could. But to cook for the whalers seemed to push me to the very limit of my forbearance. As I say, it was not even the fact of the extra mouths to feed—it was the lack of appreciation for my efforts. Not enough salt? Then here, sir—have the entire container, upended over your fat head.

Another difficulty we faced in feeding the whalers was that in order to carry down their slops from the kitchen each evening, we were required to "run the gauntlet" of a pair of masked plovers known to us as Mr. and Mrs. Maudry. These plovers had for some years staked their claim to our front garden and, by unhappy coincidence, timed the great drama of their annual nesting with our whaling season. I cannot say for sure why we came to know them by these names, or even if it was the same Mr. and Mrs. Maudry who year after year tormented us; it is entirely possible, since they are indistinguishable from each other, that succeeding generations took over the roles. Suffice to say, these ill-tempered birds provided a wholly unwelcome element of annoyance to the short but dreary journey down to the sleeping huts each evening—and back.

For that part of the year when they were not preoccupied with matters nesting, Mr. and Mrs. Maudry contented themselves with stalking broodingly about the garden and glowering at us. Mr. Maudry in particular possessed a malevolent air similar to that of a Land and Tax officer or Customs agent, an effect enhanced by the plovers' plumage, in which nature appeared to be imitating the black-collared suit coats of the kind favored by my late paternal grandfather. By all accounts entirely capable of flight, the Maudrys for the most part elected not to, preferring to spend their days instead lurking ominously amongst the jonquils. Occasionally they might materialize suddenly out of "thin air" where previously they were not, prompting the thought that wings may have been utilized in some fashion in order for them to do so. For reasons of their own, however, Mr. and Mrs. Maudry felt it necessary to maintain the illusion that they were solely ground dwellers.

Soon after whaling season commenced each year, Mrs. Maudry would get broody, and from that moment on, any interloper (by which I mean any person who ventured foot in the front garden) was set upon at once by Mr. Maudry and summarily issued with his marching orders. First he would charge towards the hapless wanderer, emitting a series of short staccato cries (I mean Mr. Maudry would emit the cries, not the wanderer); all the while, Mrs. Maudry urging him on shrilly from the sidelines. Should the unhappy party not immediately desist from his or her intended journey, then Mr. Maudry would launch at them with his wings extended, revealing a fearsome kind of spur he had hitherto concealed in his plumage and which he wielded wildly, all the time with a look in his eye that meant to say he would have no compunction in using it if pressed. No amount of stick-waving or shouting at Mr. Maudry would discourage him, and this is what we faced every evening in carrying down the pots to the ungrateful whalers. If one of us was assigned the task of distracting Mr. Maudry whilst the other scurried past, then Mrs. Maudry would willingly abandon her nest to tackle the other party, proving herself every bit as spirited as her husband. Nor were the dogs of any assistance to us: alas, cruel experience had taught them well, and in the height of nesting season they simply refused to accompany us at all.

Eventually the Maudrys stepped up their campaign to the point where we had no choice but to take an alternative route around the back of the house and through the blackberry bushes, the last section of which journey required sliding perilously down a steep set of rocks onto the beach. Thus we arrived scratched, bruised and pulling off leeches; scant wonder the whalers received short shrift if they complained that their slops had gone cold.

Commencement of Whaling Season, 1908

I HAD RISEN EARLY TO MAKE THE DAMPER, AND NOW I HURRIED down the hill to the boat ramp with tucker-bags for the whale men. They stood about beside the boats, flapping their arms in a bid to warm themselves and grumbling as usual about their conditions. Our Aboriginal crew members had recently returned, as they did annually, from Wallaga Lake: Arthur Ashby, my father's long-standing harpooner; Albert Thomas Senior and Albert Thomas Junior; and Percy Madigan and his son, Darcy. We were always relieved to see them, for without them my father would have struggled to continue. They were stronger oarsmen overall; Darcy especially had extraordinary eyesight, and their nerve was better in a pinch. Consequently, my father preferred to use them on the Number One boat, which saw most of the action. As well, electing to return finally after protracted consideration was Salty Mead, one of my father's longest serving whale men (in fact, he had served as an oarsman for my father's father), and

Walter Bastable, a veteran of the Great Shearers' Strike of 1891, who now considered himself the "whale man's shop steward." I spotted John Beck almost immediately; he was standing to the side with two other new chums.

"And what brings you here to try your hand at whaling?" asked my father of one of these newcomers, a tall, stooped man with a drooping mustache.

"Well, sir, not a soul on this earth cares whether I live or die, so I suppose I have naught to lose," responded the man in a thick Scottish brogue.

"We haven't lost a man in thirty years, Mr. Shankly," said my father, glancing up from his ledger book. "So I'd be pleased if you'd adopt a more optimistic outlook. Can you row hard?"

"I can," said Mr. Shankly.

"All right then, I'll try you out as oarsman in the pick-up boat. You'll get a seventieth lay, less board and slops, take it or leave it as you please."

"I'll take it, sir, thank you kindly."

"And you?" said my father, turning to a callow, pimpled youth of seventeen.

"Yes, sir, Mr. Davidson, my name is Robert Heffernan, I'm a mate of Harry's."

"I know who you are," said my father. "Why are you so keen to go whaling all of a sudden?"

"Well, sir, I thought as a way of meeting girls."

Harry gave Robert a shove in the ribs, but it was too late. The whale men stared at him; Bastable, removing the pipe from his mouth, surveyed the young man balefully.

"There are no girls whaling, lad," he said. "I believe you've been a laboring under a terrible misapprehension."

"I've worked on whaleboats forty years and never met a girl yet!" cried Salty, and judging from their responses, it would seem that this had been the experience of most of the whale men.

"No, you want to be trying the Presbyterian Sunday school picnics," offered Uncle Aleck. "Now there's a way to meet ladies of all shapes and sizes."

"That's right," concurred Salty. "Or the Plain and Fancy Dress Balls up at the School of Arts, though it will cost you five shillings to get in."

"I haven't got five shillings," said Robert.

"Ah well then, I see your point. You might as well try the whaling."

My father held up his hand to indicate that that was enough on the subject.

"Listen to me, young man," he said. "If you've volunteered for whaling in the hope of getting yourself better acquainted with Louisa, then I had better put you out of your misery. She won't be courting till she's eighteen years of age."

"Yes, sir," said young Robert, his cheeks aflame.

"So, in light of that information, are you still keen?"

"Yes, sir. I'm still keen, sir," he replied.

My father nodded, and signed him on. The young man did not look very keen. I imagine the prospect of having to go out in all weather and row back and forth across the bay in endless pursuit of enraged leviathans must have seemed exceedingly grim, especially now any chance of courting Louisa on the side had been discounted. He threw a dirty look at Harry; it seemed this might have been all his idea.

I have the ledger book in front of me now, and in my father's handwriting is the following, inscribed on that blustery morning:

Boat Number One	Boat Number Two
Headsman: Geo. Davidson	Headsman: Harry Davidson
Harpooner: Arthur Ashby	Harpooner: Salty Mead
Oarsmen: Walter Bastable	Oarsmen: John Beck (Rev.)
Albert Thomas Senior	A. Shankly
Albert Thomas Junior	Robert Heffernan
Percy Madigan	
Darcy Madigan	

"Right, men," cried my father, handing the ledger to Uncle Aleck. "Let's get the boats in the water. We're off to the Lookout!"

"And here's to a prosperous season, this nineteen hundred and eight!" cried Salty.

There were general grunts of "Hear, hear!" as the men dragged the boats into the water.

"And let's hope it's a damned sight better than last year," I heard someone mutter.

Urged on by my father now, the men bent to the oars and the two dark-green whaleboats pushed past the first line of breakers. My father stood at the stern of the first boat, wielding the mighty steer oar with expert authority; he was much practiced at negotiating the moods of the bar, and his crew had a better time of it than those in the second boat. On the jetty, Violet and Annie jumped up and down, shouting goodbyes and whinnying. Our two dogs, Patch and Bonnie, raced up and down the beach, barking in excitement. Bonnie even had the notion of swimming after the boats in a show of enthusiasm, and leapt into the shallows determined to do so; once testing the temperature of the water, however, she thought better of the idea and clambered out again, shaking herself miserably at my feet.

"Louisa!" cried Salty. "How old are you now?"

"Sixteen!" she called back. "Why?"

"No reason! None at all!" Over the water, we could hear him chortling. "Two years of whaling, you poor hapless b-----d!"

Once the boats had rounded the Point, we headed back to the house. Glancing back, I saw that Uncle Aleck was standing in the shallows, clutching the ledger, unaware that water was now washing around his knees. I called out to him, and as he turned and came towards me, I saw that tears were streaming down his cheeks. This was not unusual; he had only stopped whaling a few years ago, and it was on occasions such as this that he seemed to miss it most keenly. Knowing better than to offer any soothing words, I put my arm through his and together we made our way back up to the house, the children galloping on ahead, all mad with the cold and excitement.

Once inside and warmed by the fire, Uncle Aleck soon recovered himself and was within half an hour berating me over the consistency of the oatmeal. In fact, he only ate a few spoonfuls before pushing it away and stomping off down to the tryworks to see that things were in order for the men's return. The oatmeal was not wasted, however; Louisa applied the rest of it to her face and throat as she had read in the newspaper of its improving effects upon the complexion.

A Most Prepossessing Young Lady

I SHALL NOW PAUSE A MOMENT AND DESCRIBE MY SISTER Louisa, as I notice she is creeping into my story and perhaps warrants an explanation. At that time (I have decided to confine my literary endeavors to an account of the whaling season of 1908), Louisa was sixteen years of age and widely admired for her appearance. Her hair was a pale straw yellow in color, her features dainty and her figure slender, with an overall effect which many found pleasing. (I myself value qualities such as kindness and consideration for others above mere symmetry of form; however, it seems I am out of step with public taste in this regard.) That same year, I had painted Louisa's likeness in a bid to try my luck in the Portraiture section of the Eden Show. While it too failed to secure a ribbon, the portrait nonetheless attracted a great deal of interest. Certainly, I had captured a reasonable facsimile of her appearance, even in spite of the fact that, at Louisa's insistence, I had elongated her neck untruthfully and painted out a small blemish on her chin. But beyond the relative accuracy of its physical representation, I felt that the portrait also indicated something of her character; a glassy vacancy about the eyes, perhaps, and a sullen insolence in the pouting of her lips. For whatever reason, whether in admiration of Louisa's pleasing physiognomy or the skill that I had demonstrated with my brush, there seemed always to be a small assembly of men gathered about this portrait as it hung in the Exhibits Pavilion. After several offers were made to me, I finally agreed to sell the painting for the sum of ten shillings to Mr. Caleb Cook, a sheep farmer from Burragate. Mr. Cook then went on to award Louisa the prize of Best-dressed and Most Prepossessing Young Lady, a sum of one pound in the form of a gold sovereign which he himself had personally donated.

It is true that, even at this young age, Louisa seemed to exert a mysterious power over the opposite sex. If I was down at the try-works, for example, perhaps bringing the men their evening slops, the whalers might manage to restrain themselves for fully five minutes before they reverted to blasphemy and expectorating. My father was often forced to rebuke them on this matter, with little lasting effect. And yet if I succeeded in having Louisa accompany me, they would come over all quiet and queer and generally conduct themselves with far greater decorum. It seemed they were mesmerized by the aforementioned dainty features and the will-o'-the-wisp way she floated about, avoiding anything that might look like work. The various flaws of her character seemed to pass undetected by these fellows.

I will say in Louisa's defense, however, that in one area she did contribute to the household, and that was in the matter of dressmaking. After the particularly prosperous whaling season of 1899, in which twelve whales had been captured (five of them right whales), my father had purchased as a gift for my mother a Singer sewing machine from Mr. Crowther, the traveling agent. I recall clearly the great day of its arrival on the back of Mr. Crowther's sulky, for it was the first time we realized how much afternoon tea Mr. Crowther was capable of ingesting, and in fact he went on to stay for dinner and a hearty breakfast the following morning. Still, if the larder was depleted, it was worth it, for never had we seen anything so beautiful as the machine he unveiled to us in the front room.

It was an especially fine example of the Singer, with a handsome timber cabinet and an ornately detailed Egyptian Sphinx emblazoned in gold upon the black lacquer of its chassis. I can remember feeling even then, at the age of ten, a sense of shame, as its startling glamour seemed only to throw into stark relief the shabbiness of our dwelling and furniture. The haughty demeanor of the golden Sphinx did nothing to ameliorate this feeling.

In between slices of Madeira cake and long anecdotes about unpleasant cows he had had run-ins with in his travels, Mr. Crowther took some trouble to demonstrate to my mother the various features of this wonderful machine. By the time he had departed the next day (with corned beef and mustard pickle sandwiches to be going on with), my mother had sewn all by herself a flannelette chemise and an apron made from a fifty-pound calico flour bag. Her next task was to sew together hessian wheat bags, which she then painted with cal-

cimine to form dividing partitions between rooms. She sewed
singlets and underpants, petticoats and bloomers; shirts and
trousers for the boys and pinafores for the girls. Her work
was plain and straightforward; she rarely bothered with anything so fanciful as lace trimmings or ruffled hems; there were
no crocheted necklines or blue embroidered forget-me-nots
about our collars. I suppose this was the Presbyterian in her
nature, or perhaps she just simply could not be bothered. It
was not like there wasn't already enough to do about the place.

Much of my memory of my mother, I realize, is of her
leaning over her Singer in the evening, murmuring quietly to
herself as she strained to thread the needle, and the gentle
comforting whirr of her treadling as we drifted off to sleep.
Although she attempted to teach me how to sew on it, she did
not meet with much success. A dull child, I was always slow
to acquire any new skills, and the footwork involved in con-
trolling the machine was beyond me. Further, the hand wheel
seemed to wish to deliberately defy me, revolving in the opposite direction to that which it was bid, thereby causing the
thread to snap. Even when I finally got it going, the furious action of the plunging needle frightened me, causing me to leap
back and the needle to veer wildly from its path. For these
crimes, the Sphinx regarded me scornfully.

Louisa was always too flighty a child to be bothered with
such a tedious task as sewing; on the one occasion in which
my mother coerced her into sewing a pillow case, she registered her protest by sewing the wispy curls at the end of her
own plait to the linen. The half an hour spent unpicking the
stitches in order to release the furious child was enough to discourage my mother from further attempts in this direction.

Thus, when my mother died, the sewing machine sat silent and still, the Sphinx glowering at us accusingly from across the room. My father must have been very sorry about this, not only for the memory it held of my mother, but also because he was still paying it off on Mr. Crowther's hire-purchase plan (he would continue to do so till November 1912). I attempted a few simple garments for the little ones, but the Singer did not choose to cooperate with me; its bobbin jammed and its stitches looped and finally I gave up in frustration. I put the cover over it, ostensibly to keep the dust off, but truthfully to stop the Sphinx from judging me. And then one day, around her thirteenth birthday, Louisa removed the cover and began to sew.

A Cinderella ball was approaching. Admiring an illustration of a pretty girl on a biscuit tin, Louisa decided she would attempt to copy the girl's dress for the occasion. Right from the beginning, she demonstrated an uncanny ability. Pulling apart a blue percale skirt of my mother's, she fashioned for herself a very reasonable approximation of the biscuit-tin dress, though deeming it too plain ("too Presbyterian" were her actual words), she embellished it with a ruffled hemline, and made the sailor collar and sleeve cuffs of a contrasting white cotton, trimmed with a fine pink ribbon she had had my father purchase in Eden.

I would like to report that she sat quietly at the Singer, constructing her garment with a minimum of fuss. This was not the case. She spent most of the week in a vile temper, snapping at anyone who dared approach her, and hurling at the Singer all manner of briny epithets she had picked up from the whalers. By the end of the week, however, she had gained the upper hand; the Singer had cowered into submission. The contest had been hard fought, with casualties on both sides, but now the Sphinx seemed to have lost some of his hauteur. The dress turned out very nicely, and Louisa was singled out in the *Eden Observer and South Coast Advocate* as a *"budding beauty in cornflower blue."*

I would also like to report that from that point on, she took upon her slender shoulders the entire burden of clothing her family, but in this regard Louisa again thwarted hope. She would not condescend to sew such workaday items as shirts and trousers and undergarments—these items my father was forced to purchase at Howard the Price-Cutter. However, if a ball or a concert or the Presbyterian picnic was approaching, and my father could spare the money, she and I would hasten into Eden and choose ourselves a floral cretonne of some description (there were prettier fabrics, but they were too expensive), and Louisa would apply herself to the task of making our dresses. As long as I made no suggestions as to what I would prefer by way of trimmings or style, they always turned out very well indeed. She would study the pictures in catalogues and newspapers, and without aid of any pattern, produce something very similar; I say "similar" because invariably Louisa improved upon the original. She had mastered the Singer's many fancy feet, and she pintucked and ruffled, smocked and shirred and puffed. And although squalls of foul temper continued to pass through the front room whenever a dress was in progress, for the most part the activity greatly improved her moods and certainly improved our wardrobes. She had bent the Singer to her will; but then Louisa's will was always formidable.

The Bandages

WHEN MY FATHER AND HIS MEN RETURNED FROM South Head after their first day of lookout, I had boiled a flap of mutton for their dinner, and served it with white sauce, cabbage, carrots and potatoes. We had a reasonable supply of stores since my father's trip into Eden, so I also fixed a tapioca pudding with marmalade sauce. The men were pleased to have meat and pudding, and spoke in a complimentary way of my cooking.

"You keep this up, we'll have to change our name for you," said Salty.

"Oh, and what is your name for me?" I inquired.

Here, the men grew fidgety and feigned great interest in whatever small activity they were engaged in at the time.

"That's all right, I have names for you also," I said, and they took this in good part, chuckling humorously. The truth is, I was pleased that the men had enjoyed their meal, for I was keen to make a good impression on John Beck.

I had espied him when Dan and I carried down the food; he was sitting on a log outside the sleeping hut, ruefully examining the palms of his hands. Like any new chum, he had incurred blisters from rowing. Further, he sported a fresh bruise upon his chin, for at one point the oar had apparently slipped from his grasp and smacked him soundly in the jaw. It seemed he was somewhat less experienced at rowing than he had claimed to be.

"You'll want to bandage those blisters," offered Dan. "Mary has some rags up at the house if need be."

"No," said John Beck. "I don't need bandages."

"They'll be a damned sight worse after tomorrow," said Dan, who often lapsed into language around the whale men. "And what if a whale hoves to? You can't chase a whale with girl's hands."

John Beck's face darkened, and he stood abruptly and walked away. He did not return, so I left his portion in a tin dish and covered it with a saucepan lid.

Later that night, as Louisa and I washed the dishes, I came across this same dish scraped clean, and took it as a sign that my culinary efforts had met with his approval. I immediately set about planning what meal I might prepare for the following evening. It would have to involve mutton, but perhaps there was some new way I might enliven it. As I was reflecting on the limited possibilities available to me, I heard the shrill cries of Mr. Maudry in full attack: several moments later, a small knock sounded on the kitchen door. There outside in the darkness stood John Beck, looking somewhat harassed.

"I have just been set upon by an unpleasant bird," he said, as if to account for the state in which he presented.

"Yes," I said simply. "That is Mr. Maudry."

"I see," said John Beck, regarding me strangely. "Well." He paused for a moment. "I was wondering if you might have some rags to spare."

"Yes, of course," I replied. "Is it for your blisters?"

"Yes," he said.

"May I see?" I asked.

He gave me his hands, palms facing upwards, and I took them by the wrists and examined them closely. (I had to examine them closely, as for some reason I was not wearing my spectacles.) They were good hands, well-shaped and strong—perhaps stronger than one would reasonably expect of a Methodist minister—the pads of each palm sporting a set of fresh blisters.

"You should wash them in salt water," I instructed.

"I did, in the sea," he replied.

"And rub in some sand."

"You mean rub sand into the actual blisters?" asked John Beck.

"Yes, several times daily."

"Did you just make that up?"

"Yes. I mean, no. No, it's actual advice that I have read somewhere. In a medical text of some kind. I believe the coarse granules, ah, slough away the damaged skin."

"Won't that hurt?" he asked.

"It may."

"Can you recommend something less painful?"

I glanced up at him; he was smiling at me.

Many times in the ensuing years, I have run this moment through again in my mind; taken it out of my small box of precious things and turned it over, examining its every facet minutely. There was something about his smile that was unlike that of any minister, Methodist or otherwise, that I had ever encountered. It was a gentle smile, amused but not mocking, the subtle, curving movement dispersing small creases around his eyes and mouth; even the purple bruise upon his jaw did not detract from the effect. How fortunate had been his congregation, I marveled, to have had that kind, handsome face beam down upon them from the pulpit, intoning a psalm perhaps or leading them in a Wesleyan hymn.

A small movement of his hands alerted me to the realization that I had been holding on to them for a longer period of time than was appropriate; I dropped them at once.

"Well, of course, you could simply bandage them," I said. "Let me fetch some rags."

I hurried back inside and rummaged about, and in fact it was several minutes before I was able to put my hands on anything suitable. Upon returning to find him waiting patiently, I held them out to him. He hesitated.

"I don't suppose…would you?" he asked. "It's just that it's awkward to do it oneself."

"Yes, of course. I would be happy to," I responded, and set about bandaging his hands in as business-like a fashion as I could muster, given my own hands seemed to be trembling violently.

"Do all the whalers get such pretty bandages?" he asked softly. (I had torn a strip of *broderie anglaise* from the bottom of my clean petticoat, as there were no other suitable rags available.)

"Not all of them," I responded, not daring to look up at him.

"May I ask, is it from a petticoat?"

"Possibly."

"Then when I am chasing whales tomorrow I shall think of that poor petticoat's sacrifice, and it shall spur me onwards."

So overcome was I at the unexpected turn that the conversation had taken (albeit somewhat at odds with my image of him leading the congregation in a Wesleyan hymn), I was unable to think of any response, and simply tied the bandages as securely as I could. When I had done so, he thanked me and moved off into the darkness; several moments later the piercing shrieks of Mr. Maudry resounded through the night.

I stepped back inside the kitchen and closed the door. I would have valued a moment of quiet to reflect upon this exchange; however, Louisa was keen to pass judgment on our newcomer. Initially, she expressed surprise that he had incurred blisters from simply rowing the short distance to South Head and back. When I reminded her that new chums often suffered blisters, she responded that this might well be the case if they had rowed eight or nine times across the bay in pursuit of a whale. I was then compelled to remind her that since John Beck was formerly a Methodist minister, it was small wonder his hands were more delicate than those of our regular whale men. Louisa twisted her mouth into a scornful expression, and said nothing; I then informed her that this was most unbecoming and made her look like she had recently ingested something disagreeable, to which she responded, "Yes, dinner."

"What kind of bandages do you call them?" asked Salty the following morning, as they pushed the boats into the water.

"Why, I'm not sure," said John Beck. "I think it's *broderie anglaise.*"

"Looks like a lady's undergarment is what it looks like!" cried Salty. "Oi!" he called out to the occupants of the other boat. "You should see the Reverend's bandages!"

"What's that?" called Arthur Ashby, unable to hear him properly across the water.

"Reverend's got some girl's bloomers as bandages! Show them, Father!" Here, he raised one of John Beck's hands so they could see it more clearly. "All frilly and lacy! Some lady's pantaloons, I'll wager!"

John Beck pulled his hand away in annoyance, and bent to the oars. He did not look to be enjoying Salty's ribaldry. Nor did it appear from his expression that my father much liked the sound of what he heard. It was fortunate that he was pre-occupied in guiding his boat across the bar, otherwise John Beck would have felt the full force of Fearless Davidson's whale-killing gaze.

The Old Gray Kangaroo

THE OLDEST CHILDREN—THAT IS, HARRY AND LOUISA AND I—had been taught to read and write by our mother, who had herself been a governess before she met our father. She had come out from England at the age of twenty-five on a loan from the Female Middle-Class Emigration Society (I know this because they continued to write for many years after her death, demanding that the loan be repaid). There was no one to meet her when she arrived, and she was forced to impose on the goodwill of strangers; not wishing to be a burden, she proceeded to endure a series of situations, each worse than the last, until finally she arrived at the Walcotts' near Pambula. Soon after her arrival, she took ill with the measles and very nearly died; in a bid to reduce her fever, they cut off all her hair. Considering her too sickly to work, the Walcotts subsequently discharged her. As luck would have it, my father was called upon to convey her back to Eden (he had been cutting railway sleepers in the area at the

time, a job he often took out of whaling season). He did not
think much of her immediately, as she was thin and pasty and
her hair was cut short like a boy; also, any attempts at conversation were thwarted by her continual crying and blowing
her nose. However, my father, always a kindly man, felt sorry
for her and he took her back to stay at his mother's house
(this house in which we still live) as she had no place else to
go, and barely a shilling in her pocket. Over ensuing weeks,
they developed sufficient feeling for each other that they became engaged. He was thirty years of age at the time and she
was twenty-nine; each of them had given up hope of ever marrying, and yet they shared thirteen happy years together and
produced six children. I was the firstborn and named Mary,
after my late maternal grandmother.

It was January when they met and March when they married, and although my mother knew my father was a whaler,
she little realized what that meant until the first whale of the
season was captured and tried out in July. My mother suffered
frequently from sick headaches, and the stench and the blood
and the ramps awash with whale oil greatly exacerbated her
condition; however, she did her best to keep the extent of her
suffering from my father. I well remember the sight of her returning from the try-works after delivering the men their
meal; scrambling up the hill with her hand clasped tightly
over her mouth, veering suddenly into the shrubs to retch violently. Once inside, she would bid me squeeze a lemon and
add a teaspoon of baking soda, and this she would force herself to drink down to quell her biliousness. I don't think that
she was ever a woman of strong constitution. Even on her
good days, I can only recall her eating small portions of dry

toast, dipped in a little Worcestershire sauce. "It's my nerves," she would tell me. "They get raggedy sometimes."

We have a photograph of her which I sometimes find myself studying. She had broad cheekbones and prominent teeth; people say I take after her, although I cannot see it myself. She has baby Dan on her lap and I stand very close beside her, as if attempting to hide behind her skirts. She is smiling (in fact, she is the only one who smiles, as the rest of us children are either glowering or grimacing), but there is a look about her, almost in the slope of her shoulders, that indicates a person who struggles with her health. Nonetheless, her expression is one of gentle kindness, and that is how I remember her. The *Eden Observer and South Coast Advocate*, in noting her passing, commented: *"She was highly esteemed by all who knew her."* This was true; I could only add that small children and animals esteemed her most of all.

One of my strongest memories of my mother is the way she used to talk to an old gray kangaroo that would come and graze about the house in the dawn and the early evening. My mother liked this kangaroo, and whenever she saw him, she would go out and talk to him in a kindly fashion. "Watch him, Mary," she would say. "Watch him go all sleepy when I talk to him." She would then proceed to tell him how handsome he was, what a fine kangaroo, how nicely his fur gleamed in the sunshine. On and on she would murmur these compliments; after a little while, the old kangaroo would start to close his eyes as if falling asleep. His battered old head would start to sink. Occasionally he might open his eyes and gaze at her dreamily, then close them again as if in a trance. He seemed to like to listen to the sound of her voice. I liked to listen to her, too. I would sit very quietly on the back step and watch. When it was time to resume her chores, she would bid the old buck goodbye; he would rouse himself softly, as if from a reverie, and hop slowly away.

The morning after she died, I was standing in the kitchen, feeling rather sad and lonely for our mother, when I looked out the door and saw the old gray kangaroo. He was standing beneath the jacaranda tree, and he seemed to be gazing at me in a very deliberate way. A sudden feeling of hope lifted me; I felt at once compelled to go outside and talk to him, just as my mother had so often done. Approaching him carefully, I began by assuring him that he was indeed a fine old kangaroo. I told him that our mother was dead, but that his handsomeness was beyond question. I remarked on his fine posture and how magnificently his fur gleamed in the morning sunshine (in truth, he was rather battle-scarred and moth-eaten in appearance). All the while, the old kangaroo eyed me steadily. As I continued, I noticed that his expression seemed to be growing increasingly indignant. Every now and then, he would swing his head around sharply, as if in scornful disbelief. Then, after several minutes and with an air of the greatest disdain, he turned his back upon me and hopped away. I have never forgotten it. A feeling of the utmost despair came upon me. I was thirteen years old and motherless; I wanted only that he stand there and listen to me. The old gray kangaroo could not have chosen to hurt me in a more deliberate fashion.

On subsequent occasions, whenever I saw him about the place, I would greet him curtly and continue on with my chores. After a while, he stopped visiting at all. I assumed he was dead, and felt glad about it. However, some months later, while taking baby Violet for a walk in the bush up behind the house, I suddenly came upon him. He had been basking in a patch of sunlight, nearly asleep; I had caught him by surprise. He lurched to his feet in a most ungraceful manner, and hopped away into the scrub. This unexpected sighting infuriated me. The fact that he was still alive but chose no longer to visit us seemed to be his final insult; I felt that he could scarcely have been more pointed in indicating what a poor substitute for my mother he thought me to be. Overcome with anger, I flung at his retreating form all the various anathemas I could think of; startled awake by my shrill cries, Violet commenced howling afresh. She was teething and unhappy, I had taken her for a walk in a bid to settle her. This was the last occasion on which I saw him. Over the ensuing years, we have had many wallabies come to eat the new grass around the house. I much prefer their company; they are timid and deferential by nature.

But I see I have gone on at length about my mother, and in fact I only mentioned her by way of explaining that she had taught us older children to read and write. After her death, our father employed a governess briefly, a Miss Gurney; however, she did not stay with us for long. I do not remember much about her except that she was very tall, and took the largest size in boots and gloves; also, we were a little afraid of her as she seemed very harsh and once referred to my brother Harry as a "bl---y b-----d." On one occasion, she asked my father if she might accompany them on a whale chase; of course he was horrified and would not hear of it. He did consent to let her take the rheumatism cure for her lumbago, and she was subsequently submerged up to her head in the carcass of a dead whale. (This treatment was quite a popular sideline for my father at the time; the combination of the natural benefits of whale oil and the heat generated from the fermentation process was known to have a curative effect.) I remember her staggering up the hill afterwards, looking as if she might faint; shortly after this she departed abruptly without giving notice, a paltry thanks for my father's kindness.

Preoccupied as he was with his own concerns, it seemed not to occur to him to employ another governess, and we were left to our own devices. Years passed and the little ones grew out of babyhood. One day I realized that Dan, almost nine years of age at the time, did not know so much as his ABC. I immediately took it upon myself to educate the younger ones, and from that day on devoted an hour or so daily to their schooling, sometimes including the Aboriginal children in my "classroom"—that is, the children of our Aboriginal whalers, if it was whaling season and they were willing to be confined indoors.

They were good little children on the whole, and eager to learn, with the possible exception of Darcy, whose natural high spirits seemed to incite mischief in others, especially Louisa. I remember the pair of them once encouraged the younger children to eat tree sap wrapped in tinfoil, claiming it was caramel toffee. My classroom rapidly became the sick room; I spent the afternoon administering salt water and ground mustard as a purgative. On another occasion, I found Darcy terrifying the younger children with an account of a bunyip he claimed to have witnessed emerging from our creek.

"The water was bubbling and the ground started shaking,

and there he was, with a huge white head like a bull, and terrible rolling eyes..." And here Darcy rolled his eyes alarmingly while the little ones clutched at each other and whimpered. "They say if you done something wrong, he'll come looking for you. You'll hear him panting like this"—and here Darcy began to pant stertorously—"and then he'll start to roar, and you better watch out, because if he bites you, you die." At which point, the little ones erupted into shrill screams, and I was forced to intervene. Fortunately for me, Darcy commenced whaling at thirteen. As fond as I was of the boy, I was glad to banish further talk of the bunyip from the classroom, for reasons of my own which I will now describe.

As a very young child, perhaps two years of age, I had once wandered away from the house as far as the creek that runs along the back of our property—that same creek where Darcy claimed to have seen the bunyip. It was most unlike my mother to let me roam so far; her anxiety of losing us was such that she used to tie a small bell around each of us so she knew at all times where we were. It occurs to me now that on this occasion she may have been indisposed with another of her sick headaches; perhaps she had been lying down in a darkened room. For whatever reason, I nonetheless disappeared for several hours, and it was only as darkness approached that my mother found me, playing happily with a pile of stones I had collected by the side of the creek. My little bell had apparently been caught on a branch and broken free, and I was soaking wet from head to toe, as if I had fallen in; however, the creek runs deep at the point at which I was discovered, so if that had been the case I would surely have drowned. I certainly have no memory of having fallen in, or indeed of anything prior to my mother's discovery of me, but that I recall very vividly; in fact, it is my earliest memory. Her face was very red and her features contorted with fear as she gathered me up and clutched me tightly. Suddenly, almost as if we were being chased (although I don't believe there was any pursuer), she began to tear wildly through the undergrowth so that it ripped her skirt and scratched our arms and faces.

Even now, I can make no sense of this memory when I think of it. Why did she take off like this? Why did she not simply return the way she had come, where she would have emerged very quickly from the scrub and returned safely to our house? If there was no one pursuing us, why did she run? Of course, the only explanation for this was my mother's terror of the bunyip, for she had heard the blackfellows talk of it.

As the creek was our primary source of fresh water, my mother was required to venture there several times a day. She claimed that on one occasion she had seen the bunyip scampering through the trees; also, that she heard it crying out at night and, on several occasions, had even come upon the ragged bones of the creatures it devoured. She was convinced it was the bunyip that had lured me up to the creek, torn my bell from my clothing and thrown me into the water; she feared it would very likely have eaten me had she not stumbled across the scene in time. When we asked her what the bunyip looked like, she would clamp her lips tightly shut and shake her head, as if its appearance was too monstrous to describe. At night, sitting by the fire, especially if my father was out chasing whales, she would suddenly stop what she was doing and motion for us to be quiet. In silence, we would listen. Mostly, we heard nothing but the sound of our own panicked breathing; sometimes the crack of a branch outside. *"Bunyip,"* she would whisper to us triumphantly. "Prowling about."

Of all of her children, I became the most frightened. Having been lured away by the bunyip once, I became very fearful of venturing far from the house lest he entice me again. My fear of the bunyip was such that I felt a great need to stay close to my mother at all times, and became very agitated when separated from her. When my mother died, my fear of the bunyip only escalated. I now refused to go to the creek at all, even in broad daylight. This was a great nuisance to my father, as he had enough work to do without having to fetch water for our domestic needs.

"Don't be foolish, Mary!" he said to me one day, in exasperation. "There's no such thing as bunyips. Don't you realize your mother only told you that to keep the little ones away from the creek?"

At first, I was deeply shocked by this, for if it was true, then she had lied to us, and my memory of my mother was sacred to me. But after a great deal of thought on the subject, I concluded that my father had only told me this in a bid to dispel my fears. Of course my mother had feared the bunyip; I remember vividly her great panic on the occasion on which she rescued me. This was something I had witnessed which my father had not: her terrified whimpering, her wild blundering through the undergrowth. Naturally, she would have tried to keep her fears from him, not wishing to concern him with her private anxieties when he had already so much to worry about. Also, and this was something I could not emulate, my mother was, in spite of her terror, somehow still able to visit the creek to fetch water every day. Given this, it is perhaps little wonder that my father concluded that her fears were not genuine.

The situation was only alleviated by the arrival of a book entitled *Mr. Bunyip,* charitably bestowed upon us by Mrs. Pike of the Great Southern Hotel, along with several other books her own children had outgrown. I opened it with some trepidation; however, once I commenced reading I could not stop until I had finished it (admittedly it is a slim volume of twenty-four pages). By the time I put it down, I felt altogether differently about bunyips, and my one regret was that my mother had not had an opportunity to read it also.

The story concerns a little girl named Mary (coincidentally the same name as my own) who is sitting by the river one day when a huge monster (the bunyip) rises out of the water and approaches her. Paralyzed with fear, she is surprised when the creature addresses her not with a fearsome roar, as Darcy had described, but with a mild, gentle voice: *"Don't be in the least alarmed, my little dear," says the Bunyip. "I know who you are. You are Mary Somerville, the best-conducted girl in your class. I wouldn't hurt a hair of your head for all the gold in Ballarat."* He then describes to her something of his life (he is one hundred and eighty years old), and talks of how important it is for boys and girls to apply themselves to their schoolwork. He advises all children to put money away for the orphanages in Melbourne, to listen to old people and not be too trusting of strangers. He talks of how he dealt with a cruel white settler, Peter Hardheart, who used to shoot down the Aborigines as if they were wild beasts.

I kept my eye on him till one day I saw him chasing some of the poor fellows along the bank here, and I was out of the water and had him in a moment.

He dealt similarly with Tommy Turbulent, a small boy who used to steal other boys' marbles and play truant.

> When you see Susan Slattern, tell her I have my eye upon her, too. I know all about her capsizing the perambulator and throwing her baby out in the thistles.

Although I knew it was only a story, it nonetheless made a great impression on me, for this was an altogether different bunyip to the one of my terrified imaginings. This bunyip seemed a gentle fellow. He acted harshly only when appropriate, and his words were remarkably instructive and of value to all. But the greatest revelation for me was the way in which the bunyip's physical appearance was described:

> He had fins at his sides, which gave him the appearance of a whale, and as he had a difficulty in moving along the ground, and seemed much more at home in the water, she came to the conclusion at last that he must belong to the whale species.

I found this remarkable, given that we are a family of whalers and surrounded by whales, mostly dead, and from that point on, my fear of the bunyip diminished. What did I have to fear? My father was a whale-killer. Even a bad bunyip (presumably there were bad bunyips as well as decent bunyips) would be no match for his lance. I myself had stood upon the bloated underbelly of the ninety-foot blue whale whose ribs now form our pergola, as it lay belly-up in the shallows (this was for Mr. Wellings, our town photographer, in order to best demonstrate the whale's vast dimensions); how could a bunyip be more fearsome than that? I read the description aloud to my father, who raised his eyebrows thoughtfully and considered it a moment.

"Next time you go up the creek, take the whale gun with you," he said at last. "If there's no whales, we'll try bunyips."

And in fact, I did take the whale-gun with me up to the creek the next few times in the hope of contributing to our family's fortunes; however, I soon desisted as it was a cumbersome great thing and the water was enough to carry. Suffice it to say, the terrible fear I had suffered was now gone; I could go to the creek alone. For this reason, *Mr. Bunyip* remained a book close to my heart, and I endeavored to use it as a means of instructing the youngest two in particular. They had much they could learn from a little girl like Mary Somerville, *"who seemed to carry sunshine with her wherever she went, and was a universal favorite."* Annie and Violet did not think much of the book however, except to cackle in the most uproarious fashion at Susan Slattern throwing the baby out of the perambulator into the thistles.

An Unhappy Experience

THREE WEEKS INTO THE SEASON, AND NOT A WHALE WAS sighted. Please God, we prayed, not another season like the last. Every night my father would return from another fruitless day of keeping lookout at Boyd Tower; every night he would seek something different to blame. It was a parasite, a worm of some kind burrowing into the whales' brains and thus diminishing the population. It was the Norwegians with their factory steamers and their explosive harpoons. The whales had changed their breeding grounds. The water was too warm, or possibly too cold. After his dinner, he would sit by the fire and forbid us from speaking, lest he miss the call of a wandering humpback. Please God, we prayed, bring our father a whale. Make it a big one, with plenty of whalebone. Let him pay off all his debts, and stop from worrying.

To add to my discomfort, I was becoming increasingly pre-occupied with my feelings for John Beck. Since our exchange over the bandages at the kitchen door, I had seen him only briefly when I served the whale men their slops; thus I found myself looking forward to this time of day with a mixture of eagerness and nervous dread. Unlike some of the other whalers, John Beck was invariably pleasant towards me; sometimes he even joked with me a little or teased me in a friendly way. Although I tried to respond in kind, I found I was often at a loss to know how best to reply to his remarks. Having lost my mother at an early age, I had no feminine example in matters concerning intercourse between the sexes. (I do not wish to give the impression that I am forever moaning about the loss of my mother. Most of the time, I do not think about it.) Being somewhat earnest by nature, I greatly feared I would make a dull companion; consequently, I had looked to romance novels for direction in these matters (the School of Arts had a small collection available for loan, although the waiting list was long). In so doing, I had often noticed a certain archness deployed by the heroines when addressing members of the opposite sex and I strived to emulate this tone whenever the opportunity arose, which was infrequently. I had been forced to practice on my brother Harry, or my father; however, I did not meet with much success, as my playful tones seemed only to irritate the former and bewilder the latter. In desperation, I had even attempted to engage my Uncle Aleck in repartee, but it was difficult to sparkle when constantly having to repeat things in a louder voice.

I now attempted to adopt this lightness of manner when speaking with John Beck, to the extent that I became quite nervous and excitable in his company and had even been cultivating what I had hoped to be a gay and tinkling laugh. However, my brother Harry took me aside one evening and said to me, in his surly fashion: "Stop with this dreadful false merriment you've been assuming of late. You're greatly embarrassing me." Admittedly, as my brother and closest sibling, Harry was the least forgiving of my foibles; be that as it may, I was nonetheless aghast that I had perhaps been creating an unfortunate impression of myself. I now seemed to lose what little self-confidence I possessed; I began to find it difficult to simply look at John Beck in a casual, nonchalant fashion, or even to meet his gaze when he spoke to me. The responses I gave to his queries seemed to suffer, at best, from a stilted quality. In trying not to be falsely gay my conversation became overly self-conscious and strained. It soon reached the stage (over a period of two to three weeks) where, in my anxiety not to offend, I seemed to be losing the capacity for speech altogether. And what was the reason for all this agony? Because I had bandaged John Beck's hands and he had smiled at me.

I had suffered a similar experience before, in fact, during the previous season, with a man called Charley Burrows. He had been one of my father's best oarsmen; in fact, my father thought so well of him that he had elevated him to the position of headsman of the second whaleboat. Burrows was a ruddy-faced young man, well-liked by all for his readiness with a joke or a quip. He was at first very amiable towards me; we had a little joke together where he would call me "Curly" or "Curly-Top" (owing to my hair) and I would call him "Ginger" or "Gingernut" (owing to his hair). He would often volunteer to carry the pots and dishes up to the house for me after dinnertime, and it was always "Curly, let me get the door" and "Curly, have we got any jam for our bread and butter?" and "Curly-Top, tell us what's new in the newspaper."

Flattered by his attentions, I found myself rapidly developing feelings towards him. As with John Beck, these feelings manifested themselves in my becoming rather nervous in his company, and unable to converse with him any longer in a relaxed fashion. The other whalers noticed this and began to tease me, making a great joke of my blushing and so forth. Hoping that Burrows would speak up for me, I found that his manner seemed instead to become increasingly cool towards me. He no longer called me Curly, nor would he volunteer to carry the pots and pans for me. When I attempted to engage him in conversation (and I was careful to keep my subjects general, some topical issue in the newspaper perhaps), he would respond in a surly fashion if he responded at all. One night, as I passed him his meal, I said to him, "Here you are then, Gingernut," and he scowled at me and told me not to call him that. Needless to say, I was exceedingly hurt and bewildered by this apparent change of heart: after all, he had been very civil towards me at first. However, I was soon to discover the true reason behind it all.

It transpired, in fact, that Burrows was a drinker. One evening, on bringing down their meal, I found that several of the men had procured a quantity of rum. Burrows in particular was intoxicated and reeling about the sleeping huts, singing a song about a jolly tinker which contained several lewd verses. He followed me up to the house on the pretense of helping me with the pots; instead he lunged at me and attempted to kiss me. I broke free and scrambled away, whereupon he hurled insults at me and accused me of having encouraged him and led him on unfairly. Horrified, I returned to the house, saying nothing of this at all to my father.

Instead, I took myself off to my bed, and lay there wide awake, going over and over in my mind this dreadful development. Although I had many times tried to imagine myself being kissed, even somewhat roughly, by Burrows, the reality had in fact been most unpleasant and rather upsetting. His breath had smelled of liquor and his beard had scratched my face; also his tongue had become involved, which I had not expected and found alarming, as if a sea slug was flailing about in my mouth. Perhaps I should not have been surprised by his behavior; whalers were inclined to imbibe heavily, especially if they had recently captured a whale (which had not been the case in this instance). Well aware of their propensity towards ribaldry when inebriated, my father usually ensured that we kept well away from them if there was any sign of them carousing in the sleeping huts. However, on this occasion, my father had been preoccupied with his own concerns (brooding on the absence of whales and so forth), and had thus unwittingly allowed me to venture down to the sleeping huts alone.

However, even more upsetting to me than his intoxication was the fact that Burrows had so rudely attempted to make love to me after lately treating me with such coldness. If he liked me well enough to want to kiss me, why had he been treating me with such indifference? Could it be that he drank more than I realized, and the drink was causing him to behave in such a way? I sat down and wrote Burrows a long letter, in which I discussed my bewilderment at his conduct towards me. I suggested as delicately as I could that this might be a consequence of his dipsomania and that, if he could adopt a more abstemious way of life, then indeed there might be a chance of our friendship developing into something deeper. I indicated that if he was prepared to embrace a life of abstinence, then I was certainly prepared to overlook the unfortunate incident of the previous night and start afresh.

The next morning, the crews were away early as usual to spend the day on lookout at South Head. Realizing I would not have an opportunity to see Burrows until evening, I worked all day on polishing and refining my letter. I crossed out entire paragraphs and reinstated them; I fretted over misspellings and attempted as far as possible to improve my childish, back-sloping handwriting. By evening, I had completely rewritten the entire five pages several times over.

That night, the crews returned later than usual; in fact, Dan and I had been waiting for them at the jetty for some time. We had hoped that their late return might be a consequence of them capturing a whale; however we soon learned that this was not the case. It seems they had rowed over to Eden for the purposes of letting Burrows off; he had "had a gutful" of whaling (according to Harry) and was not coming back. Whether he had indeed given up in disgust at the shortage of whales or had been released from his duties by my father, I was never able to discover. I had certainly said nothing of the incident the previous evening to anybody, and yet my father instructed my brothers to accompany me to the sleeping huts that night and from thenceforth. The men were exceedingly subdued that evening; I felt a tension in the atmosphere that I could only surmise contained a degree of resentment towards me. As I say, Burrows had been well-liked by the men; I imagine they were sorry he had gone.

But I was also sorry, and I kept my letter in the hope that he might return.

The reason I go on at such length about this unpleasantness is in part because Harry himself had introduced the subject of Burrows on the occasion that he had taken me aside to berate me for my false merriment and for being an embarrassment to him. "Don't be doing to the Reverend what you did to Burrows," he had cautioned me. When I asked him to explain more fully what he meant, he indicated that I knew very well what he meant, and on that note ended our conversation. I can only conclude by this that my personal feelings for Burrows had been so plainly evident that they were somehow construed as granting him permission to make improper advances to me.

"Why don't you talk to me anymore?" asked John Beck one night, as I gathered up the dirty dishes outside the sleeping huts. "Have I offended you in some way?"

"No," I stammered. "You have not offended me."

"Because you used to like to talk to me, and now you don't."

"That's because I am busy with my chores," I said.

"Did you not want to see how my blisters have healed?" he asked, with a smile coming over his face again.

"No, I don't," I replied quickly, and scurried away just as fast as I could.

Tom Raises the Alarm

I AWOKE SUDDENLY TO HEAR A DISTANT BUT DETERMINED *smack!* It was a Killer whale flop-tailing, surely? *Smack!* There it was again, and no doubt about it this time. I jumped out of bed and hurried out to the veranda—my father was running stiff-legged down to the sleeping huts, shouting, "*Rush oh! Get up, boys! Rush oh!*"

Hurrying around the side of the house, I climbed up the ladder to where the boys slept inside the roof. Both Harry and Dan were sound asleep—what heavy sleepers boys were as a rule! I sometimes thought it might be necessary to detonate the whale gun in order to rouse them. "Harry, get up, there's a whale!" I cried, shaking him vigorously. He opened his bleary eyes, and lay there inert for a moment; however, upon poking him sharply and reiterating my point, he finally seemed to rouse fully and started groping for his trousers.

I clambered down the ladder and rushed to the kitchen now to hastily fill two waterproof canvas bags with yesterday's damper and some salted beef. I thrust these at Harry as he scrambled down the ladder. "Don't forget the kegs!" I cried, and he scooped up a keg of water with his free arm. "Dan, take the other!" I instructed, as Dan jumped down off the last few rungs. He picked up the second keg and set off down the hill at a gallop, although with some difficulty as the keg was heavy for a small boy.

Back on the veranda, I could see the men now rushing for the whaleboats. There was John Beck, scrambling to jump in. Annie and Violet were awake now, and at my side. "Come on, girls, let's see them off," I cried. We ran for our coats, which we pulled on over our nightgowns, and we raced up the hill to where we could gain a reasonable vantage point of the bay.

"It's Tom!" cried Annie, and there he was, our famous Killer whale, leaping out of the water and crashing down his tail, impatient for the whalers to join him. As ever, I felt something of a shock when I saw him. He was so crisply illustrated, as it were; his black head so shiny and his white patches so luminous that he struck me as absurdly cheerful in his appearance as a carousel horse at a fairground. He had none of the dismal, barnacled gray of the humpback: no, he was a portly and dapper fish in white tie and dinner jacket. How homely and dull humpbacks were in comparison, I thought to myself. (Or at least they certainly seemed so as the men at the capstan prepared to haul off their blubber, which is when I had had most occasion to observe them.) Sometimes, at night, when we heard the anguished cow-like moan of the humpback, my sister Louisa would say: "Listen! A humpback has just seen its own reflection," which set the younger ones to giggling. My father told us that on several occasions he had witnessed younger humpbacks bedecked in seaweed, as if in a bid to improve their appearance.

The girls occupied themselves by calling out excitedly to Tom, in the hope that he might somehow acknowledge them. He paid us no direct attention, except to perform more spectacular breaches; perhaps he was showing off for our benefit. Meanwhile, I scoured the bay in the hope that I could spot the whale, and thus assist my father. Was that a plume of smoke rising up near Snug Cove? My eyesight was not reliable at a distance, but yes, I felt certain that that was smoke. Somebody had obviously sighted the whale, perhaps a fisherman at Eden wharf, and had lit a fire in order to alert my father as to its whereabouts. Now my father's boat appeared below, his men pulling hard at the oars. *"Smoke!"* I cried out. My father, at the steer oar, looked up at me; I pointed towards Snug Cove and cried out, "Smoke at Snug Cove!" I could see him squinting in that direction. He called out to me, "Where?"

"Snug Cove!" I cried again. Was there smoke at Snug Cove? I wondered suddenly. It was certainly quite difficult to see at the moment, given the heaviness of the clouds.

"I don't see any smoke," said Annie, standing beside me.

"Smoke at Snug Cove!" my father was now calling to Harry. Harry was headsman of the second boat, which was coming up quickly behind my father's boat. I could see every head turn in the direction of Snug Cove, straining to see. Where had it gone, that plume of smoke? Perhaps the fire had been accidentally extinguished?

"Where did you say?" cried Harry.

"Snug Cove!"

"I don't see any smoke at Snug Cove!"

"Nor me!" This from Darcy, who had the best eyes of all.

"Mary thought she saw smoke!"

"Mary?" riposted Harry. "She's blind as a bat, for Christ's sake!"

I could see John Beck look up towards me now and felt suddenly mortified. I had leapt out of bed in such excitement that I had not considered my appearance and my hair was now blowing about wildly in the stiff breeze. Just then, providing a welcome distraction, Tom rushed up suddenly out of the water and flop-tailed directly between the two boats, thoroughly drenching the occupants. The men cursed the Killer whale vehemently.

"Stop your complaining!" I heard my father cry. "At least now you might wake up a bit! Come on, put your backs into it!"

The men leaned in to their oars and took off in pursuit of Tom, all talk of smoke now forgotten. I felt a rush of excitement as I watched the two dark-green boats fighting their way through the breakers. A hard northeasterly wind ripped across the bay; it was not at all a good day for small boats such as these, and now as I gazed upon the churning sea I wondered that they were going out in it at all.

"Good luck!" I cried to my father, and also to John Beck, although they were well past the breakers now and could not hear me. The girls jumped about in excitement; also in a bid to keep themselves warm. Uncle Aleck staggered up the hill to join us; Dan bounded up as well, anxious to see them off. Together, our little group watched until Killer whale and whaleboats had rounded the point and disappeared from view.

"Godspeed," said Uncle Aleck. "Bring us back a humper, Georgie boy."

We spent the rest of the day trying to occupy ourselves with the usual mundane chores; however, I doubt that many minutes passed between one or other of us scampering up the hill in the vain hope of witnessing our warriors engaged in battle. I should add that Tom had led them off towards Honeysuckle Point, which is in the opposite direction to Snug Cove, so perhaps I had been wrong about the smoke.

Canst Thou Draw Out
Leviathan with a Fish Hook?

MY FATHER AND HIS CREW RETURNED AT ABOUT FOUR in the afternoon, covered in whale blood, weary but triumphant. The second boat returned some forty minutes later with Harry in a foul temper and his crew looking exceedingly shame-faced. A humpback had been captured; however, another had somehow managed to escape. The crew of the second boat had been found sadly wanting.

In short, from what I could glean, the chase and ensuing capture had gone as follows: Tom had led the men to where the Killers were engaged in harassing two whales; they succeeded in separating the whales just as the boats arrived and the Killers subsequently applied their attentions to the smaller of the beasts. My father and his men immediately set off in pursuit of the larger whale. It zigzagged desperately in a bid to shake them off, and considerable time elapsed before my father was sufficiently close for his harpooner to throw his iron. My father always used Arthur Ashby in this capacity; he was one of our longstanding Aboriginal whalers, and tremendously accurate with his aim. From this point, I will quote from the *Eden Observer and South Coast Advocate,* in which an account of the chase appeared several days later:

> The Killers had been engaged with the smaller whale, but no sooner had the larger animal been harpooned than they were present, attacking it with desperate energy; and its loud and continuous bellowing told clearly the deadly battle that was being waged beneath the troubled waters of the bay. The spray flew continuously over the frail craft, in quantities sufficient to dampen the ardour of any but George Davidson and his plucky men, who don't seem to understand the meaning of the word danger or have a total disregard for it.

We were fortunate to have such a fine writer as Mr. Phillips, the editor of the *Eden Observer and South Coast Advocate* at the time. Although the men would often mutter that he'd got some small detail wrong here or there, his accounts nonetheless offer a tremendous record of my father's work. We made sure to cut out every article and preserve them in a scrapbook, sometimes making small annotations in ink on the side. Uncle Aleck would often have me read aloud his favorites by the fireside of an evening, and although my father acted like he didn't much care, you could tell he was listening intently.

> Crowds of people occupied the different headlands, and, notwithstanding the bitterly cold wind which was blow-

ing, watched the chase with keen interest. From the heights of Cattle Bay could be seen almost every movement of the whale as it tore onwards from Quarantine Bay, from time to time rising above the surface of the water and throwing great bodies of foam in all directions, as attack after attack was made upon it by the Killers, whose persistent onslaughts were witnessed with great wonder by visitors. While a number of Killers always remained close by the head of the whale, tearing at its jaws and impeding its progress by many methods, others were acting as sentinels well ahead and in its wake, and as they rose to the surface, spouting up the water, exhibiting their bodies and long black fins, they presented a sight never to be forgotten.

The roughness of the water prevented a free use of the lance for some time, and then one of the Killers, being in a frolicsome rather than a business mood, caught the whale line in its mouth and hung on to it for considerable time...

Although Mr. Phillips has refrained from naming the guilty party, clearly this was Tom up to his usual tricks.

...and as the whale turned in the middle of the bay and steered a course for the open sea, it was feared the crew might suffer a loss; but nearing the lookout, George Davidson, standing in the bow of the boat, was seen to be using the lance with great effect. Just here the whale made a quick turn and for a minute or so whale, Killers and boats seemed to be an inextricable mass, and the crowds of people on shore looked on with feverish excitement lest an accident should happen. It is such a position as this that coolness, seamanship, and complete knowledge of the tactics of the whale show out to great advantage, and all these qualifications are possessed by George Davidson. Another turning movement and the whale was bound seawards again; but his life was a short one for, as it rose to the surface, upwards went a volume of blood, and the whole surface of the water was seen to be dyed with the crimson fluid. Onwards, however, the whale went until off Lookout Point, when suddenly it collapsed, and a few final thrusts of the lance and the first whale of the season was killed.

The second boat, led by my brother Harry, meanwhile made several attempts to fasten to the smaller whale, but, as reported in the same account:

> his somewhat amateurish crew were either unable or unwilling to get within the required distance to throw the harpoon with any chance of success and consequently he had to be content with following the "fast" boat to render aid in the event of an accident taking place.

Here I see that I have underlined the words *unable or unwilling* and inscribed a tiny question mark in the margin.

I should explain that the second boat is often relegated to the role of "pick-up boat"; that is, if the whale line, tearing out of the boat, flicks a man into the water, then the second boat picks him up. Similarly, if the whale stoves in a portion of the boat (this happened rarely, again mainly due to the afore-mentioned qualities of my father). Sometimes, if a whale was particularly large or possessed of unnatural vitality, or if the first boat's harpoon had not gained a secure purchase within the whale's flesh, then the second boat would also make fast to this same whale; however, this was dangerous in practice as the two lines could become crossed in the ensuing chase, and the two boats end up plowing into one another at high speed. If the Killers had apprehended more than one whale, then the duty of the second boat was to harpoon and capture the second whale or, at the very least, to remain fast to the whale until such time as the first boat could render assistance. In this instance, it seems that the crew of the second boat was deemed *"unable or unwilling."* Certainly the crew included three new chums (John Beck amongst them), but I wonder if the blame could not be at least in part attributed to my brother's inexperience in the role of headsman.

I should perhaps pause here to outline in more detail the duties of the headsman. He is sometimes described as the chief officer of the boat; he steers the boat from the stern with the long sweep or steer oar, until the boat has gained sufficient proximity for the harpooner to employ his tool. It is a highly skilled position and calls for a man with experience; when a whale has sounded, it falls upon the headsman to predict where it might resurface and set his course accordingly. Here it must be said (and perhaps Mr. Phillips of the *Observer* was alluding to this when he referred to my father's *"complete knowledge of the tactics of the whale"*) that my father had an uncanny instinct for the underwater maneuverings a whale might attempt. Frequently was a whale surprised by the cold steel of a harpoon when it at last came up for air.

At this point, once the boat is attached to the whale by means of the harpoon, the headsman then changes position with the harpooner in order to lance the whale from the bow of the boat. This "changing of the guard" between the headsman and harpooner is a time-honored practice, but puzzling to the uninitiated. Here is the whale stung by the harpoon and desperately trying to outrun its tormentors, yet just at this critical and dangerous moment, the headsman and the harpooner must each scramble to opposite ends of a thirty-foot boat, doing their utmost not to become entangled in the whale line which is whipping out of the boat at such speed that the friction as it pulls around the loggerhead will sometimes cause it to ignite.

"But why does the headsman not simply harpoon the whale himself?" I once asked my father.

"Because that is the job of the harpooner," he replied in a kindly fashion, as if to a halfwit.

"Then could not the harpooner just stay at the bow and lance the whale?" I asked, feeling as if I may have unwittingly stumbled across a simple solution to a vexing problem.

"Oh no. No. No chance of that."

"Why not?" I persisted.

"Because that is the job of the headsman."

I could tell by the tone of his voice that he did not wish to continue this line of conversation, so I desisted. However, I do not pretend to know better than my father; there is much about whaling that my father chose not to explain to me, although I took an avid interest; indeed, there is much about whaling that he tried to spare me. The truth is that throwing the harpoon and wielding the lance are two quite distinct disciplines. Certainly, great skill was required of the headsman to hasten the whale's demise; a mortally wounded whale in its "death flurry" is extremely dangerous. The headsman would take aim at the whale's vulnerable spot, about three feet back from its side fin; sometimes, a single thrust of the lance, a mighty shudder and it would all be over. At other times, however, many more thrusts of the lance were required; occasionally, the vitality of the whale was such that it simply would not die. On one moonless night in 1905, a large humpback set such a determined course out to sea after having been repeatedly lanced and even fired upon by the whale gun, that my father was forced to cut it loose, deeming the operation too perilous to continue. They had chased this whale for six hours and over many miles; in spite of its injuries, it showed no sign of weakening, and yet my father considered it could not possibly live. In cutting adrift, my father lost a harpoon and eight fathoms of line.

I go into detail here about the role of the headsman because I feel it is important to understand that it is a demanding and difficult position, the headsman's skill in both steering and lancing being crucial to the outcome. Harry at that time was only eighteen years of age, and had been promoted to the position of headsman of the second boat only owing to my father's extreme difficulty in finding crew members. Harry maintained, in this instance, that his crew had not rowed hard enough, that they seemed leery of getting too close to the whale, but I wonder, was that really the cause? Surely it is up to the headsman to steer the course whereby they are best positioned to encounter the whale when it next resurfaces? Surely it is up to the headsman to encourage and inspire his men with his own steady nerve? These are questions that I felt needed to be asked of Harry; however, given his foul temper that evening, I thought better of doing so.

At mealtime that night, the crew of the second boat was given a pretty thorough bucketing by the others. When Dan and I brought down the evening meal, John Beck seemed not his normal self, but rather pale and shaken; he took his plate from me without a word and moved off to sit alone, some distance from the others. This concerned me; it was not unheard of for new chums to "do a runner" after their first taste of whaling, and my father could ill-afford to lose an oarsman.

I brooded over this as I washed the dishes, and as soon as I was free of my duties, I sought him out with the idea of offering him some words of encouragement. Night had fallen and, apart from a slush lamp flickering within a sleeping hut, all was in darkness. It seemed that the whale men, worn out by their exertions, had taken themselves off to bed. With some difficulty, I negotiated the path down to the try-works and stood for a moment on the slipway, holding up my lantern in a bid to peer further into the darkness.

"Well, you were right, Mary," said a voice behind me.

I turned quickly and saw that John Beck was leaning up against the capstan behind me.

"What about?" I responded.

"There's a great deal of blood in these whales."

"Ah," I said. "Yes."

Although pleased to be vindicated, I had no wish to gloat at this moment, so I said nothing further. Moreover, I felt suddenly uncertain as to what I might say that would best offer comfort or encouragement at this time. John Beck also remained silent, seeming greatly preoccupied, although owing to the darkness it was difficult to be sure. Several moments passed; it was John Beck himself who finally spoke.

"*Canst thou draw out Leviathan with a fish hook?*" he asked.

"I beg your pardon?" I said. In truth, his comment startled me.

"*Or press down his tongue with a cord? Canst thou put a rope through his nose, or pierce his jaw through with a hook?*" he intoned.

I was now genuinely at a loss; unfamiliar as I was with much of the Bible, I was uncertain whether a response of some kind was expected of me.

"*Wilt thou play with him as with a bird?* No, that's not right....How does it go again, I wonder? Do you know the passage I mean, Mary? I find I cannot quite remember it, and yet it now seems so important that I do."

As I feared, he certainly did sound discouraged.

"I gather you found your first encounter with a whale to be startling," I said, summoning all my nerve to speak directly. "It put you in mind of something biblical."

"Yes," he said. "Yes, it did. Oh, Mary, such a sight to behold."

"I have never seen one actually alive," I confessed. "A spout in the distance, perhaps. Mind you, I've seen plenty of them dead, of course, belly-up here on the slipway."

"Ah yes," said John Beck. "That's a pity. For it's a sight to surely fill one with awe."

"I gather that you were perhaps too filled with awe to bring yourself to row close enough to the drat thing?"

There was silence in the darkness.

"Who told you that?"

"That is just the general impression I have formed."

"Has there been a complaint?"

"No. Not really. Look, it's common for new chums to be scared—"

"I wasn't scared."

"Filled with awe then—whatever you wish to call it. Frankly, I mostly blame Harry. He doesn't have the experience to be headsman yet. I don't know what Dad was thinking. Anyway, first whale of the season! Plenty of time to get your nerve up! I'm sure on the next occasion you won't be letting one get away." I gave a light laugh. I had meant this speech to instill in him a sense of optimism and verve, but even as the words spilled out, I began to doubt their efficacy. For although I could see him only dimly by my lantern light, I could sense in him a mounting irritation. There was silence; then a short sigh, as if of exasperation.

"Well, Mary, I will try not to let you down again," he said. "Goodnight."

And with that, he wandered off towards the sleeping hut.

The Trying-out

HERE I WILL ATTEMPT TO DOCUMENT THE INTERESTING process of "trying-out"; that is, rendering the blubber into whale oil. Although the smells were abhorrent and the spectacle gory, I often tried to find time to study at least part of the trying-out process, and sometimes brought with me my sketchbook. Looking at these sketches now, I see that I had a great deal of difficulty with the subject; in fact, the longer I stare at them, the less I am able to make sense of what these earnest scratchings are supposed to represent. For if a whale is difficult to draw when alive and kitted out in all its blubber, it is nigh on impossible when just a mountain of indeterminate, unwholesome flesh, denuded of blubber, fins and features, and left abandoned in the shallows. I would sometimes catch our house cat Philly sitting on the slipway staring at these remains—as keen as she was on fish scraps, the very sight of these seemed somehow to defeat her.

The humpback recently captured had "gassed up" within a

day or so and risen to the surface; the Killers had taken their portion, and now the whalers towed it back to the try-works and immediately set to the task at hand. It was not a job they greatly relished, yet they applied themselves to it in a deter-mined fashion, the new chums learning from the old. First, armed with the blubber spade, my father clambered to the top of the carcass and, making an incision near the tail end, cut a piece along the length of the whale about twenty feet long and six feet wide. A rope was then attached to one end of this piece and fastened to the capstan. Seven or eight of the men (includ-ing John Beck on this occasion) then put their weight to turn-ing the capstan, thus slowly prizing the "blanket" away—for it did not come easily—my father hacking at it with his blub-ber spade whenever it should stick. In this laborious fashion, the belly side of the whale was flensed of its blubber, and with aid of heavy tackling and much heaving and grunting on the part of the whale men, the whale was then turned over for the same process to be repeated on the other side. This particular humpback was not an especially large one, yet the process still took a great many hours.

Those men not engaged in flensing would commence cut-ting the "blankets" into "junks," which were then sliced into smaller pieces, called "horses," and tossed in a vat to render into whale oil. After a period of time, these pieces were pulled out again and placed on the mincing horse to be sliced into thin leaves, and thence into the try pot itself, where they would liquefy into valuable whale oil. The oil would then flow automatically into a series of coolers, and from there be ladled into large iron tanks, and then into casks for storage.

Uncle Aleck himself took the task of supervising the try

pots, standing by with his skimmer and every so often pulling out a piece of crispy blubber and examining it closely. Only when he was satisfied that every last ounce of oil had been extracted would he toss it aside. It could then be used to fuel the fire, although the smell was not pleasant.

"I have a question for you, Father," said Uncle Aleck. Glistening with blood and oil, he looked like a creature from the bowels of hell as he stirred the foul contents of his cauldron.

"Oh yes?" said John Beck. He also glistened with blood and oil, yet somehow the effect on him was more pleasing.

"It's a theological question of sorts."

"By all means. Ask away."

"I believe you were a minister of the Methodist church?"

"That's right, for a time."

"In your frank opinion then, Father," said Uncle Aleck, "how do you find the Methodist ladies compare with Presbyterian girls? I'm speaking purely of appearance—never mind personality for the moment."

Uncle Aleck had never married, and his thoughts often lingered upon such topics.

"Well, I couldn't rightly say," said John Beck, and at this point he glanced over to where I sat sketching, some small distance away. "I've not had a lot to do with Presbyterian girls."

"More's the pity! Presbyterian girls are the prettiest by a country mile!" volunteered young Robert. Some of the whale men then proceeded to offer their own opinions on the subject; Bastable took the case for the Anglican lasses while Salty admired the good women of the Salvation Army. The conversation was just turning to the Little Sisters of the Sacred Heart when my father instructed me to get back up to the house.

"But why? I've nothing to do up there."

"This is no place for you, that's why."

Annoyed with him, I gathered my drawing implements and headed off up to the house; the whole area was awash with blood and whale oil, but thankfully I did not slip.

Excursion to Boyd Tower

ITUATED ON THE CLIFF TOP AT SOUTH HEAD, BOYD Tower was built by Benjamin Boyd, one of the founding fathers of the Eden district. He was a pastoralist, banker, adventurer and whale man who later went broke and took off in his schooner, only to be killed and eaten by natives somewhere in the Pacific. Such is life. The structure is some sixty feet high, and constructed of sandstone: across the four stones at the very top of the monument is carved the word BOYD. Inside, a series of perilous ladders lead to the top, and if one is game to climb them, tremendous views of the ocean may be enjoyed. It was from this uppermost vantage point that our whale men took turns in keeping lookout each day from dawn to dusk.

It was now seven weeks into whaling season, and we had captured only the one moderately sized humpback. Since then, any whales that passed by on their journey north must have veered so wide of the coast that they eluded even our vigilant Killers. Could it be that the whales were growing more cunning? Strange to think that after almost a century of whaling in Twofold Bay, the whales might finally be concluding that it was better to avoid the place.

Boyd Tower

"You've never engaged in this line of work before then, Father?" asked Salty. They were leaning against the base of Boyd Tower, idly surveying the horizon. Other whale men were playing cards or draughts, or fishing off the rocks below.

"No," said John Beck. "This is my first time whaling."

"Well, then. That's grand. Good luck to you," said Salty,

sucking at his pipe. "Can you bear a word of advice from an old hand?"

"I'd be glad of any advice you could offer me."

"I've been doing this for thirty years now, and I've encountered a few whales in my time. I think I might know what I'm talking about."

"I would not doubt that," said John Beck.

"Nevertheless, you may dismiss it as the rantings of an old fellow, if you so choose. It is entirely up to you."

"Anything you have to tell me would be of great interest to me."

"I was not fortunate enough to get much in the way of schooling as a youngster; however, there is one area in which I am learned, and that is the subject of whales. In fact, some folk call me the Professor of Whales."

"I have no doubt that you are a great authority on the subject," said John Beck. He was beginning to think that Salty was something of a blowhard, and might never get to his point.

"An authority? Some may consider me so. The truth is, I would estimate that I've harpooned over two hundred whales in my time."

"Over two hundred whales in his imagination," said Darcy, rather cheekily. But Salty did not appear to hear him.

"And that is why I say to you, Father, do not fear the humpback. Nor fear the black whale, the blue whale or the white whale."

"All right," said John Beck. "Thank you. I will bear that in mind."

"No," said Salty, for he had not finished, "it is the spotted whale you must fear."

Darcy coughed quietly to himself.

"Spotted?" said John Beck.

"Aye. That's what I said. Spotted." At this point, Salty paused to stoke his pipe.

John Beck began to wonder if Salty was having some kind of joke at his expense, although he could not be entirely sure. He looked to Darcy, but Darcy was now bent over his work. He was carving a serpent out of a piece of driftwood.

"Do you know why it is you must be fearful of the whale who has spots, Father?" resumed Salty, having satisfactorily tended to his pipe.

"No, I do not."

"Those spots are old harpoon scars."

"I see."

"What I am telling you is this: *the whale has been harpooned before.*"

"I understand."

"Three things you must bear in mind now. First up, she'll be a boat-breaker, for likely that is how she got away. And if a whale has broken a boat once, she likes to do it again; oh yes, she enjoys it, as a child enjoys jumping on a sandcastle. Secondly, the whale knows all our tricks; oh yes, she has our measure. We can no longer surprise or outsmart her. Thirdly, and this is the worst of it…"

"Yes?" said John Beck.

"She is consumed with thoughts of vengeance."

Here he puffed away on his pipe to such a degree that his face became momentarily enshrouded in smoke. Again, John Beck looked to Darcy, but Darcy was now bent so intently over his work that his face was entirely hidden from view.

That day, I had decided to take the children on a picnic to Boyd Tower; they had been fighting amongst themselves and we had all been feeling cooped up. The fact was that we lived a long way from anywhere, and had not much in the way of transportation. Three or four seasons ago, we had had three good horses, ten head of cattle and several sheep, but the varying fortunes of whaling were such that we were now reduced to Two Socks, a good pulling horse although moody in temperament, and Betty, our milking cow. Betty was by no means an especially prepossessing cow, and yet she comported herself with an air of great self-satisfaction which oft times reminded me of my own sister Louisa. Certainly what bovine charms Betty possessed worked their spell upon Two Socks, for over the years he became inordinately attached to her and demonstrated the strength of his feelings by protesting strenuously if any attempts were ever made to separate them. Never a cooperative horse even before this infatuation, he could now only be persuaded to venture from the back paddock if Betty felt inclined to accompany him. This was not such a problem if we proposed a short journey, such as this one to Boyd Tower, which Betty could manage comfortably. However, it was a different thing altogether to have Betty accompany us all the way into Eden. Not only did the journey take three times as long, for Betty was a terrific dawdler and must sample the foliage, but also the exercise exhausted her and was bad for her milk. Suffice to say, there were times when, owing to a shortage of provisions, we had no choice but to go through this ordeal with cow in tow, but wherever possible, we waited till our father was going into town by means of his motor launch *Excelsior*. Of course, at the moment he was always on lookout, so this was not a possibility. Thus, the long months of whaling season loomed before us, stranded at Kiah, with slim possibility of outings.

Our three remaining chickens had managed between them to lay two eggs. In a rush of excitement I attempted the Economical Madeira cake from my mother's Presbyterian Women's Missionary Union cookbook. It turned out presentably enough and, while it was still warm, I wrapped it in a tea towel and we set off. Louisa and Uncle Aleck decided at the last minute that perhaps they would come after all, then the dogs took exception to being left at home, so all in all, we made quite a procession. The six of us would not fit in the buggy, so had to be taking turns walking, except Uncle Aleck, who was suffering with his lumbago. A lengthy and heated discussion ensued. Finally, it was resolved that there would be a changeover every two hundred paces; however Violet, the youngest, considered that somehow she should be exempt from this ruling and registered her protest by taking tiny, tiny steps and Annie, in her customary fashion pretending to be a horse, insisted on being a very nervous horse that shied at the slightest leaf rustle and finally balked altogether. At this point, our real horse, Two Socks, decided that he would only continue if Betty walked alongside him (up until then, Betty had been tied to the rear of the buggy), but Betty did not care to walk ahead because she did not like Patch, and Patch always had to take the lead in any expedition as he imagined himself to be our advance guard. So that meant we had to make Patch ride in the buggy, sitting across our laps, but he struggled so much that finally I walked just ahead of Betty and Two Socks, carrying Patch in my arms so he wouldn't annoy Betty. This worked well enough until a magpie got it into her head that we were after her babies so she began to swoop us; this frightened Betty and she balked, whereupon Two Socks balked, so now Dan had to get out of the buggy in order to hold Louisa's parasol above Betty's head so she could not see the magpie. But then Bonnie (who had been the least trouble of anyone) got a prickle in her paw, and made such a performance of bravely limping onwards that it was agreed she should ride in the buggy, at which point Patch decided, somewhat contrarily, that if Bonnie got to ride in the buggy, then so should he. I was glad of this, because Patch had been getting very heavy, but once in the buggy he became excited and commenced jumping about from one side of the buggy to the other until everybody screamed at him to "Sit!," whereupon he sat himself down on my Madeira cake.

"Stop yelling at Patch, Mary!" implored Annie.

My nerves were frayed and I had lost my temper; it was the way Patch was grinning at me whilst wagging his tail stump about in my Madeira cake.

"He's just a dog!" cried Violet, hugging him violently. "He can't help it!"

At which point, Patch noticed he was sitting in the Madeira cake and so commenced to eat it.

Soon after, we arrived at Boyd Tower, where the whale men stared at us perplexed.

"Why is the boy holding an umbrella over the cow?" asked Albert Thomas Senior, to which there was no sensible answer.

The magpie had stopped swooping some distance back, but Betty seemed to enjoy the shade that the parasol provided her.

One of the pleasures of visiting Boyd Tower was that it afforded, on occasion, an excellent vantage point from which to observe the marvelous work of the *Orca Gladiator*. The steep cliffs overlook Leatherjacket Bay, the preferred headquarters of the Killer whales when residing in Twofold Bay, and often they would pass the time between the real action of chasing whales by teaching the younger Killers the complex tactics and maneuvers involved in such a sport. Sure enough, much to the children's great excitement, a game of "Chase the Finback" was underway. An unfortunate finback had been enticed into the bay, and now found himself being herded back and forth and roundabout by several squads of Killer whales.

Each squad, consisting of seven or so Killers, seemed to have its own responsibilities. The first squad was involved in the direct chasing and harassment of the finback; the second concerned itself with heading off the creature from its desired course while the third squad formed a sentry line across the bay to contain any attempts at escape. The entire business was conducted at tremendous speed, and on several occasions the finback (who we estimated to be thirty feet in length) leapt entirely out of the water in his desperation to escape his tormentors. At one point, he charged towards the shallows as if to beach himself, but Hooky and Charlie Adgery would have none of that; they darted ahead and turned him round again, as if to say, "Oh no you don't, sir, we're not finished with you yet!"

As the finback grew more exhausted and began to slow

down, he was dealt a sharp nip to the tail by Tom and instructed to get a move on. Up and down and roundabout and do-si-do your partner; in this fashion, the game continued for most of the morning. Finally, they tired of it and got down to the real business. There was a great threshing and foaming of the water, and the finback disappeared from view.

My father watched their antics with amusement; however, I imagine he wished that the Killers were expending their efforts on chasing a real whale. Occasionally, if the Killers had driven a finback onto the beach, the men might tow the carcass home and go through the rigmarole of trying-out, but as there wasn't much blubber on them, it was hardly worth the effort. As for myself, I had found the Killers' play discomforting. Although the other spectators laughed and cheered as each bid to escape was thwarted, it struck me that the Killer whales were nothing more than a pack of schoolyard bullies. Their behavior demonstrated that they had not one ounce of compassion between them. I found myself overcome with sorrow for the hapless finback, to be hounded to death in such a fashion.

John Beck was on lookout in the tower for much of this time, and then he came down and said hello, to which I responded, "Hello."

We stood side by side in complete silence watching the blood and the oil spread across the water, and then he turned to me and said: "I would not much like to be a grampus, would you?"

"A grampus? Why do you say that?" I said sharply. I was sensitive on the subject as Harry used to tease me and say that I reminded him of a grampus he had seen washed up on a beach, and that it was lucky that the grampus had not been wearing spectacles, otherwise we would have been virtually indistinguishable from one another, and everybody would say, "Oh look, there's poor Mary Davidson washed up on a beach and covered in kelp." This never failed to upset me, and finally my father had ordered him to desist.

"Well," said John Beck, "because it has just been torn apart by the Killer whales."

"That was not a grampus; that was a finback. They are completely different."

"Really? Are you sure? Because Salty told me it was a grampus."

"Oh, Salty calls everything a grampus," I said dismissively. "What would he know?"

For some reason, I was sounding very bad-tempered, although I did not mean to. It was probably because I was hungry and had not thought to bring any food besides the Madeira cake which Patch had sat in. Yet even as I spoke, I recalled an article that I had cut out from the newspaper, entitled *"How a Woman Becomes Popular,"* from which I quote below:

She was not a pretty woman, rather plain than stylish, but of a cheerful temper. When asked to give a reason for her popularity, she answered: "A man is a sensitive creature, and in dealing with him, I bear that in mind. He does not like to be reminded of his shortcomings, nor does he care to hear another man praised for the attributes he lacks. He dislikes to be interrupted when telling a story, or set right over unimportant matters. I always try to talk to every man as he talks to me, and treat young men as if they were old and old men as if they were young. I can think of no other reason for my popularity."

The homely woman had made it her practice never to remind men of their shortcomings or set them right on unimportant matters, and here I was this very minute setting John Beck right on the subject of the grampus.

"Well," said John Beck, "I might take myself for a walk along the rocks then."

"Yes, all right then, why don't you," I said. I could certainly not be described as being *"of a cheerful temper."*

If he was going for a walk along the rocks, then I would take myself for a walk in the opposite direction—along the cliffs, perhaps, where I might spot a whale and be the heroine of the day. I was just setting off when I saw ahead of me Louisa sitting on a rock, with her young admirer Robert Heffernan in doting attendance. She made no attempt at concealing her boredom, and when she saw me jumped up eagerly and called out: "Can we go soon?"

"For goodness' sake, we have only just got here!" This was not true; we had been there for almost two hours. But for some reason, I was feeling oddly contrary. Louisa was forever setting men right or reminding them of their shortcomings, or in this case openly yawning out of boredom, and yet men admired her all the more for it! It was simply not fair. The homely woman did not know what she was talking about.

As I walked, my thoughts returned to the Killer whales, and their conduct regarding the finback. I realized that my discomfort in watching the harassment may well have stemmed from my own experiences at the hands of one Eunice

Martin and her friends at Sunday school. (Incidentally, this was the same Eunice Martin who had gone on to receive the blue ribbon at the Eden Show for *Towamba Eventide*, the depiction in watercolors of a five-legged cow at sunset.) She and her friends had poked fun at me because of my spectacles and said that I smelled like a dead whale. Also they had once shoved me into the sand at the Sunday school picnic. This sort of behavior went on for some time; however, when my mother died, my father lost all interest in attending church and so my torment finally ended. But it seemed to me that day, as I pondered what I'd seen, that the Killer whales were the Eunice Martins of the marine world.

And yet, had I known at the time what was to become of Eunice Martin, perhaps I would have judged her less harshly. For only several years hence, she was found in Towamba cemetery after attempting to poison herself. She had left several letters indicating where she might be found, placing the blame squarely on Constable Weston, who it seems may have molested her in some fashion. My sister Annie took a dim view of this, and said, "How difficult is it to poison yourself? And how convenient that she left so many letters indicating where she might be found so that she may be revived before it was too late." Certainly she recovered fairly promptly, but the family was obliged to leave the region shortly thereafter. In the meantime, Constable Weston had been hastily moved on to Barmedman, where it was expected that he might engage in further unwholesome activities involving young ladies of hitherto spotless reputations; there was a brief furor about it in the newspaper.

I had been charging along through the low shrub, not looking up but just stomping angrily head down and thinking about Eunice Martin, when suddenly I heard a cry: *"Rush oh! Rush oh!"* The lookout had spotted a whale! Where? I thought, furious at myself for not having spotted it first. I looked out to sea. At first I saw nothing, and then at once I saw it—a V-shaped spout of mist and the sense of an immense dark bulk beneath the water. I stood without breathing for a moment, not daring to believe it. Then a vast set of gnarled black flukes rose up out of the water and hung there, as if suspended.

The First Black Whale of the Season

THE WIND WAS WORKING UP TO A GALE AND THE WORK WAS heavy in pulling across the water. The whale had last been seen off Jews Head but, as the boats approached, had sounded. A considerable interval had passed and it had not yet reappeared. At different vantage points along the cliff tops, groups of onlookers were gathering and their cries could be heard across the water, urging the whalers on.

"It is all very well to shout at us," muttered Harry. "Kindly tell us where the whale went, if you wish to be useful."

He was out of sorts as he had been demoted from the position of headsman and was now taking the secondary role of harpooner. This meant more rowing, which was unfortunate, as whichever way they turned the wind was against them. They had already rowed many miles with only occasional distant glimpses of their elusive quarry.

"Are we just to row round and round in the hopes it will come up beneath us?" he asked, with a note of petulance.

"These whales can certainly hold their breath for a long time," remarked Robert Heffernan.

Salty, who had taken the role of headsman, urged them to shut up. The crowd on the headland had broken into screams and shouts, and were waving their hats and handkerchiefs in the direction of Cattle Bay. There it was, spouting idly, basking in the winter sunlight. It was the length of a steamer, and even from this distance, you could see that its head was a mass of unsightly callouses.

"Black whale all right," said my father, turning the boat towards Cattle Bay. A cheer went up amongst his boatmen. A black whale (or a "right" whale as they are also known, because they are the "right" whale to catch) is the most valuable of all the whales, especially a big one like this one. Its whalebone would be long; its blubber thick.

My father's boat led the way, moving quietly so as not to startle the leviathan. Arthur Ashby rose to his feet and braced his thigh in the cleat, his harpoon poised. The whale wallowed contentedly in the water, quite unconcerned, almost as if it hadn't seen them. The boat crept up to within four or five boat-lengths away. But just as Arthur pulled his arm back to launch his iron, the whale curved its broad back and slid under the water, flicking its flukes idly. The crowd let out a cry of disappointment. Arthur Ashby lowered his harpoon.

"Where was she off to then, George?" cried Salty, across the water.

My father shook his head. He gazed intently at the circle of smooth water the whale had left behind, trying to read in its shape some idea of the whale's intentions. Up above, an albatross hovered—the men looked up at it hopefully. Seabirds often provided clues as to a whale's whereabouts; they were both, after all, interested in the same food. Sometimes, if a whale was lunging through a patch of krill with its mouth open, the cheekier birds liked to swoop in and pick off any morsels of marine life stuck in the whalebone. The albatross, however, veered off on the wind.

"Where are the Killers?" asked Bastable, disgruntled. "Have they not noticed there's a whale in the bay?"

"Too full of ruddy finback," muttered someone.

"We try calling them, boss?" asked Albert Thomas Junior.

My father leaned on his steer oar, peering intently at the water. Finally he nodded. The men raised their oars high and, at a given signal, brought the blades down hard upon the water in a single resounding *smack!*

Up on the headlands, the crowd fell quiet; all studying the water, all eager to be first to raise up the cry. A bank of clouds passed in front of the sun. There was an eerie atmosphere suddenly, and a feeling of heaviness in the air. Gently, the boats rose and fell, the water slapping at the sides. A short distance away, a cloud of mutton-birds materialized as if from nowhere and wheeled in wild formation just above the surface of the water. The men watched in silence as the birds banked sharply to one side and skimmed low across the surface, seeming to dip their very wingtips in the water.

"Mutton-birds," said the newcomer Shankly, darkly. "They are not a tasty bird, by any means."

The others looked at him in surprise. Shankly rarely spoke, and when he did say something, it generally had a portentous quality about it.

"Well, that depends!" responded Salty. "It depends on how long you boil them."

"I believe they are very good if stewed at length in port wine," offered John Beck, but Shankly just shook his head grimly. It appeared he had a set against the mutton-bird.

"Salty!" called my father, whose mind was still on matters whaling. "Head over towards Quarantine Bay. We'll go towards Snug Cove."

"Right you are!"

The two boats separated and began moving off in opposite directions. They had not traveled far when, from the cliff tops, the piercing cry of a small boy rent the air.

"Whale! Whale! Whale!"

Where? wondered the whale men, turning to look up at him, and just now, with a loud spout from its blowhole, the black whale rose up directly alongside the Number Two boat. The inexperienced oarsmen reared back; their instinct was to flee, but unable to flee, they froze and stared at the sight before them. It was difficult to make sense of what they were seeing. It was huge, unmistakably, though most of its mass was concealed underwater; gray-black in color with a flat broad back. Its ugly, misshapen head had the tumorous quality of an ancient anthill, or a tree stricken with abscesses. These tumors, one of which sat comically atop its head like a bonnet, were whitish in color with a quality similar to lichen, and within this lichen, odd dark stalagmites sprouted from which rivulets of water streamed. Its vast coal-scuttle mouth curved downwards, and at one end of this a tiny eye, rheumy like an old man's, gazed up at them. It was grotesque and prehistoric in appearance, yet not unfriendly.

"It's big, isn't it?" said Robert in a hoarse whisper, and I suppose that is what they were all thinking.

"For God's sake, get your iron up, Harry!" hissed Salty.

Harry rose to his feet and scrabbled for his harpoon. With a sigh, the whale began to move away. The oarsmen remained stunned, their oars in mid-air.

"Row!" cried Salty, and his voice seemed to have risen an octave. "Don't let it get away, you useless b-----ds!"

This epithet appeared to rouse the men from their reverie. They seized their oars and began to pull, all out of time with one another, their blades colliding.

"Take her, Harry!" cried my father, whose boat was beginning to catch up. "Don't wait for us!" My brother raised his harpoon with trembling hands. The notion of plunging such an implement into this mountain of whale seemed suddenly ludicrous, like sticking a hatpin into an elephant.

"You have her in sights?" asked Salty.

"I have her," said Harry, and he braced his thigh against the cleat in readiness. But just at that moment, the leviathan spouted a percussive *Bosh!*, and the fetid spray blew over him, stinging his cheeks. His iron was poised above his head, but for some reason he did not throw it.

"Dart, dart, you imbecile!" cried Salty. "Into the old girl's gizzards!"

"Use your iron, son!" cried my father.

"Harpoon her!" cried the people on the cliff tops.

These exhortations were not helpful to Harry. He tossed his harpoon, but in his panicked state, it fell short and landed in the water with a dispiriting slap.

The whale dived, smacking the water with its flukes and

thereby drenching the boat's occupants. The crowds howled their dismay, as did the whalers.

"God Almighty!" cried Salty, his face bright red, his gray hair dripping.

"My hand slipped!"

"He throws like a girl!"

"This is where nepotism gets you," cried Bastable. "The boy has been promoted regardless of merit."

"Shut up, the lot of you, for Christ's sake!" said my father.

Chastened like children, the men fell silent. Even the crowds on the headlands desisted from hurling their derisive comments.

My father stood gripping his steer oar, his face a study of grim concentration. Minutes passed; nobody spoke. Hearts thudded in chests.

Some distance away, a Killer whale leapt out of the water, and slammed the full weight of its body upon the surface— the sound ricocheted across the water like the crack of a whip. The crowd on the cliff top let up a cry: "*Tom! It's Tom!*" The men in the boats grabbed hold of their oars and tried to steel themselves; now the chase would be on in earnest. A strange sound rose up out of the water, hard to identify at first: a piteous kind of bellowing, like a bull set upon by dogs.

I realize that I do not paint my brother Harry in a very favorable light, first of all in his failure as a headsman and now with his harpooning. Certainly, I was very hard on him at the time, and yet even as I write this account, it occurs to me that perhaps Harry was not scared at all, but simply had no wish to kill the whale. It is entirely possible, as he was a kind-hearted boy in many ways; if not with his sisters, it was certainly evidenced in his treatment of "all creatures great and small." As a child, he would climb to the top of the run-off tank and endeavor to rescue any small insects that had apparently drowned. Gathering them gently in his palm, he would blow softly upon their lifeless forms till they revived. Then he would sit there quietly nursing them till such time as their wings had dried and they were able to fly away.

Nor can I believe that he would be put off by such an oft-seen sight as a whale spout, even a large one. My brother had the idea that when a whale spouted, it was actually saying, *"Bosh!"*; that is, vehemently pooh-poohing something, as would a curmudgeonly old man (in fact, it was a common retort of Uncle Aleck). As a young oarsman in the whaleboat, this notion tickled Harry to such an extent that he would endeavor to have a conversation with a whale if it was spouting nearby.

"Excuse me, Mr. Whale, are you aware that the dolphin is said to be the smartest of all God's creatures?"

"Bosh!"

"I believe Towamba is a dead cert to defeat Eden in the upcoming semi-final."

"Bosh!"

And so on and so forth, until he would set to giggling. It was all very distracting when someone was meanwhile trying to harpoon the whale. I know my father frowned upon it, and perhaps that is why he was so anxious to tax Harry with the more serious tasks of headsman or harpooner. As I say, I cannot know for sure why Harry failed with the harpoon on this occasion, and it has only just occurred to me that the reason may have been something other than fear.

A Celebration

THANKFULLY, OUR RETURN JOURNEY FROM BOYD TOWER
was much faster than the one we had endured on the
way out there. Once Two Socks was pointed in the
direction of home, he invariably put a sprint on, and Betty was
simply expected to keep up. We were glad about this, as we
wanted to be sure we were ready for our whale men's return.
As they had run for the whaleboats, several of them had thrust
their freshly caught fish upon me, with instructions as to how
best I should prepare them. Darcy had pulled some mollusks
and mutton-fish off the rocks below, and these were also
added to the bounty. Thus I had several whiting and three
snapper, and one fish the likes of which I had never seen before, plus five mutton-fish, a dozen or so oysters and a handful
of other unidentified bivalves. As the boats pulled away from
the cliffs, Salty was still calling out his recipe for fish stew;
much of it was lost on the wind, but it seemed to involve plentiful amounts of milk and cream. "A liberal dash of

Worcestershire will improve the flavor," was the last that I heard.

Thus when we arrived home, we set about preparing it. Such was the excitement over the long-awaited appearance of a whale that the whole family pitched in to help. Dan cut open the first oyster, but injured his thumb so badly in the process that Louisa took over (she could at times prove herself very capable), while Uncle Aleck cleaned the fish; Annie coaxed some milk from Betty, and Dan and Violet went to find parsley and chives in the garden. Meanwhile I browned some onions in a little butter, and made a gelatinous broth from the fish heads which formed the base of the stew. With a portion of Betty's cream, some boiled potatoes, salt and pepper, a pinch of cayenne powder, and of course the obligatory Worcestershire sauce, the fish morsels and mollusks cooked up very nicely indeed. It was a hearty meal for the whale men, and one they were sorely in need of when finally they returned home that evening.

"Here they come!" cried Dan. He had been keeping lookout up on the hill, and en masse we ran down to greet them. They appeared to be rowing in the most haphazard fashion; also, across the water we could hear strains of robust argument and song.

"Oh, she was wily!" cried my father, as he came lurching up the jetty. "She was a wily wily old wily old whale."

I looked at him in astonishment: he appeared to be intoxicated. In fact, it soon became apparent that they were all in this condition, to varying degrees. Darcy and Robert Heffernan were no sooner out of the boats than they began to punch one another, and had to be separated, while Percy Madigan had to be stopped from veering off the jetty altogether and into the water. It seems that so satisfied were the whalers with their efforts in capturing such a fine whale, they had promptly adjourned to the Great Southern Hotel before finally rowing back with a quantity of rum. It was most unlike my father to drink to the point of intoxication; however, it gives some indication of the intense relief he must have been experiencing in catching such a valuable whale.

"We must feed them immediately," I instructed Louisa, and while the men washed themselves, we hurried up to the house to bring down the big pot of fish stew and some freshly baked damper with which to mop up the juices. They devoured it in the most ravenous fashion, and declared it a culinary triumph. We each felt a degree of pride as we had all taken some part in its creation, and for once we stayed with the men to enjoy the celebration rather than retiring to the house as we would normally do; my father was too inebriated to care. I should hasten to add that the meal had had the desired effect of sobering the men to some extent, otherwise I should never have permitted the younger ones to remain in their company.

It was a bitterly cold night but several large campfires were lit on the beach, which we gathered around, sitting on kegs and blankets and whatever we had at hand. Our Aboriginal whalers, Albert Thomas Senior and Albert Thomas Junior and Percy and Darcy Madigan, provided the music by means of blowing upon gum leaves as you would blow upon a harmonica. To this, the little girls danced a jig while we all clapped along our encouragement. Our very own Dark Town Leaf Band demonstrated complete mastery of their unusual "instruments," and their repertoire was wide-ranging, from reels and jigs to sentimental ballads, even several hymns that they had been taught by the missionaries of the Salvation Army. We sang along as best we could whenever we could remember the words; however, it was only "Onward Christian Soldiers" to which Bonnie felt compelled to add her voice, with an outburst of the most heartfelt baying and howling, inducing much laughter and merriment amongst us all.

At one point, I looked across and saw my father gazing into the flames, wearing an expression of great weariness but also something akin to contentment. I felt a tug at my heart, for I realized I had not often seen this expression since my mother died. I went across and sat at his knee, and although we did not speak, he smiled at me and patted my hair.

As I sat there, listening to the conversations around me, I began to piece together the story of the chase and capture of the black whale. After the Killers had arrived upon the scene and set about corralling the whale, it was short work for the first boat to make fast to it. However, once stung by the harpoon, the whale—who had seemed a placid creature up to this point—put up a ferocious battle for its survival. At first, it executed a series of short, sharp turns, as if attempting to dislodge the boat now suddenly attached to it; then, when this tactic did not achieve the desired result, the creature stopped suddenly and elevated its great tail flukes to a height of some twenty feet above the water, before sweeping them most deliberately across the length of the boat. Fortunately, my father, who was of course standing at the bow, and Arthur Ashby (at the steer oar) had had the wherewithal to hastily duck down, thereby avoiding what could undoubtedly have been serious injuries. (By all accounts, the whale's tail span was twelve feet across, and of exceptional thickness.) The whale then made a spirited dash for North Head, causing the Killer whales to exert their most concentrated efforts in attempting to prevent its escape. It succeeded in rounding North Head, and was speeding in the direction of Leonards Island, still dragging my father's whaleboat after it, before the Killers managed to rein it in and turn it back into Twofold Bay.

Becoming increasingly desperate now, the whale sped towards the entrance of Lake Curalo, then thought better of the idea and skirted along Haslems Beach before proceeding to Lookout Point where, as if for the benefit of the onlookers assembled there, the Killers commenced a series of furious onslaughts. Humpy threw himself across the creature's blowhole; Tom engaged in his favorite game of pushing at the whale repeatedly from underneath, while Hooky and company endeavored to tear open the creature's mouth. They only desisted long enough to allow my father clear access to deal the fatal lance, and with each thrust of the steel, the crowds on Lookout Point let out cheer upon cheer. Soon the spouting and bellowing and the crimson-foaming of the water ceased; the whale was *hors de combat.* The entire business, from making fast to the whale to its ultimate demise, took only an hour and a half.

Remarkably, the whale was of such vast dimensions that the Killers had difficulty in pulling the carcass below. "We'll have our work cut out for us towing it over the bar," said my father, and there was talk of the possible necessity of excavating a channel in order to tow the carcass close enough to the try-works. My father estimated that, given its size, it could yield up to ten tons of whale oil. Further, its whalebone was of tremendous length and quality. All in all, it had been a most satisfactory afternoon's work.

As the exertions of the day began to catch up with everybody, and the merriment and music died down, a stiff breeze rose up suddenly, causing the flames of the campfires to gutter. My father lifted his head, almost like a dog sensing something on the wind. He looked out towards the blackness of the water; then, without saying a word, rose to his feet and made his way down towards the jetty. I watched him for a moment, then got up to follow. As I passed, a shadowy figure, seated some small distance away from the campfire, reached out and took hold of my arm. It was John Beck.

"Mary, Mary, sit with me a while," he said.

I hesitated. He had obviously partaken of the liquor, for his eyes were shiny, but had not taken so much as to be unpleasant, nor were its fumes redolent on his breath. He gave a small tug at my arm by way of encouragement, and so I sat myself down beside him.

"I have something for you," he said.

He pulled from his pocket the *broderie anglaise* bandages, now somewhat grimy from use, and for one moment I thought that he was simply about to return them to me. But instead, he carefully unwrapped them to reveal a shell, which he held up to show me in the flickering light.

"I've been making a collection of seashells," he said. "But this one is by far the prettiest."

"Oh yes," I responded. "It is very pretty."

In fact, it was a common spindle shell; undoubtedly attractive, with its brown and white markings and spindle shape, but perhaps I had seen too many of them to be greatly excited by it. John Beck, however, seemed quite delighted with it. He turned it over several times to admire its delicate contours, then pressed it into my hand.

"It's for you," he said.

"For me?"

"Yes. Do you know why?"

I shook my head.

"Because you made my blisters better."

"Are they better?"

"Oh yes. Look," he said, and he held up the palms of his hands. "I don't think your little brother would be laughing at my ladies' hands now. Do you see how they've toughened up?"

He then took my hand so I could feel the new callouses where the blisters had once been.

"Yes, they have toughened up considerably," I said. How earnest and dreary I sounded, I thought to myself. *Yes, they have toughened up considerably.* No wonder I had never been popular. Perhaps it was time to put into practice the advice of the homely woman: *"Treat young men as if they are old and old men as if they are young."*

"You should see my arms, Mary," John Beck was meanwhile saying. "See how strong my arms have got from the rowing?"

Here he rolled up a sleeve to reveal his upper arm. "Feel it," he offered encouragingly. Twisting his fist this way and that, he made several flexing motions with his arm, causing the upper muscle to bulge most satisfactorily. Scarcely aware of what I was doing, I found myself reaching out and feeling it with my fingertips.

"Like a rock, eh?" whispered John Beck. "Not many

Methodist ministers have muscles like these, I can tell you. I'm very proud of them, as you can see."

"They're very nice," I replied, and instead of removing my hand at this point, I allowed it to slide down to his forearm, which was also of pleasing firmness and strength.

"I've been wanting you to admire them all night," he continued softly. "It's been rather chilly in my shirtsleeves too."

He was smiling at me and his eyes were shining in the darkness, and at that point, I'm afraid that something within me seemed to seize up in a kind of panic. Any girlish gaiety that I had been blessed with at birth had stiffened and stuck from lack of use, and although I was only nineteen years of age, I felt unable to rise to the obvious demands of the occasion.

"I'm sorry. I'm no good at this. I can't do it," I said, lurching abruptly to my feet.

Swiftly he reached up and pulled me back down again.

"Do what?"

"This light-hearted banter between the sexes that you are obviously hoping for."

"Of course you can do it! You've been doing it extremely well up to this moment."

"That is kind of you to say, but I am only too aware of my shortcomings. And although I've been trying to picture you in my mind as Uncle Aleck—"

"What?" he said. "Please don't do that. Please don't picture me in your mind as Uncle Aleck. Why in God's name have you been doing that?"

"Because that way I might perhaps be less stilted in my conversation."

"No, no. I must insist that you stop it at once. It is undoing all of my good work with my muscles."

"But you see…" I hesitated for a moment, but then all of a sudden it came tumbling out. "My fear is that you view me as some earnest, bespectacled *whale painter*—a blue-stocking—which of course is not helped by the fact that I was wearing my blue stockings when we first met, but only because I had not been expecting company, let alone a Methodist minister—"

"*Former* Methodist minister."

"—otherwise, of course, I would have been wearing my black silks—"

"Yes, but putting aside the Methodist minister bit for the moment," said John Beck, "and even the much more interesting question of your black silks—do you think your father would mind terribly if I kissed you?"

"*Oh!*" I exclaimed. "Yes, possibly he would mind terribly."

"What do you think he would do? Would he harpoon me?"

"Oh, I doubt he would waste a harpoon on you."

"Ah! You bantered!"

"No, no. That wasn't banter. That was the truth. He is very careful in his use of harpoons."

"I see. Is he looking?"

"Looking?"

"At us."

"No."

"Then dare we have just one little kiss?"

Rendered unable to speak, I simply nodded; he leaned forward and kissed me tenderly on the lips. And because I did not resist, he kissed me again, longer and more tenderly this time. Until finally I opened my eyes and found him gazing at me.

"Please don't tell me you were imagining Uncle Aleck," he whispered.

"Oh no!" I replied. "No, I wasn't at all—"

And at this moment, a fierce gust of wind whipped around us, pulling a sheet of tin from the roof of the try-works. It crashed down upon some empty barrels, causing them to thunder down the slipway and setting the dogs at once to barking.

"Get the boats—we're going out!" my father shouted from the end of the jetty.

The whale men cried out in disbelief; various epithets were tossed about in bitter disappointment; and yet they clambered to their feet and moved towards the boats. Such was the loyalty my father inspired.

"Wait!" I cried. "I'll get some food for you! Dan, fill the water bags!"

"What's happening? Why are we going out?" asked John Beck.

"Because the wind has come up!"

"But what does that mean, that the wind has come up?"

"We'll lose the whale! It'll blow out to sea—oh, shut up, you stupid dogs, from barking!"

In all that commotion, I must have dropped the shell that he gave to me. The next morning, upon realizing my carelessness, I went down to the beach and spent several hours combing the area thoroughly. I found a multitude of spindle shells in the vicinity, and because I could not be entirely sure which was the one he had given me, I have kept four of which seemed to most closely resemble my memory of it.

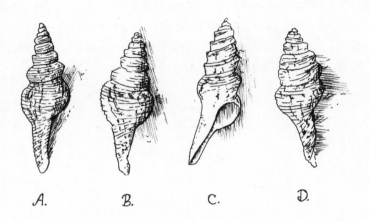

A.   B.   C.   D.

Although, as I say, I cannot be entirely sure, I feel that A may be the shell that he gave to me, as it could be argued that A is slightly prettier and more delicate in its ridges than the other three. Then again, C has a more elegant fold to its opening, and is very softly colored in this area. D is not really a contender as it is somewhat battered, and I cannot believe that he would have pressed that upon me so ardently; however, as it is a spindle shell and was found closest to the log on which we were sitting, I feel I must include it. All in all, it is a great pity that I did not take the trouble to examine the shell more carefully when he gave it to me.

(Of course, the thought occurs to me now that he may have simply picked up the nearest shell and pretended that he had been saving it up to give to me. Perhaps he had hastily wrapped it up in the bandages as he saw me approach. But no, I cannot really believe this of him, for he seemed so genuine in his appreciation of its prettiness, and so ardent in the manner in which he pressed it upon me. I do not understand this impulse I have developed in later life whereupon some small part of me seems to want to find fault in my memories of him, to "burst the balloon," as it were.)

Sitting Tight

A S A RULE, A DEAD WHALE TAKES TWENTY-FOUR HOURS TO bloat with gas and rise to the surface; in fact, sometimes, for unknown reasons, it takes longer than this. So the reader may wonder why my father insisted they go out when the black whale had been dead for only a matter of hours. The only answer I can proffer is that his fear of losing the whale was so great that he felt it necessary to take every precaution possible. Thus, in the bitter cold and darkness, the weary men rowed back across the bay and, with some difficulty, finally located the marker buoys bobbing upon the surface. The Killers had long since finished their feast and departed. The carcass of the whale lurked deep down below. Arthur Ashby held up his lantern. He tugged at the marker buoys, and peered into the black water.

"Looks like the anchors are holding all right," he announced. Not wishing to look as if he did not wish to be there, he perhaps made his voice sound a little overly cheerful. The men looked hopefully at my father. Perhaps they could now row back home again?

"We'll sit tight," said my father.

A low murmur of frustration went round the whalers. They did not fancy the thought of keeping watch over the sunken remains of a dead whale. They would rather have been asleep in their bunks, especially since the rum was wearing off.

"Excuse me for saying so, boss," said Arthur Ashby. Being my father's harpooner and right-hand man, Arthur was the only one who would dare to say what he was about to: "The old girl's not going to gas up till tomorrow at the earliest. We might as well—"

"We'll sit tight," repeated my father, with such a firmness of manner that Arthur deemed it better not to press the point.

And so the long wait commenced.

The great gust of wind that had knocked the sheet of tin off the roof of the try-works had been the harbinger of a biting northwesterly gale, bringing with it squalls of icy sleet. The whale men hunched over and huddled together; they pulled up their collars, pulled their hats down low over their ears and buried their hands deep within their pockets. Any part of their anatomy exposed to the elements began to turn blue and stiffen with the cold.

"We shall have frostbite of the nose," said Salty grimly. "And it shall not be pretty."

This prompted Bastable to recount the story of the Parisian streetwalker he had once met. It had been a cold night and, moved by her plight, he had taken her to a small cafe that she might warm her innards with a bowl of pea soup. For in spite of her occupation, maintained Bastable, she was the most elegant and gracious lady you could ever hope to meet. In the course of their conversation, she assured him that although her work exposed her to many dubious characters, she was never afraid, for she knew how to protect herself. If any man tried to force himself upon her, she would simply bite his nose off. Then she would spit it at him.

"Spit what at him?" asked someone who had not been following the story closely.

"His nose."

"But the nose is all gristle!" argued Albert Thomas Senior. "It would be next to impossible to bite it off!"

"I am only repeating what she told me," said Bastable. "She herself had a good set of teeth."

Generally speaking, the whale men were not so fortunate in the way of teeth, and so they refrained from commenting on this.

"Furthermore," continued Bastable, "after having his nose bitten off, the offender would now find himself stigmatized by his crime. If he attempted to stroll through the boulevards of Paris *sans* nose, then all would recognize at once the foul nature of his deed."

"Why are you telling us this story?" demanded Salty. "Are you saying that everyone in Eden will assume we have had our way with your Parisian prostitute, simply because we have had the misfortune of losing our noses to frostbite?"

Some of the men considered it unlikely that Bastable had ever spoken to a Parisian prostitute in the first place, and thus there was probably little to worry about. Nonetheless it was decided that a notice could be placed in the *Eden Observer and*

South Coast Advocate to clarify the issue, if indeed it became necessary. My father, who had not entered the discussion up to this point, spoke up to say that, for God's sake, no one was going to lose their nose to frostbite, for to do so they would have to be a lot colder.

"I assure you," said Bastable, "the only occasion on which you will find me colder will be at my funeral."

"Hear, hear!" the men grumbled.

"In which case, you need not worry about the frostbite," said my father.

The men slumped into silence. Another squall arrived, the sleet as piercing as if each icy drop had been sharpened on a whetstone. The men hunkered down into their sodden clothing, their misery complete. When the squall had passed, Salty shifted in his seat and shook the water out of the brim of his hat. To John Beck's surprise, he began to sing:

"Shallow Brown, you're going to leave me."

It was slow and solemn, like a dirge. His rich baritone voice seemed to cut through the howl of the wind. The older whale men responded with a mournful refrain:

"Shallow, Shallow Brown," they intoned.

"Shallow Brown," sang Salty, *"don't ne'er deceive me."*

"Shallow, Shallow Brown," averred the men.

"Ye're going away across the o-ocean."

"Shallow, Shallow Brown."

"You'll ever be my heart's devotion."

"Shallow, Shallow Brown."

And then the song was over. The men had sung it without comment, and indeed without looking at each other. If anything, their gaze seemed fixed upon the water, as if it was the carcass deep below who might deceive them, who might go away across the ocean.

"All right," said my father. "We'll go ashore and light a fire."

They rowed ashore to a rocky and inhospitable beach, where after the most treacherous landing, in which their boats very nearly capsized in the breakers, they staggered ashore and found a patch of sand protected by a rocky overhang. Here they succeeded in lighting a small fire with what little bit of dampish driftwood they could scratch up in the darkness. Around these thin flames they huddled. They ate some salted beef from their tucker-bags and then almost immediately fell asleep, curled up tightly together on the wet sand. Only John Beck and Salty remained awake, and they sat silently staring into the flames, occasionally rearranging the burning embers in a bid to improve the fire's heat. After a while, Salty produced a small flask of rum, which up to this point he had kept secreted on his person. He offered it to John Beck, who gratefully accepted.

"Tell me, Father," said Salty, as he watched him take a swig. "John Wesley—was he not the founder of Methodism?"

"Yes," said John Beck. "That's correct."

The rum felt good and warming. He passed the bottle back to Salty, who himself took a fulsome draught.

"Unfamiliar as I am with his teachings," said Salty, "I believe that Wesley held some pretty strong opinions regarding—well, how can I put it—*licentious behavior*."

"That's correct," John Beck acknowledged.

"By which I mean, gambling, fornicating, turf plunging; the drinking of hard liquor and so forth."

"Yes, yes, I am clear on the definitions of licentious behavior," said John Beck.

"And this is part of what's puzzling me," said Salty. "I note that you yourself imbibe liquor with some evident enjoyment."

"In moderation."

"Yes, and who's to blame you? Who's to blame you, Father, for having a drink? John Wesley himself would agree, whaling is a thirsty business."

As if to illustrate this, he swigged again from his rum bottle in a vehement fashion. Then he stashed it away in his coat pocket and pulled out his pipe, which he commenced to stoke.

"Also the card games, Father," he continued, when he had completed the difficult process of lighting his pipe in the wind.

"What's that?" said John Beck.

"I've noticed you partake of the card games. Occasionally for stakes, I might add."

"Only when the fellows have needed an extra hand," said John Beck.

"And very expertly, if I may say so," said Salty.

"Well, that's as may be—"

"No, no, it begs to be remarked upon; you play with a great deal of *proficiency*."

His eyes twinkled pleasantly at John Beck across the flickering flames.

"Also," he added, "and here's the rub, I could not help but ponder the nature of your attentions to Mary this evening."

"I was a minister once, but not anymore," said John Beck. "Have I not made that perfectly clear?"

"Ah, yes, yes. Perfectly clear. But as I say, it's the *proficiency* that puzzles me."

John Beck slept poorly on the cold damp sand, and awoke at the first glimmering of the gray dawn breaking over the beach. The other whale men were still sleeping. They were a pitiful sight in the contortions of sleep, having each tried to find shelter by nestling tightly against one another, arms flung across faces, legs entangled. Robert, in the grip of a nightmare—possibly a nightmare about a large black whale—was moaning and muttering incoherently. With a sigh, John Beck unfolded his stiff limbs and clambered out of their dismal grotto. He looked out to sea. It was gray and roiling, its whitecaps blowing foam. He strained to see any sign of a floating whale carcass, but could not. He began to search for driftwood with which to build a fire, for he was keen to put the billy on.

Up ahead in the distance, he noticed a dark stooped figure standing on the shore. His heart started, for from this distance in the ghostly dawn light the figure looked almost like a large black crow, or an undertaker, or some other harbinger of ill fortune. As he drew closer, however, he realized it was Shankly. John Beck had not exchanged many words with Shankly up to now, and those words that had been exchanged had tended to leave John Beck feeling somewhat on the back foot.

"Good morning!" John Beck called out cheerfully, determined that Shankly not get the better of him this time. Shankly turned and surveyed him gloomily. He wore a long black coat that was flapping in the wind, and his thin hair was plastered over his scalp.

"No sign of it," he remarked, with a sweeping gesture out to sea.

"No," said John Beck. "It is not risen yet."

"Or else it has blown away while we lay sleeping," said Shankly. This appeared to be an attempt at levity, for he bared his long teeth in a kind of smile or grimace.

"Yes," said John Beck, with a short laugh. Shankly's grimace vanished.

"A curious thing to find humorous, Father. Given that the livelihoods of twelve men depend upon it."

"Yes indeed," said John Beck, annoyed that Shankly had once again got the better of him. "Well, I am just off to gather firewood."

"Would it be an imposition if I were to trouble you with a theological question, Father?"

John Beck stopped, and turned back to him.

"In the Methodist church, we are customarily addressed as Reverend," he responded, somewhat testily. "You may be thinking of the Catholic or the Anglican faiths, where the priest is referred to as Father."

Shankly stared at him. "I understood you had left the church."

"That is so."

"But you wish to be still known as Reverend?"

"No, I am simply—I am simply mentioning that it is customary for a minister of the Methodist church to be addressed as such."

"As you wish," said Shankly. "I daresay such questions of

nomenclature are important to clergymen, even though they seem of trifling concern to the rest of us."

John Beck sighed inwardly. He was beginning to wish he had never mentioned his clerical background in the first place, for the whalers could not seem to let go of it.

"In your experience then, Reverend," Shankly continued, "how does the Lord regard the act of *mudder?*"

His Scottish accent was such that at times John Beck found him difficult to understand.

"Mudder?" he queried.

"You heard me the first time, Reverend. I will not repeat it."

John Beck stared at him a moment, nonplussed. Then the penny dropped.

"Oh," said John Beck. "Well, not very favorably, I'm afraid. In fact, that is one of His Commandments—*Thou shalt not kill*—so it's something that I think He feels rather strongly about."

Shankly said nothing, but returned his brooding gaze to the horizon.

"Why do you ask?" asked John Beck, after a moment.

"Well, I killed a man, Reverend."

"What, just now?"

"No. Some time ago."

"I see."

"I killed a man and I ate his kidneys, and then I was satisfied."

"I see," said John Beck. "Did you say that you ate his kidneys?"

"Yes, Reverend. I cooked them up in a frying pan."

"Well, no. The Lord does not view such things favorably."

"He was a wretch, Reverend, and deserved his fate."

"Nonetheless."

A silence fell between them. They both gazed out to sea. After a while, John Beck felt that he really must resume his search for firewood.

"Well, I'd best be off then," he said.

"As you wish, Father," said Shankly.

Twenty-four hours had passed since the whale had been killed, and still it had not risen to the surface. The two whale-boats sat tight by the marker buoys. It had been a miserable day; the wind blew, squalls came and went, and throughout it all, the sea had had a nasty lurching jobble which kept them all in a state of digestive discomfort. As day drew into night, the wind began to freshen once more into a gale. Still their prize lurked deep below. The men stared at the marker buoys as if willing the carcass to materialize. Surely it had to be imminent.

Hungry and exhausted, cold and sodden, the men now barely spoke to each other, and did so only to offer a terse rebuke for some perceived misdeed. "Shallow Brown" had been cycled through many times now, and they were heartily sick of it; yet none had the inclination to sing anything more cheerful. Not long after midnight on the second night a spat broke out. Robert Heffernan had fallen asleep, and in his unconscious state had slumped heavily against Shankly. When shoved off, Robert had briefly regained consciousness only to slump against him again, and again a third time, and this had roused Shankly to anger and he leapt to his feet wielding a boat spade and shouting: "Violate me, would ye, so brazenly?" John Beck and Harry managed to wrench the boat spade from him, but in the ensuing struggle, the boat had come close to capsizing.

Finally, amidst my father's shouts for calm, some semblance of civility was restored to the second whaleboat. John Beck was instructed to sit between the two men to deter any further infractions. This did not stop Shankly from muttering dark threats at Robert Heffernan out of my father's earshot. Further, as his own weariness threatened to overtake him, John Beck became concerned that he might himself inadvertently violate Shankly. He did not fancy having his kidneys cooked up in a frying pan, no matter how satisfying Shankly might find the result.

For some time, Robert Heffernan could be heard crying softly in the darkness. Far from appealing to their compassion, this seemed to work as an irritant upon the men, yet shouting at him to stop blubbering or punching him hard on the shoulder seemed only to induce fresh bouts of weeping. These small sobs the young man attempted to stifle, producing an effect all the more pathetic and exasperating.

"For pity's sake," cried Salty. "This is beyond all endurance!"

"All right," said my father heavily. "We'll go ashore and light a fire."

Once again, they rowed to the rocky and inhospitable beach; once again they almost capsized and drowned in the breakers; once again they lit a scrap of a fire and fell into a deep and dreamless sleep atop the cold wet sand.

Dawn broke to find my father standing alone on the beach, peering out to sea. Amongst the sleeping whalers, Arthur Ashby stirred. Seeing my father, he dashed the sleep from his eyes and stumbled over to him.

"What can you see, Arthur?" asked my father, turning to

him anxiously. "I don't know if my eyes are playing tricks upon me."

Arthur looked out. It was difficult to see with the breakers and the spray and the size of the swell. His eyes narrowed, and he studied intently for several moments the vicinity where they had left the carcass only a few hours before. Seeing nothing, his eyes shifted out to sea. There he caught a flash of something. It was a marker buoy bouncing jauntily over a wave top.

"She's adrift," he said.

The Perils of Whaling

N O SOONER HAD THE BLACK WHALE RISEN TO THE surface than a whole gale rose also from the southwest, sweeping the bloated carcass before it and causing it to break free of its anchors. Now the huge body was bowling out to sea unrestrained, its marker buoys crashing along behind it. The whale men set after it, their thoughts focused solely on their vanishing prize: twelve hundred pounds worth of blubber and whalebone, now apparently en route to New Zealand. Once they had made it out of the bay, however, they were struck by seas so vertiginous that the headsmen began to experience great difficulty in handling their boats.

"Pull, for God's sake, men!" cried my father as he grappled with the steer oar. "Pull! Pull!"

As they bent to the oars, their weary muscles burning, one or other of the men would throw a look over his shoulder and snatch a glimpse of the marker buoys, then turn back to my father in disbelief. Not only were the buoys a great distance away, but the two small boats were pursuing them further and further out to sea. Even if they managed to catch the break-away whale, they still had to face the prospect of the long and perilous journey back, towing a mountain of blubber. As this fresh horror dawned upon them, the precarious morale of the new chums began to waver, and the second boat staggered fit-fully up each precipice of water. Even the hardened men of the first boat found their resolve flagging when they realized they had now lost sight of land.

"Keep going!" cried my father. "Why do you slow down?"

I imagine it can only have been out of loyalty to my father that the men continued to pull at all, for the chase must have surely seemed hopeless.

"I can't see her," cried Salty from the other boat. "Where's she gone?"

My father gripped the steer oar for support and squinted against the spray. It was true: the marker buoys and carcass seemed to have vanished.

"Darcy!" he cried. "Stop rowing and look. Can you see any-thing?"

Darcy had the best eyes of all the whale men; it was extra-ordinary what he could see. Where we could see a tree on a distant hill, he could identify the birds that sat in it. He rose to his feet now and stood looking for several minutes. Then he turned and faced my father.

"I see her, boss," he said. "She's too far."

My father stared at him. Darcy was Percy Madigan's boy, cheeky and good-humored and well-liked by all. But to tell my father that he deemed the whale too far was an act of unheard-of defiance. The other men kept their heads down, even Bastable. In their hearts, they agreed with Darcy; the whale was too far away to catch, and had been from the beginning.

"How far?" said my father, eyeing Darcy steadily.

"Miles."

"How many miles? Two? Three?"

"Four maybe."

"But the marker buoys—"

"Those marker buoys have come loose, boss."

My father reeled. Albert Thomas Senior leapt up to support him, but he regained his equilibrium and motioned him aside, instead leaning heavily upon his steer oar. (We wanted that the steer oar be buried with my father. It was of course twenty-two feet long and would not fit in the grave; but the fact that it seemed appropriate will give an indication of how much a part of him it was.) The men stared up at him. They had been chasing after marker buoys that were no longer even attached to the whale? Then where in God's name was the whale?

"Home," said my father hoarsely. "Turn your boat, Salty. We're going home."

Turning the boats around, the long journey back now confronted them. At best reckoning, they were seven miles out. The wind was against them and every wave that rose up threatened to engulf their frail crafts. There was no choice except to tackle it; their only other option was to sink and drown. It was all too terrible to contemplate. And yet, as they rowed, calling upon every last ounce of energy from their exhausted reserves, the boats seemed to barely progress. Instead, they slid sickeningly up each new wall of water, only to be dashed into the trough below. Then the next wave presented itself. It seemed impossible that both whaleboats and men could continue to withstand such a battering.

"This isn't funny anymore," said Robert Heffernan, not that at any point he had shown signs of amusement.

Salty looked at his exhausted men, rowing as if already dead, their faces haggard with disbelief.

"A prayer! That's what we need!" cried Salty. "Give us a prayer, Father, now as we row! Is there not a special prayer for whale men in distress?"

John Beck looked up at him in dismay. A prayer? When it was all he could do to keep his hands on the oars, he must suddenly come up with a prayer—and not just any prayer, but one appropriate to the dire circumstances in which they found themselves? The fact that the hardened whale man and self-proclaimed Professor of Whales felt it necessary to appeal to the Almighty surely meant that things were worse than he could imagine. The other oarsmen turned to him now, feebly hopeful. They needed something perhaps he alone could give them, some small words of encouragement, some promise of salvation.

"O God," John Beck began tentatively. "Give to the wind our fears—"

"Speak up, Father!"

"O God," he repeated, raising his voice. "Give to the wind our fears. Hear our sighs—"

"We can't hear you back here in the cheap seats!"

"Hear our sighs and count our tears!" He had to shout to be heard above the elements. "Lift up our heads and carry us through waves and clouds and storms!"

"Yea, O Lord," cried Salty.

"Yea, O Lord!" agreed the whale men.

"Dispose our hearts that death may not be dreadful to us—"

"Not that prayer, Father!" cried Salty abruptly.

"No. No, of course," said John Beck. They were riding up an especially vertiginous wave. The boat hovered horribly at its crest, causing their bellies to lurch with fear, then smashed down bow first into its trough.

"Oh Jesus," whimpered Robert Heffernan, and nobody blamed him.

"Yes, Jesus, hear us now!" cried John Beck. All this shouting against the elements and rowing at the same time was making him short of breath, and the words came out in staccato bursts. "You have—taken from us—the great Leviathan—whose empty carcass must now rot—uselessly—upon the ocean floor—"

In fact, he was quite pleased with this style of delivery. It seemed to suggest a passion and urgency that had perhaps been lacking in his sermons, and his straining voice was acquiring a commanding timbre.

"Where once—its precious bounty—might have lubricated—cogs—of great machinery," he continued. "Or served perhaps—in the construction of umbrellas—or indeed corsets—to enhance the silhouettes of our womenfolk—"

"Not a sermon, Father, just a prayer if you would!"

"Right, yes," said John Beck. "O God," he commenced afresh, "who hath embarked our souls in these frail boats—preserve us from the dangers that on all sides assault us—give Your oarsmen the strength to pull against this tempest—that we might arrive at last in the haven of eternal salvation—"

"Haven of eternal salvation, Lord," cried Salty.

"Yea, O Lord," cried the whalers, who would welcome a haven of any description.

"Hear the cry of our hearts, and have mercy upon us, Lord. Have mercy upon whale men who have lost their cargo—"

"Yes, Lord!"

"—and seek only to return home."

And just as these last words blew away on the wind, by all accounts of those who were present, the dark clouds above broke apart just enough to permit a shaft of pale crepuscular sunlight to shine down upon the two small boats. The men gazed up to the heavens in amazement, and none more so than John Beck.

"Amen," he said.

"Amen, Father," said Salty.

"Amen," said the whalers.

Importance of Preserving Memories

I REALIZE, ON LOOKING BACK AT THESE PAGES, THAT IN MY anxiety to hurry along to the exciting part of the story, I have moved on from the moment where John Beck kissed me without perhaps acknowledging that this was, and remains, a moment of great significance to me. Our lips met again on other occasions (and I will get to them in due course), but this was the first kiss, and here I will state that it is not for nothing that these first tender caresses between lovers are so treasured. Unlike the time when Burrows had kissed me roughly and conjured up the unpleasant image of the live sea slug or bivalve flailing about inside my mouth, John Beck's kisses on this occasion were more tentative, indeed almost chaste. And yet even to attempt to describe this moment between us seems to diminish it somehow, so I shall desist from going any further. I have only these memories to hold on to, and am anxious lest I wear them out.

Several years ago, in my anxiety over this possibility, I in-

troduced a ration plan whereby I permitted myself to summon these most precious memories only once a day (usually
at bedtime, after extinguishing the lamp). It was difficult, but
I felt I had to do this, so concerned was I that the *tangibility*
of the memory (where I could bring it to mind so vividly I
could smell and taste, and feel the roughness of his cheek and
so forth) was fading, or at least somehow becoming *less*. Not
long after the introduction of this plan, I noticed that I was
beginning to compensate for the deprivation by allowing myself, once a memory was summoned, to dwell in that pleasant
state for longer and longer periods of time, as if reluctant to
relinquish it for another whole day. Again I had to be firm
with myself and impose a greater self-discipline. That is, I
permit myself to linger in the memory state for a period of no
more than two minutes. And yet, even in spite of these efforts,
I find the memories are continuing to recede. Thus I have put
in place a new regime of allowing myself to indulge in these
memories only once every few days, trying to stretch the period between them for as long as possible each time. If I catch
myself wanting to summon the memory more frequently, I
pinch myself as hard as I can on the underside of my forearm.

The Whale Men Return

I DID NOT HEAR ABOUT THE SHAFT OF MIRACULOUS SUNLIGHT that had answered John Beck's prayer until sometime later, and it did much to explain the puzzling behavior he manifested from the moment of his return.

But I am getting a little ahead of myself. For although the crepuscular beam pierced the clouds so marvelously that bleak morning, inspiring in the men a sense of hope and salvation, the effect lasted barely a minute and did nothing to assuage the wild seas or ameliorate their ordeal. Their journey continued in the same arduous and terrifying manner until finally they reached the shelter of Leonards Island, and then of Twofold Bay itself. Sometime in the afternoon, they made it back to the whaling station at Kiah. We watched much of this last stage of their journey from the headland (where we had been taking it in turns to keep lookout); it was pitiful indeed to see the laborious progress they made in these conditions, the smaller second boat huddling in the wake of the first.

I was unable to linger, though, for it was necessary that I turn my attention promptly to the problem of how to feed them. They would of course be extremely hungry; I had packed only small quantities of salted beef and damper in their tucker-bags, little expecting that they would be gone for two whole nights. In their absence, the family had subsisted on porridge and griddle scones; our stores were getting worrisomely low. Now, as I untied the last of the salted beef, hanging in muslin from the roof of the cellar, I leapt back in fright. The muslin was alive; that is, the salted beef had become completely infested with larder beetles.

"We can't feed them that," said Louisa, as we stared in horror at the seething hunk of meat, now lying on the floor where I had dropped it.

"Of course we can't feed them that. I had no intention of feeding them that," I snapped. Leaning in to examine it more closely, we could see that the industrious beetles were busily laying their eggs in it.

"Dan!" I bellowed. "*Dan!*"

"What?" said Dan, from the top of the cellar stairs.

"Run at once and check the bandicoot traps."

The reader may not be familiar with the long-nosed bandicoot; it is a slight creature, about the size of a small rabbit, with bright eyes, pointy ears and a nervous, querulous disposition. It sleeps by day, and spends its evenings scurrying around in the undergrowth, grunting and squeaking and fighting with other bandicoots. If you come across one unexpectedly, it will jump straight up in the air out of fright; "Startle the Bandicoot" had long been a popular game amongst the children. I bear no ill-will to the bandicoot, nor is its meat particularly flavorsome; however, "needs must" and, thankfully for us, Dan returned with one such creature found in the trap. We then sent him off with the rifle to try to pot a rabbit. Not that we held out much hope of this; Dan was somewhat near-sighted, like myself.

Louisa and I stared at the bandicoot in dismay; they do not have a lot of meat at the best of times, and this one appeared to be a juvenile.

"Well, you had best hurry up and skin it," I told her.

"We can't feed all twelve of them on this!" she cried in a high-pitched tone that was bordering on hysterical. She was right, of course. I turned my attention back to the lump of salted beef, still lying on the floor, swarming with beetles. It looked for all the world like they might at any moment lift it up and carry it out the door.

"Perhaps if we were to wash it free of beetles?" I suggested.

"Have you taken leave of your senses?" cried Louisa. "Have you gone completely insane?"

"Well, what else are we going to do?" I was beginning to ac-quire the same hysterical tone that I had observed in Louisa. There was nothing for it; the men approached in their whale boats even as we stood there. Promptly we filled a large bucket with water and a dash of vinegar, and then I scrubbed away at it furiously while Louisa cowered in the corner, covering her eyes and making sounds as if she were to be violently sick.

"Do not tell a living soul about this," I warned her. I must have made a pretty sight, standing there with my lump of disintegrating beef, surrounded by a colony of drowned and sodden beetles.

We made a kind of hash of boiled bandicoot combined with

those portions of salted beef which were not infested with larvae, onions, potatoes, milk, flour and a liberal amount of Worcestershire sauce to improve the flavor.

"It's a pity we can't feed them the larder beetles," observed Louisa ruefully, as we slid down the rocks towards the sleeping hut. Suddenly we came to a halt. Over in the try-works, the whale men could be seen taking their baths, no doubt in a bid to thaw themselves out. They had filled the try pots with water and lit fires beneath then, and now they were wallowing contentedly.

"*Quelle horreur,*" hissed Louisa. "Naked whalers."

We stood there for a moment and watched them. It was not a sight we had ever seen before. There amongst them, I glimpsed John Beck, ladling hot water over his shoulders with a skimming spoon. I will not go into further detail on this; suffice to say, it is one of the memories I am trying hardest to preserve. Rousing myself from my reverie, I nudged Louisa and we continued our journey to the sleeping huts.

"What's this then?" asked Robert Heffernan, as we doled out the hash. He was staring at his plate and, to my horror, I saw what appeared to be a larder beetle lying legs up in a murky pool of Worcestershire. Deftly, I flicked it from his plate.

"Never you mind," I replied. "Just eat heartily. We need to fatten you up, young man."

"Why do we need to fatten him up?" asked Louisa. "Are we going to cook Robert next?"

I was distracted then by the sound of tapping on a tin cup, and turning, I saw John Beck standing amongst the whale men. There was something oddly cherubic about their appearance freshly bathed, reminding one of large ruddy-faced bad-tempered babies. Except for John Beck, of course. He had a blanket wrapped around him, and a light beard growth, and looked for all the world like Jesus of Nazareth amongst his Apostles.

"Men," John Beck was saying. "Perhaps after our experience out at sea this morning, you will permit me to offer a small prayer of thanksgiving."

There was grumbling at this, but most of the men put down their forks and some even lowered their heads solemnly.

"How typical of the clergy," muttered Salty to Bastable. "Give him a little encouragement, now we can't shut him up."

"Oh, most great and glorious God," intoned John Beck, closing his eyes and holding up his right hand. "Who art mighty in thy power and wonderful in thy doings; accept, I beseech thee, our unfeigned thanks and praise for our creation, preservation and all the other blessings which in the riches of thy mercy thou hast from time to time poured down upon us. Amen."

A mumble of "Amens" issued forth from the whalers but I found, in my astonishment, that my lips could not form the word. A feeling of bewilderment overwhelmed me. What had become of the John Beck of two nights ago, stealing kisses and forcing me to admire his muscles? Here he stood, avoiding my gaze and offering grace in the most doleful and pious tones. Behind me, I heard a mutter of disgruntlement.

"I'll not be thanking the Lord for a piece of boiled bandicoot," said Bastable.

Some Words About My Father

I AM AGHAST, LOOKING BACK AT THESE LAST CHAPTERS, AT HOW selfish I appear. Here I am relating the story of the devastating loss of the black whale through the prism of my feelings for John Beck, when in fact my thoughts should have been only of my father. Certainly now, looking back at it from a perspective of thirty years, I wonder that my memories of him at this time are so hazy; the vigilance I have demonstrated in collating and preserving any memory of John Beck has not been exercised to the same degree in the case of my father. The one memory I do have of Father upon their return that afternoon is something of a distressing one. So exhausted was he by the ordeal, both mentally and physically, that he had had to be helped, almost carried, down the jetty. Seeing his bandy legs buckle as the men supported him, I turned and took hold of the little girls and hurried back up to the house so that he would not suffer the embarrassment of knowing we had witnessed him in this condition. I remember also that Louisa picked the very best portions of bandicoot for his plate, and made sure that he did not partake of any of the beetle-infested beef (she could be a loving daughter in her own way). But these are my only memories of him on that occasion, for I was obviously too preoccupied with my own feelings to think about how he must have been suffering.

The black whale we lost that season was not the only whale that had ever been lost in such circumstances. Allowing the Killers to take possession of the carcass always carried with it the risk that the weather might turn before the men were able to recover it. Perhaps the profits incurred by whaling would have been more consistent if the whalers had been able to tow the carcass back to the try-works immediately after the kill; however, the Killers would never have permitted such a thing and I daresay would have torn the whale to pieces had my father attempted it. Not that he would have dared, of course; he had too much respect for their longstanding "gentlemen's agreement." Besides which, as he readily conceded, without the assistance of the Killer whales, they would likely not have captured the whale in the first place.

The point I was getting to, however, is that although we had lost whales before in similar circumstances, I feel I can trace the beginning of the despondency that characterized his later years to the loss of this black whale in 1908, coming as it did in such a poor season, and after the dreadful season of the year before. And although we went on to have some few reasonably successful seasons after this, there was never a return to the great numbers of whales that were sighted and captured in Twofold Bay in previous generations.

On top of this, whale oil no longer commanded the prices

it had in former times; for this, my father would always blame the Great War, although in truth the decline had commenced much earlier, with the ready availability of kerosene. Similarly, as the fashion for corsetry diminished, the demand for whalebone also began to decline. (My father strongly disapproved of these advances in ladies' fashions, and would cast a baleful eye over Violet and Annie's short skirts and drop-waists when they were old enough to attend the Kiah dances. Indeed, it was a full year or two after he died before I felt that I could dispense with my own whalebone corset.) Yet although these larger forces of wars and fashion and kerosene were outside my father's control, I think he felt badly that he was the last of three generations of Davidsons to whale in Twofold Bay. By 1929, he had put the whaling station up for sale, although it took some years to sell.

> *There's many a time I've quivered with fear*
> *As I've passed by Twofold Bay*
> *And many a time I've shivered to hear*
> *"Fearless Davidson's on his way!"*
> *"Look smart, boys!" cries Fearless George*
> *"She's a humpback fifty feet!"*
> *And he holds aloft the piercing steel*
> *His mission to complete.*

This poem, written from the whale's point of view and published in the *Eden Observer,* continued for some ten to twelve verses, and yet I find I can only remember portions of it. (As a child I knew the entire poem by heart and would stand on the back step and declaim it to the chickens, although I was always too shy to recite it to anybody else.) It described my father doing battle with a particularly ferocious humpback into whose gizzards he plunges his lance in the last stanza, crying out, "*O dark heart, beat no more!*" This caused my father some embarrassment, for of course he knew the humpback to be a mild-mannered creature, nor would he ever cry out such a thing. The only other part of the poem I can recall is:

> *I beg of you, (something something)*
> *Please heed my anguished pleas*
> *But now he deals the fatal blow*
> *Which brings me to my knees.*

Which we found very funny at the time, since obviously whales do not have knees. My point is, however, that while not entirely factually accurate, this poem (and there were others in a similar vein) demonstrates some measure of the esteem in which my father was held by the townsfolk of Eden. I suppose his quiet courage and his cool head when confronted by danger were qualities the civic fathers wished to call their own; certainly they made full use of his reputation to advance the public image of Eden.

Thinking about my father, I feel the urge to recount an event which occurred only a couple of years before he died. By then, it was just him and myself living at Kiah; whaling had been abandoned, much of the equipment already sold, even the Killer whales had stopped returning. I was then employed as a teacher at the Kiah Half-time School; my father spent his days now either sitting on the front veranda or "tidying up" down at the try-works. On this occasion, he had spotted a whale spout from the headland up behind the house. Living where we did, we frequently saw whale spouts during the season; in fact, they seemed especially plentiful now that our livelihood no longer depended upon them. But for some reason, this particular whale captured my father's attention, and he watched it spout and play for some time from the headland. (It is necessary sometimes to remind oneself that these passing whales are undertaking an epic journey of many thousands of miles, for in fact they seem to dawdle and meander in the manner of recalcitrant schoolboys on their way to school; if there was a bottle, they would kick it. It is truly a wonder that they ever get anywhere.) Returning home from school, I saw my father going down to the jetty and getting into his dinghy; I imagined that he was going to row into town, as he sometimes did on the spur of the moment. But instead, unbeknownst to me, he rowed out some considerable distance to where the whale was still idly cavorting. As he approached, the whale sank below the surface; my father—who clearly still possessed an instinct for such things—then rowed to where he believed it might reappear. Sure enough, some minutes later, the whale rose to the surface directly alongside his boat, whereupon he drove his lance into it.

He lanced it just once; the whale immediately dived, then surfaced again in a distressed state and swam off at great speed. My father attempted to pursue it but, needless to say, an old man in a dinghy was no match for it, so after a while he gave up and returned home.

When he came inside for tea, I noticed what appeared to be blood on his clothing, though it seemed he had attempted to sponge it off. When asked about it, he remarked that he had rowed out and lanced a whale, in as casual a fashion as if he had said that he had walked to the letterbox to pick up the mail. I put down my cup and stared at him. For a moment, I truly believed that he might be in the grip of some kind of senile delusion, but his eyes were clear and lucid and he seemed to be entirely his normal self.

"Why did you do that?" I asked, and I realized that my voice was shrill. I did not like whales to be killed for no reason. Besides, it was not as if we had eleven extra men to tow the carcass back and render it into whale oil. Even if we could render it into whale oil, we almost certainly couldn't sell it.

"Why did you do that?" I repeated, and I realized I was angry. I was so angry I felt I could fling something at him, especially since he sat buttering his bread and not responding to my question. He wore a faint, silly smile upon his face, and I noticed his hands were trembling: I suspect he may also have been privately wondering why he had done it, and was unable to provide a satisfactory answer.

Several days later, the dead whale (a young humpback) washed up on the rocks near Green Cape lighthouse, its lance wound plain to see. The story of my father's deed soon became known, and was widely interpreted as somehow heroic; there was even a small article about in the *Sydney Morning Herald*, under the headline: *"LONE WHALER. VETERAN'S FEAT IN DINGHY."* My father's demeanor was considerably more cheerful for some time after this event; he concocted various excuses to go into Eden that he might sit in the bar at the Great Southern and have drinks bought for him on the strength of it. Looking back on it now, I am still somewhat bewildered as to his motive, yet overall more sympathetic in my attitude. I suppose after a lifetime of chasing whales and "staring down the gaping maw of destruction," it must be difficult to allow them to swim past unmolested. I do not mean to sound glib in saying that; I simply mean that he probably just wished to have one more shot at it.

The postscript to the story is that various attempts were made by my father and his old mates from the Great Southern to somehow float the carcass off the rocks, with the vague idea, I imagine, of rendering the blubber into whale oil. They never succeeded; thus the whale rotted over several months in situ, much to the annoyance of the lighthouse keepers, especially when the wind blew in towards them.

A Missing Clergyman

I T WAS AROUND THIS PERIOD—THAT IS, AFTER THE LOSS OF THE black whale, the period in which John Beck was apparently overcome by a resurgence in his faith—that we first came across the story of the missing clergyman. An old newspaper article had been discovered pasted over a crack in the wall in one of the sleeping huts; the first I became aware of it was overhearing Salty recounting the contents of the article for the other whalers' enjoyment one evening at mealtime. John Beck was subsequently on the receiving end of a good deal of speculative commentary on the subject, and I noted at the time that he became quite "hot under the collar."

The next morning, after the whale men had left for the lookout, I entered the sleeping hut, found the article in question (with some difficulty, as there were a great many newspapers plastered over a great many cracks) and copied it out in its entirety.

To summarize the contents of the article: in April of 1906, a Reverend T.A. James, a Methodist minister from Albany,

Western Australia, had traveled to Sydney on a visit. Sometime later in the same month, his wife, Mrs. James, received a telegram stating that her husband had unfortunately drowned in Sydney and his body had not been recovered. Even amidst her grief, Mrs. James considered it odd that the telegram which bore these sad tidings had been posted from Suva, the capital of Fiji, and she at once asked the police if they would commence inquiries. They soon discovered that there had been no drowning accident to speak of in Sydney Harbor at that time. Further, they learned that the Reverend James had last been seen on 15 April, Easter Sunday, at a boarding house in Wynyard Square; he was clean-shaven (up to this point, he had always worn a beard) and, notably, was not dressed in clerical attire. The very next day, a mail steamer, the *Maheno,* had left Sydney for Vancouver. It stopped at Suva on 23 April, the very day the telegram had been posted.

The article concluded with the following postscript:

> Important developments have occurred in connection with the missing clergyman. A photograph of the Rev. T.A. James has been identified as Mr. Lee, who, with Mrs. Lee, stopped at a Sydney boarding house at Easter week. Inquiries show that Mr. and Mrs. Lee were amongst the passengers by the mail steamer "Maheno," which left Sydney for 'Frisco on 16 April. There is now not the slightest doubt but that Lee and James are one and the same person.

The whalers derived a good bit of sport from teasing John Beck on the subject, asking him how he liked 'Frisco and what had become of Mrs. Lee and whether he shouldn't let poor Mrs. James know his present whereabouts. He had borne all this with good humor initially, but after a while seemed to become irritated by their incessant jibes, and requested somewhat tersely that they desist. (This was not in itself surprising; the whalers would often carry a joke too far, and not infrequently something that had begun as a little light jesting would culminate in fisticuffs.) After a while, the whalers lost interest in the story, and it soon faded from general conversation. As for me, I do not recall thinking there was any great cause for concern; rather, the article simply piqued my curiosity. Yet even as I write these words, it seems to be dawning on me for the first time that given the voyage to 'Frisco occurred fully two years before John Beck came ambling up our front path, then there *was* a possibility, albeit a slight one, that John Beck and Reverend James were indeed "one and the same person."

I raise the following points for consideration.

On more than one occasion, John Beck had mentioned Western Australian place names in passing, indicating that he had almost certainly been there. For example, I remember overhearing him mention to my father that Busselton, a town in Western Australia, had a jetty that was a mile long. Another time, he said something about there being a large jail in Fremantle.

Albany (the town in which Reverend James had originally resided) was a whaling port. So it is interesting that there is a whaling connection.

Also, John Beck was clean-shaven (at least he was when we knew him).

Even so, and all things considered, I find I cannot really believe it. It would mean that he had traveled to 'Frisco only to return to Australia again within two years. You would think that he would be reluctant to return to Australia, given the dubious circumstances of his departure, but then again, when I think on it, the police were presumably looking for Rev. James (or, rather, Mr. Lee) in 'Frisco, and I imagine that could have made things uncomfortable. (Indeed, the West Australian Methodist Conference recommended his expulsion from the ministry, and sent a statement of his offenses to be posted in every Methodist church in the United States.) Then there is the whole question of Mrs. Lee. What became of her? I can only assume that the pressure of being "wanted," combined with guilt and shame at his conduct towards his wife— and perhaps even a spiritual turmoil, given that he was a man of the cloth—led to the breakdown of their perhaps somewhat rash and ill-considered liaison.

In truth, it distresses me to think of John Beck as Reverend James in fresh incarnation, with a Mrs. James left behind in Albany, and a Mrs. Lee lingering in 'Frisco. It conveys the impression that he was some kind of Lothario, yet I cannot believe that of him. It is simply a striking coincidence that both men were formerly ministers of the Methodist church.

The Ungraspable Phantom of Life

I T WAS NOT UNUSUAL FOR THE RIGORS OF WHALING TO INSPIRE in new chums a sudden and fervent interest in the hereafter, and for a time I hoped that John Beck's newfound absorption in the Bible, and his readiness with only the slightest provocation to vouchsafe a psalm or lead the whale men in prayer, might simply be another manifestation of this condition. However, it seems that the meteorological coincidence of the crepuscular beam breaking through the clouds in apparent heavenly response to his prayer that grim morning had had the effect of inducing in John Beck a violent reawakening of his faith. This, in turn, induced in me a sense of creeping disappointment. I found I much preferred the old John Beck; the John Beck with the interest in my black silk stockings, the John Beck of the flexing arm muscles; the John Beck with the twinkling eyes and the pleasingly lascivious grin. Most of all, I missed the John Beck who wanted to kiss me, even if it meant risking my father's ire.

I had the distinct sense now that this new John Beck was uncomfortable in my presence. At mealtimes, I gazed at him imploringly as I doled his portion onto his plate, but he kept his eyes firmly downcast, murmured his thanks and moved on. Offering an extended prayer before each meal had become his regular custom now, often taking the opportunity to expound upon theological themes and draw analogies with some small event that had happened during the course of the day. One day, he pontificated for twenty minutes on the fact that just as there were twelve disciples, there were indeed twelve whale men. Needless to say, this sort of talk made the whalers uneasy. Nor did they ever wait for John Beck to finish saying grace before they commenced eating, but I suppose they could scarcely be blamed for that. Thus his invocations were offered to the noisy accompaniment of derisory comments and spoons scraping upon tin plates.

All this was most distressing for me. Was this a repeat of the Burrows episode? I wondered. An ardent pursuit followed by a period of distinct coolness? If so, it seemed very unfair. After all, it was John Beck who had insisted he kiss me; yet now it seemed that I was an unpleasant reminder of a side of his nature that he wished to suppress. At least I was able to examine my own behavior and truthfully state that, in this instance, I had not thrown myself at him. Certainly, I had acquiesced willingly, but was that the same thing? Did my compliance in allowing myself to be kissed amount to "throwing myself at him"? If so, I was beginning to grow very tired of the whole thing.

One day some repair work had to be done on the second whaleboat, and the crew of that boat stayed behind whilst repairs were effected. As it happened, that very morning I had come across my mother's flute and decided I would make a renewed attempt to teach myself to play it. I had attempted several times over the years, and had got to the stage of mastering the "embouchure" and extracting some not unpleasant sounds. Now, with aid of my mother's music book, I intended to work on my fingering. Encouraged by Louisa to move as far away from the house as possible, I took my flute down to the beach below, and there I espied John Beck, sitting alone on a rock some distance away. At first, my impulse was to veer away without him seeing me, but then some contrary spirit within urged me to proceed as I had originally intended. Bonnie, who had elected to accompany me, led the way.

"Oh. Hello there," I said as we approached.

"Hello, Mary," he said.

"What are you doing?"

"Well, I am studying my Bible."

I nodded bitterly. Of course he was. Uncertain as to what to do next but anxious not to end the exchange immediately, I picked up a pebble and skimmed it across the surface of the water. Then I picked up a much larger rock and, with some effort, hurled it into the water. It created a great splash— some droplets even landed on the open pages of his Bible. He glanced up at me briefly, but made no comment.

"Would it be all right if I practiced my flute over there?" I asked, pointing to a cluster of rocks a small distance away.

"Yes, that would be all right," he said.

"I won't disturb your study?"

"No, I don't think so."

"Will you let me know if it does disturb you? Because of course I would stop right away."

"Thank you. I think it should be all right."

I gazed at him unhappily. How handsome he was. I had never noticed it before, but his neck was particularly appealing; strong and well-formed, masculine without being bullish. A clerical collar would have set it off to perfection. However, there was little to be achieved by standing there and staring at his neck, so, with heavy heart, I moved off to the rocks with my flute.

I soon discovered that, in the months since I had last practiced, my mastery of the embouchure had lapsed, and my attempts at producing any decent sound from the wretched thing were thwarted. I pursed my lips and blew in a variety of different ways through and at and over the mouthpiece, but only the most dismal squeaks emerged. What an infernal instrument this was. How did anyone ever learn to play it? Why must my attempts at self-improvement be continually frustrated?

"May I join you?"

I looked up in surprise. John Beck was standing beside me on the rocks.

"If you wish," I replied.

He sat down beside me on the rock, his Bible on his knee. I glanced at it resentfully.

"I do hope you have not come to recite psalms at me," I said curtly.

"No," he said. "Not if you do not wish me to."

I said nothing, but instead pulled my flute apart and proceeded to shake it angrily. I was hoping to convey the impression that there was something the matter with it which prevented me from producing the lilting airs that one normally associates with the instrument.

"Mary," said John Beck, "I think you might be annoyed with me. Perhaps if you would allow me to explain myself."

"I assure you, I am not annoyed with you," I responded crisply. "I just find you extremely changeable, much like the weather we have been having lately."

"Yes. I realize I must seem that way. But you see, something happened out at sea the other day, and I suppose I am trying to make sense of it."

I said nothing, but put my flute back together. Then I rested it on my knee. I had no wish to embark upon more blowing and squeaking in front of him.

"Up until now, you see, Mary," he continued, "I have not always been...entirely straightforward in the way I have represented myself."

"Oh yes?"

"Sometimes I find in life we are all too ready to judge a person's worth on what we perceive of their demeanor or appearance or indeed their past history—"

"I'm sorry, you have lost me altogether."

"I beg your pardon."

"I hope this is not an indication of what your sermons were like."

"Not at all," said John Beck, somewhat tetchily. "In fact, my sermons were on the whole well-regarded. It's just that I am trying to express something rather difficult—"

"Oh, then do forgive my interrupting, simply because I have no clue what you are talking about."

"Well, to speak more plainly, perhaps you have formed an idea about me—"

"I assure you, I have formed no ideas whatsoever."

"I mean, based on the fact that I was once a Methodist minister."

"You are very pleased with the fact that you were once a Methodist minister."

"But that's my point, you see. Perhaps I have no right to be pleased about it."

"Then why do you go on about it so?"

The word "harpy" suddenly leapt into my mind. I sounded like a harpy, sitting there on my mossy rock berating him. Ashamed of myself, I fell into silence. We both stared at Bonnie, who was rolling happily in the remains of a dead mutton-bird she had found on the beach. Every now and then she gave a joyful bark. How nice it must be to be a dog, I thought wildly. Simple pleasures. A nice dead mutton-bird to roll in.

"You wonder why I seem changeable," said John Beck after a moment. "It's because I have always been troubled by a kind of restlessness. I have always been in search of something."

"Goodness," I said. "What have you been in search of?"

"I don't know, you see. That's the problem." He gazed down at his Bible. "Perhaps I am searching for 'the ungraspable phantom of life.'"

He turned to me then, and when I look back at this moment, it seems to me that his face wore a hopeful expression, as if anticipating from me a sympathetic response. A wise nod, perhaps; a gentle smile; a thoughtful word or two murmured in a low voice.

"The ungraspable phantom of life?" I repeated. My voice had now assumed an unpleasantly sardonic tone. "Do you expect you will find it whaling, amidst the blubber?"

He said nothing. Reaching down into a small rock pool

near his feet, he prodded a lowly sea cucumber that resided there. It hunkered down and spat out a murky substance in protest. Then he rose to his feet and walked away (by which I mean John Beck walked away, not the sea cucumber).

I sat on my rock meanwhile, stewing in my own juices. *"Restlessness,"* I muttered to myself scornfully. Was the humble sea cucumber troubled by thoughts of its restlessness? I very much doubted it. More likely, it found contentment within the confines of its rock pool. Had that mutton-bird Bonnie just rolled in been tormented by restlessness also? Actually— I hesitated here—perhaps it had. Perhaps it was restlessness that compelled the bird to fly many hundreds of miles on its annual migration, only to drop dead out of the sky from sheer exhaustion. These hapless whales, driven by an unknown force to travel up the coast each year—perhaps they, too, were plagued by this cursed restlessness, and much good it did them, with the Killer whales waiting to pounce. Such was the confusion of thoughts that darted about in my mind like sheep taking fright in a paddock.

I had failed to recognize, you see, the phrase that John Beck had held out to me. Certainly, I had made several attempts with *Moby-Dick,* and in fact I had read that first chapter through on several occasions. But it was only years later, in another of my efforts at improving myself, that I decided once again to make a renewed attempt. And there, in the first few pages, I stumbled across it:

Why did the old Persians hold the sea holy? Why did the Greeks give it a separate deity, and own brother of Jove? Surely all this is not without meaning. And still deeper the meaning of that story of Narcissus, who because he could not grasp the tormenting, mild image he saw in the fountain, plunged into it and was drowned. But that same image, we ourselves see in all rivers and oceans. It is the image of the ungraspable phantom of life; and this is the key to it all.

That night, in the darkness of our bedroom, I confided in Louisa that I had feelings for one of our whale men.

"Which one?" She propped herself up on an elbow to look at me, her interest roused. "Which one do you fancy?"

Immediately I wished that I had not said anything, for she began poking at me with her bony forefinger.

"Well, John Beck, if you must know," I finally admitted. It felt thrilling, somehow, to give voice to my feelings, as if in doing so, they might actually amount to something.

"Oh, him." Louisa flopped down against her pillow. "But yes, I suppose I can see how he would appeal to you."

"What do you mean?" I asked.

"Well, he's such an old nanny goat," she said.

"Hardly!" I cried hotly. "He is by far the handsomest of all of them."

"Even if that were true, Mary, it would not be saying much."

I deeply regretted telling her, and was thankful that I had not gone into more detail. Although of course now, with the benefit of hindsight, I have come to realize which one of the whalers she personally considered more worthy of admiration.

A Visit from Mr. Crowther

I T WAS AROUND ABOUT THIS TIME THAT WE RECEIVED AN
unwelcome visit from Mr. Crowther. On top of his responsibilities as local agent for Singer sewing machines,
Alfa Laval cream separators and Griffiths Brothers tea, he had
lately taken on the Wunderlich ceiling account, and "wun-
dered" whether we did not feel our small homestead could
benefit from such an improvement. His habit was to sing out
"Hell-o-o thar!" long in advance of his arrival, in the hopeful
expectation that it would allow the lady of the house sufficient
time to rustle up a cake, or at the very least a batch of scones.
Mr. Crowther was a hearty eater, and expected a decent
spread; if he did not get one, he was inclined to let the neighbors know that a traveling man could go hungry at the
Davidsons', at least since Mrs. Davidson had died. He was
well-known for timing his arrival around three in the afternoon, and then stringing out his stories to such an extent that
evening would fall and he would consider it too late to depart.

That is, he would gladly depart if it were not for his fear of bushrangers, who would view Mr. Crowther's sulky—loaded as it was with tea samples and miscellaneous sewing-machine parts—a welcome booty. Thus his hosts were obliged to offer him a bed for the night and full breakfast.

Upon hearing the first distant "Hello-o thar!," Louisa and I looked at each other in fright. The men were all at Boyd Tower, and we wondered if we could not perhaps gather the children and try hiding in the store shed. He would sniff us out, though, we conceded, or the dogs would give us away (we had once tried hiding before, and the dogs, thinking it a game, had commenced barking shrilly in their excitement). Besides, if the house was left unattended, he was just as likely to help himself to whatever victuals he might find. He was known to be especially partial to apples; one family had arrived home unexpectedly to find him perched amidst the branches in the process of stripping their small orchard. Thus we found ourselves with little choice but to open the gate for him and greet him in as cheery a manner as we could muster. Our difficulty was this: not only did we not wish to share our dwindling rations, but also our repayments for the Singer were well overdue.

We fashioned an attempt at rock cakes using dripping instead of butter and the last of our currants; they turned out edible enough if partaken immediately and washed down with plenty of hot sweet tea. Indeed, Mr. Crowther made no complaints but demolished half a dozen of them whilst allowing us to pore over the catalogue for his Wunderlich ceilings. Louisa expressed her admiration of a frieze representing the four seasons, to which Mr. Crowther nodded his approval.

"There is no doubt the Wunderlich ceiling would form the crowning feature of any decorative scheme," he said, casting a doubtful eye over our kitchen. The whitewash on the walls was in need of fresh application, and there were greasy marks where the menfolk leaned back in their chairs of an evening and rested their heads. "Further, you will find them durable and fire-resistant; nor will they crack, warp or fall on top of you."

"I am glad to hear it," I said. Surely "not falling on top of you" was the least one could hope for from a ceiling, and not a bonus feature deemed worthy of advertisement? "Unfortunately, it has not been a good season for whales, so we find ourselves unable to contemplate such improvements just at the moment."

"But it is only the first week of October," said Mr. Crowther. "I am surprised at you for taking such a pessimistic view. Is this not the month when the whales become more plentiful?"

"Ordinarily, yes," I said. "However, we suspect the Norwegians may have greatly depleted their numbers. They have factory steamers, you know, with explosive harpoons. They capture five whales a day without difficulty, but it is not fair on the rest of us."

"No," said Mr. Crowther. "Nor very fair on the whales either. Tell me, how is the Singer running?"

"It is running satisfactorily at present," said Louisa.

He nodded, eyeing her coolly. Then, briskly wiping the crumbs from his shirtfront, he stooped to pull from his bag his receipt book. Our hearts sank at the sight of it: clearly, all pleasantries were over. He had decided it was a waste of time to tempt us with ornamental ceilings and now, given the low standard of our comestibles, he thought he might just as well get down to the unpleasant business.

"Treadle belt still holding firm?" he inquired, frowning down at his book. He had had occasion to replace the belt once, and had never forgotten it: we had learned from our nearest neighbor that he considered Louisa to be "very rough on belts."

"Yes, I have had no trouble," said Louisa. I could see her cheeks beginning to flush, which was usually an ominous sign.

"Purchased November 1899 at a sum of seven pounds, sixteen shillings and sixpence," he read from his receipt book. "To be repaid in quarterly installments of fourteen shillings threepence. The last payment I have received was…" Here he paused, and flicked through the pages of his receipt book. "Can this be correct? A part-payment of six shillings only, March 1907?"

"No, that's not correct," said Louisa. "We gave you three shillings in July."

"July of this year?"

"No, last year."

"Ah yes, here it is. Three shillings, 21 July 1907." He sighed and looked up at us. "You have defaulted on the last four installments. Do you have the outstanding amount for me today?"

"What is the outstanding amount?" I asked.

"Four payments of fourteen shillings threepence, plus this quarter's due."

"And how much is that altogether?"

"Do you wish me to work it out?"

"Please."

"It may be quicker for you to simply tell me how much you are able to pay."

"Oh. Well, none of it just now. We have no money at all, unfortunately."

Mr. Crowther sighed heavily and closed his receipt book. "Then I am very sorry to say I have no choice but to reclaim the Singer. I have strung you out for as long as is possible. Mr. Singer will not tolerate it any longer."

Here it was: the death knell we had feared. Louisa rose up out of her seat at once and fled the room, which I took to be a sign of her emotion.

"There, you have upset my sister!" I cried. "I hope you are satisfied."

And certainly, Mr. Crowther seemed concerned, for he broke into a light sweat. I suppose he understood how important the Singer was as a memento of our mother, let alone as the only thing that kept us looking faintly presentable.

"Miss Davidson, I am very sorry about this," he said. "But you must realize I am answerable to Mr. Singer himself, and he is expecting his money. I have put him off and put him off, but he will have no more of it. You understand, he must pay the wages of his employees."

It was an odd conceit of Mr. Crowther's that he professed to be in direct personal contact with the founding fathers of the firms in which he dealt. He had even gone to the trouble of devising particular character traits for each of them: the brothers Griffiths were prone to spells of nervous disquietude if they learned you had lately been enjoying a rival's tea, and Mr. Singer was always fretting about his employees.

Just at this moment, Louisa returned.

"Here," she said. "Take this. It might count towards some of it." And she handed him the gold sovereign awarded her by Mr. Caleb Cook for being the best-dressed and most prepossessing young lady at the Eden Show.

Mr. Crowther's mood immediately lifted; he thanked her profusely and said that Mr. Singer would be delighted; that of course Mr. Singer understood about the whales and the Norwegians and whatnot, and that the last thing Mr. Singer wanted was for us to lose our machine. Hastily he wrote out a receipt, and then took it upon himself to give the Singer a look-over and apply a bit of oil to its moving parts, and while he was at it he had a look at our cream separator also. By which time, of course, evening had fallen, the men had returned home from another fruitless day on lookout, and Mr. Crowther thought he may just as well stay for tea.

We had stewed several rabbits (augmented with giblets and potatoes) for the evening meal, and now Mr. Crowther helped us carry the pots down to the sleeping hut. There his interest seemed excited by the spectacle of John Beck saying grace, and in a low voice he questioned me as to the identity of our new whale man.

"That is the Reverend John Beck," I responded. "He is an oarsman in the Number Two boat."

"Reverend?" queried Mr. Crowther.

"Yes," I responded unhappily, for once again I noted that John Beck was avoiding my gaze. "He was formerly a Methodist minister."

"How interesting," said Mr. Crowther, stroking his beard thoughtfully. "Would you be so kind as to introduce me?"

Happy to have a reason to approach John Beck, I led him over. John Beck was now hunched over his plate: he seemed startled by our looming out of the shadows, for he at once jumped to his feet, as if he might run.

"Excuse me for startling you," I said. "I would like you to meet Mr. Crowther. He is the agent for Singer sewing machines. Mr. Crowther, this is Reverend Beck."

They each said, "How do you do?," and Mr. Crowther shook John Beck's hand in a bracing fashion.

"May I join you?" he asked. John Beck nodded his consent, and Mr. Crowther at once sat down beside him in a manner which struck me as oddly familiar. He patted John Beck on the knee, and urged him to eat up and not to mind him.

"I hear from young Mary that you were formerly a Methodist minister," he remarked, by way of conversation.

"That is correct," responded John Beck. He seemed reluctant to elaborate more on the theme, although Mr. Crowther smiled at him encouragingly. In truth, he was having difficulty with his portion of meat—I noted with dismay that it appeared to be the shoulder girdle of one of the more senior rabbits.

"Tell me, are you aware of the recent scandal involving one of your kind in Milton?" inquired Mr. Crowther.

"I have never been to Milton," said John Beck. "So I would not know anything about it."

"Never been to Milton?"

"No."

"Did you hail from Sydney originally?"

"Yes."

"Then you must pass through Milton to travel down to Eden! It is a pretty little town—you would not easily forget it."

John Beck said nothing but instead concentrated on eating his rabbit. The very act of pulling the meat from the bone appeared to be hurting his teeth.

"Are you able to furnish us with some detail as to the nature of the scandal?" asked Uncle Aleck. He was seated nearby and sucking on a thigh bone. "Did you say it concerned the Methodist minister?"

"It did," replied Mr. Crowther, settling into the story with an air of enjoyment. "Very popular was he, and well-liked by all. It is a small parish, but the congregation had been steadily growing in numbers since he took it over a year or so prior. This minister, by all accounts a fine-looking man—I have forgotten his name—took it upon himself to start a fund, the purpose being to raise money for a church organ. He worked assiduously at this task, enlisting the support of many of his churchwomen. Letters were written petitioning some of the more prosperous townsfolk. In short order, the fund had reached a little over forty pounds, whereupon the minister absconded—"

"Absconded?" cried Uncle Aleck.

"Taking the organ fund with him—"

But just at this point the story was interrupted, for my father approached Mr. Crowther, looking very upset. He had just learned that Louisa had given over her gold sovereign in payment for the Singer, and he demanded that Mr. Crowther return it to her at once.

"It is my responsibility to pay for that machine, and pay for it I will. But you will not take money from my children, especially in my absence."

And opening his leather purse, which he normally kept secured in a safe place, my father emptied its entire contents into his hand and thrust it at Mr. Crowther. It was the sum of about twelve shillings and a few odd pence—all he had to see us through till they captured a whale.

"Now give that sovereign back to the girl, and be on your way," said my father, and his voice shook discernibly.

The scraping of plates had stopped; everyone had gone quiet. It was very unusual to witness my father so inflamed, and the whale men recognized the significance of the occasion. Without delay, Mr. Crowther dug deep into his breast pocket and handed the gold sovereign over to me. Then, counting the scattered coins quietly under his breath, he secreted them into his pocket.

"I have no wish to offend, I'm sure," he said to my father. "But this is not a full installment. You are very much in arrears. You will need to pay more next time."

"Next time I will pay it off in its entirety," said my father. "On that I give you my word." (Unfortunately, the fortunes of whaling were such that my father was unable to pay the Singer off in its entirety for another four years.)

"Very good," said Mr. Crowther. And tipping his cap, he rose from his seat and headed off into the night. He made no mention of what Mr. Singer might say about this.

"Gather the pots and get back up to the house," said my father, turning to me. He seemed embarrassed and irritated that I had witnessed this exchange.

"And if you must feed us these aged vermin, kindly allow the rigor mortis to subside before you stew them," added Bastable.

Now here is a very odd thing. It took me some several minutes to gather the pots etc., and as I headed back up to the house, I could hear that Mr. Crowther was in the process of harnessing his horse as best as he could manage in the darkness. It seemed by the sound of it that the horse was giving him some trouble, for I could hear scuffling noises and low curses emanating from that area. Taking pity on him, I went over with my lantern, and as I did so, I was suddenly aware of a dark figure moving off abruptly at my approach. Mr. Crowther himself seemed somewhat agitated, and I noted his shirt was free of his trousers, as if some kind of struggle had ensued.

"Most kind, most kind," he murmured, but all the while his eyes darted nervously about.

I stood over him till he had lit his lanterns; in fact, I had to take over at one point for his hands were trembling so much he had difficulty in lighting the matches. Then, in great haste, he climbed up into his sulky and drove off into the pitch-black night. The question of bushrangers seemed suddenly not to bother him.

A Sermon Interrupted

JOHN BECK SUGGESTED TO MY FATHER THAT WE CELEBRATE
the Lord's day by conducting a short non-
denominational service for the whale men and family
early on Sunday morning, before the men rowed to the
lookout. Perhaps he had hinted that this might be beneficial
in terms of whales, for somewhat unexpectedly my father
embraced the idea, and not wanting to displease my father,
the whale men felt obliged to attend. Benches were arranged
on the sand as if pews, and John Beck stood before us. In
lieu of cassock and surplice, he had donned a clean white
shirt, and it complemented his suntanned complexion admirably.

"Today I would like to talk on the subject of Temptation,"
said John Beck, after we had sung what we remembered of
"All Things Bright and Beautiful." This was in fact only the
chorus, and the verse about the rich man in his castle and the
poor man at his gate.

"For who amongst us has not been buffeted by temptations?" John Beck continued. "I know I most certainly have, and sadly I yielded to them, and that is why I am no longer a minister of the Methodist church."

I found myself sitting upright now. This had become rather more interesting than I had anticipated.

"If you are no longer a minister of the Methodist church, then why are you imposing upon us this sermon?" demanded Bastable.

"Well, I suppose I am acting today as a kind of lay preacher," John Beck replied. "But back to the subject of Temptation. Who amongst us has not been buffeted by temptation?"

"Father, since you ask, I have not been buffeted by temptation in a long time," said Uncle Aleck.

"Me neither," admitted Arthur Ashby.

"I would very much like to be buffeted by temptation, but sadly no one is buffeting me," said Salty.

"I wonder if we could get on to the business of praying for a whale," said my father.

"Yes, in a moment, but first—I understand that some of you may not have been to church for some time and may have forgotten the procedure, but the idea is I talk on a theme for twenty minutes or so—generally there are no interruptions—then we might have another prayer and a hymn or two. Does that sound all right?"

"Yes, yes, by all means."

"As I was explaining, whilst I was serving as a minister of the Methodist church, I was greatly buffeted by temptation."

"Bragging," muttered Bastable, behind me.

"Would this be some of the ladies in the congregation buffeting you, Father?" asked Uncle Aleck.

"Yes, in fact it was."

Louisa nudged me sharply in the ribs. A murmur of interest passed through the congregation.

"You see," John Beck went on, "I have always been greatly
susceptible—"

"They're not shy then, Father, the Methodist lasses?"

"As I say, Uncle Aleck, generally speaking a sermon is not
a question-and-answer style of discussion. Rather, I expound
at length on a certain—"

"Just get on with it, Father, pay no attention to Uncle," said
my father.

"Yes, yes, proceed; pay no attention to me," agreed Uncle
Aleck.

"Thank you. Now, where was I?"

"You were telling us about your susceptibility," I said.

"That's right," said John Beck, and here I seemed to notice
a flush of color rising up from his collar. "You see, my difficulty was that I have always been burdened with a natural
susceptibility to whatever is amiable"—here he glanced at me
nervously—"in a woman."

"More bragging," said Bastable.

"Well, not really bragging—you see, it was my undoing,
and the reason that I stand before you as an oarsman in the
Number Two boat."

"There's no shame in being oarsman, Father," cried
Bastable. "I have been an oarsman for nigh on fifteen years and
proud of it."

"What he means is, he is only oarsman in the Number Two

boat," said Darcy, who was of course an oarsman in the Number One boat.

"No, no—" John Beck protested.

"Oh, so the Number Two boat isn't grand enough for you?" declared Salty, ever quick to take umbrage.

"No, you have me all wrong. What I mean is, I am now an oarsman—forget the Number Two boat—where once I was a minister of the Methodist church."

"And that makes you a better man than us, does it?"

"No, not at all, I am simply saying that temptation has brought me greatly undone."

"Are you referring to your exploits with Mrs. Lee in 'Frisco, Father?"

"I have no knowledge of Mrs. Lee."

"Then is it regarding the organ fund?"

"Once again, I must reiterate that I have never been to Milton—"

"Back to the buffeting, if I may," said Uncle Aleck. "What were the ladies doing exactly? Were they pressing up against you in the sacristy?"

"I have no wish to go into details—that is hardly suitable—"

"Could we pray for a whale now?" asked my father.

"If you could just let me finish. You see, I thought that God had abandoned me, given the depths to which I had fallen—"

"Is that Tom?" cried Dan suddenly.

"Yet the other day when we were out at sea—"

"I saw him! I swear!"

"—and we prayed—do you remember?"

"Where?"

"Where's Tom?"

"—well, it seemed to me that Somebody heard us."

And just at that moment, directly behind John Beck, Tom rose out of the water, revealing the full length of his magnificent black and white body. He curved gracefully—surprisingly lithe for such a corpulent fish—and seemed almost to hover in mid-air a moment before re-entering the water and slapping his tail down hard upon it with a sound like the crack of a whip. *Come now!* was unmistakably his terse instruction.

"*Rush oh!*" cried my father, leaping to his feet.

The whalers clambered over each other in their haste to get to the whaleboats. Tom had sounded his clarion; now they must do his bidding. The children ran off, relieved to be let out of church. Only Louisa and I remained in our seats. John Beck glanced over at us, a little embarrassed.

"Well, it would appear that I have lost my congregation to a Killer whale," he said.

"What a shame, for the sermon was very interesting," I said.

"Yes, well—I am a little out of practice."

"No, not at all."

"It was all right?"

"It was extremely enlightening."

"Thank you, Mary," he said, gazing at me earnestly. "That's kind of you to say."

"Perhaps you had better go now and catch the whale," said Louisa, for the whale men were dragging the boats into the water.

"Yes. Yes, I suppose I had better, especially since I am oarsman in the Number Two boat." He laughed nervously. "That bit didn't go over so well, did it?"

"Whalers can be very prickly about such things," I said.

"Yes, I see that now. Well…" Here Salty shouted at him to get into the boat. "Please excuse me, ladies."

Throwing off his coat and tossing aside his sermon notes, he ran down to the water and jumped impressively into the whaleboat. How magnificent he looked rowing, and how well that white shirt set off his physique. There was certainly nothing of the nanny goat in his appearance today, as I pointed out to Louisa.

"I admit he looks quite nice in that shirt," she conceded. "But don't you find him awfully dull?"

I did not find him dull. I was in love with him. And as I watched him bend to the oars as the whaleboats pulled over the breakers, it became clear to me that I could not remain passive; I must act. I must buffet him with temptation as he had never been buffeted before, not even by the good ladies of the Methodist church.

The Boat-Breaker

AS A RULE, WHALES ARE DISTINCTLY BOVINE IN TEM-
perament. If they lived in a paddock, they would
stand about chewing their cud and staring into the
middle distance. If they saw another whale sitting down under
a tree, they would think to themselves, "Maybe I will sit down
under the tree also." Then, when they got to the tree, they
would think, "Why did I come over to the tree again? I can't
remember." And they would start to wander off again. And
then they would think, "Oh, look at that whale sitting under a
tree. Maybe I will sit under a tree also." (I will desist from this
allegory now as I feel it is becoming rather strained.) Suffice to
say, whales are placid, dull creatures and mean no harm. But
every now and then comes a whale different to other whales,
and that whale is known as a boat-breaker.

Such was the whale to whose tail, by means of harpoon,
my father's boat had just attached itself. As mentioned previously, the harpooner Arthur Ashby was an excellent aim, but

so fast was this whale and so erratic its movements that on this occasion his harpoon fell short and found purchase on that narrowing section between the whale's flukes and body. This is perhaps the least desirable part of a whale's anatomy to which to attach oneself, for it seems to be extremely sensitive, as was demonstrated by such wild thrashings on the part of the whale that my father had no choice but to cut loose for fear of damaging his boat. The second boat, in close attendance, was then ordered to fasten on, and here my brother Harry did himself credit by landing his harpoon just at the back of the whale's blowholes. So stunned was he at his success that he forgot that it was now necessary to change positions with Salty.

"Change over, boy, change over!" cried Salty. "Oars up, men! Let's let the old girl run!"

The men lifted their oars up high out of the water, locked their handles into the peak chocks and braced themselves for the wild ride. Doing their utmost not to become entangled in this lethal line, the two men scrambled over the oarsmen to assume their new positions. Reaching the bow now and jamming his thigh in the clumsy cleat, Salty took a good look at their adversary. "Damn it to hell! White spots! Say your prayers, men!"

For sure enough, the monster had two distinct white spots—old harpoon scars—clearly visible on its back. The Killers were doing their utmost to contain the whale's flight, but the canny whale embarked on a series of sharp zigzags in a bid to throw them off. Finally, in desperation, it dived. The Killers dived as well, and for several frightening moments it appeared that the whale might travel down so deep as to pull the entire whaleboat down with it. But the Killers drove it up

again and as it broke the surface of the water, it suddenly came
to a complete standstill; the second boat, still attached to it
and compelled by forward momentum, headed straight for it.

"Stern all, boys! Hard astern!" cried Salty.

The men scrabbled to get their oars back into the water, but
it was too late; they collided, the boat sliding onto the whale's
vast back. Infuriated, it reared out of the water, lifting the
boat up with it. There the boat floundered sickeningly, oars
flailing, before sliding down the ridge of its back and smash-
ing into the water.

At once the great flukes rose up and, with a vicious swipe,
knocked Harry clean out of the boat. At this, young Robert
panicked, and endeavored to jump out of the boat to avoid
being struck himself, but as he did so, the flukes pinned him
down on the gunwale, half in and half out of the boat. As he
squealed and squirmed, the flukes rose up again and released
him; he at once effected his escape into the boiling seas. Only
John Beck, Shankly and Salty remained in the boat now, and
they stared transfixed as the giant flukes rose with majestic
stateliness to a height of twenty feet above them, harpoon and
line still dangling.

"Father," said Shankly, turning suddenly towards John
Beck.

"Yes?" said John Beck, feeling a wave of irritation. What in
God's name did Shankly want of him now?

"Is it too late to ask for forgiveness?"

As if by way of answer, and with only the subtlest quiver
to warn of its impending action, the tail slammed down upon
John Beck and Shankly, pinning them to the bottom of the
boat. With great presence of mind, Salty set to beating the

weighty tail muscle with an oar in a bid to free the men, and at this the enraged creature tipped the entire boat over into the water.

It seems John Beck may have lost consciousness with the first impact of the flukes, but the sudden immersion in freezing water revived him and he opened his eyes to glimpse a flurry of black and white amidst the blood and foam and bubbles. Propelled towards the surface, he came up beneath the overturned boat, so was at once forced to dive again and this time, with the last bit of oxygen in his lungs, came up beneath the whale itself. But the capsizing of the boat had released the tub containing the whale line, and the whale, sensing its chance, gave a last mighty flick of its tail and headed for the open sea, bearing two harpoons, eighty fathom of line (much of it coiled around its girth), and even the tub itself, tumbling along the wave tops in its wake.

Once the whale escaped for deeper waters, the Killers called a meeting amongst themselves and voted to "down tools"; whales can dive deeper and stay under longer in the ocean and this puts the Killers at a disadvantage. One or two of their number saw the whale off with a nip or two to remember them by, but most of them elected to stay close by the men in the water, both solicitous and curious about their predicament. My father, of course, was wasting no time in effecting their rescue—most of the men wore heavy coats and sea boots, and were in grave danger of drowning.

John Beck was in particular strife; barely conscious, he clung feebly to the upturned hull. Feeling a powerful nudge to the small of his back, he opened his eyes blearily to see Tom's beknobbed dorsal fin close by. A black snub-nosed snout rose out of the water and the famous orca surveyed my battered paramour in evident amusement, for he seemed to be grinning, and he waved a stumpy side fin at him as if by way of greeting. He then opened his mouth to reveal his sharp teeth and made a strange noise as if clearing his throat in preparation for a speech.

John Beck panicked now, for a glimpse of those pointy white teeth brought back memories of the hapless finback he had witnessed torn apart at Leatherjacket Bay. In desperation, he tried to scramble onto the hull, but in his weakened state only slid back into the water. This prompted Tom to embark upon a series of high-pitched squeals, as if sharing a joke with his friends; they responded in a similar vein, and several swam over as if to observe John Beck for themselves. It was at this point that John Beck began to make preparations to die, for he could not seem to keep his head above water; his last conscious thought was that if the Killer whales were laughing at him, then they would surely soon commence to eat him.

Fortunately, my father and his whale men were at once by his side, and pulled him out of the water. Even in his unconscious state, his limbs were still futilely scrabbling, as if trying to get away from the Killers.

Yet he did not need to fear. On past occasions where boats had overturned and whalers had found themselves in the water, the Killers had been known to act with the greatest concern and solicitude, to the extent of propping one drowning whaler up with a side fin till help arrived. According to our Aboriginal whalers, some of their people, in finding themselves in a similar situation, had been towed ashore by hanging on to the dorsal fins of these good Samaritans of the deep.

I have no doubt that in this instance Tom was simply keeping a friendly eye on John Beck, ready to offer his assistance the moment it should be required.

It now became apparent to my father that of the five men in the second whaleboat, only four remained; there was no sign at all of the Scotsman Shankly. It was concluded that he had been knocked unconscious by the impact of the flukes, and then drowned amidst the general turmoil of the boat over-turning. The men scoured the sea calling for him till such time as it was decided that the surviving whaleboat was in danger of sinking if they dallied further; also, John Beck was injured and in need of first aid. With the sun sinking low in the sky, they made the sad journey home—eleven men in one boat, the gunwale almost level with the water; the stove-in hull of the second boat towed behind; an escort of Killer whales swim-ming alongside.

The Sermon Notes

I N THE MEANTIME, WHILST ALL THIS WAS HAPPENING OUT AT sea, we had changed out of our good Sunday clothes and resumed our chores. I was in the process of turning over an area of soil in preparation for planting a new crop of celery and parsnips, and as I tilled the soil, I mulled over the various interesting insights that had arisen during John Beck's sermon. Suddenly a thought occurred to me. As he dashed for the boat, John Beck had tossed aside his sermon notes along with his coat; perhaps if I was to find these notes, they might prove to be edifying in both the personal and the spiritual sense. Abandoning my shovel, I hastened down to the beach and, after some little difficulty, eventually managed to locate the notes floating face down in a small rock pool some distance from where he had discarded them. With great care, I retrieved the sodden, solitary page and took it back to the house, where I allowed it to dry in the sunlight in a sheltered position on the veranda. In fact, I have this same page beside me now as I write; it is the only example I have of his hand-writing, which alone affords it enormous value to me. But more than this, the words that I found there on the page—words that were left unsaid owing to Tom's unexpected appearance, and yet give proof positive of the direction in which John Beck's thoughts veered—these have ensured that this tattered, yellowing scrap remains for me one of my dearest personal possessions. It is a simple piece of lined paper, nothing more, seemingly torn in haste from a notebook, on which his thoughts are marked out in pencil, in a neat, forward-sloping hand:

> *Dangers of Temptation to God-fearing life.*
> *Talk about own exp. & where it has brought me*
> *Matt 26:14 spirit indeed willing but flesh weak etc.*
> *Benefits of marriage in this regard (1 Corinthians 7) let every*
> *   man have his wife*
> *In conclusion, poss. humorous remark whaling vs marriage?*
> *   Both fearsome adversary?*
> *(NB pray for whale.)*

Once again, it is tempting to lay the blame on Tom, for had he only delayed his call to arms by ten to fifteen minutes, then perhaps John Beck might have finally been permitted to get to his point. For close study of his sermon notes seems to make clear: here was a man who had grown weary of temptation, and saw that his salvation could be found within the blessed confines of matrimony. *"Let every man have his own wife, and every woman her own husband"*: these were the words he intended, and perhaps his glance would have fallen upon me just as the words fell from his lips, for I have little reason to doubt that his thoughts were beginning to settle in my direction. However, Tom had his business to attend to, and therein lay my misfortune. That, and the blow to the head that John Beck received in the subsequent whale chase, whereby any further thoughts along these lines seem to have been summarily knocked out of him.

Repercussions

WE MADE UP A BED FOR JOHN BECK IN THE FRONT room, and there I devoted myself to the task of nursing him back to health. He was still in a stupefied state when they brought him up and not conscious of his surroundings; I sent everybody away, drew the curtains and set about bathing his forehead where it had been gashed. My tender ministering did not rouse him; occasionally his eyes stirred behind his lids if a drop of water trickled from his brow, but that was all. At one point, he murmured something I could not make out. I leaned in more closely to hear it and felt his soft breath upon my cheek, but he soon lapsed back into unconsciousness. I gazed down at his fine battered features—his blackened eyes, his bruised cheek—and a rush of intense feeling overwhelmed me. How grateful I was that he had been spared, and not banished to the dismal depths like poor Shankly, but *oh!* how anxious I was that he now pull through.

Louisa entered quietly with some clean rags for the purposes of bandaging his head wound. She placed them on the table, then hesitated a moment to watch me.

"Well, you seem to be enjoying yourself," she said, with an unpleasant smirk.

"How dare you," I retorted hotly, though still keeping my voice modulated to a whisper. "The man is gravely injured, and yet you consider it appropriate to make improper suggestions."

"All I am saying is I have difficulty imagining you tending to the other whale men in this doting fashion."

Whereupon I pinched her hard on the fleshy part of her arm, so hard that she squealed. Then I instructed her to prepare the supper for the whalers, and to make it a good one, for they had had a bad day. At this she balked, but I insisted, for I could not be pulled away from my present duties. Amidst vigorous protests and more pinches, she finally submitted and left the room to attend to the evening meal.

Returning my attention to my patient, I found that his eyes were now open and he was gazing at me in a puzzled way. It seemed that our heated discussion had roused him.

"Rest now," I said softly. "Do not worry; I have sent her away."

Thus reassured, his eyes drifted shut again, and I returned to the task of bathing his forehead.

Of this most difficult season, this day—18 October 1908— marked the nadir. The experience had shaken the men badly. Morale was at its lowest ebb. To add to their woes, provisions had almost completely run out and Louisa was in charge of the kitchen.

"What is this? Dishwater?" asked Arthur Ashby, gazing down at his soup. A good-natured chap as a rule, he was not normally one of our complainers.

"No, it is soup," said Louisa crisply.

"What sort of soup?"

"Larder beetle soup."

At this, young Robert Heffernan, who had just taken a mouthful, spat it out violently.

"Oh, for goodness' sake!" said Louisa. "I was only joking."

Darcy was the only one who chuckled; then again, he always seemed to find Louisa amusing.

"I wish it *was* made of larder beetles," muttered Bastable. "If it was made of larder beetles, then it might offer us some nourishment. Expecting us to catch whales on a diet of dishwater."

"Well, if you would only *catch* a whale instead of letting them get away all the time, we might be able to think of offering you some nourishment," said Louisa, turning upon him. "Heavens, we might even be able to think of offering *ourselves* some nourishment!"

"Louisa…" said Dan anxiously. She was known for her hot temper, and once unleashed, it could not easily be reined in.

"I never met such a collection of whining, lily-livered namby-pambies!" she continued. "We'd do a better job if it was me and Violet and Annie out there! I tell you what, we'd have better sense than to let a piddling thirty-foot humpback get away!"

And with that, she threw down her soup ladle and stormed back up to the house, leaving the whalers to stare after her in dismay. A sense of shame overcame them. The young mistress had described them as namby-pambies.

"It's all very well for her to say," offered Albert Thomas Senior. "That humpback was at least thirty-five, maybe forty feet. And it was cranky."

The others said nothing, however, but meekly supped their soup. It was Darcy who later gathered the pots and plates and carried them up to the house.

The Trees They Do Grow High

THAT EVENING, AFTER THE MEN HAD EATEN, MY FATHER took himself down to talk to them. "Men, I just wanted to say a few words about Shankly," he said.

"Aye, poor old Shankly," murmured the men, and some of them lowered their heads out of respect.

"We none of us knew him very well, I know, but I want to pay him tribute nonetheless," my father continued. "He proved himself to be a decent oarsman and pulled hard when it counted."

"Nonetheless, he was a strange one, if you ask me," said Uncle Aleck. "There was something about him that made me uneasy. I cannot put my finger on it."

"He owed me a shilling," said Percy Madigan. "I daresay I have no chance of seeing it now."

"Anyway, he is gone," said my father, wishing to discourage the direction in which the conversation was veering.

"And, men, I wouldn't blame any of you if you decided you'd had enough. We are having a bad season, and no mistake."

"This was the last straw, boss, what happened to Shankly," said Bastable, and some of the men muttered in agreement.

"I realize that, Bastable. We haven't lost a man in thirty-five years. It weighs heavily upon me."

There was an uncomfortable silence. My father was a retiring man, and speaking to the men in this fashion did not come easily to him. He stuck his thumbs behind his braces and stared fixedly at the ground.

"Men, I wanted to say this to you. I reckon we should be able to get the second boat back in the water in a day or so— and if you'd consider seeing the season out with me till the end of November, or at least for as long as the Killers stay, then, well, I'd appreciate it. November is usually a pretty good month for whales—"

"Not last November it wasn't," said Bastable.

"Well, you're right, Bastable, I can't argue with you there. But if November doesn't bring us a whale, then I'll sell the boats and the harpoons and lances, and we'll divide the proceeds up between us. You're good men, all of you, and I feel you should have something for your efforts."

"You'll not sell the whaling station!" cried Salty.

"I may have to, Salty, if it comes to it."

"Then you'll have to sell me with it. For I will not be leaving!"

"Hear, hear!" said Arthur Ashby, and several of the other men concurred.

"I appreciate the sentiment, men. But I want you to consider the matter carefully. As I say, I'll not think the worse of any man for quitting, given the circumstances..."

And here his voice trembled, so he turned abruptly and marched back up the hill to the house.

Having bandaged John Beck's forehead as best I could, I settled down to watch over my patient. He seemed to be resting more comfortably now and, in the lamplight, I took the opportunity to gaze at him fully. His chest rose and fell as he dozed; a lock of unruly dark hair fell across his brow. One arm rested on the blanket, his calloused palm lying upwards as if in expectation of something being placed in it. Without thinking, I slipped my own hand into his, and his fingers closed reflexively around mine. I sat there for several moments like this, then I leaned forward and kissed his cheek tenderly. He responded with a sigh. Emboldened, I then kissed him full on the mouth—once, twice, and as I kissed him a third time, his eyes flickered open and he looked at me.

"Oh! I'm sorry!" I said, pulling back.

"That's all right," said John Beck, somewhat dazedly.

"I hope you don't think I was taking advantage of your—of your susceptibility."

"Oh. Well, I suppose you were a little."

"Only in that I thought you were deeply unconscious. I do apologize."

"Oh, that's all right."

"Are you feeling better?"

"Yes. Considerably."

"Does your head hurt?"

"A little."

"Are you hungry?"

"A little."

"I will fetch you some supper then."

Only then did I realize that I was still clutching on to his hand, so I released it and hurried towards the door, astonished at my own actions. Had I been taking advantage of him? Perhaps I had. Certainly, I had resolved to buffet him with temptation, but was it appropriate to buffet a person when he had recently been stupefied by a whale? The truth is, the compulsion to kiss him had simply overwhelmed me; I had not considered it, I had simply done it, as if driven by forces I was powerless to fight.

Reaching the doorway, I stopped and turned to him. "I hope you do not think I am like those ladies who pressed themselves up against you in the sacristy," I said.

He stared at me for a moment as if confused, then waved his hand wanly. "This talk of the ladies in the sacristy, that was Uncle Aleck's invention—I would not put too much store in it," he replied.

I had no sooner stepped out of the room, closing the door behind me, when my father materialized.

"How is he, Mary?" he inquired.

"He is feeling better and about to take some nourishment," I responded, thankful that it was dark and my father could not see the color in my cheeks.

"You go and see to it then, girl," said my father. "I am going in to talk to him." And knocking lightly on the door, he entered.

"Sorry to disturb you," he said to John Beck. "Is it all right if I have a quiet word?"

"Yes, of course," said John Beck.

My father sat and gazed down at his battle-scarred hands. Nervously, he rubbed the stump of his right index finger which Tom had famously crushed between his teeth—a habit of his when worried. (That is to say, it was my father's habit when worried—not Tom's habit. That is, it was not Tom's habit to crush someone's finger when worried. I think he had merely been irritable.)

"You're feeling better, I hope?" he said, after a moment.

"Much better, thank you, sir."

"Mary has been looking after you?"

"She is a tonic for any invalid, sir."

(To be honest, I am not entirely sure if these were their exact words—I am reconstructing this conversation from an account given to me later by John Beck, and he supplied only the basic details.)

My father nodded absently. It was clear that he was preoccupied with weightier matters.

"Father, the men have just about had enough, and I don't blame them. I've asked them if they'll at least see the season through to the end of November. I don't know how you feel about this, given you've just copped the flukes in the old noggin."

"Oh, I'll see the season out, sir. No question at all."

"Well, Father, I appreciate it. I can't promise anything, of course, but we'll…we'll do our best."

John Beck nodded. A short pause ensued.

"Father, just on another note altogether, some of the men have asked if you would kindly stop with the hymns and the saying of grace and what-have-you. It doesn't sit right with them somehow."

"I see."

"As I say, it's the men, Father, not me. If I had my way, you'd be singing hymns till the cows came home."

"Think no more of it," said John Beck. "I understand completely." A silence. "Do you mean a suspension to the Sunday services?"

"If you wouldn't mind, Father."

"Of course not. Whatever you think best."

My father stared down at his hands again. It seemed he might be working up to ask something else.

"Father," he said finally, "I wonder if we might pray for a whale, just the two of us?"

"Why, of course."

"For a good-sized whale, Father, preferably a southern right. I'm fairly desperate, Father, or I would not be bothering you, on your sickbed and all."

"It is no trouble," said John Beck, and my father immediately lowered himself to his knees. Yet for some reason, John Beck seemed to hesitate. "I am happy to do what I can, of course, but there is something I feel you should know," he said.

"What's that, Father?"

"Well, I must be honest with you. I was never really a proper Methodist minister."

"Ah," said my father, and he was silent for a moment. "Not ordained as such?"

"Not ordained, that's right," said John Beck. "In fact, the truth is that I borrowed the papers of an actual Methodist minister who had the misfortune to expire on the passage over, so you see..." Here he trailed off.

"Did you say you borrowed them?"

"Yes. Well...I suppose it could be argued that I stole them."

"The gentleman had expired, you say?"

"Yes. The truth is, he fell overboard in mysterious circumstances."

"I see," said my father. "That does cast a different light on things."

"Yes, it does, sir. I'm sorry."

My father said nothing. He simply gave a deep sigh, as if this just about capped things off. He had pinned all his hopes on John Beck's celestial connections, and now he found these hopes extinguished. His shoulders slumped; his whole physical demeanor seemed to speak of unendurable weariness and despondency.

"Nevertheless," said John Beck, who had been studying my father with some concern, "it is said that God hears us all in our hour of need. You and I are as much entitled to pray for a whale as the Archbishop of Canterbury himself."

My father looked up at him hopefully.

"A large southern right, if you would then, Father," he said. "And long in the whalebone preferably."

Later that night, my father, Uncle Aleck and Dan sat outside on the veranda together. Nobody spoke; the men simply sat in somber reflection, smoking their pipes. Dan briefly wondered if the events of the day were such that he might pull out his own pipe without provoking an incident, but better sense prevailed and his pipe remained concealed in his pocket. After ten minutes or so, however, Dan began to grow fidgety. He started breaking a stick into smaller and smaller pieces; *snap,*

snap, snap! This got on my father's nerves, and eventually he asked Dan to desist. That was when Dan finally decided he must speak.

"Dad?"

"Yes, son?"

"Now that you are a man short, can I go out, do you think?"

"Go out?"

"In the whaleboat, I mean."

My father turned to survey him then, his face set grim as granite.

"How old are you now?" asked my father.

"Thirteen. Or at least, I will be thirteen in December."

"Can you row hard?"

"Yes, sir, I can," said young Dan. "And I was only thinking, since you're a man short..." My father gazed at him a long moment and sucked on his pipe.

"Well, Uncle, what do you think about it?" he said finally, turning to Uncle Aleck.

Uncle Aleck shook his head. "It's a dangerous business."

"That it is," said my father. "His mother would never forgive me. A boy of twelve in a whaleboat."

"I was eleven when I started," said Uncle Aleck. "And I rowed as hard as three men."

My father nodded. The age at which Uncle Aleck started whaling was a variable thing, but it was consistent in the fact that it was always younger than anybody else's.

"I will row as hard as six men," averred Dan.

"D'you know what it is to stare down a whale?" asked Uncle Aleck. "For you must stare down a whale, or they will try to get the better of you."

"I'm a good starer," said Dan. "I can stare down any whale."

"And how do you calm a whale when he's angry? D'you know that?"

"Sing to him," said Dan, for he knew all Uncle Aleck's stories as he'd heard them a thousand times.

"Sing to him? What would you sing to him? Just any old song that comes into your head?"

"I would sing to him, 'The Trees They Do Grow High.'"

"Yes, and why?"

"It will make the whale cry, and he'll stop his thrashing."

"He'll do," said Uncle Aleck, turning to my father.

And the saddest part of this whole story is that Dan himself died young, just like the bonny boy in the song, not in a whaleboat but at Pozières, France, sometime around the 26th August, 1916.

Having Gone to Be
Wasted in Battle

UFFICE TO SAY, IN WRITING WHAT WAS SUPPOSED TO BE A straightforward account of the whaling season of 1908, I did not intend to be side-tracked by the vagaries of fortune that affected our family as they affect all families. Thus I had not supposed I would dwell upon what happened to Dan any more than I had dwelled upon the loss of our mother. So I was taken aback at the way in which my recounting of that conversation on the veranda in the previous chapter affected me, for it brought my progress with this memoir to a standstill; I found myself tearful and downhearted and had no inclination to return to these or any memories for a period of some weeks. Only now do I feel myself sufficiently strong enough to sit at the typewriter again.

Of course, there is something deeply poignant in a small boy asking the older men if he can join them in doing battle, particularly as for me it brought to mind so many of Dan's qualities: his pluck, his earnest enthusiasm, his eagerness to grow up. But in fact, more than this, I found I was affected by the reference to the song itself. "The Trees They Do Grow High" was an old song that Uncle Aleck used to sing to us, always with a show of great reluctance and only after the most prolonged pleadings on our part. "Don't make me sing it, for it will only set you to bawling," he would say, and we would promise that this time we would somehow manage to retain our composure. But of course the power of the song was such that it would inevitably send us flung across our beds and weeping.

The trees they grow high,
The leaves they do grow green
Many is the time my true love I have seen
Many an hour I have watched him all alone
He's young,
but he's daily growing.

Uncle Aleck had a thin reedy voice which warbled in a wayward fashion on the high notes, and yet it was capable of making one's heart lurch with sorrow.

At the age of fifteen, he was a married man
At the age of sixteen, the father of a son
At the age of eighteen, the grass grew over him,
Having gone to be wasted in battle.

I suppose it is a song about life's hopes dashed, and perhaps that is why it affected us so; as a whaling family, we were familiar with disappointment. And yet I still cannot fully account for the seemingly prescient grief that afflicted us all upon hearing it. For Dan was amongst us then, and as affected by the song as any of us.

When Sergeant Piesley came to Eden to encourage the local lads to enlist, Dan volunteered immediately along with his best mate, Charlie Oslington, and several other lads from the cricket club. It was hardly surprising. As a very small boy, when the Salvation Army missionaries had visited to minister to our Aboriginal whale crew, Dan had been fiercely attracted to the military appearance of their uniforms and had readily joined up, that he might bang his kettle and pipe in his boyish voice:

Thousands of children Jesus has saved
Making them pure and holy
Teaching them how to fight and be brave
In the Salvation Army!

I remember Dan came galloping home on Trinket (Two Socks had passed away by then) with the news that he would be embarking within two weeks. This came as a terrible blow for my father. I suppose he had hoped that Dan's poor eyesight would prevent him from being accepted; it was right at the beginning of the whale season of 1915, and our father could not easily spare him from the whaleboats. A farewell social for the boys was hastily organized at the School of Arts, decked out with flags for the occasion, and the fathers of each young man took turns in speaking. Mr. Oslington said he knew nothing but good of all the boys, and he felt certain there was not a one that would shirk when hostilities got thick. Mr. Walsh said he had played cricket with each of them and found them to be true sports. Mr. Strickland drew comparisons between whaling and warfare, both starting with the letter W, and went on to liken the humpback with the Hun, my father to Lord Kitchener and Tom the Killer whale to General Douglas Haig. Then Mr. English got up and said he felt like the man sitting down to dinner after the turkey had all been served, for there was very little left for him to say. He then went on to expound at length on the theme that the single man had no more duty to go and fight than the married one, and if this war continued, then he would certainly offer his services if he could only pass the medical test. (This produced laughter, for Mr. English had only one leg, the other having been crushed by a tree while timber-felling.) It was my father's turn to speak then and he walked in a determined fashion to the stage, but when he turned to gaze upon the five boys all standing there beneath the Union Jack, his lower jaw began to tremble violently.

"I wish you all a speedy and safe return—" was all he could manage to get out, for helpless tears had begun to slide down his face. The gathered families and townsfolk stared in dismay; there stood Fearless Davidson, leviathan-killer, weeping into his handkerchief whilst the other fathers patted his back and nodded grimly. Dan himself simply seemed embarrassed. He shifted on his feet and joked about with the fellows next to him while all this was going on.

Sergeant Piesley leapt up then, obviously anxious that the paternal anguish not spread to the room at large, and told the lads in a loud cheerful voice that there was nothing in the world to worry about if they would just heed this one piece of advice from an old soldier, and that was never to become separated from their greatcoat and rifle. The band launched into "God Save the King," light refreshments were served and a whip-around conducted, with the proceeds of ten pounds three shillings being divided up between the five boys.

Less than a week later, they embarked from Tathra wharf for Sydney. It was a dismal, drizzling day with a bitter wind; we huddled under those umbrellas that had not yet been ripped inside out. Dan was tense and distracted and did not want to linger much in saying goodbye. Also, he had a sweetheart at the wharf, a freckled lass from Lochiel, of whom we had hitherto known nothing. He took her aside, and there was much fervent whispering between them while the family was left to stand about awkwardly. When the ship moved away from the wharf, the girl cried more than anyone.

"God, she is certainly bunging it on," said Annie.

And yet if we had realized that the offhand wave he had given us from the gangplank was the last we were ever to see of him, we would have howled like babies.

After we learned that Dan was missing in action, the girl came to visit us. (I realize I have completely forgotten her name, but I think it was something like Maud or Maeve.) She said little and refused any refreshments, implying by her manner that she was surprised we could think of such things given the circumstances. Only after much encouragement did she tell us that she and Dan had met at the Convent School Ball only three weeks before he embarked, at which occasion they had shared a piece of jam sponge "as light as air." She asked us if Dan had ever mentioned her in his letters, and we had to answer truthfully that he had not. She blushed angrily then, and told us Dan had always said we would try to keep them apart, for she was a Roman Catholic. We told her this was not the case; we had simply been unaware of her existence until her sudden appearance at Tathra wharf. She became upset and left abruptly. I felt bad about it. I imagine she had been fondly nursing the hope that Dan had spoken of her incessantly, a hope we had casually quashed. Looking back, I wish that we had not been so truthful, and simply invented something. All she had to remember her sweetheart by was a shared piece of jam sponge, "as light as air." That was not much to keep you going.

The last missive we had from Dan was this postcard:

Hello All, well, I hope the whales will soon be visiting, say hello to Tom and all the gang for me. London is a fine city but not a patch on good old Eden. There is nothing of interest to tell you so I will ring off, yr affectionite Dan.

It is undated, but the very fact that he is even talking about whales makes me think it might have been written in early June. In September we learned that he was missing in action. Then we heard nothing whatsoever till the following January, when Reverend Forbes came to visit us, bearing the following cable:

Officially reported that No. 2460 Pte. D. Davidson, 21st Batt, previously reported wounded and missing, is now reported killed in action between 24 August and 26 August, 1916. Please inform Mr. G. Davidson, Eden, and convey deep regret of their Majesties, the King and Queen, and the Commonwealth Govt., in the loss that he and the army have sustained by the death of this soldier.

Having gone to be wasted in battle, the grass grew over our brother Dan before he reached his twenty-first birthday. Or at least, we can only assume it did, for there were no remains ever to be found; we had simply to take their word for it.

I find myself once again reluctant to go on, except to comment briefly on the effect Dan's death had on my brother Harry. He was six years older than Dan, but had not enlisted, owing to the fact that he was by then married with a small child and working as assistant light keeper at Green Cape lighthouse. In the recent letters leading up to his death, Dan had taken to insinuating that Harry was a shirker.

A toothless old man can keep a lighthouse lamp burning, yes the job is necessary but it does not take an ABLE BODIE YOUNG MAN to do so, just so long as he can climb the steps. I think if they had a few showers of shrapnel instead of the rain he is always complaining about at Green Cape, he might realize what we are all putting up with over here and decide to lend us a bit of a hand insted of living the life of Riley.

We did our best to keep these letters from Harry, but it was difficult. He and Grace would come to visit with the baby and always ask what news of Dan. Letters were so infrequent that when we had received one he would want to read it himself; this he would do silently, and without making any comment regarding the contents. In the awkwardness and embarrassment of the situation, we did not say anything, and I feel now that this was our mistake, for he must have imagined that our silence indicated our agreement with the sentiments Dan expressed. I know my father wrote back to Dan and tried to convey the responsibilities a married man owed to his family, especially since Grace was expecting again; not to mention the responsibilities of lighthouse work for the safety of navigation, never more so than during wartime. But who knows if Dan ever received the letter.

After Reverend Forbes came with the cable, my father and I traveled over to Green Cape to break the news to Harry. I remember it clearly, for we stood on the veranda of his cottage, and force of habit was such that my father kept turning his head to gaze out to sea on the off-chance he might see a whale spout.

Harry stood there in silence for a long time, and then finally he spoke. "I suppose you're wishing it was me, not him, if I hadn't been such a shirker."

Well, my father told him not to talk nonsense, but Harry became belligerent then and said he knew that's what we all thought of him; that he was a coward and that he scarcely deserved to be called a Davidson. He turned on me then and said I was right to depict him wringing his hands like a girl in that painting, and wasn't I happy it had turned out to be true? And then he said to my father, who was looking out to sea again, "That's right, look for whales, at a time like this. And I'll bet if one swam by, you'd chase it."

Poor Grace came out then, and seeing at once that we had received the news we had been so dreading, insisted we come inside for some tea. Harry, however, went off somewhere on the pretext of work needing to be done, and we did not see him again before it was time for us to head home.

From that point on, Harry seemed to want nothing more to do with the family. I urged my father to write to him to convince him that we had never thought him a shirker, but for some reason my father seemed disinclined to do so and simply responded, "He will get over it eventually." Harry took up a position shortly thereafter at Gabo Island and after that we scarcely heard from him except for a card at Christmas, and even that was written by Grace. So, in truth, my father lost both his sons and we girls lost both our brothers. It was another sad aspect of the whole terrible thing.

It fell upon me, of course, to write to Maeve or Maud in order to convey the dreadful news. I spent a good deal of time in drafting the letter, for I wished it to bring her some small measure of comfort, a comfort we had failed to provide her when she visited. One line in particular stands out in my memory: *"I have no doubt that the memory of your dear freckled face provided Dan tremendous solace, even as he faced his final moments."* I showed the letter to Annie, who urged me to strike that passage out. "Do you really think now is the time to start concocting fantasies? Besides, she may not wish to be reminded of her freckles." To which I responded, "How do you know it is a fantasy? It may very well be the truth, for all we know. He certainly seemed keen on her at Tathra wharf." Ignoring Annie's continued protests, I went ahead and posted it. I hope it afforded

Maeve or Maud some small consolation; at the very least, I hope she did not take umbrage at the reference to her freckles. Perhaps in retrospect, given her sensitive nature, I would have been wiser to omit that particular adjective, or use another expression, such as "sun-kissed." In any case, we never heard back and I cannot say whatever became of her.

The Flukes

I T WAS SUNDAY WHEN THE WHALE UPENDED THE BOAT; BY
Tuesday the boat was repaired and the men set off to the
lookout. Young Dan took the place of Shankly, and Uncle Aleck stood in for John Beck, until such time as John Beck
could return to the oars. This was felt to be within a day or so,
as he was considerably improved and keen to return; however,
my father deemed it prudent that he rest a little longer. Thus
John Beck sat on our front veranda in the morning sunshine
reading the *Eden Observer and South Coast Advocate*, while
Louisa and I labored over the week's washing.

My father had erected three solid posts, crossed at the top,
from which hung a big cast-iron pot, and under this we lit a fire
to boil the water. I did most of the hard scrubbing, as Louisa
felt that the steam rising off the tub caused an unattractive rud-
diness of the complexion (here indicating my own complexion)
and that the Rumford's Blue was too harsh on one's hands. Thus
she concentrated most of her efforts on jamming the mangle

and hanging out the wet sheets in such a pointedly bad-tempered fashion that inevitably a pole would collapse and the whole lot would end up in the dirt. Rarely did we get through washing day on speaking terms with one another.

Normally, as a matter of strong principle, we did not tend to the whale men's laundry, but as John Beck was still recuperating in the front room, it was a small matter for me to ask if he would like me to launder his white shirt. He gratefully accepted and requested that perhaps I might starch and iron it also, to which I agreed somewhat hesitantly, as our laundering standards were such that we rarely bothered with starch and were somewhat uncertain as to how best to get satisfactory results from the process. However, I found a small amount of corn starch and boiled it up with water and hoped for the best. Whilst I was plunging the shirt into the starch bowl, I noticed it had been darned very neatly near the cuff; perhaps it had become caught on something and torn. As I studied the tiny stitches, I found myself wondering if this was not the handiwork of whichever lady had caused John Beck such problems with Temptation. Certainly there must have been some attentive gentlewoman offering her services, for the needlework was far too dainty to have been done by any man. It was on this matter that I was thus preoccupied when a series of muttered maledictions caused me to glance in Louisa's direction. She was struggling with our mangle, the cogs of which frequently jammed and could only be released by employing a dangerous and intricate maneuver involving great risk to one's fingers. My vantage point was such that I saw at this moment a plume of fine spray apparently emanating from the top of her head; that is to say, the plume emanated from the sea directly behind her, at a point behind the breakers, not far removed from where Tom would often come to marshal troops. Saying nothing for fear of having imagined it and thus invoking my sister's derision, I put down the shirt and fixed my eyes upon the sea, waiting for another such appearance. Surely, if I had seen a spout, then it must have been the spout of a Killer whale, for it struck me as remarkably reckless, even foolhardy, of a whale to swim up to a whaling station and draw attention to itself in this manner. But no, there it was again! The size of the spout and the glimpse of gray bulk beneath the water confirmed it.

"*Whale,*" I said in a strangulated tone, for excitement had gripped the muscles of my throat.

"Whale?" said Louisa.

"There! See it?" I said, pointing triumphantly. For now the mass of whale had surfaced and was rolling idly with the swell.

"Is it dead?" said Louisa, staring.

"No, I just saw it spout."

"How have the Killers not seen it?"

"I don't think anyone has seen it." For there was no sign of whaleboats bearing down upon it, nor indeed the familiar tall black dorsal fins.

"Louisa, saddle up Two Socks at once and ride over to the lookout," I said.

"Are you mad? I will have to take the cow as well."

"Then—run over!"

"I can't run all that way!"

"Well, what else do you suggest then? Should we row out and catch it ourselves?" And even as I said it, the idea took form before my eyes. "Yes. We will row out and catch it our-selves."

"Are you mad?" she repeated shrilly. "How can we?"

"We'll take the dinghy."

"But we don't have any harpoons."

"We'll use the whale gun."

At this, Louisa gasped and clapped her hand to her mouth, but without waiting for another query as to my sanity, I took off as fast as I could down to the boatshed. Forced to choose between finishing the washing or chasing down a whale, Louisa opted for the latter, for she at once hitched up her skirts and came tearing down the hill after me. Patch and Bonnie rose up in a startled fashion from their sunbathing and joined in the chase, barking excitedly but with little notion as to what they were actually barking about; all the while the Maudrys shrieked their protests.

The whale gun was kept up on a high shelf in the boatshed, wrapped in a blanket and oilcloth. It was rarely used for, as pre-viously mentioned, the loudness of its report was known to scare the Killers away; however, since the Killers had failed to show up at all in this instance, I was not unduly concerned by this. It was also said to have a fearsome recoil, but that too was something I did not pause to ponder, so consumed was I by the desire to surprise our father with a whale. In truth, I suspect that the main reason my father preferred not to use the whale gun was that he felt it somehow dishonorable to do so. Far bet-ter to have the battle play out hand-to-hand, as it were, in close quarters, than to fire a bomb at the whale from a safe distance.

My first shock was how brutishly heavy was the whale gun—far heavier than you would reasonably expect by looking at it. It was just over three feet in length, with a wide round muzzle and a curious skeleton stock of cast iron. I passed it down to Louisa, who staggered back a little with its weight, then I seized a rectangular wooden box inscribed in my father's lopsided capitals *"BOMB LANCES,"* along with a small bottle of Black Powder.

"Well now! How are you going to load the stupid thing?" cried Louisa.

"Oh, I expect it cannot be too difficult," I responded, anxious that Louisa not detect any sign of uncertainty in my demeanor. I was no expert at armory, but I imagined I knew enough to load a bomb lance, having heard my father once describe the action and having frequently loaded our muzzle-loading rifle which we used for potting the occasional rabbit. I say "occasional" because the aim of the ancient rifle was infamous—if one wanted to hit a rabbit, it was best to aim roughly four feet to the right and slightly upwind of it. It was the same weapon with which my great-grandfather, Alexander Davidson, had infamously shot dead Uncle Aleck's beloved pony Nimblefoot when she made the mistake of bailing him up once too often on his morning walk. It was offered in my great-grandfather's defense that perhaps he had only meant to teach Nimblefoot a lesson, and had been surprised when the weapon had unexpectedly fired straight. I know for certain, however, that Uncle Aleck (who had been a small boy at the time) considered this unlikely, and still thought very bitterly of the old man. "She was the grandest little pony you ever saw," he would say, if ever the subject came up in conversation, and it did, remarkably frequently. Louisa averred privately that grand the pony may have been, but none too nimble-footed if she had managed to get herself shot by this most unreliable of weapons.

The whale gun required that the sharply fluted arrowhead of the bomb lance be forced down the muzzle with a ramrod. The bomb lance itself was about thirty inches in length and its latter section was hollow to contain a fuse which was lighted by the flash of the powder; this would cause the weapon to explode once embedded in the whale's flesh. Having jammed it in the muzzle as securely as I could, I set the hammer in the half-cock position in readiness. Now gathering up some rope, a marker buoy, the box of bomb lances and a kellick, we hurried towards the jetty, at which the dinghy was moored. Hearing a cry, we saw John Beck running down towards us.

"God help us, not the nanny goat," muttered Louisa. "He will want to say a prayer over us."

"You're not going after it, surely!" cried John Beck as he caught up with us.

"Well, what else are we going to do?" I responded. "Let go a perfectly good whale simply because no one has seen it?"

"All right—then I am coming with you," he said, and we clambered down into the dinghy. Compelled by sense of duty to protect us, the two dogs jumped into the dinghy also, causing us to waste several valuable minutes in hoisting them back upon the jetty and sternly admonishing them with little effect, however, for they jumped directly back into the boat again. Fortunately, at this point Violet and Annie appeared and were instructed, by means of our screaming at them, to hold on to the dogs till we had gained some distance from the jetty. We had only managed to row a short distance when Violet must have relaxed her grip, for Bonnie—always a plucky little dog—leapt heroically into the water and proceeded to paddle after us with an expression of deranged determination on her face, intermittently barking and disappearing underwater. This of course necessitated that we turn about and rescue her. All the while, Patch yelped his outrage from the jetty (he had a horror of water, and did not care to get his paws wet).

Realizing we had little choice but to continue our mission with Bonnie on board, we squared up to the breakers now, and it was here I felt the first pang of doubt as to the wisdom of our proposed adventure. With three of us on board and one small wet dog, our aged craft sat worrisomely low in the water. In truth, the dinghy, like the rifle, dated back to Alexander Davidson's time and was now mostly retired from use; I was not entirely confident that it would withstand the rigors of crossing the bar. However, it surprised us by plowing gamely through, although not sparing us from a terrific drenching.

"Ease up now, there it is!" I cried, once I had dashed the stinging water from my eyes and resumed my position at the steer oar. For there indeed the whale drifted, only fifty feet away. I could tell at once that it was a humpback whale, and a very good-sized one at that.

"Let me see," said Louisa, pausing in her rowing to swing about and look at it.

"Keep rowing!" I hissed. "But quietly does it. We must sneak up upon it, as a cat would a mouse."

We rowed to within twenty feet of the vast creature, at which I signaled to my crew to lie on their oars. The three of us now took the opportunity to gaze at the creature in wonderment; certainly it was the first time in my nineteen years that I had ever seen a living whale at such close quarters. It was dark gray in color and approximately forty or so feet in length, though this was difficult to determine precisely as most of its bulk was underwater. Its back (which was the only part above water) was rounded, yet surprisingly sleek in appearance, its modest dorsal fin forming part of a ridge or "hump" from whence I suppose it got its name. It seemed perfectly aware of our presence but not in the slightest concerned; it lifted its knobbly head and spouted, *Bosh!*, as if by way of casual greeting. It conveyed no sense of purpose but seemed content to simply drift about aimlessly, as if enjoying the gentle motion of the swell; if a whale could whistle, I imagined it would be whistling just now, or humming to itself some small snatch of song it vaguely remembered. It was remarkable to me how different it was in its affable demeanor to the determined intent and ruthless purpose of the Killer whale.

Having admired it long enough, I reached down now and picked up the whale gun, and as I did an odd feeling of calm descended upon me. Given the remarkable ease with which my plan was unfolding, it felt almost as if this day, this moment, had been laid out for me by Fate. I would capture this creature which floated so obligingly within range of my whale gun and, in doing so, I would turn around my family's fortunes. My father would be surprised and delighted; even proud of me in his own quiet way. "Good work, lass," he might say, placing his knotted hand upon my shoulder. Perhaps one of the Eden townsfolk would write a poem about me.

"I really don't think we should be doing this," said Louisa. "Dad won't be at all happy when he finds out."

"He'll be happy if we catch a whale," I responded, moving the hammer to full-cock.

"He won't be happy that you're using the whale gun."

"May I ask a question?" said John Beck. "Is it loaded?"

"Of course it is loaded!" I said, turning to him.

"Don't wave it at us!" cried Louisa, and even John Beck cowered involuntarily as if I was about to shoot him.

"Oh, for goodness' sake," I said crossly.

Raising the gun to my shoulder, I now took careful aim at the mass of gray that lay before me. There was so much of this whale, it seemed almost impossible that I could miss—if I could only control the muscles of my right arm, which had begun to tremble involuntarily with the great weight of the weapon. I braced myself as best I could till the muzzle steadied, but just as my finger moved to the trigger, Bonnie—who had up till then been gazing off eagerly in the other direction— turned about in her seat, and seeing the whale for the first time, took strong and vocal exception to its presence.

"Grab the dog!" I cried, struggling to retain my balance with the weight of the gun and the dog leaping about. "Shut the dog up! We will scare away the whale!"

But it was too late. The whale curved its back and tipped up its tail flukes, suspending them in mid-air momentarily as if for our inspection, then disappeared from view.

This was the first time that I had seen a humpback's tail flukes in situ, and I remain convinced, thirty years later, that there is no more wondrous and stirring sight to be seen. Though dark gray on their topside, they are quite white on their underside, which is the side the whale revealed to us now. The flukes were outlined heavily in black as though drawn with a thick nib; several splodges of black were speckled across them, as if the artist had been careless with his pen, and yet the end result was as endearing as freckles on a small child. In the delicacy of their movement, the flukes seemed possessed of a charming insouciance; the overall effect was of a strange flower upon its thick stem, its twin petals opening to the sun. They were beautiful flukes, and we were hushed by them, and remained so for a long moment after they had disappeared. Even Bonnie broke off from her barking and stood with her front paws on the gunwale, staring at the water, now oddly still.

"Don't whales look different up close?" I said, lowering my whale gun. "Alive, I mean."

John Beck turned to me and nodded. We looked about us at the empty sea. A strange atmosphere of melancholy stillness came over us as we waited, and it brought to mind the feeling as we had sat in church at my mother's funeral, waiting for the service to commence. The organist had played "Abide with Me," and I suppose he had been instructed to keep playing till the congregation settled, for I remember feeling that he would never stop, and at one point, when we thought he had finally finished and he started up afresh, Harry had got the giggles and had had to be spoken to. Yet as long as that mournful dirge continued and we sat in the presence of my mother (for she lay in her coffin at the front of the church), it felt to me as if the family were suspended together (for the last time) somewhere between the earthly world and heaven. Why I should suddenly think of it at this moment, I cannot say.

I clutched onto the whale gun, its muzzle pointing to the sky. Bonnie leaned her wet body against me and made small anxious noises. *This isn't right,* she seemed to say. *We shouldn't be here.* My eyes scanned the sea for a disturbance of the water, but the conviction I had felt formerly that I was acting upon my Destiny had begun to evaporate. In truth, some small part of me was beginning to hope that the whale might not reappear at all.

But there it was! It had surfaced on the other side of the boat now, some thirty feet away. *Bosh!* it spouted. *Here I am again! Over here!* I recognized that I must summon my resolve; I could do this, if only I steeled myself. Rising to my feet, and lifting the whale gun to my shoulder, I took aim.

Again, the muscles of my arms commenced shaking violently, and as my finger closed on the trigger, I was struck by how tremendously heavy was its action, almost as if it might have jammed from years of disuse. As I endeavored to overcome this resistance, I screwed up my face with the effort, and as I felt the trigger begin to give, I thought, *Oh, I must look where I am firing,* and I opened my eyes and saw—at that exact instant, as the whale rolled with the swell—a small calf nestled beneath its side fin. Louisa screamed, "Don't shoot! There's a calf!" and I at once pulled my finger away from the trigger.

It seemed to me (in retrospect) that the whale did not recognize as threatening the great weapon I was aiming at her; in fact, she had, at that moment, deemed us sufficiently friendly to reveal to us her cherished baby that she had been hiding beneath her fin. She was proud as any mother of her newborn, and with good reason; it was the dearest little thing (when I say little, it was probably ten feet long) and a perfect miniature of its mother. Even its spout was its mother's spout in miniature; the knobbles upon its small head were tiny versions of hers. It tipped up its flukes (the prettiest little flukes you ever saw!) and together, in unison, they dived out of sight.

"Why did you not shoot?" said John Beck, looking up at me.

"Because it had a calf," I responded. "My father never kills a whale if it has a calf."

This is indeed what my father used to tell us as children, knowing how sensitive we were to small creatures being left without their mother. But in truth, although he may have wished otherwise, the Killers did not share his compunctions and would set upon a calf immediately.

"Did you see its flukes?" cried Louisa. "How sweet they were! Oh, Mary, thank God you didn't shoot!"

Just then, John Beck put his hand upon my arm. Surprised by this action, I looked at him. He said nothing, but pointed towards Honeysuckle Point, from where, unmistakably, slicing through the water in their haste to join us, appeared the tall black dorsal fins of the Killer whales. I have never forgotten it, for there seemed a great many of them and they were traveling at such speed. It was as if the Indians were descending from the hills, for if the Killer whales could have waved their tomahawks and hollered their war cries, so they would have. It was a chilling spectacle, for we knew at once that they would tear the baby apart, even before they began on the mother.

Now the next part is difficult to describe for it happened all very quickly. Without being aware of consciously deciding to do so, I found myself lifting the whale gun once again and this time taking aim at the Killers; that is to say, I aimed in their direction, for I must make it perfectly clear I had no wish to kill one; my intention was simply to frighten them away. Again my arms set to shaking, and again I felt the great resistance of the trigger beneath my finger. I was startled by a loud extended squeaking noise, like a creaky door opening, and I realized that this was the call of a Killer whale, now almost alongside the boat. I had no time to stop and identify its dorsal fin, but I felt instinctively that this was Tom, the leader of the pack. At once I felt a great confusion—should I aim four feet to the right of this creature, as if Tom was a rabbit; or should I aim directly at him, if I did not want to hit him—for what if I were to compound the misadventures of this afternoon by inadvertently blowing up this most beloved of all cetaceans, my father's favorite? All this went through my mind in the instant my finger closed on the trigger, and to my surprise, the resistance suddenly gave way. There was an almighty report, and as if collected by a steam train, I was hurled backwards into the bottom of the boat, which itself rocked violently almost to the point of capsizing.

There I must have momentarily lost consciousness, for I opened my eyes to find John Beck leaning over me, while some great weight sat upon my chest and prevented me from breathing. This turned out to be Bonnie; John Beck shoved her aside and peered down at me.

"Are you all right?" he inquired.

And there I must have passed out again.

I have only the groggiest memories of what followed, although apparently I rallied and indeed set about attempting to load another bomb lance, before John Beck, with some difficulty, removed the whale gun from my grasp. I was told that the Killers had vanished and I have the briefest memory of Louisa crying, "There they are!" and pointing to something I could not see, which she seemed to think were the whales' spouts, some distance away. Apparently I insisted that we row after them in a bid to ensure the whales' safety, and when John Beck argued that it was not possible to take our dinghy into the open seas, I became agitated. In the end, he had to pretend they were rowing after them in order to get me to lie down again. I spent the remainder of the trip at the bottom of the dinghy, with my arms wrapped tightly around John Beck's boots, while Bonnie licked my face encouragingly.

My father and the whale men had heard the report from Boyd Tower, and thinking it sounded suspiciously like the whale gun, and thinking that it emanated suspiciously from somewhere near home, my father had ordered the men to the boats to investigate. Fortunately, by the time they intercepted our dinghy, the whale and her baby had long since departed. Nor at any time were the Killers sighted after that initial report of the whale gun.

Sensing from his stern expression that my father required an explanation, John Beck proceeded to recount the whole story from the beginning. He had just outlined in detail the moment in which the whale had revealed her calf, and was about to launch into a description of the dramatic approach of the Killers, when Louisa suddenly interrupted him in the midst of his sentence.

"Mary fired at the whale but she missed—she is as blind as a bat," said Louisa.

John Beck turned to look at her. Of all the Davidson children, Louisa alone had inherited my father's whale-killing gaze; thus John Beck sensed that she was willing him to keep quiet.

"That's correct," he agreed, though somewhat confused.

"Why did you not then have a shot?" Bastable demanded to know. "Are you telling me that when the girl missed, you threw your hands in the air and gave up?"

"Yes, I suppose I did," said John Beck unhappily, his color deepening.

"Leave Father alone," said Salty. "He has just had the flukes to the head. Is it any wonder he does not wish to be blasted into the hereafter by the bomb lance?"

"Did the *Beowas* come?" asked Percy Madigan.

"Beowa" was the native word for Killer whale. Up until then, the Aboriginal crew members had kept quiet, although John Beck noticed that some of them had been surveying the surrounding waters intently.

"No," said John Beck, for by now he had begun to suspect why Louisa had cut him off. "No, they did not come."

"I thought you said something about them coming?"

"No, no," said John Beck. "I may have simply said that we…we wished they would come. But they did not come."

I, of course, was still lying on the bottom of the boat, dimly conscious of what was transpiring, yet still not aware of the potential seriousness of the situation. It was thought that I may have cracked several ribs and suffered a concussion; thus, upon our return, I was put to bed at once.

My father had a stern talk with Louisa, who wavered between brazen defiance and pinning the blame in its entirety on me. However, at no point did she let on about the presence of the Killers. (I know all this because Dan informed me later; he and the little girls were eavesdropping in the next room in the hopes that Louisa would get a thrashing.) "Very well, Louisa, I can see I am getting nowhere with you," my father concluded. "You may leave the table."

To which she responded, in her typical fashion: "Well, I can't very well take it with me."

This set the younger ones to giggling; when they were unable to stop, my father gave up and went out on the veranda to smoke his pipe.

Interesting Beliefs of the Aborigines

VERY EARLY THE NEXT MORNING, AT THE FIRST GRAY glimmering of daylight, my father came into our bedroom to talk to me. Bidding Louisa get up out of bed to pack the tucker-bags (to which she acquiesced hastily and without complaining), he sat on a hard-backed chair and surveyed me somberly. Rarely had I seen his countenance so grim as he outlined to me the foolishness of my actions and the gravity of their possible consequences. He was, of course, rightly concerned that I had endangered our lives in going out to sea in the old dinghy; also in using the whale gun, which was strictly prohibited, not to mention attempting to ensnare a whale by ourselves when we should have more sensibly alerted the whale men.

"I just wanted to capture you a whale!" I cried out, unable to halt the tears that were rolling down my cheeks.

"It is not your responsibility to capture me a whale," he responded. "Any capturing of whales to be done around here

is up to me and the whale men. Just imagine if you had succeeded in hitting that whale. She would have upended the boat
in her death flurry and you would all be drowned."

I nodded mutely, horrified at this possibility, which I had
not till this point ever considered.

"Mary, I must ask you this, and I want you to answer me
honestly," he continued. "Am I right in believing that the
Killers were in attendance?"

I hesitated for a moment and then I nodded, for I could not
easily lie to my father.

"And is it that you fired upon them to keep them away from
the whale calf?"

How was he able to know such a thing? Were my actions so
predictable, my motives so transparent? My tears started up
afresh; I dabbed at them futilely with a sodden handkerchief.

He sighed heavily and looked down at the floorboards.

"Mary," he said finally. "If it happens that you have slaughtered one of the Killers, then I am afraid we have a very serious
situation on our hands."

I stared at him for a long moment and then, suddenly, I
saw for the first time, with terrible clarity, what I had done.
For it was the deeply held belief of our Aboriginal whale men
that each individual Killer whale represented the reincarnated
spirit of a deceased tribe member. If I had taken the life of a
Beowa, their respect and loyalty towards my father notwithstanding, the Aborigines might well feel compelled to take my
own life in order to avenge that of their spirit ancestor.

Many years ago, in my grandfather's time, a headsman
named Higginbotham, but known affectionately to all as
"Flukey," was in the process of lancing a whale when a Killer

whale reared up before him and was accidentally struck by the lance and killed. The natives were so greatly distressed by this that they armed themselves with spears and, by all accounts, would certainly have killed Flukey had not an elder of the tribe intervened on his behalf. His life was spared, but only on condition that he leave the region at once. This he did, with the utmost haste, and was never heard from again. My father was very mindful of this story in his own actions, as amidst the chaos of trying to lance a whale, with the Killers working closely all around, it could easily happen that a Killer be accidentally struck.

I remember when I was quite small, there was an infant Killer whale of whom the Aboriginal crew members were inordinately fond; his name was Jimmy, and it was believed that he was the reincarnation of a small boy of their tribe who had not so very long ago died of sickness. When Jimmy first made his appearance alongside his seniors, the Aboriginal whale men greeted him with loud cries of excitement and recognition, as if overjoyed to be reunited. Whilst out chasing whales, they would call to the infant orca in their own language, "Jimmy, do this," and, "Jimmy, do that," and Jimmy would respond to the very best of his abilities. (The Aborigines often called to the Killers in their own language; they seemed to be calling instructions, as you would to a sheepdog.) One day, the infant Killer whale was playing with the anchor rope of a whaleboat (for Killer whales have a fondness for ropes and anchors, as we have seen) when he became entangled within these ropes, and drowned. It was nobody's fault, of course, but even though I was quite small at the time, I well remember the terrible grief displayed by the natives over the loss of this young Killer. The men wept openly and wailed, and cut themselves with shells until they bled, so intensely felt was their sorrow.

"I must ask you this," continued my father. "Can you be sure that you did not injure any of them?"

I shook my head miserably. I could not be sure, for I had been too busy being "blasted into the hereafter," or at least into the bottom of the boat, to pay much attention to what became of the Killers. Nor did I dare admit to my father how close to the boat one of them had come: the leader, no doubt it was Tom. Nor could John Beck or Louisa say for certain what had happened; their impression was that the Killers had dived. Had the bomb lance itself exploded? Amidst all the smoke and confusion, no one was able to confidently say, least of all myself.

My father eyed me gravely, then stood up. "You must say nothing of this to anyone, not even the children."

He and his men, including John Beck, left for the lookout. Bruised and wretched, I dragged myself out of bed and limped through my chores. I felt sick to my stomach at the thought of what I might have done, not just for the terrible consequences I would undoubtedly and deservedly face, but also for the sheer, ghastly fact that I might have, in the heat of the moment, destroyed so horribly such a noble beast. Surely, pray God, I had missed? But what if the swollen corpse of a Killer whale were to wash up on a beach somewhere, a bomb lance embedded in its flesh? And what if the corpse was that of Tom, most beloved of all orcas, himself a reincarnation of an ancient tribal warrior greatly venerated by the blackfellows? What would happen then?

I climbed up to the headland and gazed out, willing Tom to materialize at the breakers. He was welcome to eat as many whale calves as he liked, I thought to myself bitterly, if only he would kindly leap out of the water this instant. Him and all his cohorts, especially Cooper, who was believed to have been a tribal king, and Charlie Adgery, who was known to have been a distinguished and beloved whale man in his former life. But as far as I could see from the headland, the watery world seemed utterly devoid of life, ancestral or otherwise.

Further, I was plagued by the feeling that the rest of the family was avoiding me. Louisa assisted me in completing what remained of the washing, but was churlish and silent throughout. Uncle Aleck stayed in his shed and did not even come down for his lunch. Even Bonnie seemed anxious to stay clear of me, leaping out of the way in a startled fashion whenever I drew near. (We later discovered she had been rendered completely deaf by the explosion of the whale gun.) Thus I passed a most miserable day, compounded by the fact that the injuries to my ribs meant it hurt to draw breath.

That evening, the whale men returned from the lookout to report that there had been no sign of the Killer whales in their favorite haunt of Leatherjacket Bay. This was not in itself completely unusual, as the Killers often occupied themselves with activities elsewhere of which we knew nothing, and yet for them to be absent that day of all days felt to me like the death knell of all hope. There was a degree of tension evident amongst the whalers that evening as I doled out their stew: Arthur Ashby and Percy Madigan, and Albert Thomas Senior and Darcy and Albert Thomas Junior (that is, our Aboriginal whalers) all seemed deliberately to avoid my gaze, while Bastable and Salty were evidently still brooding over the fact that we had let the whale get away.

"As I said to the Reverend, in no uncertain terms," muttered Bastable, making sure that I might hear it, "if you cannot find the gumption to kill a whale, then summon the men that can."

Not surprisingly, perhaps, given that he had passed much of the day being tormented in this fashion, John Beck seemed somewhat withdrawn; he asked briefly if I was feeling better, then retired a small distance away to eat his meal. It was only later when he saw me struggling with the pots that he jumped up to help me carry them. We walked together in silence up to the house, for I felt somehow mortified by everything that had happened and sure that he must think me worthless.

"Mary," he said finally, when we had reached the kitchen door, "I feel as certain as I can be that your shot did not injure the Killers."

"Really?" I said, turning to him. I felt as if a thin shaft of sunlight was revealing itself from behind a bank of dark clouds.

"Yes," he said. "I am fairly confident that you missed them by a wide margin."

"Oh, I hope so!" I exclaimed, and it hurt my ribs so badly to do so that I cried out in pain. That hurt also, making me gasp, which also hurt.

"Are you all right?" he asked. He had been watching my gasping and wincing with some concern.

"Yes," I said. "Although my ribs are quite sore."

He nodded. And then he hesitated a moment before he next spoke.

"Mary, I just wanted to say this also. I thought what you did tremendously brave."

"Tremendously brave?"

"Yes."

"Which bit?"

"I'm sorry?"

"Which bit was tremendously brave? I mean, of what I did?" You see, I had to be sure of his meaning, for I knew his words would stay with me for my lifetime, and I could not afford to suffer any confusion about it.

"Well, all of it, really. But especially the action…" (here he looked around to ensure he would not be overheard) "…regarding the Killers."

"Thank you," I said.

Such tender memories as I have! So much more fortunate than poor Maeve or Maud, with only her jam sponge "as light as air." For although his eyes were still blackened and his cheek bruised, his face as he gazed at me, so troubled and earnest, had never looked more gravely beautiful. And things no longer seemed so terrible nor did it hurt so much to breathe.

An Unexpected Revelation

I N FACT, THE KILLERS DID NOT REAPPEAR TILL ALMOST A WEEK
later, and true to form, they made sure to stage their
reappearance in the most spectacular of circumstances.
But I am getting ahead of myself. The most pressing problem for us at that time, apart from the non-appearance of the
Killer whales, and the non-appearance of whales in general,
was our desperate shortage of provisions. We were now at the
stage when my father's terse instructions to "eke 'em out" were
to little avail; our provisions could withstand no further ek-
ing. Anxious not to miss a day on lookout (and presumably
anxious not to have the difficult conversation with Mr.
Howard, the storekeeper, that I would inevitably have to endure), my father arranged for Mr. Caleb Cook to come over
in his sulky and convey Louisa and myself into Eden. It is
an indication of how distracted my father must have been at
the time that he permitted Mr. Cook, of all people, to be our
driver and escort: for as observant readers will be aware, it

was Mr. Cook who had put up the prize money and then selected Louisa as the Best-dressed and Most Prepossessing Young Lady of the Eden Show. I may not have mentioned previously that Louisa had been rather insufferably pleased with herself when awarded this prize, but significantly less so upon meeting her admirer.

Mr. Cook had a sheep farm in Burragate, and was very keen to find a wife; it seems that the prize he offered in the Eden Show may have been an opening gambit towards this end. I should explain that Burragate is tremendously isolated and accessible only by the most arduous journey over many precipitous ridges, and if the axle did not snap or the brake fail or the horses take fright at a snake and bolt down a hill, then you considered yourself to have had a reasonable trip to Burragate. It was funny to imagine Louisa spending her days up there married to a sheep farmer and occasionally we teased her on the subject, but only if we wished to have our heads bitten off, for Louisa did not regard the topic as humorous. While happy to accept the prize money and bask in the glory of being Eden's "Most Prepossessing," she nipped in the bud any further attentions, and Mr. Cook had returned to his sheep farm still a bachelor.

He was an extremely tall man of about twenty-eight years with a ruddy face, prominent ears and a diffident manner; his mother had passed away several years ago, and it seems the loneliness was beginning to affect him. He wanted a companion, and who could blame him, for there is not much companionship to be had from three hundred and twenty-one sheep. That is the exact number; I know, because he mentioned it several times during the long trip into Eden.

"Last year I had twenty-eight cows and fifty-three sheep; this year, I got no cows and three hundred and twenty-one sheep," he volunteered, apropos of nothing, but just because the numbers seemed to appeal to him.

"What happened to the cows?" asked Louisa. "Did they run away?"

There was once an article in the newspaper entitled *"Women Who Should Never Marry,"* which seemed to have been written by someone of intimate acquaintance with Louisa, for I felt at the time that it described her to a tee:

Sweeping as the assertion may appear at first sight, there are women who should never marry, and whom young men would do well to avoid. Someone has said that a girl who comes under this category is one:

Who is so utterly selfish that she could not consider or love another more than herself.

Who prides herself on her domestic incompetence, and boasts of her inability to cook a dinner or scrub a floor.

Who displays no love for children, and who would rather fondle a pug dog than a baby.

Who is cross and miserable unless she is the center of attention or is engaged flirting with the best-looking man in the company.

Who does not hesitate to pronounce old and ailing people "bores," or to show impatience with the recital of their aches and pains...

I mention this article, because I was reminded of it whilst sitting in the sulky with Louisa and Mr. Cook, and I found myself contemplating copying it out in its entirety and sending it to him anonymously. What on earth he was doing driving all the way from Burragate to pick us up and then convey us all the way into Eden, I do not know. I imagine he had hoped that the long trip would give Louisa ample time to warm to him, but if her frosty demeanor was an indication, this was not eventuating.

"Who is looking after your sheep?" I asked politely, for I felt a compulsion to make up for Louisa's coolness.

But he looked at me in scornful amazement. "They're not like cows, you know—you don't have to milk 'em," he said, and when Louisa gave a snort of laughter, he began to guffaw at his own joke, and from then on kept alluding to the fact that I apparently thought sheep needed milking.

After that, I decided I did not much care for him. Let Louisa do her worst, I thought, and sat in silence. (I suppose I will not spoil the ending if I say that Louisa did not marry him, and as far as I know, he remained a bachelor.)

The trip into Eden was uneventful, except for when we came to a dead echidna on the road. Mr. Cook's ponies took great exception to it, and would not go past it for anything. Instead, they decided they might simply back up all the way home again, and this they commenced to do, with the unhappy effect of unscrewing the sulky wheels in the process, causing us to have to hastily dismount before the entire contraption fell apart. Fortunately, Mr. Cook seemed to have come prepared for an event of this nature, for he produced a large wrench and screwed the wheels back on again. After removing the offending corpse from within a hundred yards of the vicinity of Mr. Cook's ponies, we were eventually able to continue.

"Let us try to not draw attention to ourselves," Louisa whispered to me as we finally approached the post office. "I would rather not be noticed with Mr. Cook."

No sooner had the words fallen from her lips when, as if to defy her, Mr. Cook's ponies began to buck and plunge, and then at once took off at a terrifying speed across Imlay Street, along Mitchell Street and then down the hill towards Aslings Beach. I remember little of the incident clearly except clinging on for dear life and thinking the sulky would surely break apart as we hurtled down the hill. People in the street were screaming and running in all directions. Mr. Cook lost his hold of the reins amidst the initial bucking, but I will say this for him: he managed to clamber forward over the dash board and take hold of them again whilst our sulky was careening down the hill. He had almost succeeded in reining the ponies in just as we reached the cemetery, whereupon the ponies slewed sharply to the right, capsizing the sulky and tipping us into the sand on Aslings Beach, directly in front of the cemetery in which rested the remains of our great-grand-father, Alexander Davidson.

At once, a crowd of people came running down the hill in the hope of our having incurred death or serious injuries; many excitedly declared it the worst runaway they had ever witnessed. But in fact, despite a few bruises from being bounced about in the sulky, we were relatively unscathed; shaken up and covered in sand, certainly, but mostly just very annoyed with Mr. Cook. To our mind, he did not seem sufficiently apologetic. In fact, he offered by way of explanation that his ponies were used to the peace and quiet of Burragate, and did not much care for town; they particularly did not care for town horses, and it seems a town horse may have slighted them in some way outside the post office.

"Slighted them in what way?" asked Louisa.

"Well, I daresay he looked at them funny," said Mr. Cook.

Mrs. Pike, proprietress of the Great Southern Hotel, insisted we come back to her establishment and lie down in a darkened room for an hour or so to recover from the shock. We accepted her offer gratefully, leaving Mr. Cook to tend to the injured feelings of his ponies. We were very glad of one thing, and that is that we now had a perfectly acceptable reason not to travel back with him; Mrs. Pike kindly offered to make arrangements for us to travel home later in the day by means of Mr. Jessop's motor launch. She brought us up corned beef sandwiches with mustard pickles and a bottle of lemon barley water, and when we thanked her profusely, she said that she'd do anything she could for George Davidson's girls, she thought so well of the man, and so did everyone in the whole of Eden and surrounding areas; in fact, she went on about our father to such an extent, we began to wonder if she harbored feelings for him. When she had left us, with assurances that we must consider the room ours for as long as we needed it, we washed up with a soap that smelled of roses and drank our lemon barley water and ate our sandwiches; then we lay down on the big bed with the pink satin eiderdown and giggled about Mr. Cook and his sensitive ponies and his three hundred and twenty-one sheep. And that is when Louisa confided in me that she loved Darcy.

I was surprised of course, stunned even; and yet I also experienced the not disagreeable sensation that pieces of a puzzle that had never made sense to me (the puzzle being Louisa) suddenly fitted into place, and I saw her at once clearly and wholly and compassionately, for possibly the first time in her sixteen years. Of course Louisa loved Darcy! It seemed suddenly obvious—and yet not obvious at all. Certainly, they had been great playmates in childhood, for we had known Darcy since he was very small; his father Percy had been a whale man for my father for many years. When whaling season came around, our Aboriginal crew members would materialize (their usual home was Wallaga Lake, some distance north); the men would stay in the sleeping huts, but the women and children would oftentimes in those days camp up the hill behind the house. We would rush up to greet them, so excited were we to have our little friends return. After a period of initial shyness, lasting all of about half a day, we would pick up where we had left off the previous year; fishing with spears we had fashioned ourselves and building humpies and "startling the bandicoot"; all the normal fun of childhood. Louisa was a contrary sort of child, but Darcy seemed to have a knack with her, and her oft-declared boast as a child was that her bare feet were almost as tough as his. At thirteen, Darcy began whaling, which meant we saw a good bit less of him, and if you asked me to relate any particular sign of their enduring closeness, I would say only that they were inclined to surreptitiously toss small stones and sticks at one another whenever circumstances drew them in near proximity.

But now that I thought of it, quite recently, when she had been charged with the cooking whilst I tended to the injured John Beck, I had entered the kitchen to fetch his meal and there they were, just the two of them, for Darcy had carried up the pots. It was odd to see him standing in the kitchen, for he would never normally venture into our house, and seeing him silhouetted in the doorframe made me realize how tall he had grown. However, I was too preoccupied with John Beck at the time (what a familiar refrain this is becoming) to notice anything between them; besides which, Darcy made his excuses and promptly left.

"Does he love you?" I asked Louisa now, as we lay together on the bed.

"Yes, of course he loves me," she said, and she suddenly looked very sorrowful. By which I mean that the corners of her mouth pushed downwards and her lower lip convulsed violently for a moment before she regained control of it. As a rule, Louisa did not like to cry, and considered it a sign of weakness.

"Does anyone else know?" I asked.

"I think Harry and Robert may suspect."

"What makes you think that?"

"I don't know. They seem to watch us all the time."

"Don't let them find out," I said urgently, and I found I was enjoying my new role as her heart's advisor. "No one must ever find out."

"Oh well, they will find out soon enough," said Louisa.

"What do you mean?" I asked, and even as I spoke the words, I could feel my physical being stricken with a presentiment as to the answer.

"Well, we are going to run away and get married," said Louisa.

The very first thought that came to my mind, and I am ashamed to admit it, was of the Breelong murders. These had happened some years earlier, for I remember reading about it in the newspaper, and when my mother saw what I was reading she snatched the newspaper abruptly from me and hid it away. However, I found it again and, when my mother was otherwise occupied, I studied the article at length. A young blackfellow named Jimmy Governor had married a white woman (in fact they had been properly married by a Church of England minister), and he and his wife Ethel (who was by all reports a nice-looking and presentable young lady) were camping on the property of the Mawbey family, for whom Jimmy Governor was working. The Mawbey womenfolk taunted Jimmy and Ethel and called them "rubbish" and said that Jimmy deserved to be shot for marrying a white woman. Ethel began tearing her hair out, and cried, "Lord save me from the terrible things these people are saying, I cannot stand it." So Jimmy went up to the house to ask the women to stop their name-calling. But the women taunted Jimmy further, and he became so enraged that he bludgeoned the women to death, and the children also, with a tomahawk. I remember the article vividly for the description of the brains coming out of one of the victims; also because it was the first time I had ever heard of an Aboriginal man and a white woman being married. (In fact, it was the only time I had ever heard of it.)

The second thought that leapt to mind was that it was a great shame that my mother had died when we were young. It was more than a shame; I felt suddenly furious about it, for I was saddled with more responsibility than I was equipped for. Surely if my mother was still alive then she would have taken Louisa in hand, and she would not be now considering running away and marrying a blackfellow and spending the rest of her days in ignominy and ruin. But even as this thought passed through my mind, I realized with a jolt that Louisa was not "considering" this; she had already made up her mind.

My third thought was this: I had long sought to be close to my sister, but her haughty demeanor and the various differences of our personalities had always kept us at a distance from one another. Here now, as we lay side by side on the pink eiderdown, she was confiding in me, and this she had never done before. I felt honored and filled with love for her; I was proud of her pale beauty and her defiant spirit. It was somehow of the greatest importance to me to keep this thin new thread of sisterly feeling between us from breaking. I see clearly now that as her older sister, especially in the absence of wise counsel in the form of our mother, I should have urged her to consider more fully the inevitable and terrible consequences of this action. I should have reminded her that she was only sixteen, and that her feelings for Darcy were most probably a remnant of her childish fancies, distorted by the tempestuous emotions common to youth and the relative isolation in which we lived. At the very least, I accept that I should certainly have said something to our father. However, the unexpectedness of the revelation and the pleasure excited in being her confidante prompted in me a loss of reason, and in this moment, when I had perhaps my greatest opportunity, I chose not to attempt to dissuade her.

We lay on the bed in silence together, me absorbing what she had said and having all these various thoughts and so forth when, perhaps interpreting my silence as disapproval, she suddenly leapt up, quite pink in the face, and cried: "Don't be foolish! Of course, I am only joking! It is only nonsense! I cannot think why you believed me!"

At once, I felt a mixture of emotions, hurt and confusion foremost amongst them, but also a small measure of relief that I did not after all have to contend with such a complicated scenario. To vent my feelings, I berated her harshly for making up fibs and she berated me in turn for believing them and so I punched her, and once again our sisterly relations resumed their normal course. Some small part of me, however, held on to the truth, and the truth was that I had seen her lower lip tremble violently when I asked if Darcy loved her.

Antecedents

I T IS AN INTERESTING COINCIDENCE THAT, EARLIER THAT SAME day, we had been capsized out of the sulky, petticoats over our heads, directly in front of our great-grandfather's tombstone.

"Well," said Louisa, pulling her skirt down and dashing the sand from her eyelashes. "This will certainly confirm the old man's suspicions about us."

It seems that several of Alexander Davidson's daughters had been notably flighty of disposition, and thenceforth the old man regarded all his female progeny with some measure of distrust. We had only been small children when he died, and yet he would so frequently mutter the word "harlots" in our near vicinity that for a long time we believed it was the Gaelic word for "girls."

Apparently his daughters had a weakness for sea captains and, happily for them, the feelings were entirely reciprocated. How they ever came to meet these sea captains was a source of some wonder to us, for these Davidson girls were stranded and becalmed in Kiah, just as we were. Yet it seems they were somehow more resourceful in their methods, for certainly they succeeded where we did not (I have never even met a sea captain, and short of loitering hopefully about the wharf, cannot imagine under what circumstances such a meeting might ever have transpired). The eldest daughter Margaret married William Greig, the captain of one of Benjamin Boyd's whaling ships. She bore him a son (our own Uncle Aleck), and shortly thereafter Captain Greig sailed to Queensland, from which ill-fated trip he was never to return. It was presumed that the ship had foundered in bad weather and gone down with all souls.

Yet it seems in truth that Captain Greig had somehow convinced his crew that, instead of returning to Sydney, it would be a fine thing to try their luck on the goldfields of California, as had done Benjamin Boyd before them, and thus in that direction they set sail. A hurricane drove them to seek shelter on Fanning Island, and there they found the amenities so pleasing they decided that perhaps they were not in such a hurry to get to the goldfields after all. Captain Greig succumbed to the charms of a native princess (having apparently forgotten about poor Margaret languishing at home), acquired large tracts of plantation land, sired several more children and appointed himself the King of Fanning Island. This was only discovered many years later, when Uncle Aleck happened upon his obituary in a newspaper. As can be imagined, it came as a tremendous surprise to him, for he had labored under the misapprehension that his father drowned at sea. He had never imagined for a moment that all this time the captain had been lying about under a coconut tree with a bevy of dusky maidens in attendance. Poor Margaret, meanwhile, had died long ago, bereft, at the age of twenty-two. So it is a very sad story, and goes some way to explaining the fact that Uncle Aleck could at times be a difficult individual.

The story of Alexander's third daughter, Jane, had particularly piqued our interest for she had eloped at the age of eighteen with a gentleman considerably older than herself, the sea captain of the *Fancy*. Her sister Elsy had assisted in this illicit conjugation by rowing her out to his waiting schooner. Alexander got wind of the scheme and gamely pursued them, but the sea captain had no sooner hauled Jane on board than he set sail, and Alexander could not catch them. Whenever I hear this story repeated, I always find myself sympathizing with the hapless Elsy, persuaded against her better judgment to row her sister to her waiting paramour and receiving, no doubt, little thanks for her trouble; her sister scooting up the rope ladder swung over the *Fancy*'s sides with nary a backward glance. And then Elsy having to turn the little boat around and row back and face the wrath of Alexander Davidson, all red-faced from the rowing and spitting epithets at her. I would not be in her shoes. And yet it was not difficult to imagine myself in a similar scenario, for if any member of our family was most likely to elope with a sea captain and force me into rowing her out to his schooner, it would be Louisa. Except she didn't.

Unpleasant Encounter with
the Price-Cutter

WHEN WE HAD DECIDED THAT WE HAD SUFFICIENTLY recovered from our ordeal with Mr. Cook and his ponies, we thanked Mrs. Pike profusely and made our way down Imlay Street towards the vast emporium of Mr. Howard, the Price-Cutter. A sick, heavy feeling of apprehension began to manifest in my belly, for Mr. Howard was a trying man at the best of times, and we were already indebted to him to some considerable extent. I had a long list of requirements and no money to pay for them; I could only prevail upon his kindness, the one provision he kept in short supply.

Out the front of his store, we paused to survey a small poster pasted on the window:

> ### - A GRAND -
> # PLAIN
> ## —AND—
> ## FANCY DRESS
> # BALL
> will be held at the
> ### Eden School of Arts
> — ON —
> Saturday 21 November.
> —
> Double Tickets 5s, Single 3s.
> —
> First-Class Music and Refreshments.

Glumly, we gazed upon it.

"I wonder if Eunice Martin will wear her cream luster or her tinsel-thread organdy," I said.

"I imagine she will have a new dress altogether," said Louisa. "It will be sewn together from the desiccated corpses of seventeen bush rats, left out to dry in the sun."

I snorted gleefully. How fondly I felt towards Louisa

sometimes! In her meanness towards Eunice Martin, I saw that she was demonstrating her loyalty and affection towards me. In her own strange way, she was a loving sister.

"Let us look at the muslins and cretonnes and see if there is something we like," I said, squeezing her arm. "There is no harm in pretending. And choose some lace and some ribbon to go with it."

"All right," said Louisa, although her heart did not seem to be in it. We stepped inside, adopting a purposeful attitude to indicate that we had a job to do and meant to do it. Mr. Howard was engaged in serving somebody, and feeling our resolve diminish at the sight of him, we seized the opportunity to lurk amongst the bolts of chiffons and georgettes, muslins and lace. How pretty they were, and how long it had been since we'd had a new dress! After some consideration, I chose for myself a moss-green georgette with cream chiffon trimmings; it was only then that I realized Louisa had moved over to the bridal section, where I found her thoughtfully contemplating an ivory crepe de chine. Alarmed, I thrust a bolt of pink crinkle marocain at her in an attempt to distract her from the direction in which her thoughts seemed to be wandering. It was at this point that Mr. Howard pounced upon us.

"Well, here we are, the Davidson lasses! I was wondering if you'd pay me a visit, for I heard you were thrown face first into the sand at Aslings Beach! I am glad to see that you have sufficiently revived to feel equal to the task of shopping. Are you looking to buy something pretty for the ball?"

"Actually, it is for provisions we have come," I responded stiffly. "I have rather a long list, if I could call upon your kind assistance."

He took the list I proffered and surveyed it at length, and as his eyes traveled down it, his face assumed an expression of mounting incredulity.

70 lb sugar

2 cwt flour

10 lb Lipton's tea

Rolled oats, 2 bags

3 dozen eggs

vinegar (1 gallon)

condensed milk, 1 dozen tins

jam (1 doz. assorted)

5 lb tapioca

5 lb pearl barley

5 lb split peas

3 lb currants

2 lb cocoa

1 loaf cheese

2 jars mustard pickles

Lea and Perrins Worcestershire sauce (6)

5 large tins golden syrup

Biscuits (Arnotts), 5 lb

Dripping

5 lb bacon

1 side corned beef

2 flaps mutton or mutton shanks

5 bags potatoes

3 bags carrots

2 bags onions

2 lb salt
Baking powder
Tobacco (6 pkts Yankee Doodle dark)
Sunlight soap (4)
Candles (3 boxes)
4 cases Snowflake kerosene
1 bottle raspberry cordial
1 small bag aniseed balls

"Is there anything you've left off, do you think?" he asked finally.

"I don't believe so," I responded untruthfully. In fact, we required a great deal more than this, but given we did not have any money, I did not wish to appear too fanciful.

"I note that you request aniseed balls—would you not prefer humbugs instead?"

"No, thank you," I replied firmly, for I sensed where this was heading.

"Yes, I daresay there is enough humbuggery already in this list," said Mr. Howard. "Kindly tell me how you imagined you were going to pay for all this?"

"Oh! Well, of course I was hoping that you would extend our credit for just one more month, Mr. Howard," I began, and as he was already starting to shake his head, I continued on quickly: "As you know, November is traditionally a very strong month for whales—"

"Not last November, it wasn't."

"Last November was certainly the exception to the rule, I grant you. But all the signs are there for us this year. The Killers are in remarkably fine trim—"

"I heard the Killers have already departed for the season."

"I refute that utterly!" Just at that moment the bell tinkled above the door and a customer entered the shop.

"Misses Davidson, I have the greatest respect for your father—" said Mr. Howard, adopting a more obsequious tone for the benefit of the other customer.

"I am *Miss* Davidson," I interrupted.

"I meant 'Misses' as in the plural, for there are two of you."

"Mrs. Davidson is my departed mother, who had the misfortune to expire far too early," I continued, ignoring him, for a wave of fury had overtaken me, "before she could raise her children to adulthood and before she could see the statue in honor of our father that I have no doubt will be erected in the middle of Imlay Street, cast in bronze and standing thirty feet high, with a fountain spouting from it which will represent the spout of the whale, and which people will travel from far and wide to throw coins into, for it will bring tremendous fortune to all who do so." I remember Louisa staring at me, but the release of all the accumulated tension— of the day, if not of the entire whaling season—was so tremendous I did not seem able to staunch the torrent. I went on to state that while it seemed to me the townsfolk were very happy to bask in the reflected glory of my father's bravery, and write poems about him that were factually inaccurate and did not even rhyme very well, and use his reputation for fearlessness to advance their own ill-fated efforts to have Eden become the nation's capital, no one would offer a hand in assistance if he suffered two bad years in a row and was struggling to feed his family.

And just at this point, the customer, who had been standing

about impatiently and shifting his weight from foot to foot, suddenly interrupted me, and said: "Excuse me, Miss Davidson, your father has a whale in the bay right this moment and it is as big as the S.S. *Merimbula*!"

"*Rush oh!*"

Voices Whisper

—

That during last Thursday's whale chase, intense excitement pre-vailed in Eden.

That, while the chase lasted, business was suspended and homes de-serted.

That many families left the dinner table before the meal was com-pleted; and

That as a consequence, before they returned home, the cats of the neighbourhood had "sat down to all good things provided."

That two lady visitors had some trying experiences while negotiat-ing the barbed wire and other fences on whale day.

That when the whale was in the vicinity of the wharf, many feared it would be knocked down, and reached the other end, hat in hand, in even time, and

That one was the "belle" of the Eden Show.

EDEN OBSERVER AND SOUTH COAST ADVOCATE

An Intensely Exciting Chase

I AM NOW GOING TO ATTEMPT AS BEST I CAN TO DESCRIBE THE chase and capture of the whale, and I ask the reader's forgiveness in advance if my abilities are found to be somewhat less than equal to the task. I admit it is a daunting challenge, for I fear it will only invite comparisons with Mr. Melville that will not be flattering. (I mean, they will not be flattering to me; they will be perfectly flattering to Mr. Melville.) Nonetheless, it is important that I attempt it, as this particular chase was considered by old-timers to be unparalleled as regards its unpredictability and sheer excitement, not least for the fact that the Killers staged their triumphant deus ex machina in the third act. So I shall endeavor to do it justice in my depiction, and if the reader finds it wanting, then they must simply put up with it, as I will have certainly tried my best.

Upon hearing the news of the whale, we took leave of Mr. Howard and hastened out of the store, finding ourselves at once amidst a throng of people hurrying in the direction of the wharf and surrounding headlands. Some were running, some rode bicycles or went on horseback; older matrons half ran, half walked in a bid to keep an air of respectability about them. Shopkeepers hastily shut up shop; others climbed onto balconies and rooftops, peering through telescopes and binoculars. Drinkers spilled out of the Great Southern Hotel; children poured out of the school gates in haphazard lines of two by two, herded in as best they could by their teachers. "Excuse me, excuse me, we are Davidsons, our father is after a whale," we cried, as we elbowed our way through, and on the whole, the townsfolk were most obliging and made way for us: "Let them through, it's the Davidson lasses!" Suddenly, there beside us materialized Mr. Caleb Cook in his sulky, offering us a ride. I was about to demur, but Louisa, who was slightly ahead of me, at once hitched her skirt up and, taking his proffered hand, clambered on; I followed suit (without any proffered hand, I might add), feeling it arguably safer to be pulled by the sensitive ponies than trampled to death by them. With Mr. Cook's encouragement, the easily offended ponies made it down the hill in a matter of moments, whereupon we jumped off and ran full tilt along the wharf, for judging by the screams and shouts that emanated from there, it seemed to be the best vantage point. Some locals were even jumping into their dinghies and pleasure craft, eager for a more immediate experience.

We were about midway down the wharf when we heard the cry, "Look out!" and, looking out, I saw my father's boat hurtling towards us at such speed that for a moment I genuinely believed it had become airborne. The oarsmen, their oars peaked, clung on to the gunwales with looks of grim desperation on their faces; my father stood at the bow, lance in hand, and he seemed to be shouting something, for certainly his face was contorting in a way I had never seen before. At once I realized that the whale (to which the boat was attached) was traveling in a direct path towards the wharf, and even if it managed to pass under the structure, the boat would surely collide with the piles. *Cut loose!* I thought to myself. *Cut loose!* It was then I realized that my father was shouting, "Get off! Get off!" and seeing suddenly that the wharf might well collapse with the impending impact, the crowd turned as one and bolted to safety, clearing the distance, as the newspaper said, "in even time." Upon reaching the end of the wharf, we turned around in time to see the whaleboat careening under the wharf. The oarsmen ducked, Arthur and my father threw themselves down to avoid being knocked out; Louisa and I screamed in horror, expecting the very worst. But there, in a second, the boat emerged on the other side, still fast to the whale and the wharf intact. Arthur and my father sprang back up to their standing positions, and the crowd roared its approval.

The whale now headed out to the middle of the bay, causing those eager onlookers in their pleasure crafts to scatter in all directions, rowing wildly as the whale bore down upon them. One hapless man in a dinghy even dived into the water and attempted to swim before remembering that he could not, and was thence plucked out of the water by the nearest boat. The whale cleared all of them with my father's boat hurtling along in its wake, the Number Two boat rowing desperately to keep up with them.

What happened immediately afterwards we did not witness, for at that moment we were running as hard as we could up to Lookout Point, which afforded the best view of the bay. It was en route that we became entangled in a barbed-wire fence, as reported in *"Voices Whisper"* (for it seems the editor of the *Eden Observer and South Coast Advocate* had his opera glasses trained upon us, in preference to the action at sea). Caring not, we ripped our skirts loose and raced onwards, leaving snatches of worn fabric to blow in the breeze like bunting. There was already a crowd up there, waving their hats and shouting and gesticulating. We pushed to the front of them and found ourselves at the very outermost edge of the cliffs, where various men obligingly wrapped their arms around our waists to ensure we did not plunge over. The whale passed close by the rocks down below, and from this perspective we could see the length and breadth of it.

"Oh, Louisa!" I cried. "It's a black whale!"

"Fifty feet if it's an inch," offered the stout, mustachioed man who had his arms about me. (Incidentally, I recognized him to be one of the judges at the Eden Show who had deemed *"Stern All, Boys!"* to be worthy only of a Highly Commended.)

"Fifty feet!" Louisa and I exclaimed, looking at each other incredulously. The whale now veered off wildly for the northern side of the bay, before sweeping back to the cliffs again, keeping so close to the rocks that the whaleboat seemed in imminent danger of being smashed upon them.

"Where are the Killers?" cried someone. "If only the Killers would come!"

Yes, yes, where were they? At once I was stricken with a sharp stab of guilt. For at this time, I was still uncertain as to whether I had scared them off or even inadvertently slaughtered one.

As long as the whale was traveling at this speed, there was little chance of my father gaining proximity enough to lance it. From the shouts of the men below, we gathered that my father was urging the second boat to fasten on as well, in a bid to slow the great beast down. Harry stood up at the bow, harpoon in hand, and seemed about to launch it when a small bent figure rose up behind him and began waving his arms and gesticulating.

"It is Uncle Aleck!" cried Louisa, clutching her face in horror. "What is he doing?"

Who indeed knew what he was doing? Certainly no one on the Number Two boat seemed to know, for an argument ensued. There was more shouting and waving about of arms, until Dan and John Beck pulled him back into a seated position. (John Beck later informed me that Uncle Aleck had been called in to assist young Dan at the oars. Amidst the excitement, he had risen to his feet to shout advice at Harry, thereby startling him and causing him to miss his chance.) Frantic rowing now ensued in order to catch the whale again. Even from the cliff tops, we could see the spray of Salty's spittle as he urged his oarsmen on.

The next sequence of events happened very quickly. Harry landed his harpoon well, and he and Salty did the changeover, a maneuver made even more perilous by Uncle Aleck choosing this moment to take his coat off. ("The old goat! I will kill him!" cried Louisa.) The sting of this second harpoon seemed only to exacerbate the whale's desperation, for it set off on a series of precipitous zigzags in a bid to shake loose its extra burden. The final zag of the series was so sharp and so abrupt that it caused the second boat to swing directly across the first boat's path, its line passing over the men's heads. They had just time enough to duck and thus avoid being decapitated—my father, however, was knocked clean into the water. Immediately the men cut loose in order to rescue him, leaving only the second boat now attached. Of course, our attention was on our poor father; even from this distance, we could see him urging them to row on as he bobbed in the water. His men pulled him back into the boat, and they at once set to rowing to recapture their fearsome quarry.

The whale had meanwhile headed directly for the nearest cliffs, for its intention seemed to be to drive its tormentors onto the rocks. The speed and wildness of the boat's ride as it was towed along behind reminded me of our own experience with the runaway carriage, even down to the last-minute swerve executed by the whale. This maneuver propelled the hapless second boat headlong onto a rocky outcrop, from which a group of dozing terns rose up in a startled fashion—the boat then slid wildly across the rocks before becoming wedged in a crevice. A strange sight indeed: a landlocked whaleboat with its full crew aboard, its headsman standing at the bow, all looking about in a bewildered fashion. Freed of its burden, the whale headed directly for the open sea, two harpoons rising out of its flesh, fifty fathoms of rope trailing after it. And here at last, just as it all seemed utterly hopeless, the Killers finally made their appearance.

Where had they been? Why had they not participated in any of the preceding chase, which had been underway for over an hour, and crisscrossed much of the bay? Why had they waited till this last desperate moment, when both boats had been forced to cut loose? It was as if they were a troupe of vainglorious actors, waiting for the moment of greatest dramatic effect in order to make their grand entrance. All along the headlands, cheers rose up as those beloved of all dorsal fins revealed themselves, to which the Killers responded by throwing their bodies jubilantly out of the water like tumblers in a Royal Court. Here was Hooky, with Cooper leering cheerfully alongside; there was Humpy breaching and Charlie Adgery and Jackson and so on. Best of all, though, was to see the determined and portly form of Tom, up to his usual antics, with no sign of any ill-effects from the firing of the bomb lance. Perhaps he had simply been nursing a dull headache, and laid low for a while.

After announcing their arrival in this fashion and receiving the ovation they considered their due, the Killers immediately set to work. From here on, amidst the flurry of black fins and white water, it became a great deal more difficult to determine exactly what was happening. Clearly their modus operandi was to contain the whale's progress in order that my father and his men gain sufficient proximity that he might employ the lance, and the gleeful enthusiasm with which they set about the task reminded me of nothing so much as the time that the Bega football team had annihilated Eden in the semi-finals. Bega were the longstanding champions with a reputation for thuggishness; for some reason, possibly owing to being dairy farmers, they were twice the size of our lads and much faster on the field. (Also, their home ground was situated on a hillside, causing visiting teams immense difficulties in having to kick uphill towards the goalposts.) The ease with which they outclassed their opponents was such that they played with a kind of ruthless gaiety, shouting out jokes and pet names for one another, jumping up in the air and spontaneously embracing whenever another goal went through the posts. The delight they took in their play and in one another was not appealing; it was sickening, for it was at the expense of our own boys. The game ended 47–1, with the Eden lads incurring some serious injuries (Harry was amongst them; he had several toes broken when one of his boots came off in the mud and a Bega boy stomped on his foot).

I felt the same sick feeling now as we watched the Killers at work. Their amiable snub-nosed appearance seemed at stark odds with their viciousness; the poor dumb whale was no match for these warriors. Briefly, the embattled leviathan rose up out of the water, rolling its great girth in a bid to shake them free, only to be pulled back down again by the Killers hanging on to its side fins. If it tried to dive, the Killers would dive beneath it and push it back up; if it tried to surface for air, a Killer would leap atop its blowholes and push it down again. Curlicues of crimson appeared amidst the foam. Worst of all, rising up from the water came the most terrible sound—at first we did not understand what we were hearing: the piteous bellowing of the hounded whale.

The men of the first boat rowed gamely (the second boat still wedged upon its rocks) and Arthur Ashby wasted no time in fastening on to the whale again. So sustained was the Killers' attack that the whale had now practically come to a standstill, allowing my father the opportunity to apply his lance. Drawing the weapon up high, he plunged the lance deep into the poor creature; oh, a hideous sight to see. If only once had done it, but again and again he plunged his lance, and each time the heartless crowd cheered as if watching a prize-fighter pummeling his opponent in a boxing tent. The dreadful bellows grew more anguished, its last feeble spouts turned red. "Stop it!" I heard someone cry, and turning around, I realized it was Louisa, tears streaming down her face. "Stop it! Make him stop!" (I will say in my father's defense that I believe his frenzy of lancing was born of an urge to expedite the whale's demise and minimize its suffering.)

Mercifully, the poor creature's ordeal ended shortly thereafter and the great body lay lifeless on the surface of the blood-stained sea. Mr. Winston, the customs officer, offered me his telescope, and somewhat gingerly I peered through it. There I saw the whale men, bloody and triumphant, slapping each other on the back and shaking hands. The crowds on the headlands offered up a rousing three cheers, and the men turned and waved their caps in response; all except my father. He was leaning over the gunwale, and as I watched, he reached out to touch the fin of a Killer whale swimming close by. It was Tom's fin, I feel sure of that, for I saw that knob on its trailing edge. It was a brief gesture, like a handshake or a pat on the back, a simple moment of acknowledgment between two generals, but done with quiet affection, for my father esteemed Tom above all Killer whales and it would not surprise me if Tom held my father in similar regard. After this brief exchange, my father turned to the men; I could see from his gestures that he was urging them to waste no time in securing the carcass with anchors and marker buoys. They could ill-afford to delay, for the Killers were impatient; it was a matter of barely three minutes before they had pulled the carcass down below.

A Lonely Killer, He

THINKING ABOUT MY FATHER'S DEEP AFFECTION FOR THE Killer whale Tom, I include in this memoir the following obituary which appeared in the *Eden Magnet*, 20 September 1930, on the sad occasion of Tom's passing.

Old Tom: The Last of the Killer Whales Is Dead

For a century or more, there's been whaling—now there's wailing—at Twofold Bay. "Old Tom," the last of the famous pack of Twofold Bay Killer whales, is dead. On Wednesday morning, under the influence of favouring breeze and tide, his body, unheralded, came floating gently in to rest in the bay which had been the killer's battlefield and the scene of many memorable exploits during the last hundred years or more of Eden's history. Old Tom had died at sea a day or two previously, and kind

Nature had sent his body drifting in to be disposed of as might seem fit to his allies of old.

It was only last week that Old Tom was disporting off Leonards Island, in the vicinity of which he had caught a grampus, and he was commemorating the event with a display of unusual vivacity. What happened to bring about his demise is a matter of mere conjecture. Master whaler George Davidson does not know and, although he made a post-mortem superficial examination of the body, could form no opinion satisfactory to himself as to the cause of the centenarian's untimely death.

Of Old Tom's sagacity and many deeds of daring there are many yarns extant, but if anyone wants the true version there are few persons to whom one can with confidence apply, and one is master whaler George Davidson, otherwise known as "Fearless George."

Of the old "Orca Gladiator," last of the Twofold Bay killer whales—Old Tom—renowned in war—it may be said that his end was peace, and that he dies regretted by all who knew him.

There also appeared—on the front page the following week—this poem entitled "Old Tom," by Eden's poet laureate, Tom Browne:

For eighty years or more, Old Tom has whaled off Twofold Bay,
And many a humpback met its fate when passing down this way.
There's "Fearless George" and Aleck Greig who live to tell the
*   tale*

Of how the veteran helped them well with many a vicious
  whale.
And now his carcass lies afloat on peaceful Twofold Bay
Whose waters he so oft has roamed in conflict and in play.
His mates have long since passed away; a lonely Killer, he
Has gone at last to well-earned rest—the whaler's home from sea.

I don't suppose that there are many fish who could reasonably expect an obituary of several hundred words and a poem dedicated to their memory featuring prominently in the local newspaper. But as I think I have already established, Tom was not like any other fish (or cetacean, to be more accurate); for one thing, he was braver and smarter than most men and, for another, he was more loyal than any dog. I know we are all inclined to eulogize the Dead, but looking back at earlier chapters, I see that I have made much of Tom's undoubtedly more annoying qualities; his impatience at what I suppose he perceived to be petty bureaucracy (the attaching of marker buoys to the whale carcass and so forth), his hooligan antics with the towing of fishing boats and his high jinks with the whale line. But since I am taking this opportunity to mark his passing—and it hit us very heavily at the time, more heavily than even the disbanding of the whaling station and the forced sale of equipment several years earlier—I would prefer to concentrate on his more noble qualities, for there were many of them. He served faithfully as my father's lieutenant year after year as our fortunes waxed and waned; he respected their unspoken agreement, and could always be relied upon to uphold his end of the bargain. Every winter to the end, even when my father had given up whaling, Tom kept returning to Twofold

Bay—such was his sense of duty, perhaps unusual amongst his kin, for certainly the rest of the Killers had long stopped coming. Occasionally, as of old times, he would flop-tail at the bar, in an attempt to entice my father out. My father, of course, would drop everything, scrounge together a crew of whoever happened to be about, and off they would go joyously on a whale chase.

Searching for a fitting way of commemorating this friendship, my father settled on the idea of preserving Tom's skeleton, and he towed his body back to the try-works in order to carry out the necessary work himself. How tenderly did he flense Tom of his blubber, and how carefully did he boil his bones. One morning, as I tended to the washing, I heard him calling me down to the try-works; there was something he wished to show me. He had Tom's skull before him on the workbench, and was engaged in the task of polishing his teeth with a rag and some bicarbonate of soda. The skull was long in snout and startlingly prehistoric in appearance; it looked as if it might have been better suited to a crocodile or a dinosaur. The front teeth on both the upper and lower jaws were worn to stumps or broken off; they spoke of a hard life and a great deal of adventure. Only the teeth on the sides of his jaws were of normal length, and here my father pointed to a particular tooth towards the back on the lower left-hand side. There could be seen distinctly a pronounced groove, as if worn down by the repeated friction of a rope; clearly the legacy of his exploits hanging off the whale line. It was a remarkable sight, for the groove was so deep it had practically worn through the tooth; such was the force with which he had been towed through the water in those whaling days of yore. How his antics had annoyed the whalers; such briny epithets as were hurled at his gleaming head! I reached out to feel the smoothness of the hollow, and looked up at my father; he was smiling at me, his eyes shining. We had only Tom's skeleton to remember him by, and yet this rope-furrowed tooth spoke of his very essence, of the foolhardy, reckless and mischievous fish he had been.

Uncle Aleck Takes the Cure

E XTRAORDINARY AS IT MAY SEEM, GIVEN THAT WE WERE
the daughters of George Davidson, master whaler,
the capture of this southern right was the first whale
capture we had ever witnessed, and it is fair to say that we were
greatly shaken by the ghastly brutality of it all. The heart-
rending bellows of the poor tormented beast seemed to echo
around the cliffs and reverberate in our very rib cages. To see
this noble creature slaughtered by our own kith and kin was
very difficult for us, and we found ourselves unable to respond with any civility to the hearty congratulations that were
heaped upon us in the aftermath. Louisa wept openly on the
cliff top and would not be consoled by anybody, though many
tried, nor even by the thought that we would now be able to
pay for the provisions Mr. Howard had just refused us; perhaps even, I suggested (feeling it advisable not to mention the
ivory crepe de chine), the pink crinkle marocain that had
looked so becoming against her fair complexion. Upon our

return home, she would have nothing to do with any of the whalers—even, I noted, Darcy—but most of her fury she reserved for my father.

For myself, I was not so much angry with my father as stunned that I had formerly been so naive and unquestioning. What had I imagined happened out there? How had I imagined these whales met their deaths? Had I imagined that they passed away delicately of shock like the diamond dove fledgling I had once rescued from the cat? For although I understood in principle the technicalities of whaling—the harpooning, the chase to exhaustion, the necessity of a swift and vigorous lancing—I had never conceived, never understood, never imagined for one moment the horror of it all. Only now did I understand why John Beck had returned from his first whale capture straining to recall that passage from the Bible. I imagine he was trying to find some way to live with what he had just witnessed.

Of course, my father was much too busy to notice—let alone tend to—the more fragile sensibilities of his daughters. The whale proved to be one of the largest black whales ever captured in Twofold Bay. Fortunately the weather remained mild, and when it gassed up a day or so later, it was towed home without incident. It measured fifty-seven feet to the tail tips; its whalebone eight feet in length, and the blubber at its thickest almost sixteen inches deep. It was so large that a channel three feet deep had to be dug at low tide to stop it running aground on the sandy bottom. When finally it was dragged close enough to the try-works, the flensing of blubber commenced, a process that required almost two full days of the most backbreaking labor. Once the flensing was complete, a deep hole was cut into the remaining pile of putrefying flesh and Uncle Aleck duly inserted up to his head, so that the lower part of his body sank down into the whale's intestines.

"How are you feeling, Uncle?" asked Dan, whose job it was to watch him and ensure he did not pass out from the tremendous heat of the fermenting whale.

"I feel like I am roasting in the furnace of eternal damnation, lad, so shut your smart mouth. How long have I been in?"

"Forty minutes," said Dan, checking Uncle Aleck's pocket watch.

"Is that all? Christ! I will surely die in here and then you will all be happy!"

I noticed that John Beck had emerged from the try-works and was observing this spectacle with some bewilderment. After a while, unable to contain his curiosity, he wandered over to where I sat peeling potatoes for the evening meal.

"Would you mind telling me what your uncle is doing buried up to his head in a dead whale?" he inquired.

"Well, he is what they call 'taking the cure.'"

"I see," said John Beck. "Cure for what, in particular?"

"Cure for rheumatism. You will find him remarkably sprightly when he emerges."

John Beck stood there a moment, absorbing this information, while I cast furtive glances at him. He had his shirt unbuttoned and his sleeves rolled up, and his forearms were glistening with whale oil.

"How is it supposed to work exactly, this cure?" he asked eventually.

"Oh, well, I think it is something to do with the fermenting gases. Or maybe the heat and the oil. Anyway, it is very beneficial, if you have the lumbago. Although sometimes it can require several immersions."

"I see."

"Unfortunately, it can be rather difficult to remove the smell of putrefying whale meat afterwards."

"From his clothes, do you mean?"

"Oh no, he is not wearing any clothes. If he was, he would have to burn them, for the smell can never be removed."

"Yet I note he is still wearing his hat?"

We both turned now to gaze at Uncle Aleck. It did seem an odd choice, superfluous somehow, to wear a hat while immersed bodily in a dead whale, but there you have it, that was Uncle Aleck, standing on his dignity at all times. It seemed he may now have had enough, for he was bellowing to be pulled out. Several of the men hoisted him out (not easily, for the whale's grisly innards seemed to have a suction-like grip on him) and mercifully covered his scrawny nakedness with a blanket. He waded limply through the shallows, dripping bodily fluids and entrails, with Dan hovering close by lest he collapse. Various whale men stood about at a distance, offering derisive comments and laughing uproariously. Even the normally amiable Bonnie skulked away as he approached, her tail between her legs.

"Would you give me a dance at the ball, Mary?" asked John Beck, all of a sudden.

"Are you going to the ball?" I asked.

"Yes. Aren't you?"

"Yes, of course." The capture of the black whale had meant that this was now possible; however, our father had not been persuaded to relent on the subject of new dresses. Our fortunes had improved, but not to the extent of moss-green georgette and pink crinkle marocain.

"It's only that I thought Methodists didn't approve of dancing," I said.

"Ah well," he said, making a kind of grimace. "Maybe I'm not really a Methodist."

I stared at him. What an odd and surprising man he was proving to be. What had been the excuse that he had once proffered for his changeability? That's right: he was troubled by a kind of restlessness. He was in search of the "ungraspable phantom of life."

"In fact, I can't be a Methodist," he continued. "I dance too well to be a Methodist."

"Are you a Presbyterian or something?" I asked.

"I don't think so. Do they dance?"

"No. At least, not terribly well."

"I see. Well. Perhaps I'm just an oarsman in the Number Two boat." He looked at me now with a smile. "Does that sound all right to you?"

I nodded, for my mouth had become suddenly tremendously dry so that I was forced to swallow.

"I will be having a bath, so I don't smell of whale oil," he added.

Again, I nodded, having apparently lost all ability to form words.

"And Mary," he said, earnestly, "if I was to pretend I'm unconscious, do you think you might feel inclined to kiss me again?"

To which I responded readily: "You will not need to pretend you are unconscious."

"There, you bantered!" he said. "You see, you are very good at it."

He smiled at me then, and a strange, miraculous feeling seemed to overcome me. I watched him ambling back towards the try-works; along the way, he passed Uncle Aleck, who was staggering up towards the house, muttering to himself and clutching his blanket around him. There was a brief exchange between the pair of them, and I remember John Beck threw back his head and laughed, even slapping Uncle Aleck on the back in a good-natured fashion. And remembering how I sat there, potatoes on my lap, my heart bursting with happiness and hope, I realize that all I have achieved in writing this memoir is to reopen a great wound that has taken a very long time to heal over.

Louisa

A
S MENTIONED IN THE PREVIOUS CHAPTER, LOUISA HAD
been greatly distressed by the killing of the whale,
and vowed to have nothing further to do with any of
the whalers, whom she referred to as "a pack of murderers."
By all indications, this included Darcy. Certainly they appeared to have no contact with each other—I know, for I made
it my business to keep a close eye upon the pair. Louisa kept
herself up in the house and only grudgingly assisted in the
preparation of the whalers' meals (which in itself was not unusual), insisting that Dan help me carry down the pots lest one
of the "murderers" should affront her by wandering into her
field of sight.

Robert Heffernan came knocking at the back door to ask
Louisa if she might give him a dance at the ball, to which she
responded bluntly that she would never dance with a whale
slaughterer, now or ever. At this, Robert remonstrated that
he had only rowed the boat, and not very well at that; she

had only to ask Salty, who had called him a "bl---y incompetent." Louisa, however, could not be cajoled. She kept to herself, and spoke little to anyone. Our father she referred to as "George Davidson, master murderer." When he entered a room, she got up and walked out of it.

For his part, Darcy, normally so full of quips and merriment, now seemed subdued and withdrawn. After several days of having had no sighting of Louisa, he finally asked me if she was sick. "No, just bad-tempered," I replied, for her mood was becoming tiresome. Also, I thought it unfair that she was so hard on my father, who after all was only trying to provide for his family. I explained to Darcy that she was upset about the whale, and if she kept to her usual form, would likely get over it in a week or so. He seemed to accept this response but, as I say, he seemed subdued. Like Louisa, he kept to himself.

On about the fifth night after the whale capture, around the same time as John Beck had asked me if I would dance with him, I awoke and realized that the bed beside me was empty. At once, I felt a sickening lurch of my belly; *She has done it*, I thought, *she has run off with Darcy*. And as I lay there imagining various awful scenarios, yet too paralyzed with dread to get up and go and look for her, I suddenly heard from the front garden the shrill, infuriated cries of Mr. Maudry. Only a few short moments later, the door of our room opened softly and Louisa slipped back into bed alongside me. Feigning sleep, I affected to fling an arm out; sure enough, her skin was cool to the touch, which indicated that she had been outside for possibly some time. I realize now, of course, that she was undoubtedly returning from a clandestine rendezvous with Darcy, in which a great many things had been discussed, arrangements put in place and so forth. But so convinced had I been by her act, by her avowal that she would have nothing to do with any whalers, and so pre-occupied was I with my own thoughts of John Beck and the upcoming ball, that I chose not to dwell on the possibilities but simply elected to put the whole business out of my mind. It is highly unlikely, I told myself, if not impossible, that she would ever do such a thing. Had she not told me herself that she had simply been joking?

The next day her mood was greatly improved. She was civil to my father at breakfast; she even braided the younger ones' hair in the popular fishbone style, and willingly helped me with the usual chores. One incident, however, stands out to me now as significant. We had pulled our cretonne dresses out of the trunk to see what we could do by way of enlivening their appearance for the ball. After some experimentation, we decided that my green floral cretonne could be improved if we trimmed the neckline with a small quantity of lace removed from an old blouse of my mother's. I also suggested that Louisa's pink floral cretonne could be brought up to date if we removed the spangled netting from my mother's good hat and arranged it in a fashion at the bodice. At first, Louisa had seemed very tempted by the idea, but as she passed the veil netting between her fingertips, she seemed to change her mind. "No, it doesn't matter," she said. "Let's leave it. I don't mind it as it is."

This was most unlike my sister, and in itself ought to have been enough to alarm me.

"Well, then," I suggested, "you could have the lace trimming, and I could use the spangled netting."

"No," said Louisa promptly. "You use the lace as it suits the green cretonne."

"It will suit your pink cretonne just as well."

"No, I have made up my mind. You use the lace, and I will wear my pink cretonne just as it is."

As I say, this degree of unselfishness was unusual for Louisa. But perhaps, as I reasoned at the time, this was a long-awaited sign of her growing maturity.

The next night, I feigned sleep in the hope that I might catch her sneaking out on another of her midnight assignations. But instead she fell asleep promptly (I could tell by the rhythm of her breathing) and so I fell asleep also, and the pair of us slept through till morning undisturbed. The night after that, however, I awoke from a deep sleep to find her climbing back into bed. When I questioned her, she responded: "What are you blathering on about? I was just using the potty. Go back to sleep."

Yet even as I write these words, I am struck by how plainly obvious it all was, and I wonder at myself that I did nothing except vaguely hope that the dark storm clouds that seemed to be gathering might blow away of their own accord. Knowing Louisa as I did, I should have recognized the unlikelihood of this, for she had always been an obstinate, pig-headed girl, determined to have her own way. And perhaps that is the real reason why I did nothing: I knew in my heart that there would be no stopping her.

The Plain and Fancy Dress Ball

IF YOU COULD HAVE SEEN HOW PRETTY OUR SCHOOL OF ARTS looked, its walls festooned with white clematis blossoms and gardenias, so different from its usual somber municipal self! Immediately I wished that, in matters of costume, Louisa and I had not settled so readily for "plain," for certainly the townsfolk of Eden had embraced the more imaginative option. Everywhere you looked there seemed to be a picturesque tableau. In one corner, Pierrot chatted with a bearded Viking; in another, a Japanese Maid smiled coquettishly behind her fan in the company of a dusky Rajah. Eunice Martin came garbed as a Christmas Lily, draped head to toe in Louisa's coveted ivory crepe de chine, for which she won the prize for "Best-Sustained Character—Lady." I realize I may seem churlish whenever Eunice Martin wins an unwarranted prize, but many of us considered privately that a more deserving recipient was Elspeth Gilbert, who put together a very humorous interpretation of "What Percy Picked Up in the Park," or indeed Miss Watkins as "Bermagui Meat Supplies," with a chain of lifelike sausages draped about her neck. (Apparently, she was excluded from consideration because it was decided she was more of an Advertisement than a Character—her father is the actual proprietor of Bermagui Meat Supplies—and this was felt to be spoiling the tone of the evening. The Watkinses left the ball shortly after the prize-giving, Miss W. in tears.) Mr. Strickland Senior practically brought the house down as the Old Witch, chasing after the children with his broomstick and screaming curses (which was not greatly different from his usual behavior, admittedly), and for this he won "Best-Sustained Character—Gentleman," before passing out quietly in the bushes out the back.

At least the children had entered into the spirit of things— Violet came as a Housemaid in apron and lace cap and carrying a feather duster, and Annie as "Mary, Mary, Quite Contrary," for which a basket of flowers, a watering can and her customary scowl was all that was required. Harry and Robert Heffernan came as Cricketers, which was not so very clever as they simply wore their cricket whites and leaned about nonchalantly on their bats, as if in the unlikely scenario of waiting for a six to be retrieved from the back of the grandstand. Dan, however, came dressed as the Major of the Artillery, sporting his Salvation Army cap, a painted-on mustache, a riding crop and my father's spyglass; this combined with the authentic manner in which he sucked on his clay pipe ensured that he won "Best-Sustained Character—Boy," much to the Davidson family's delight.

After the Grand March and the prize-giving, the dancing began in earnest. Music for the evening was provided by the Powers family on piano, violin, cornet and tambourine, and with Mr. Oslington as MC they galloped through a selection of popular dance numbers. Borax powder had been sprinkled liberally on the dance floor, rendering it dangerously slippery in patches, but this did not deter the scores of dancers, of which none were sprightlier than our own Uncle Aleck. Thanks to the whale cure, he was reeling Louisa about the room with the vigor of a man many years his junior.

"I wonder if I should rescue your sister," said John Beck, glancing over at them. Louisa certainly looked quite flushed in the face, and had I known what I now know of her condition at the time, perhaps I would have shown a little more sympathy.

"Oh no, she adores it," I replied. "The quicker the waltz the better. She wouldn't dream of changing partners, not for anything."

I was fast to John Beck and not going to cut loose if I could help it. It was true, he danced far too well to be a Methodist; certainly he danced far better than the rest of us. Most of us had been forced to acquire what dancing skills we possessed from intensive study of Mrs. Chas. Read's *Australian Ballroom Guide*, available for loan from the School of Arts. Louisa and I had struggled at length over the years with her bewildering directions and schematic diagrams, but they simply made no sense no matter which way up you held the book. And yet, in spite of the squabbling she caused at the time, Mrs. Chas. Read became one of our greatest sources of family merriment. If ever we read in the newspaper of some wretched soul's misfortune, we would say, "I see how Mrs. Chas. Read has got drunk again and gone at her landlady with a carving knife," or, "I see how Mrs. Chas. Read has mixed too much laudanum in her hop beer and been taken to hospital with the nerve trouble." In our minds, the only possible explanation for her bewildering instructions was that she was either drunk or imbibing opium at the time of writing.

Like most Edenites, we were reasonably competent in the Spot Waltz, the Jolly Miller and the Progressive Barn Dance, but any attempts to conduct an orderly Quadrille descended into confusion and arguments. People were forever adding new parts half remembered from other dances or leaving out entire sections altogether. John Beck was clearly used to higher standards, for he became somewhat terse on several occasions with those other dancers who stood in his path saying, "What's this bit? Oh! I see! Too late! Should we be—? Oh—sorry! Beg your pardon!" For the most part, I simply clung to him, and when separated in the Quadrille, I made small skipping steps as best I could in time with the music.

The Quadrille having finished, John Beck led me over to the refreshment stalls, past Salty and Bastable, all spruced up with their beards combed and their wisps of hair plastered over their scalps, sitting on the bench eyeing us wistfully. They had placed orange blossoms in their buttonholes in an attempt to mask any remnant of whale smell, but the delicate flowers appeared to have wilted.

Dan had won five shillings as Best-Sustained Character and, filled with largesse, had decided to treat his little sisters to some lollies. Now they held up the queue at the confectionery stall as they contemplated the vast display, seeming to find the choice overwhelming. Violet loved coconut ice, but she equally loved jujubes. Annie could not choose between Turkish delight and chocolate caramels. Dan was becoming irritated and could be heard threatening to withdraw his offer if they did not bl---y hurry up about it. How often one's attempts to behave generously are thwarted, and so often because of the ungrateful attitude of the intended recipient(s). At the refreshments stall, I found myself faced with a similar, bewildering array of choice. The Persian Princess behind the counter eyed John Beck with interest from behind her spangled veil and why shouldn't she? John Beck was plainly the handsomest man in the room. Not wishing to dally longer than was necessary, I selected a blackberry cordial; a hasty choice and perhaps not the wisest, as it was found to stain one's lips and not necessarily in a becoming manner. I was not aware of this until Louisa joined us, having at last broken free from Uncle Aleck.

"What's the matter with your mouth?" she asked. "Did somebody punch you?"

Nonetheless, taking the cordial from my hands, she helped herself to it freely, for dancing with Uncle Aleck was thirsty work. Meanwhile, I rubbed at my mouth with a bit of spit on a hankie, until John Beck assured me that the blackberry stain was "barely noticeable."

"We have to do something about Uncle Aleck," said Louisa, having sufficiently quenched her thirst (oddly, the blackberry cordial left her lips with merely a delicate blush). "He smells abominable. Everyone is starting to notice."

"Surely he's harmless enough," I said magnanimously. "Besides, the whole room smells a little ripe."

"He smells of *fermenting whale gizzards*," said Louisa. "You try it and see how you like it."

My time had come, for even as she spoke Uncle Aleck was upon us, tapping at my shoulder. Off I went to face my fate. Robert Heffernan seized the opportunity to approach Louisa once more to ask if she would do him the great honor of accompanying him in the Waltz.

"All right," she said grimly.

"Gosh, this floor's slippery!" cried Robert as they danced past us. "It's hard to keep on your feet, isn't it?"

"Oh, I see," observed Louisa coolly. "You're deliberately trying to step on my feet, are you? I thought it was merely accidental."

She made a point of dancing with anyone who asked that night, no doubt in a bid to throw us off the scent. And what else could she do, for she could not dance with Darcy. He sat out the front of the School of Arts with my father and the rest of the whale crew, enjoying the balmy evening and the water views. In fact, a great many of the menfolk of Eden ended up sprawled outside on the grassy slopes. It seems they had secreted their bottles of liquor here and there amongst the bushes.

"Mary," said Mrs. Pike, taking hold of my arm as I lurched dizzily off the dance floor after several rounds with Uncle Aleck, "where's your father? Won't you encourage him to come inside and have a dance with me?"

"All right," I said, and I went outside to find him. In truth, I was hoping also to find John Beck, as he seemed to have disappeared.

My father was in the middle of telling his snake and umbrella story, and so I stood about, shifting my weight from one foot to the other, waiting for him to finish. In essence, it was not a complicated story, but my father paused so often in the telling, remembering small details that he should have mentioned earlier or becoming side-tracked by other unrelated thoughts, that the story went on far longer than it deserved to. It concerned a man who had fallen asleep in the bush, and upon waking up to find it raining, opened his umbrella. It felt rather stiff going up and there was a terrible tearing sound, and suddenly a black snake fell to the ground, split in two from head to tail.

Now while I was waiting for my father to get to the end of his anecdote, I glanced around, wondering where John Beck had got to, when suddenly I espied him, standing in the shadows beneath the mulberry trees. He appeared to be in earnest discussion with someone I could not immediately identify, for this person's back was towards me. I would not have seen them at all, had not a party of ball-goers walked past them, lanterns in hand, and momentarily illuminated them. The other person appeared to be doing most of the talking while John Beck listened intently but with some concern, for his hands were deep in his pockets and he appeared to be slowly shaking his head. The lanterns passed and the two of them plunged into darkness again; in some bewilderment, I turned my attention back to my father.

"You see, it had swallowed the umbrella whole, except for the handle," my father was saying in triumphant conclusion. And at that moment it struck me with absolute clarity that the person John Beck had been talking to was Darcy, for certainly Darcy was not part of the group of whale men that sat around now, laughing appreciatively at my father's story.

I interrupted the general merriment to tell my father that he had been specifically requested as a dance partner by none other than Mrs. Pike, the proprietress of the Great Southern. With a show of bashful reluctance, he rose somewhat unsteadily to his feet and accompanied me back inside.

"Tell us, Mary," Darcy's father, Percy, called after me, "how are Salty and Bastable faring in there? Have they had any luck in their wooing?"

"Since you ask, I did notice Salty in the company of a lady," I said with a smile, to which the whale men responded with ribald glee. In fact, I had seen Salty "tripping the light fantastic" with the widow Mrs. Guthridge; he was surprisingly nimble on his feet for a portly man, and conducted himself very reasonably in the Country Dance. Now it was my father's turn to join them, with Mrs. Pike on his arm. He was too stiff-legged to dance well, yet nonetheless he cut a commanding figure. He held himself very upright—"like dancing with a plank of hardwood," is how Louisa described it—with a look of fierce concentration on his face, moving his lips as he counted. Regardless, Mrs. Pike seemed well-pleased to be in his arms and circling the dance floor.

It was soon midnight, and supper was called; all available hands were summoned to assist. There was tea and coffee to be brewed in four-gallon buckets; cold meat and mustard pickle and fish-paste sandwiches to be served, and sponge cakes (light as air!) to be sliced.

"Where is your sister?" asked Robert Heffernan, who was suddenly standing over me as I attempted to daintily arrange some sandwiches on a serving platter. It seemed he may have had a bit to drink as he was somewhat flushed in the face. "Have you seen her?"

"No, not recently," I responded. "She is here somewhere, I'm sure."

"Oh, do you mean Louisa?" asked Elspeth Gilbert cheerfully. "I saw her outside just before with one of the black-fellows."

"One of the blackfellows?" I cried. "How peculiar."

My heart thudded in my chest, for I noted Robert's color rising.

"I think she may have been taking the poor fellow something to drink, that's all," continued Elspeth. "She has always been a thoughtful and considerate lass, taking after your mother in that way," she added.

Thoughtful and considerate! I thought to myself indignantly. If anything, I was the thoughtful and considerate member of the family, the one that took most after my mother. Why was everyone so inclined to bestow upon Louisa virtues she did not possess? Mind you, it had not occurred to me to take any beverages out to our Aboriginal whale crew, but then that was because our whale men generally looked after themselves in the matter of beverages. It has to be said they would not have greeted my offering them a cordial with much enthusiasm.

"If I were you, I would take your sister in hand," muttered Robert Heffernan ominously. "She is in danger of making herself a laughingstock." And with that, he moved away before I could think of a worthy retort.

"Well, he is certainly the moody type," commented Elspeth. "I imagine he is jealous, over such a petty thing as your sister giving a blackfellow a drink of cordial!"

The conversation changed to the more pressing need of locating more teaspoons so that people might be able to add their own sugar to their tea; Elspeth went off in search of some. I was instructed to take my plate of sandwiches and offer them to anyone who could show their entry ticket, thus easing the crush around the supper table. I set off in hope of coming across John Beck, for I fancied the thought of settling down with him in a darkened corner, perhaps sharing a fish-paste sandwich. However, I had no sooner emerged from the kitchen than I was waylaid by Salty, beckoning me over with some urgency to where he sat with Mrs. Guthridge. As I advanced upon them with my plate, I was surprised to hear that Mrs. Guthridge appeared to be laboring under the misapprehension that Salty had been, in a former life, a minister of the Methodist church.

"May I ask, what then compelled you to leave?" she inquired, an expression of intense fascination upon her face.

Here Salty passed a hand through his beard and affected a somber expression, as with his other hand he reached out and grasped several sandwiches from my proffered plate.

"Temptation," he said finally.

"Temptation?"

"That and a certain...*susceptibility*."

Glancing up to find me staring at him in frank astonishment, he broke off and popped a sandwich into his mouth, chewing away vigorously with his few remaining teeth. Just then, an unpleasantness broke out at the supper table; some riffraff had got in without paying and were helping themselves to the cakes and sandwiches. When they were remonstrated with by Mrs. Atcherley, one smart aleck issued an insolent riposte before flinging a sandwich at Robert Heffernan, who happened to be standing at the other end of the supper table, broodingly stuffing his face. Robert howled indignantly and returned fire with a lamington. At once, merry hell broke loose; all available menfolk jumped into the fray to "sort it out," including my brother Harry. The men who had been drinking outside came hurtling in as reinforcements; punches were thrown indiscriminately, women screamed, china was broken and one hapless Edenite was thrown against the tea urn, thus knocking it over and setting hot tea and tea leaves all over the supper-room floor (miraculously, no one was scalded). The melee seemed to go on for a full five or ten minutes before order was once again restored; however, the supper table was the worse for it, and many tears were shed at the sight of flattened sponge cakes and lovingly prepared sandwiches squashed underfoot. The guilty parties (three young ne'er-do-wells from Pambula) were chased off into the night, whereupon it was later discovered that they must have returned at some point and loosened the wheels of various sulkies, for a number of unfortunate accidents ensued on the journey home. In some ways, however, the supper-room fracas provided a welcome distraction, for in all the excitement, amidst which he incurred a bloody nose, Robert Heffernan seemed to forget about Louisa and Darcy.

Once everything had settled down again and the supper room was put back to rights, some additional entertainment was provided. Mr. Oslington attempted a humorous recitation of "Sandy McGlashan's Courtship," but forgot too many of the words for it to be considered entirely successful. Mr. O'Henessey sang "The Little Irish Girl" to much laughter and applause, and after this our own Eden Christy Minstrel Club proceeded onto the stage. I at once recognized Mr. Howard the Price-Cutter leering ominously at the audience, and immediately I resolved not to enjoy them. I did not so much as tap my foot during "Oh, Dem Golden Slippers," but when they launched into "My Old Kentucky Home, Good Night," the tears began, inexplicably, to roll down my cheeks.

They hunt no more for the possum and the 'coon,
On meadow, the hill and the shore,
They sing no more by the glimmer of the moon,
On the bench by that old cabin door.
The day goes by like a shadow o'er the heart,
With sorrow where all was delight.
The time has come when the darkies have to part,
Then my old Kentucky home, good night.

Perhaps I am more susceptible than others to the effects of a sentimental song, but for me at that moment, it was the humpback and the southern right that they hunted no more, and instead of the Kentucky home it was our little house at Kiah Inlet, and instead of just the darkies having to part, it was the whale men, it was all of us. For it was as if some small part of me sensed all the sadness and loss and disappointment and separation that awaited me. Dabbing futilely at my streaming eyes, I turned to Louisa (for she had suddenly reappeared by this time), expecting to see her similarly affected. But she just sat there with a scornful expression on her face, and when they left the stage to thunderous applause, she remarked, "Thank goodness for that. I thought they'd go on all night."

After the entertainment, there commenced a great washing up of the supper plates. Louisa and I were last on the roster, and so found it our duty to wash and dry every last cup and saucer in the building, a task which took us some time. When we had finally lowered our tea towels and removed our aprons, I suddenly discovered, nestling in the corner, a small blue and white teacup that we had somehow overlooked.

"Look, Louisa," I cried, for I was thinking of our kitchen superstitions. "If when washing dishes, you forget an item, it is a sign you will hear of a wedding! I haven't heard of any weddings tonight. Have you?"

"No," said Louisa wearily, and mostly she just seemed annoyed about having to wash another cup. "Here, I'll do it then," I said, for a feeling of elation had overtaken me; I proceeded to wash and dry this little teacup with infinite care. You see, I was nurturing high hopes about this wedding I might hear of and, in particular, whose wedding it might be.

When I had finished, I stepped outside. The fat full moon hung suspended over Twofold Bay. The younger lads were out on the street playing cricket; Dan, still dressed as the Major of the Artillery, was arguing the point over a fallen wicket. Bodies lay about, snoring richly. I suppose somewhere in the darkness the ne'er-do-wells from Pambula were loosening the wheels of the sulkies. The whale men sat on the grass, exchanging fond reminiscences from the whaling season just past; someone offered up a toast to whaling season, 1909.

"And may it bring with it a great profusion of humpers!" cried Uncle Aleck.

"Hear, hear!" was the rallying response. But I could not see John Beck amongst their number, so I turned and headed back inside.

The Powers family had retired for the evening, and the last remaining dancers were left to rely upon the vagaries of Mr. Aikenhead's drunken piano-playing. Having eaten a great many jujubes and run around madly all night, Violet and Annie slumped, sleepy and out of sorts, on the benches. I went over to join them; no sooner had I sat down than Violet rested her head on my lap and fell soundly asleep. It was then that I saw John Beck come in. He stood in the doorway, casting his gaze about the room, and as his eyes lit upon me, his features softened to a smile to which my heart thumped a joyful response.

"There you are," he said as he sat down beside me. "I've been looking for you."

"I have been doing the washing up," I said.

"The washing up," he repeated, gazing at me earnestly. "Yes. And I'm sure you would have performed the task admirably."

"Well, I suppose so," I responded hesitantly. The truth was that Louisa had had to pass back to me several cups from which I had failed to remove residual coffee stains. I had finally had to inform her that some of these marks appeared to be stains of long-standing and were simply impossible to remove without resorting to vinegar and bicarbonate of soda, and frankly I had better things to do with my time whilst at the ball. Also, it struck me as something of the "pot calling the kettle black," since her own washing up left a great deal to be desired and consisted mostly of dipping an item briefly in water and making a slight, half-hearted swirling motion.

"I daresay you have had a bit of practice over the years," said John Beck, still looking at me intently. "With the washing up, I mean."

"Oh yes," I responded, feeling somewhat bewildered. Why was he so interested in my washing up all of a sudden? Was it possible that men took such matters into consideration when evaluating a future wife? Could this possibly be some kind of preamble in that direction? "I suppose I am rather good at it," I added, after a moment's thought.

He nodded, as if satisfied by my response. He looked away briefly, deep in thought, and then he turned back to me.

"Mary—" he began, but suddenly Salty was upon us, all pink and shiny in the face. "Father," he hissed excitedly, "do you have a psalm or a prayer you can lend me quickly? I took your advice, Father, and I think I'm in with a chance!"

Surreptitiously he indicated Mrs. Guthridge, who sat on the bench near the door, nodding her head in time with the music.

"Oh. Well. Let me think," responded John Beck. "Was there any particular theme you had in mind?"

"No, Father. Just something of a biblical nature."

"How about this?" John Beck suggested. *"Oh ye Whales and all that move in the water, bless ye the Lord and praise Him forever."*

"That's perfect, Father!" cried Salty delightedly. "How does it go again?"

"Oh ye Whales—"

"Oh ye Whales," repeated Salty, his face a study of concentration.

"And all that move in the water—"

"Would that not be more effective if I was to say 'swim' in the water, Father?"

"Well, yes, possibly, if you wish."

"Not saying I can improve on the Bible, Father. It just rolls off the tongue better, is all. Go on."

"Bless ye the Lord and praise Him forever."

"That's it?"

"Well, it goes on about Fowls of the Air and the Beasts and the Cattle and so forth."

"No, no. I can't be bothered with Fowls of the Air, nor the Beasts and the Cattle. Let them look after themselves. It's only the Whales I am interested in."

"Well, then, there you have it."

"Thank you, Father," beamed Salty. "It will do very nicely."

"Good luck!"

"Yes, Father. And good luck to you also." This last delivered with a broad wink, and a nod towards me. And with that, the self-proclaimed Professor of Whales hurried back to Mrs. Guthridge.

"Sorry about that," said John Beck, after a moment, turning back to me.

"That's all right," I replied. "But what did Salty mean exactly when he said he had taken your advice?"

"Oh, I don't know," he responded, somewhat sheepishly. "But for whatever reason, he appears to be pretending to be a Methodist minister."

"Good heavens! Him too?" I riposted. "It is practically an epidemic."

At which he threw back his head and laughed. And leaning in towards me, he then suggested in a low voice that perhaps it would not be a bad idea to step outside and take some air, to which I agreed that yes, it was really quite stuffy in the hall. Prizing Violet off my lap, I followed him out. And there ensued a short stroll in the moonlight, the details of which I shall keep entirely to myself, except to say there was no further talk of washing up; in fact, not much in the way of talking at all.

When to Marry

Marry when the year is new
Always loving, kind and true

When February birds do mate
You may wed, nor dread your fate

If you wed when March winds blow
Joy and sorrow both you'll know

Marry in April when you can
Joy for maiden and for man

Marry in the month of May
You will surely rue the day

Marry when June roses grow
Over land and sea you'll go

Those who in July do wed
Must labour always for their bread

Whoever wed in August be
Many a change are sure to see

Marry in September's shine
Your living will be rich and fine

If in October you do marry
Love will come, but riches tarry

If you are wed in bleak November
Only joy will come, remember

When December's snows fall fast,
Marry and true love will last!

(You will have to reverse the lines to make them appropriate to
our own seasons.)

EDEN OBSERVER AND SOUTH COAST ADVOCATE
25 AUGUST 1905

If, When Washing Dishes

OMETIME IN THE SMALL HOURS OF THE NEXT NIGHT—THAT is, the night after the Plain and Fancy Dress Ball— and as foretold somewhat obliquely by the blue and white teacup left unwashed—Darcy and Louisa ran away to be married. I awoke suddenly that morning to find Louisa's side of the bed cold and empty; immediately a sense of unease overtook me. Hastily I dressed, and as I hurried into the kitchen, I saw my father standing there with a note in his hands. His face was drained of all its color and, without speaking, he thrust the note at me to read.

Dear Dad,

Darcy and I are to be married. We love each other and wish to be together. DO NOT TRY TO FIND US OR KEEP US

APART, I MEAN IT. Do not worry as we have some money and will be all right.

Your loving daughter,
Louisa

"I can scarcely believe it!" I cried, and even as I did so, I was horrified at the falseness ringing out in my voice. My father looked up at me, and for a moment I feared he had detected the falseness also.

"Did you know about this?" he asked. I could barely stand to look at him, for his face was haggard with shock.

"No, I did not," I responded. My father's grief was bad enough without having to admit to my own foreknowledge.

"Go and wake your brothers," he said, turning away from me.

When the boys were woken, my father sent Dan to rouse the whalers, for his plan was to immediately send out a search party. But here Harry had a very strange response, for he refused to participate.

"She says in her note not to try to find her," he said, and he went very red in the face because defiance of this kind did not come easily to him.

"Are you not concerned for her safety and wellbeing?" demanded my father.

"She has Darcy," said Harry. "Darcy will look after her."

"Yes, but who will look after Darcy?" said Annie. (A curious thing happened upon Louisa's departure whereby Annie, just turned eleven years of age, dispensed with all the Whinny and horse-nonsense of her girlhood, and instead assumed Louisa's place as the smart mouth in the family. In some ways, this proved a comfort to my father, although in other ways was an annoyance.)

"Anyway, you are joining the search party, and that is the end of the matter," said my father.

By this time, the whale men were all getting up, and there was much shouting and commotion and coming and going. My father went outside to speak to Darcy's father, Percy, who seemed very shocked and upset and kept shaking his head and wiping away tears with the back of his hand; others joined them and an earnest discussion ensued about the best way in which to tackle the search. I realized at this point that I could better assist matters by getting the stove lit quick-smart and putting the kettle on, and so I was busying myself with this task when I suddenly turned to see John Beck standing in the doorway of our kitchen. He looked somewhat bleary-eyed, as if he had just woken up, and he was gazing at my father apprehensively.

"You wanted to speak to me?" he asked.

"Yes. What do you know about this business?" said my father.

He passed Louisa's note to John Beck, who read it in silence before passing it back to my father.

"I don't know much," he said. "I'm sorry."

"I saw you talking to Darcy outside at the ball," said my father. "That's why I ask."

My heart started, for of course I realized he must be referring to the exchange in the shadows under the mulberry trees that I had myself witnessed. Perhaps it surprised John Beck too, for it took him a moment to answer.

"Well, it's true, sir. Darcy did tell me he was going to get married," he said. "But he did not say who to."

"He told you he was going to get married?"

"He asked me if I might officiate. But I told him I could not, on account of my not being a proper Methodist minister."

My father stared at him. "Did you ask him who he was marrying?"

"No, I didn't. But I never suspected it was your daughter, sir. That's the honest truth. I never suspected for a moment."

I had my back turned through most of this exchange, for I was now busily occupying myself with the making of damper, so I am not sure exactly what then transpired except it all went very quiet and when I turned around next, I saw that John Beck had in fact left the room. My father stood staring down at Louisa's note, and then a moment later he departed also, without a word, to join the search party.

The runaways had planned their escape with some thoroughness. Darcy had his small portion of the profits of the whaling season (not a very large amount, as can be imagined after such a season), and Louisa had her gold sovereign for winning Best-dressed and Most Prepossessing at the Eden Show. As well—I discovered after taking inventory of our supplies—they had taken half a loaf of bread, a box of matches, a portion of salted beef and some tea. As far as I could judge, however, they had not thought to take any sugar, and this grieved me more than anything, for Louisa had a sweet tooth and needed plenty of sugar in her tea. Dan went so far as to leave a small bowl of sugar on a tree stump at the very top of our property in the hope that they might venture back for it, but of course it just became infested with ants.

In spite of the best efforts of the search parties, it seems probable that the pair of them may have hidden out in the bush for several days before boarding the S.S. *Merimbula* and traveling as far as Sydney. Louisa may have disguised herself by wearing my mother's hat with the veil netting (hence her reluctance to use the veil as a trimming on her dress) and stuffing her other clothes under her coat so as to resemble a stouter person. A "Miss Nicholson" was recorded in the steamer's log as purchasing a single ticket to Sydney; further, a crew member reports seeing a "stout lady" in a coat and veiled hat sitting on deck, a sight that struck him as unusual owing to the heat of the day. He also stated that he thought he saw this woman disembark at Tathra, but he could not be sure. He only wished to state that he felt like he might have seen the "stout lady" walking up towards the township from Tathra wharf in the company of a young Aboriginal boy who he considered to be about fourteen years of age. This was odd, because Darcy did not look like he was fourteen; he was a tall boy who looked his age, which was eighteen. Also, why would "Miss Nicholson" go to the expense of purchasing a ticket all the way to Sydney only to disembark at Tathra? It made no sense. Years later, when the S.S. *Merimbula* ran aground off Bermagui, this same crew member was found to have been drinking below deck in the company of several women, so it is doubtful whether his story can be entirely relied upon.

Late on the morning of their disappearance, while most of the men were out combing the surrounding bushland in

search of them, I stepped outside the kitchen and to my surprise saw John Beck standing there beneath the jacaranda tree.
It appeared that he may have been preparing himself in some
way, for he seemed startled, as if he was not quite yet ready for
our encounter.

"Good morning," I said, for in truth I was startled also. He
stood in exactly the same position as had the old gray kangaroo who had regarded me so contemptuously on the morning
of my mother's death. It was odd that I should think of this at
that moment, but I did.

"Yes, good morning," he responded.

"Are you off then with the others to go searching?"

"Yes, I believe we are shortly rowing into Eden." At this,
he turned his head suddenly, and again I was reminded of that
old gray kangaroo. But it seemed he was simply checking to
see that no one else was in earshot.

"I shouldn't worry," he said quietly. "If I were you."

"Why not?" I responded, for it seemed such an odd thing to
say, given the circumstances. As far as I could see, there were a
great many things to worry about, whichever way you viewed
the situation.

"It will be all right," he said. "I feel sure." And he gave a
small nod of his head, as if to reassure us both.

I stared at him. A flower, a small violet trumpet, drifted
down between us from the jacaranda tree and, looking down,
I saw that fallen flowers surrounded us where we stood. He
looked down too. The flower had landed on his boot—he
moved his foot impatiently, as if this was the last thing he
needed at the present time, a flower on his boot, and then suddenly he spoke.

"Mary, I had been going to ask your father something, but now I find I cannot."

"Why not?" I asked, for a strange constriction had gripped my heart.

"Circumstances have arisen," he said. "And so…"

"And so?"

"And so…"

We stood there for a moment, the two of us. Then he took my hand and he kissed it, and it seemed for a brief instant that he might be about to say something else. But he must have thought better of the idea, for instead he simply tipped his cap. He turned and headed off down the hill—and that is the last time I ever saw him, with Mr. Maudry going after him, wings extended, shrieking shrilly.

A Letter from Louisa

SOME EIGHTEEN MONTHS AFTER SHE'D RUN AWAY WITH Darcy, a letter turned up from Louisa, quite out of the blue, addressed to me:

Dear Mary,

I believe there is a story going about that Darcy and I were never legally married. Will you kindly inform those that seek to spread this muck that we were married by the Reverend John Beck (Methodist), and I have the documents to prove it, which I would be pleased to show anybody upon request. Certain people should spend more time minding their own business and looking after their own affairs than seeking to spread lies about others. I hope this letter finds you all in good health. We are exceedingly well and the parents of a fine fat boy (Albert George) expecting another any day now.

With fondest wishes to all, especially Dad,

Louisa
    P.S. We have our own dog now, a cattle dog named Jack he is 100 times smarter than Bonnie or Patch.

This was the first that we had heard from Louisa since their departure, and it is not untypical of her that she found the space within this brief missive to brag that her new dog was smarter than our own dogs. For some reason, miss her as I did, this boast infuriated me. What did I care about her smart dog? Perhaps Bonnie and Patch were not so very clever, but nor had we ever claimed them to be; still, they were nice enough dogs in their own way, and companionable to a fault. I felt the urge to write back immediately and ask if this Jack could sing along with "Onward Christian Soldiers," but remembering Darcy's skills on the gumleaf, the chances were that Jack could sing along, and in harmony. Besides which, Louisa had not thought to supply a return address.

The envelope, however, was postmarked Coonabarabran. It arrived in early July 1910, right at the commencement of what looked to be a promising whaling season; a pair of good-sized humpbacks had been captured right off the bat. While many (myself included) felt that my father should "drop everything" and travel directly to Coonabarabran to bring her home, he did not. I urged him to at least write to the police sergeant stationed there and beg him to make inquiries as to her whereabouts and wellbeing. Here also my father demurred, and although he said nothing of it to me at the time, I have since come to believe that perhaps he was concerned about the possible ramifications for Darcy if he did so. My father had been fond of Darcy, and although understandably distressed by this liaison, he did not like to hear Darcy referred to disparagingly by others. I remember one visitor, in the weeks following their departure, telling my father he must not blame himself. "You must remember," said this visitor, "that these people are several rungs below Paleolithic man in the ladder of civilization. It is a wonder to me that they were able to invent the boomerang." My father got up at once and left the room, and did not return until this visitor had left.

Instead, my father wrote to a gentleman of Mrs. Pike's acquaintance who lived on a property near Coonabarabran and asked that he make inquiries on his behalf. The gentleman responded that he had conducted discreet investigations around the township, but had learned nothing of any white woman living with an Aboriginal man in the area. However, he continued, it was possible that they were living out at the Aboriginal mission at Forky Mountain; he would make inquiries forthwith. A short while later, the gentleman wrote to say that he had visited the mission, and there had been told of a white woman living "as a lubra" with an Aboriginal man and two half-caste babies; it seems they may have camped there briefly before moving on in search of work. By all accounts, the woman appeared to be in good health, although one of the babies was colicky.

"What will we do?" I asked my father, upon reading this letter.

"Well, there is not much we can do," he responded. "She has made her own bed, let her lie in it."

I cannot adequately describe how dismayed I felt, how sick at heart, to hear this from my father. I wanted more than anything that he go and find her and bring her and her babies home as soon as possible, for I would happily help care for all of them. The thought of Louisa struggling in camp with those two small babies filled me with a gnawing anxiety. How on earth did she manage? My own sister, who would never willingly lift a broom or wipe a dish and had no time whatsoever for small children, how was she surviving out there? Did her love for Darcy make all these hardships endurable? *She has made her own bed, let her lie in it.*

But now I wonder if perhaps my father was right to leave her be, for what point was there in dragging her away from her husband, no matter how reduced their circumstances? This was Louisa, after all, who could never be induced to do anything against her will; she would not come easily, we all knew, and my father had a horror of any kind of shouting or unpleasantness. Looking back, I wonder if my father was not in fact a little scared of Louisa. Well, why not? I suppose we all were. She had a sharp tongue and a very forceful personality.

And certainly, when I went back to reread her letter, she did not sound as if she was struggling, what with her "fine fat boy" and her smart dog Jack. In fact, the more I thought about it, the more it seemed to me that she was feeling sufficiently like her usual self to stir up some trouble for me. For in stating that John Beck had married them, without parental consent and without the requisite publication of the banns, she was making a very serious allegation; in fact, it was tantamount to accusing him of a criminal offense. And yet for all she knew, given her knowledge of my feelings for him and his attentions towards me at the ball (which did not pass unnoticed by many), I could very well have been married to John Beck by this time. Looking back at our friendship, I do not think I imagined the fact that he had grown fond of me. I may as well admit that since my discovery of his sermon notes, I had begun privately to entertain the possibility that he might ask me to marry him. Furthermore, I know that my father considered it practically a certainty. In fact, he informed me sometime later that, on the occasion of the ball, several of the whalers were wagering even money that John Beck would ask my father for my hand that very evening. Hence, in making these allegations, Louisa must have reasoned that she might be causing a person *who might well be my husband* (but was not) an enormous amount of embarrassment and difficulty. And yet this was so typical of Louisa: although apparently content with her own domestic situation, she wished to set the proverbial cat amongst the pigeons for me.

"Well, at least one thing is clear," my father said. "I was a fool to believe a word the Reverend said. That man couldn't lie straight in bed."

It was distressing to hear my father say this of the man I had nurtured such feelings for, but perhaps it was also understandable. I need to explain, of course, that by the time we received Louisa's letter, John Beck had long since disappeared. Shortly after that last exchange we had shared under the jacaranda tree, he and Harry had rowed over to Eden with instructions to conduct further investigations in town. When John Beck did not return the following day, I learned from my brother that they had met a gentleman in the front bar at the Great Southern Hotel who, upon hearing that they were whale men, had bought them a drink in tribute to their courage. He then offered to give them a ride out to the gold diggings at Yambulla with the idea of pooling their money and trying their luck out there. This gentleman had made a great impression on Harry, for he wore a snakeskin band upon his hat and his boots were made of iguana, and while Harry had had to decline on account of the fact that they were searching for Darcy and Louisa (although I do not know why they were searching for Darcy and Louisa in the front bar at the Great Southern), John Beck had decided to take the gentleman up on it.

Of course, everyone knew that the goldfields at Yambulla were practically worked out, so although I was surprised and disappointed at his sudden disappearance, I comforted myself with the thought that he would not be gone for long. I even imagined that he might be attempting to "strike it lucky" in a bid to improve his situation and better provide for me. And although the weeks turned into months, summer turned to spring and spring to autumn, I continued to hope that he would come strolling up the path again, whale bones crunching underfoot, just as soon as the whaling season came around again. But he didn't.

When the whaling season of 1909 passed by and there was still no word of John Beck, my thoughts grew darker. I began to entertain the hope that he may have fallen down a mineshaft and died of his injuries or perhaps inadvertently blown himself up with a stick of dynamite or become entangled in the crushing wheel and pulverized, for such were the only possible explanations I could bear for the fact that he had utterly deserted me. I scoured old newspapers dating back to the time of his departure for reports of calamities. I questioned anybody I met who had been to the area, but no one had ever seen or heard of him. After a while, feeling foolish, I stopped asking.

Did his sudden departure, so soon after that of Darcy and Louisa, add weight to her charge that he had assisted in their elopement? Certainly my father thought so. My own natural inclination was to believe that in denying knowledge of their elopement, John Beck had given a truthful account to my father, and thus I argued in his defense that Louisa had simply invented the story as a way of saving face. (What contact did she have with Edenites, I wonder, to learn of this supposed gossip concerning her marital status? I myself had not been privy to any such talk, but perhaps I was excluded owing to the fact that I was her sister. Certainly I was familiar with the abrupt cessation of conversation whenever I walked into a shop; the glancing over shoulders, the whispering behind hands. Nonetheless, my general impression was that the question of whether or not Darcy and Louisa were legally wed paled into insignificance when compared to the larger scandal of her running away with a blackfellow.)

Besides, I argued to my father, when would this supposed marriage have taken place? Somewhere in the darkness outside the School of Arts on the night of the ball? That seemed preposterous; also, the note that she had left in the kitchen indicated that they were "to be married," not already married. This leaves us with the unlikely scenario that they had somehow met up in Yambulla, whereupon John Beck had seized the opportunity to preside over their nuptials. It is all simply implausible, or so I argued to my father. But since that time, I have grown gradually less certain. For I began to think about the dates.

Checking the envelope of Louisa's letter from Coonabarabran, I saw that it was postmarked June 1910. She and Darcy absconded sometime on the night of 22 November 1908. In her letter, she writes of having a son, and expecting her second child "any day now." It takes only the most rudimentary arithmetic to work out that Louisa was expecting Darcy's child when they absconded; in truth, I imagine the knowledge of her condition is what compelled them to run away in the first place. I can also see how, in desperation, Darcy might have confided in John Beck under the mulberry trees outside the School of Arts, and begged him to marry them so that the child might at least not be born out of wedlock. Clearly plagued with misgivings (for had I not witnessed him shaking his head amidst Darcy's pleadings?), John Beck may nonetheless have seen that he could not well refuse. The horse had already bolted, as it were; confronted with this, he may have felt it his duty, as a decent man and a Christian, if not as an actual Methodist minister, to ensure that at the very least their child was born within the holy ties of matrimony.

As I say, I cannot be certain; I merely see that it is possible now, whereas at the time I could not. In some ways, accepting Louisa's version of events makes his abrupt departure less painful to me, for I can see how he may have feared that his role in events would eventually be revealed, as indeed it was. No doubt the consequences for him—had he stayed to suffer them—would have been calamitous. Thus the unhappy chain of circumstances combined in such a way as to render it impossible for him to stay, even in spite of his evident feelings for me. In seeking happiness with her true love, my sister— who can say? perhaps inadvertently—deprived me of my chance of the same.

Our Aboriginal whale men had a strange story about green frog mussings. I never understood it completely, but they said that if you powdered up a green frog, then put it in a handkerchief and waved the handkerchief around with the "mussings," people would go all funny. If you liked a woman and you waved the mussings, then she would follow you and never leave you. They said it was possible to get any woman you wanted if you had these mussings. The woman would never even realize she'd been mussinged.

There were murmurings at the time that maybe Darcy had used the green frog mussings on Louisa, but I did not believe this. Those two had liked each other since childhood; it was plain enough to see. But particularly as the years went by, I did sometimes feel as if I had been mussinged by John Beck.

The Silverware in Situ

A FEW WEEKS AFTER THE DEPARTURE OF LOUISA AND Darcy and John Beck, Dan and I were in the kitchen cutting up plums for jam when I heard the first distant "Hell-o-o thar!" of Mr. Crowther's approach. We looked at each other very sadly, for of course this made us think of the handsome Sphinx which sat silently in the front room.

"Perhaps we should hide the plums, or he will eat them all," said Dan, which we proceeded to do. On this occasion at least, I had no need to rustle up any cakes for Mr. Crowther, as Louisa's elopement had brought on a flurry of visitors anxious for more details, each of them bearing fruitcake. I suppose due to its somber, substantial nature and the fact that it keeps indefinitely, fruitcake was considered the appropriate offering. And yet none of us liked it much. We were much more in need of something really delicious to lift our mood— a good sponge with whipped cream and strawberries, or a

chocolate cake. But perhaps that would have seemed too festive, even frivolous, given the circumstances.

My father heard Mr. Crowther too, and he came into the
kitchen and emptied his money pouch onto the table. He
counted out fourteen shillings and threepence, and passed the
coins to me.

"Here is our installment," he said. "Tell Mr. Crowther that
I have gone into Eden. And don't mention the business with
Louisa."

"But maybe we should mention it," I said. "After all, he
travels all over the district. He might keep a lookout for us.
Perhaps he may even have heard something."

"He is a gossip," said my father. "That is why he is coming
here in the first place. Normally he would not be expected till
the New Year."

And with that, he headed off to hide out down in the try-
works, leaving us to slice the fruitcake and open the gate for
Mr. Crowther.

It was Mr. Crowther himself who brought up the subject of
Louisa and Darcy, within minutes of settling himself down to
his afternoon tea and asking us once again if we did not consider
the Wunderlich ceilings to be at once durable and fire-resistant,
and yet stylish and attractive. He accepted the installment of
fourteen shillings threepence with a slight raise of his eyebrows, and as he wrote out the receipt he remarked that he had
wondered if we would continue to pay off the Singer's installments, seeing as how Louisa could have no further use for it.

"No further use for it?" I cried. "What do you mean?"

"Well, forgive me for mentioning it, but did she not run
away with one of the blackfellows?"

I suppose it gives some indication of the efficacy of our self-protective armor that in a bad situation such as this, where something is changed irrevocably, some small part within us keeps desperately hoping that things are not truly as they as seem, and in fact will very soon be restored to order. Although I knew the reality to be otherwise, this small deluded part of me continued to blithely hope, perhaps even *expect,* that Louisa would shortly return and conduct her life exactly as before, scowling and avoiding the dishes and doing battle with the Sphinx in the front room. It was not until Mr. Crowther expressed Louisa's departure in terms of "having no further use for the Singer" that this small hopeful voice within me seemed to finally comprehend the reality of her being gone. It was as if he had slapped me hard across the face. I began to cry and found myself unable to speak for several minutes. Dan stood awkwardly by my side, patting me on the shoulder.

Of course, Mr. Crowther was aghast that he had reduced me to tears in this fashion. He leapt up at once and volunteered to give the Singer a look-over and a touch of oil, and then he disappeared into the front room until he considered it would be safe to return. Whereupon he informed us that the Sphinx seemed to be in excellent working order; and that with Christmas upon us, he had much to do and regrettably must be on his way. I was so delighted to hear this that I wrapped up a slab of fruitcake and pressed it upon him, and then I accompanied him to his sulky.

"Mr. Crowther," I said, as he climbed up to the driver's seat, "if you hear of any news of Louisa in your travels, we would be most grateful if you could let us know."

"Of course, of course. I will keep my ear to the ground," said Mr. Crowther. "You may be sure of that."

"By the way," he said, as he picked up the reins, "what became of that Methodist minister fellow you had here?"

"Oh, do you mean John Beck?" I responded, happy to have a reason to say his name aloud. "I believe he may be currently working a small lease at Yambulla."

"Yambulla? Is that so?" he said, and a slight smile spread across his face. "As it happens, I am headed in that direction."

"Will you please pass on my best to him, if you do see him?" I said.

"Pass on your best? Well, I suppose I could," he said. "After I have notified the relevant authorities."

"What do you mean?"

"I believe him to be an imposter, with a string of prior convictions, including larceny and attempted murder. If he left you with any of your silver, then you can consider yourself very fortunate."

I stood there and stared at him, my mouth gaping open. He tipped his cap and urged his horse to move; the sulky rattled out the gate. I closed the gate behind him, and stood there waving till the sulky had disappeared around the curve in the road; then I turned and ran full pelt back inside, straight into the front room. The only silver we possessed was a cruet set, some napkin holders and a soup ladle, which were kept in the top drawer of the old bureau. It was a sticky old drawer and required a certain technique to pull it open; nonetheless, using brute force, I managed. There was our silverware, in situ and in need of a polish, just as I knew it would be. Mr. Crowther had been wrong about John Beck.

The Rawleigh's Ointment Man

FOR THE PAST FIVE YEARS, SINCE MY FATHER DIED, I HAVE
been living in the suburb of Ryde with my younger
sister Vi (Violet), her husband Jim, and their three
children, Margaret, Lionel and George. It is not an especially
large house, but I have the back room, a covered-in veranda,
and I find it quite suitable for my needs. Certainly it is a thor-
oughfare, as it leads to the backyard and the WC; also the
laundry. However, I find that by hanging a thick curtain,
which can be drawn or left open, I can retain a sense of privacy
when required.

Further, the house is situated two streets from the
Methodist church, with which I am now quite involved. I am
a member of both the choir and the Ladies' Guild, and for
two years now I have served as secretary of our branch of
the Methodist Women's Fellowship, in which capacity I have
taught myself to type. At one point, I was considering perhaps even becoming involved in missionary work, inspired

by the great work of a visiting missionary, Reverend Loftus,
amongst the Aborigines near Alice Springs. (What a great
shame there are no whales in Alice Springs, for the Aboriginal people are such excellent whalers.) Ultimately, however,
he discouraged me, citing that it was no place really for a
woman, and that perhaps I was doing more useful work here
with my coconut tartlets (this said with a smile), of which he
was a great admirer. A pity, as I should very much like to
have seen Ayers Rock. Nonetheless, he was correct in suggesting that we perform our share of good work here on the
home front. In fact, I was earlier typing up a list of our activities for our annual meeting (Mrs. Lunn, our president,
would have me type up the Old Testament if she could, and
then mimeo a hundred copies—she feels it somehow impera-
tive that I be "kept busy" with these innumerable petty tasks
she dreams up for me). Anyway, I shall copy it out here, for
it offers an interesting indication of the breadth of our activities:

M.W.F. (Ryde Branch)—Annual Report of Pastoral
Activities—1938

77 visits to the sick
109 trays of food distributed
26 bouquets
63 visits to shut-ins
48 letters and cards sent
250 garments repaired and sent to Aboriginal Mission (N.T.)
and Foreign Mission (East Bengal)
£35 raised for the Church Building Fund through various teas

and socials etc., which went a long way towards assisting in
the much-needed recent addition of the WC.

Our minister, the Reverend Davis, is somewhat elderly and his sermons rather dry; however, he is shortly to retire, and we are promised that his replacement is to be a good deal younger and known for his "great sense of humor." I confess to looking forward to the change; occasionally Reverend Davis will attempt a humorous quip to enliven proceedings, but mostly he abstains from much in the way of frivolity. He is certainly not the type to roll up his sleeves and show me his arm muscles, nor do I imagine him to be proficient at cards; still, I suppose these are hardly prerequisites for the position.

Vi and Jim run a small printing business which keeps them quite busy, so I have been able to make myself useful by looking after the children whilst they are at work (although admittedly the children are getting older now and don't require much looking after; in fact, Margaret is nineteen and engaged to be married). I would gladly cook for the family except Jim is finicky about food and prefers that Vi do most of the cooking: I sometimes joke with him that he is as bad as the whalers as regards his digestive intolerances. Still, I make a lot of cakes and slices, which keep the boys content, especially after school when they are always ravenous.

I am very fond of all the children, and I like to think they are fond of me; we rub along together reasonably well. The youngest, George, takes a great deal after his late uncle Dan; he is only twelve years old and yet he has taken up smoking! As we are often home alone together after school, it is a secret we keep from his parents: at times, I have even found myself procuring his tobacco. Of all the grandchildren, he is the one most interested in whaling, and I suppose it is particularly for George that I set out to write this memoir. When he was a few years younger, he would insist that I tell him whaling stories at bedtime, particularly those that involved the heroic antics of Tom and his chums. "What did Tom do then?" he would always ask at the end of the story, with the whale dead and the Killer whales leaping out of the water triumphantly. "Well, then Tom was feeling very sleepy, and so he took himself off to Blanket Bay," I would reply. "Goodnight."

I often think it a great pity that George cannot bend to the oars and chase down a whale himself, as have the generations of Davidson men before him. I feel similarly about Lionel, who at fifteen is worrying his mother by knocking about with a crowd of local lads who consider themselves hoodlums. There has been some drinking and some broken windows; once a policeman brought him home after he had been caught trying to break into the local bowling club. Vi is very hard on him, understandably, yet I find myself saying to her: "What do you expect? He is a Davidson! He should be out whaling." To which she replies, especially if Jim is present: "He is not a Davidson, he is a McGynty." Yet I know deep down she agrees with me. There was something about whaling that straightened a boy out. ·

Telling George these stories and having to go back to the scrapbooks to refresh my memory set me to thinking about writing some of these stories down in more detail, particularly now that I have a typewriter. Jim has even suggested he may print up several copies, so that various members of the family might have one; that is, he always goes on to say with a smile and a roll of his eyes, if I ever finish it. And so almost every morning during the working week, if I have had no other activities involving the church, I have set up my typewriter on the kitchen table, and typed up my recollections to the very best of my ability. Dusty, our house cat, keeps me company, sitting at the back door making small squeaking noises at a pair of mynah birds who visit each day to steal the remains of her cat food. Occasionally she will sit beside me as I type and stare disapprovingly at my work, but as she is not really allowed on the kitchen table, I only tolerate this in small doses. She was sitting here a moment ago, but now she has become bored and jumped down to go and wash herself in the afternoon sunshine spilling through the back door.

The process of writing has brought back a great many memories, and although many of them have been painful, it has nonetheless been a rewarding experience to go back and live for a few hours each day in that particular year of my life. Reading it through, I see that I have gone on about John Beck rather more than I intended, and certainly I will remove those chapters before I allow anyone else to peruse it. After all, it is simply meant to be an account of one particular whaling season, concerning itself mostly with the trials of whaling and the antics of the Killer whales, perhaps lightly touching on some of the characters of the time. I find these days when I tell new acquaintances that my father was a whaler, many of them respond in a horrified fashion, and that is before I even go into the details, and so now I am inclined to keep mum on the subject altogether. I'm sure some members of the congregation would be astounded to learn that Miss Davidson with the gray frizz in the second row of the choir once fired a whale gun at a Killer whale! (And missed, I am relieved to say.)

Quite recently—only a few months ago, in fact—as I sat typing in the kitchen, there came a knock at the front door. I opened the door to find a nice-looking young man in his early thirties, swarthy in complexion. Hung from his neck was an open display case which contained an array of salves and ointments. "Excuse me for bothering you," he said, "but I wonder if I could interest you in some Rawleigh's ointment today. We're also pleased to announce a new product, Rawleigh's Ready Relief, containing eucalyptus oil. You'll find it beneficial for a variety of conditions, suitable for man or beast."

In fact, we already had an ancient container of Rawleigh's ointment in the bathroom cupboard which Vi used on George's chest whenever he had catarrh; nonetheless, mention of the Ready Relief, suitable for man or beast, piqued my interest. Dusty had at the time a rather large and unsightly abscess on her face from brawling with our neighbor's tabby, and I wondered aloud if this might help her. He listened with interest as I described her condition, and then he inquired if he might have a look at her; "that is, if she is up to receiving visitors."

There was something about this young man and his ready smile to which I responded, and so I led him into the kitchen where Dusty lay on the towel I had put down for her in front of the stove, quite wan and miserable and out of sorts. Squatting down, he held out his hand to her. She sniffed it gingerly and then, to my great surprise, stood up, arched her back and commenced to rub against him. Dusty is a stand-offish cat by nature, with little time for anyone except those that feed her, so this display of excessive friendliness was most unusual. She purred and rubbed against his leg and threw herself onto her back and waved her legs in the air; all the while he told her what a fine-looking cat she was and gently admonished her for getting into scrapes. Finally he picked her up and examined her swollen face.

"If you would permit me," he said to me, "I'd like to try some Ready Relief on it. I've found it works on Mum's cats, although they don't enjoy it much."

"All right," I said.

Removing his jacket and rolling up his shirtsleeves, he asked me for a clean rag soaked in hot water from the kettle, to which he applied a small amount of Ready Relief. With Dusty purring in his arms, he then pressed the rag gently against the swollen area of her face. She stiffened but did not immediately struggle, and after a moment or two, he began gently to massage it.

This caused her some discomfort and so she began to struggle and scratch and loudly protest, but nonetheless he continued to massage, talking to her soothingly all the while. A foul-smelling pus commenced to seep from her face and she began to settle a little, as if sensing he was trying to make her better. He asked me for another rag soaked in hot water to which he applied more Ready Relief, and continued to bathe the area until he had it quite clean. Finally he permitted her to escape, whereupon she shot out the back door like a bat out of the gates of hell. When I looked at him, I saw to my horror that his forearms were covered in scratches and some of the pus had found its way onto his shirt. I directed him to the bathroom so that he might sponge his shirt under the tap, and when he emerged he bathed his scratches with the Ready Relief.

"They will be healed in no time," he said with a smile.

Seeing as how he had gone to such trouble for Dusty, I felt the least I could do was purchase a bottle of Ready Relief. He accepted my coins, recommending that I use it to bathe Dusty's abscess twice daily for the next day or so, to which I nodded my head in agreement even though I knew privately that Dusty would never permit me to do such a thing, and then he pulled out his receipt book.

"What name should I make it out to?" he inquired.

"Mary Davidson," I responded.

"Mrs.?"

"Miss."

"Davidson," he murmured, as he wrote out the receipt. "Not one of the Davidsons of Eden, by any chance?"

"Yes, as a matter of fact," I replied.

"Well, that's a coincidence," he said, looking up at me. And even before he said it, I seemed to know exactly what he was about to say: "My mother is a Davidson."

"What's her name?" I asked.

"Louisa."

And that is the funny story of how Louisa came back into our lives again.

Or, I should say, it is the funny story of how Louisa has *almost* come back into our lives, for she is not quite back yet, although we are working on it. For it seems that her characteristic stubbornness and pride may have only exacerbated over time, and she is proving somewhat resistant to being pulled back into the familial embrace.

In the thirty intervening years, we have had no contact with Louisa, nor had we any idea where she lived; our last communication was the letter from Coonabarabran. When my father died, I had hoped that she might somehow learn of it, for notice of his passing had appeared in many newspapers. As I sat in the front pew, I kept straining around to peer at the front entrance, willing her to materialize. But she did not come. I can only imagine that the thought of being amidst the gossipmongers of Eden, even for my father's funeral, was simply too much for her to bear. And yet now, suddenly and unexpectedly, here was her eldest son Albert, standing in the kitchen before me.

"She is my sister," I cried. "I am your aunty!"

And at once I embraced him. For suddenly I so clearly saw the resemblance that I wondered how I could have not been struck by it the instant I opened the door! He was tall with dark curls like Darcy (although his skin color was considerably lighter), and yet something about his droll, half-scornful smile as he endured the kisses that I planted on his cheeks was for me the very essence of Louisa.

Of course, immediately I begged him to sit down and stay for lunch, and to fill me in on his mother and father and brothers and sisters, and indeed his own wife and children, should he have any. But the young man—up to that point so friendly and open, and I would say even delighted to have discovered the family connection—grew suddenly wary. He seemed anxious not to stay long, insisting that he had a large area to cover that day and his boss would not be happy if he dallied. However, he stayed for one cup of tea, and in that short space of time, this is the information that I managed to glean from him:

That he has two brothers and two sisters, though not all of them are "still around." I do not know what he meant by that; whether he simply meant that they might be living elsewhere, perhaps interstate. His youngest sister Marian (or Maryanne?) is unmarried and lives with Louisa.

That his father Darcy died some years ago. The circumstances of his death Albert did not make clear to me, but I gathered that it might have been from injuries resulting from a fight of some description, for there was an inquest and he mentioned witnesses, or a witness who had failed to show. But he seemed very sad about it all, and I did not like to add to his unhappiness by pressing him for details.

That prior to Darcy's death, the family had been living in Queensland, "near the border."

That since Darcy's death, Louisa had moved to Sydney and was living in Surry Hills. She makes her living as a seamstress in a garment factory, and does some additional piecework on the side, if she can get it. She has been unwell recently with some problem relating to her womb, but seems to be on the mend now. "She's a tough old lady, that one," said Albert admiringly.

That Albert himself was married, with four children of his own, the youngest a baby.

At around this point, Albert got up and said that he really needed to get going or he would get a walloping, so I took a piece of paper and hurriedly wrote a note for him to give to his mother. Of course, I had no time to make a copy, but I believe it was something along the lines of the following:

Dear Louisa,

I am so happy to have met your son, Albert, and to hear news of you! I am now living in Ryde, with Violet and family. Anne still lives in Eden, married to a Strickland! We all miss you very much. Please come and visit us soon.

Your loving sister,
Mary

I pressed the note upon Albert with instructions to pass it on to Louisa. I walked him to the door and made him promise to visit again soon, and next time to bring his mother with him. Just as he was turning to leave, a sudden thought occurred to me.

"Just one more minute," I implored. "I need to show you something quickly."

And taking him by the arm, I ushered him back through the house to my small alcove. And there, removing some small ornaments I had on top of it, I lifted the wooden cover to reveal the Sphinx.

"This belongs to your mother," I said. "We have kept it for her. Tell her it is all paid off now. Tell her it is hers whenever she wants it."

He stared at the Sphinx uncomprehendingly.

"She has a machine," he said simply.

"Yes," I cried. "But this is the Sphinx! Tell her it is the Sphinx. That we still have the Sphinx."

"All right," he said, but I don't know if he understood the significance.

When Vi returned home that evening, I rushed to the door and told her the news; we hugged each other in our excitement, and shed tears at the prospect of reuniting with our sister. But as I say, this was some months ago now, and we have heard nothing further of either Albert or Louisa. We have stayed in every weekend, even though we usually like to go to the pictures, for fear of missing her if we should venture out. Every Saturday morning, I bake a cake in expectation, and even as I put it into the oven, I have to caution myself not to allow my hopes to rise along with the mixture. Louisa was very partial to cake—any sort, it didn't matter.

"Perhaps it is difficult for her to get out here," said Vi one afternoon as we sat in the lounge room, looking hopefully out the front window to the street. It was, after all, a long bus trip from town, possibly even warranting a complicated changeover.

"It is a shame that you didn't think to get her address," Vi continued, and indeed I regret this bitterly, more bitterly every time she mentions it, which is frequently. It *is* a shame, but was I to be blamed for simply assuming that Louisa would respond as I did—with joy and excitement—at the prospect of a reunion with her kin?

Thinking on it further (although I haven't shared these thoughts with Vi), I wonder if perhaps I have inadvertently offended her with my note. Writing it in haste as I did, with Albert hovering there anxious to go, there were things I omitted to say. I am particularly sorry that I did not pass on my sincere condolences regarding Darcy's passing, or indeed even mention him. Perhaps this seemed callous and hurtful to her. Perhaps Albert did not mention to her the hurried circumstances in which I wrote the note, and so she assumes that the fact that I scrawled it so carelessly is an expression of how little she matters to me. Of course, nothing could be further from the truth.

My other thought is that perhaps Louisa's circumstances are

so reduced that she is simply too embarrassed to visit us, for fear we see what has become of her. After all, she was a proud beauty of sixteen when last we saw her; Albert described her now as a "tough old lady." Certainly young people are not sensitive to the small but important gradations of age in those older than themselves, but instead regard us all as ancient crones. And yet, at the age of forty-nine, with my hair almost completely gray, I find I hesitate to describe myself as "old." I think I would be more aptly described as "late middle-aged," if there is such a definition. I queried Vi on the subject and she agreed, adding that she herself was in the "early middle-aged" category, to which Margaret snorted derisively. My purpose here is not to talk admiringly of my own appearance, for I have never been an oil painting, still less so now; I simply wonder if Louisa's difficult life has aged her harshly and whether her knowledge of that is contributing to her apparent reluctance to see us. (She was always very slender, too, and I do wonder sometimes if carrying a few extra pounds isn't kinder on the face in the long run, somewhat softening the effect of wrinkles.)

In any case, I have a plan. I may have mentioned that Margaret is engaged to be married, and Vi and I are planning a kitchen tea in her honor. I had noticed that as well as his ointments, Albert carried an interesting selection of cake flavorings and extracts, along with disinfectants and White Rose perfume. If we don't hear anything within the next month, then I shall call up the Rawleigh's head office and ask that they send their man around again, as I would like to place a sizeable order. I have already looked up the number in the telephone book. And this time I will not let Albert get away without securing Louisa's address.

For I am determined that they be with us this Christmas. I have this picture in my head which only grows more detailed every time I summon it up; it is of the family gathered around the dining-room table for Christmas lunch. It is going to be a challenge to fit everyone, but I have more or less worked out a configuration for the tables. I will put George on the children's table (the card table) with Albert's older three (George enjoys the company of small children and likes to play big brother when he can). The unmarried sister (Marian?) I will seat next to Margaret (in my head, I see them both gossiping about film stars; Margaret is mad on them) with Margaret's fiancé Peter on the other side of her, rolling his eyes in his good-humored way. On the other side of the table, I plan to place Albert and his wife (whose name I did not catch), with Lionel on the end; he is no great conversationalist, but hopefully Albert will be able to draw him out. We may have to squeeze a high chair in for the baby, in which case I will put Albert's wife on the corner end (I am fairly sure the young family next door may be able to lend us a high chair for the occasion). At the kitchen end of the table, for convenience's sake, I will place Vi and Jim, for Vi will be up and down and back and forth; and down the opposite end, myself and Louisa. I can almost see her sitting there now. She has a paper hat on her head, and she is leaning her chin in one hand and making her sly jokes the way she used to do; except in my mind's eye, I realize, she still looks sixteen.

In any case, I can't be moping around waiting for her this Saturday. We are having our "Welcome" afternoon tea in honor of our new minister, the Reverend R.H. Trinder, for which I have been called upon to bring my Chocolate Honey Roll, as well as a plate of cheese and celery sandwiches, the preparation of which will take me a good part of the morning. This will be our first opportunity to meet him, as he does not commence officially until October; however, we have gleaned some interesting morsels of information. Apparently he has a superb singing voice, and according to Reverend Davis, who has met him, he was very keen to know if any of the congregation possessed a pianola, for he loves a sing-along. (Reverend Davis seemed to be offering this up as an indication that Reverend Trinder might be a bit of a Flash Harry, but in fact we could not have been more delighted to hear it. So much so that I found myself suggesting to Vi later that evening that if Louisa does not wish to claim the Sphinx, I might very well sell it and buy ourselves a pianola with the proceeds.)

The other nugget of information came from an acquaintance of our treasurer, Mrs. Purcell, whose sister resides in his previous parish of Wangaratta. Apparently, his marriage is not a wholly happy one; Mrs. Trinder struggles with various ailments, some of them apparently imagined; in fact, the terms used to describe her by the sister of the acquaintance were "dreary" and "a bit of a spoiler." So that is interesting. Not that I wish them any ill; as I say, I have yet to meet them. Vi likes to tease me on the subject, however, for the other day I happened to comment in passing that after sweeping out the kitchen, I had accidentally left the broom in the corner of the room. I reminded her of our old superstition, to wit: the sweeper would shortly meet her true love. I made no mention of Reverend Trinder, and yet she immediately assumed he was the likely prospect, even in spite of the fact that he is obviously married; all of which is rather tiresome of her. Also, she insists I left the broom in the corner deliberately, but I know for a fact that it was entirely accidental. It has to be accidental, or the effect is otherwise null and void.

The Boat Trip Home

I N FACT, THE MAKING OF THE CHOCOLATE HONEY ROLL DID
not take as long as I thought it would, and it has turned
out very nicely (some slight cracking is inevitable, but I
have covered it up pretty well with a mixture of cocoa and
sugar). I find I still have two hours before I need to even start
assembling the sandwiches, for if I commence them too early,
they will simply dry out and wilt or, alternatively, become
soggy. I have pressed my brown wool suit and laid it out on
the bed, and cleaned my good brown dress pumps. The family
is out and about engaged in various errands and activities, and
so, finding myself with time on my hands, I have been glancing through some of the previous chapters of this memoir.

I see that in my anxiety to explain the circumstances of
Darcy and Louisa's elopement, I had left the chapter concerning the Plain and Fancy Dress Ball unfinished, at the point
where John Beck suggested we step outside to "take some air."
It is tempting to perhaps document in more detail the various

small sighs and tender caresses and whispered endearments that followed—yet I must stop myself. After all, there hardly seems much point when I shall simply have to go back and excise these more intimate moments for fear of inadvertently startling my nephews. Nor does it seem entirely appropriate to be lingering amidst such memories when I am shortly to be making the acquaintance of our new minister over cheese and celery sandwiches.

To be honest, I am beginning to feel somewhat impatient with myself about it all. There are moments when I find myself thinking, "Well, he was simply a cad." There are even moments when I say to myself, "He may have been a cad but you, Mary Davidson, were a fool." Certainly, a wiser, more experienced reader might conclude that John Beck led me up the garden path and back again. I, of course, have drawn my own conclusions and, on most days at least, am inclined to give him the benefit of the doubt. So I will provide this one small detail before moving on with the story: that upon kissing me beneath the mulberry trees that night, he murmured softly that my lips tasted deliciously of blackberry cordial (excise all this later).

The Plain and Fancy Dress Ball drew to a close around three in the morning with "Auld Lang Syne" and "God Save the King," and then the Davidson clan and the various whale men who were not immediately departing us made our way down Imlay Street to the wharf, where the *Excelsior* awaited us. It is a funny thing, but whale men were always hard to dislodge at the end of the season (like splinters, is how Louisa referred to them). They had grown used to the food and the lodging, and they had come to rather like it, as much as they complained about it. It suddenly seemed a big effort to have to go and worry about sleeper-cutting or whatever it was that they were going to busy themselves with in the meantime. My father, ever mindful of the difficulty of procuring whale men next season, was never one to peremptorily boot them out, and often the situation dragged on like this for several weeks. So in fact the only whale man we had succeeded in shaking off that evening was Robert Heffernan, who went home to his mother, but not before accompanying us to the wharf. He had drunk so much liquor that he now felt exceedingly affectionate towards everyone, including Darcy, whom he embraced and called "brother" and told him he was "a fine gentleman, I don't care what anyone says." He then stood on the wharf and waved forlornly as the men tossed off the ropes and the motor launch putt-putted out.

The full moon was high in the sky and the bay unusually illuminated by its eerie silvery light. A great weariness, a kind of happy exhaustion, descended upon us. Dan and Violet and Annie fell asleep almost immediately on the bench seats, covered over by blankets. Harry and Uncle Aleck appeared to have passed out altogether, and lay snoring underfoot; in fact, we left them there, covered in blankets, when we got home. Of the rest of us, no one talked much, but instead just sat staring out to sea, listening to the gentle sputtering of the motor as we crept across the bay.

"Well, Father," said Salty after a while, slapping John Beck companionably upon the knee, "how did you enjoy your first season whaling?"

"I've enjoyed it very much," replied John Beck. "It has truly been a memorable experience."

"Indeed," said Salty, taking out his pipe and proceeding to

light it, enveloping himself for a short while amidst a cloud of smoke. "I daresay you fancy you know a bit about whales now?" he continued, once his pipe was lit.

"Oh well," said John Beck. "I suppose I know a little more than I did before."

"I see." Another cloud of smoke. "Then I wonder, Father, can you tell me why it is that whales breach?"

"Breach, did you say?"

"That's right. By which I mean leap out of the water in their entirety."

"Yes," said John Beck. "I am aware of what breaching is."

"You are aware of what breaching is, but are you aware of what causes it?"

"No, I am not."

"Hazard a guess, if you will."

"I'm sure I do not know."

"I imagine you might think it an expression of high spirits. Glad to be alive, is that it? Possessed of the joie de vivre?"

"Perhaps," said John Beck in a noncommittal tone.

"*Perhaps?* Of course it is obvious! Here is a lovely big humper swimming along with not a care in the world! Why shouldn't he leap up in glee?! He would click his heels, if he had any."

"I suppose so."

"Then you suppose incorrectly, for that is not the reason," said Salty. "Hazard another guess. For example, perhaps the whale is of a sportive disposition?"

"Why don't you just simply tell me why the whale breaches?" A note of irritation had crept into John Beck's voice. "It would save a lot of time and effort."

"Very well then, I will," said Salty, smiling pleasantly. "It is because the whale has an earache."

At which Darcy, who had been following the back and forth between the two men in some amusement, burst into a peal of laughter. For some reason, the idea of a whale having an earache tickled him enormously.

"An earache?" queried John Beck, and he was smiling a little because Darcy's laughter was rather infectious. Others began chuckling also. In fact, even my father was smiling.

"Yes, that's right, an earache," said Salty, seeming a little annoyed at all the merriment. "And I can assure you, young man"—turning to Darcy, and becoming more vehement in his tone—"that it is no laughing matter for the whale. A minuscule crustacean is pestering the poor beast to the point of endurance, scampering up and down in the ear cavities. The whale is breaching in a desperate bid to rid himself of the pest."

"I was not aware that whales had ears," remarked John Beck.

This set Darcy off again.

"Indeed they do," cried Salty. "Indeed they do have ears! Granted, they do not have the fleshy appendages of land mammals—"

And just at this moment, as if directly refuting Salty's claim, we heard a mighty and unmistakable *Bosh!* and a plume of fine silvery spray rose within twenty yards of the launch. At once we all cried out, and there we saw in low silhouette against the water the sloping curve of a humpback commencing to dive. Up turned the insouciant flukes, a glimpse of their snowy undersides in the darkness, then down they slid into the water, disappearing from view.

"Well, that is a very late whale," said Arthur Ashby thoughtfully. "A straggler of sorts."

The men turned to my father at the wheel. I suppose they were wondering whether they would now be expected to give chase. My father desisted from the throttle and let the motor idle. The little ones roused blearily from their sleep.

"What's the matter? Why has the boat stopped?"

"Sshhh. We are waiting for a whale to reappear."

At once the children sat up, wide awake. They were not going to miss seeing a whale close up.

"There she is!" cried Darcy. The whale had reappeared a short distance ahead and lolled about, spouting amiably. The children hastened up to the bow and clustered together there, watching it reverently.

"Gee, I wish I had my whale gun," said Dan earnestly.

"It's a juvenile," said my father. "I suppose that's why it's lagging so far behind the others."

"It is Robert Heffernan, in whale form," remarked Bastable.

"What do you think, boss?" asked Arthur Ashby, and all eyes turned to my father in trepidation. I suspect none of them felt very much like having to suddenly do battle with a whale. Really, everyone wanted to just curl up in their beds and sleep for twelve hours. "We try calling the Killers?"

"Well, we could try, I suppose," said my father. "But I doubt they'll come."

He did not sound very enthusiastic himself. Perhaps he was aware of the stony disapprobation rising up from Louisa, who sat quietly at his side. Or perhaps he also wanted to go to bed. After a good bit of fumbling about in the dark, the men unclipped the *Excelsior*'s oars and slapped them over the side in a haphazard attempt at unison. Then they all stood around and scoured the water, waiting for the happy miracle of those raking dorsal fins. The children and I waited too, wrapped in our blankets.

"Come on, Tom," urged Annie in a small voice. "Come on, Hooky. Come on, Humpy."

"And Kinscher and Cooper," continued Violet. "And Jackson and Little Ben and Jimmy and Charlie Adgery and Stranger and Typee…" In fact, she went on to list nearly every Killer whale she could think of, living or deceased, and was admonished for her errors by her brother.

Minutes passed. The men tried slapping the oars a couple more times, increasingly more half-hearted and less in unison at each successive attempt. No Killers came; nor was anyone much surprised, for they hadn't been sighted now in well over a week. They had moved on to colder waters, presumably, to wherever Killer whales liked to go when the whaling season was over. Meanwhile, Robert Heffernan in whale form drifted further away, ambling along in his aimless, distracted fashion, making his journey south.

"We'll let him go," said my father, opening up the throttle. "He'll be bigger next year."

Author's Note

George "Fearless" Davidson, Master Whaler, was born in 1863, in Eden, New South Wales. He was the grandson of Alexander Davidson, a Scottish immigrant who was the first in the line of Davidsons to take up whaling in Twofold Bay. In 1890, George married Sarah Galli, who bore him eight children. George and Sarah both lived to a ripe old age. In 1936, several years after he had put the whaling station up for sale and by now an old man, George rowed out in a small dinghy and lanced a whale single-handedly. *"Davidson's feat of attacking and killing a whale without assistance is unparalleled in the history of local whaling,"* claimed the *Sydney Morning Herald* (12 November 1936).

In the interests of fiction, and with sincere apologies to the descendants of the Davidsons, I have taken a few liberties with some details of his life, in particular by making him a widower and inventing a whole new set of offspring for him.

Regarding the killer whales, however, I have endeavored to be as truthful as possible. Much of my research centered on the local Eden newspapers of the time, held in the archives of the State Library of New South Wales. Here I discovered an abundance of extraordinarily vivid and detailed eyewitness accounts of the whale hunts, often referring to specific killer whales by name. These newspapers seem to have followed the ups and downs of the Davidsons' fortunes and the killer whales' activities obsessively, even to the extent—in this instance—of documenting the killers' pursuit of an unfortunate "grampus" (most likely a minke whale):

After travelling somewhat about a mile he again altered his course for North Head expecting to get away, but his attempt was foiled by the appearance of "Cooper." He then trended his way towards the entrance to Curalo Lake, only to find laying in wait for him on the verge of the breakers, "Typee." By a skilful bit of manoeuvring, the grampus succeeded around the killer "Typee," who, finding himself outclassed, immediately took up a position with his confederates. After travelling slowly along the breast of the sandy beach, "Humpy" thought he (the grampus) was not going fast enough, so he took a hand in the game, and gave the unfortunate grampus a reminder that he was in close attendance....After floptailing a while, there were to be noticed Hooky, Cooper, Jackson, Typee, Tom, Kinscher and other killers known by their distinctive dorsal fins, ranged in semi-circular form between Lookout Point and North Head....

Eden Observer and South Coast Advocate, 3 August 1909

The whale chases themselves make tough reading, at once exciting and horrifying:

> ...the Killers were attacking them in the most ferocious manner, and the unfortunate creatures seemed lost as to which course was best to get rid of their tormentors. The bellowing the whole time was of the most awful and pitiful nature, and it would be a hard man indeed who could not bestow a little sympathy on the poor harassed creatures. Getting slightly away from the Killers, the whales made for East Boyd Bay. There a number of erratic movements were made, but the whales, getting out of the bay, steered a course for the open sea...instinctively (the Killers) knew that if the whales were once outside the bay in deep water their chances of capture were limited and so, like dogs on a beast, they were at the whales' heads and, after a great effort, turned them around again. During all this time, many efforts were made by George Davidson and his crew to fasten to one of the whales, but in vain. Their constant twistings and turnings rendered it impossible....After a while the whales and Killers took a course direct for Quarantine Bay, the whaling crew following in hot pursuit. Here success crowned the efforts of the crew, and one of the whales had the harpoon driven well home into its body, and the hopes of the crew went high; but only for a few minutes as an event, not uncommon, happened. It is well known that the Killers will often take hold of a piece of line hanging from a boat, or at times a kellick, and run away with it; and this is just what one of them did on Sunday night; and the extraordi-

nary sight of a Killer having the whale line in his mouth and being towed about by a whale was witnessed. The result of the Killer taking the line was that the crew had to take the oars and row hard for about two miles before they managed to again secure the whale line....

Eden Observer and South Coast Advocate, 1 September 1905

In fact, I found several examples of frolicsome Killer whales taking the whale line:

...At this stage an incident occurred which fortunately is not frequent although a similar one took place last season. A Killer, known to the whaling crew as Tom, took the whale line in its mouth, dragging it out of the boat, and for a while threatening the loss of the whale. Fortunately Tom held fast to the line, the whale towing him about the bay, and presenting an unusual sight to the few onlookers who were about at that early hour....

Eden Observer and South Coast Advocate, 3 August 1906

Here is the famous Tom making an appearance! On the same page of the very same newspaper, in miniscule print, I found this fascinating tidbit:

A painful, but fortunately not serious accident happened to Mr. George Davidson on Friday afternoon last at the site of the dead whale off South Head. While explaining the names of the Killers, one of them rose immediately at the bow of the launch and catching the whale line of which Mr. Davidson had hold, in his mouth, crushed his finger in such a severe manner that the top of it burst. For his playful habits, Tom, the name by which this particular Killer is known, received sufficient anathemas to last him till his dying day—and after.

Tom died in September 1930, and the obituary and poem included in this book are taken verbatim from the Eden newspapers of that month. His skeleton was preserved by George Davidson, and is on display to this day at the Eden Killer Whale Museum. Although other explanations have been offered for it, there appears to be a conspicuous rope groove on one of his back teeth.

George Davidson's whale crews appear to have consisted of various Davidsons, a few itinerants and, notably, a regularly returning group of Aboriginal whale men: Arthur Ashby, Albert Thomas Senior (Charaga) and Albert Thomas Junior (Boukal) among them. By most accounts (although this is difficult to verify), the Aboriginal whale men received the same pay and conditions as the white whale men. Certainly, they were highly regarded for their superior eyesight and ability, and Arthur Ashby in particular is mentioned in newspaper accounts for his skill as a harpooner (or boat steerer). Of particular interest is the great significance that the killer whales held for the Aboriginal people:

The older race of aboriginals around Eden had strange beliefs about the Killers, holding the opinion that when they departed from this sphere of usefulness they at some time later returned as Killers, and the one which

bears the name of Cooper was so-called after an old aboriginal who had in the flesh been king of the Kiah River
tribe. Just as a small Killer, on being seen for the first
time, was said to be the recently deceased child of one
of the natives changed into a Killer. There is no doubt
that these animals are looked upon as being supernatural, and held consequently in great reverence. Many
years ago, an old whaler named Higginbotham (Flukey),
in throwing the lance, by accident caused the death of
a Killer. The same night, the natives armed themselves
with spears, with the intention of taking his life in re-
venge for what they considered a great crime, and it was
only owing to the intervention of some of the more powerful of the tribe that Flukey was allowed to live.

Eden Observer and South Coast Advocate, 27 November
1903

It is informative of the times to note that "Killers" warrants a
capital letter, while "aboriginals" does not.

Further study of these newspapers reveals that whaling in
Eden does not appear to have been a hugely profitable enterprise in the early 1900s:

The whaling season at Twofold Bay was practically
brought to a close with the ending of last week, when
the two crews dispersed to their homes. Mr. Davidson
will keep a lookout for chance whales a little while
longer, but the fact that the Killers have not been seen
for some time renders it probable they have taken their
departure for other fields and oceans blue, and there

is poor chance of obtaining whales without their assistance....The season opened auspiciously with the capture of ten whales between July 19 and September 5,
the last being a black whale....Since the latter date,
however, the long weary watches have been fruitless.
During 1903, not a single whale was taken, with the
exception of a small finback, which was driven ashore
by the Killers at Haslems Beach. After all expenses are
paid, there will unfortunately be small profit for the
adventurous work of whaling in the last two years in
Twofold Bay. The total quantity of oil secured was 25
and a half tons. Had the Killers remained and the last
two humpers and right whale been captured, the story
would have been slightly different. As it is, we can only
hope that captures may yet be made, late as the period
is, and that next year's work may recoup plucky George
Davidson for past losses.

Eden Observer and South Coast Advocate, 11 November
1904

In fact, 1905 proved to be worse than 1904: only five whales
were captured, quite late in the season, and two of these were
blown away in gales before they could be towed to the try-
works. These losses were a bitter blow for the whalers, but
perhaps even more disappointing for the gentleman below:

Mr. James Hogan, of Moruya, who came to Eden this
week to be immersed in one of the whales as a cure for
rheumatism from which he is a great sufferer, returned
to his home on Monday. Owing to the loss of the whales

after they were killed, Mr. Hogan could not try the remedy.

Eden Observer and South Coast Advocate, 15 September 1905

For those interested in reading further about the Davidsons and the killer whales of Eden, I recommend the following:

Tom Mead, *Killers of Eden,* Angus & Robinson, 1961; republished Dolphin Books, 2002.
Danielle Clode, *Killers in Eden,* Allen & Unwin, 2002.
Rene Davidson, *Whalemen of Twofold Bay,* self-published, 1988.
W.J. Dakin, *Whalemen Adventurers,* Angus and Robertson, 1934; republished Sirius Books, 1963.
killersofeden.com

It is well worth visiting the area, not only for the Eden Killer Whale Museum, where Tom's skeleton may be admired and much of the Davidson whaling paraphernalia is on display, but also for the charming, rough-hewn Davidson cottage at Kiah, which stands preserved just up the hill from where the try-works used to be. At South Head, it is possible to visit the whaler's lookout post of Boyd Tower, where one can plainly see, carved into the sandstone, an epitaph for the whale man Peter Lia, who died when a whale smashed a whaleboat with its flukes in 1881. There's even the faded remnants of an old checkerboard, painted on a flat rock—no doubt a means of whiling away the long hours, waiting for a whale.

Happily, these days during whale season there always seem to be plenty of whales passing through Twofold Bay, relatively untormented—even the whale-watching boats must keep a respectful distance. Killer whales, however, are much less frequent visitors. While one would never wish for a return to the brutal days of whaling, it's hard not to be slightly nostalgic for a time when the killer whales' annual arrival in Twofold Bay warranted an excited snippet in the local newspaper, under the headline *"Voices Whisper"*:

That the "Killers," true to their custom, are about, and whales may be expected soon to show—or cry "hello" and bellow.

About the Author

Shirley Barrett is best known for her work as a screenwriter and director. Her film *Love Serenade* won the Caméra d'Or for best first feature at the Cannes Film Festival in 1996. In 2010, the script for her film *South Solitary* won the Queensland Premier's Prize and the West Australian Premier's Prize. *Rush Oh!* is her first novel. She lives in Sydney, Australia.